Pacific Alliance

Pacific Alliance

Reviving U.S.–Japan Relations

Kent E. Calder

Yale University Press

New Haven & London

Published under the auspices of the Johns Hopkins University, SAIS,
Reischauer Center for East Asian Studies, and with assistance from
the foundation established in memory of Philip Hamilton McMillan
of the Class of 1894, Yale College.

Set in Adobe Garamond and Stone Sans types by The Composing Room of
Michigan, Inc.
Printed in the United States of America.

Library of Congress Cataloging-in-Publication Data

Calder, Kent E.
    Pacific alliance : reviving U.S.–Japan relations / Kent E. Calder.
        p. cm.
    Includes bibliographical references and index.
    ISBN 978-0-300-14672-1 (alk. paper)
    1. United States—Foreign economic relations—Japan.   2. Japan—Foreign
economic relations—United States.   3. United States—Foreign relations—Japan.
4. Japan—Foreign relations—United States.   I. Title.
    HF1458.5.J3C35 2009
    355'.03109730952—dc22

                                                                    2008045582

A catalogue record for this book is available from the British Library.

This paper meets the requirements of ANSI/NISO Z39.48-1992 (Permanence
of Paper). It contains 30 percent postconsumer waste (PCW) and is certified by the
Forest Stewardship Council (FSC).

10 9 8 7 6 5 4 3 2 1

To the people of U.S. Embassy Tokyo, and their vital role in bridging the broad Pacific

Japan and the United States face each other, but across the broadest ocean of them all.
—*Edwin O. Reischauer*

Contents

Figures

Preface

In a very real sense, this has been the project of a lifetime—and in some ways more. Transpacific relations began for my family on December 7, 1941, only minutes into the attack on Pearl Harbor, when my father's cousin, Captain Mervyn Bennion of the battleship *West Virginia,* was felled on the bridge of his ship by an aerial torpedo. A cousin of my mother spent fourteen hours in the East China Sea off Okinawa, after his ship was hit in a kamikaze attack. My wife's uncle, conversely, was an instructor at the kamikaze instruction school in Kyushu, and *hibakusha* victims of Hiroshima, which was bombed three years before I was born, are acquaintances as well.

For me personally, U.S.–Japan relations have fortunately been a more peaceful proposition. Japan was the first foreign country I visited, at eight years of age, together with my family, en route to Burma, where my father served for three years as part of the Ford Foundation's development team. I will never forget my first sight of Mt. Fuji, hovering exotically above the clouds of early monsoon season, across the wing of our DC-8, as we approached Honshu from Wake Island in the early morning light. The Tokyo that I first glimpsed on landing was still faintly redolent of the war and the occupation, with U.S. troops walking along the imperial moat, many cars still American, and Japanese veterans visible here and there on street corners in Asakusa. John Foster Dulles was still serving as secretary of state.

Just over half a century has passed since that monsoon day on which my encounter with Japan began. Over the intervening years, I have studied, worked, and traveled the length and breadth of Japan, spending eleven years there since the first Oil Shock of 1973. Nearly half of that time has been in U.S. government service, which allowed me to gain extraordinary insights into the Pacific alliance, including sixteen trips to Okinawa. I have also spent enough time elsewhere in the world—six years in Southeast Asia, Africa, and Europe—to realize that Japan is one of the most remarkable yet misunderstood nations on earth.

This book represents my major effort to make sense of how the United States should relate to the world's first non-Western modernizer, an unassuming colossus which has grown to become the world's second largest economy. As the reader will soon gather, I see the Pacific alliance as a "high-maintenance" relationship, one which desperately needs well-functioning interpersonal networks and balanced economic and cultural interdependence at its core. Yet there are unsettling questions as to whether the maintenance is being performed properly or even, in some cases, performed at all. Over the past decade the alliance has grown markedly more ambitious in political-military terms, but economic and cultural relations have not kept pace. This imbalance is especially serious because U.S.–Japan relations today operate in both a transpacific and a U.S. domestic political context, where Tokyo faces dynamic rivals for American attention, just as Washington, D.C., does to a lesser degree in Tokyo. Those third-party rivals have grown much more influential and assertive over the past decade.

The basic notion on which this book is based—that an alliance is a comprehensive, living, socioeconomic, and sociopolitical reality extending far beyond the military realm—emerged from my academic work with former Ambassador to Japan Edwin O. Reischauer, who was my mentor and dissertation advisor at Harvard. He continually spoke of the "broken dialogue" with Japan and feared the political-military consequences thereof—so unsettlingly tangible as he was writing, in the shadow of the 1960 U.S.–Japan Security Treaty crisis. My understanding of the political-military dimensions was deepened during four and one-half years as Japan Chair at CSIS in Washington, D.C., and another four and one-half as Special Advisor to the U.S. Ambassador to Japan. Academic work at Harvard, Princeton, and recently SAIS/Johns Hopkins University has deepened my thinking, which began to take book form in the wake of a catalytic kitchen discussion with my bicultural daughter Mari in the spring of 2004, in which we coined the title, *Pacific Alliance.*

Several people have had an important hand in helping create this book, although I implicate none in its idiosyncratic failings. In the early stages Min Ye, then a Princeton doctoral candidate and now a promising young assistant professor, contributed significantly, especially in helping me research and more deeply understand the generic concept of alliance. For more than three years Yukie Yoshikawa, currently Senior Research Fellow at the Reischauer Center, has been an invaluable colleague, greatly transcending the normal definition of research assistant. Highly adept with computer graphics and statistics, she contributed enormously to the figures and tables presented here, while also providing insightful, influential comments on both Japanese domestic and comparative matters. She worked with me longer and harder on this book than anyone else, and I deeply appreciate her efforts. Arthur Lord, finally, added greatly to the comparative analysis, with insightful, detailed surveys of British, German, and Chinese approaches to relations with the United States, particularly in the cultural sphere.

Apart from these three key researchers, several others have contributed significantly to the final product. Rust Deming, distinguished career diplomat and now Senior Advisor at the Reischauer Center, read and commented in detail on the whole manuscript, as did Mariko de Freytas. Yamazaki Juri and Junko Dyokas—the latter a former colleague at U.S. Embassy Tokyo—provided valuable administrative support. David Abshire, Howard Baker, Ted Baker, Susan Basalla, William Breer, William Brock, Harold Brown, Zbigniew Brzezinski, Toshiko Calder, Kurt Campbell, Jessica Einhorn, Dick Fairbanks, Bob Fauver, Thomas Foley, Jim Foster, Fujisaki Ichiro, Francis Fukuyama, Jeffrey Garten, Paul Giarra, Carl Green, Larry Greenwood, John Harrington, Andrew Horvats, Ito Eiichiro, Karl Jackson, Kato Ryōzō, Myron Kunka, Kusaka Kazutoshi, Christopher LaFleur, David Lampton, Mike Mihalak, Matsunaga Nobuo, Walter Mondale, Okawara Yoshio, Hugh Patrick, Torkel Patterson, Susan Pharr, Robert Reis, Danny Russel, Sano Izumi, Satō Yukio, David Shear, James Shinn, Toyoda Masakazu, Ezra Vogel, Robin White, Yachi Shotaro, Yamazaki Takuya, and Jim Zumwalt have all contributed significantly also, and I am grateful to them.

Yale University Press, including Michael O'Malley, Alex Larson, Mary Pasti, and many others, has been a delight to work with. That I am deeply and eternally grateful to Edwin O. Reischauer, who led me first along the path of scholarship in U.S.–Japan relations, goes without saying, as does my responsibility for this work, imperfections and all.

A Note on Conventions

Japanese personal names throughout the text are presented in Japanese form—that is with the surname followed by the given name, in reversal of standard Western practice. Exceptions to this convention are made only in the case of Japanese scholars long resident outside Japan, whose names are conventionally presented in Western fashion in the English-language literature. In such cases Western conventions are observed here. Macron marks have been used where relevant in all cases except where the word in question appears so commonly in English discourse without macrons that such usage has become relatively standard. Tōkyō and Kyōto are the two major cases in which macrons would be relevant where this convention is employed. Most figures are given in yen, but when currency translations are undertaken, they are made at contemporaneous exchange rates for the item in question, unless otherwise indicated.

Acronyms

ACCJ	American Chamber of Commerce in Japan
ACSA	Acquisition and Cross-Servicing Agreement (U.S.–Japan)
APBC	Asia-Pacific Economic Cooperation
ASDF	Air Self-Defense Forces (Japan)
ASEAN	Association of South East Asian Nations
ATSML	Anti-Terrorism Special Measures Law (Japan)
BJOCC	Bilateral and Joint Operations Coordination Center (U.S.–Japan)
BMD	ballistic missile defense
BOJ	Bank of Japan
BRIC	Brazil, Russia, India, and China
CCP	Chinese Communist Party
CENTCOM	Central Command (U.S. Forces in Middle East)
CFC	Combined Forces Command (Korea)
CIA	Central Intelligence Agency (U.S.)
CSCC	Committee on Scholarly Communication with China
CULCON	U.S.–Japan Conference on Cultural and Educational Interchange

DCI	Director of Central Intelligence
DFAA	Defense Facilities Administration Agency (Japan)
DMZ	Demilitarized Zone (Korea)
DOD	Department of Defense (U.S.)
DPJ	Democratic Party of Japan
DPRK	Democratic People's Republic of Korea (North Korea)
EROA	Economic Rehabilitation in Occupied Areas
EU	European Union
FDI	foreign direct investment
FIL	Foreign Investment Law
GARIOA	Government Appropriations for Relief in Occupied Areas
GATT/WTO	General Agreement on Tariffs and Trade/World Trade Organization
GCC	Gulf Cooperation Council
GDP	gross domestic product
GMF	German Marshall Fund
GPR	Global Posture Review (U.S. DOD)
GSDF	Ground Self-Defense Forces
HNS	host-nation support
ICBM	Intercontinental ballistic missile
ICU	International Christian University
IRBM	Intermediate-range ballistic missile
JDA	Japan Defense Agency
JMTC	Joint Military Technology Commission (U.S.–Japan)
JSDF	Japan Self-Defense Forces
JSP	Japan Socialist Party
KMT	Kuomintang
LDP	Liberal Democratic Party
MCAS	Marine Corps Air Station
METI	Ministry of Economics, Trade, and Industry
MITI	Ministry of International Trade and Industry
MNC	Multinational Corporation
MOFA	Ministry of Foreign Affairs
MOSS	Market-Oriented Sector Selective talks
MSDF	Maritime Self-Defense Forces
NATO	North Atlantic Treaty Organization
NCUSCR	National Committee on U.S.-China Relations
NGO	Nongovernmental organization

NHK	Nippon Hōsō Kyōkai
NIE	newly industrializing economy
NPT	Nuclear Non-Proliferation Treaty
NSC	National Security Council
NTT	Nippon Telephone and Telegraph
ODA	official development assistance
OECD	Organization for Economic Cooperation and Development
OMA	orderly marketing agreement
PACOM	Pacific Command (U.S.)
PKO	peacekeeping operation
PLA	People's Liberation Army
PRC	People's Republic of China (mainland China)
R&D	research and development
RIMPAC exercise	Rim of the Pacific exercise
ROC	Republic of China (Taiwan)
ROK	Republic of Korea (South Korea)
SAIS	School of Advanced International Studies
SCAP	Supreme Commander for the Allied Powers
SDC	Subcommittee for Defense Cooperation
SDF	Self-Defense Forces (Japan)
SDI	Strategic Defense Initiative
SII	Structural Impediments Initiative
SOFA	Status of Forces Agreement
SRBM	short-range ballistic missile
SSC	Security Subcommittee
UK	United Kingdom
USCBC	U.S.-China Business Council
USCPF	U.S.-China Policy Foundation
USFJ	U.S. Forces in Japan
USFK	U.S. Forces in Korea
USJBC	U.S.–Japan Business Council
USSR	Union of Soviet Socialist Republics
WMD	weapons of mass destruction

Pacific Alliance

Introduction

Japan specialists in the United States take it as gospel truth that the U.S.–Japan alliance relationship is sacrosanct. It is an immutable reality, they contend, as fundamental to global order as a law of nature. They often cite the former ambassador to Tokyo Mike Mansfield on the alliance: "The most important relationship in the world, bar none."[1]

It is time to reexamine that proposition. And indeed, it is time, in a globalizing, post–Cold War world, to reexamine the classic notion of alliance as well. Half a century and more has passed since U.S. Secretary of State Dean Acheson and Japanese Prime Minister Yoshida Shigeru partnered in signing both the San Francisco Treaty and then the U.S.–Japan Mutual Security Treaty, only hours apart. The Cold War is waning, and China and India are rising, while international political-economic relationships throughout the world are growing much more fluid than they have traditionally been. Why do the U.S.–Japan alliance ties really matter any more?

Acheson's key advisor John Foster Dulles, if queried in 1951, as he was conceiving the architecture of post–World War II transpacific

1

accommodation, would have thought the question ludicrous. Memories of World War II, in which the United States had lost over 150,000 men in the Pacific, and Japan 3 million citizens in all, not to mention a nation laid waste, were still fresh. Dulles, as the nephew of Secretary of State Robert Lansing, had been at Versailles in 1919 and feared Japan would become a second Weimar Germany if subjected to a victor's peace. With every fiber of his being, Dulles believed that an equitable U.S.–Japan alliance, with a generous economic dimension, was crucial to avoiding the resurgence of Japanese militarism.[2]

THE EARLY RATIONALE

The Pentagon, with Americans dying on Pork Chop Hill and scores of nearby bloody sites on the Korean peninsula, strongly concurred on the importance of the alliance. It provided, after all, the bases from which UN forces could bomb North Korea and organize logistics to support the Korean War. Following the fall of China, America had no alternative, secure Northeast Asian bastion from which to stop the broader expansion of Communist power.

Important American business leaders agreed also. The banks and the oil companies, in particular, had already set up shop again in Japan, reviving their prewar relationships, with others in their wake.[3] Japan might not loom as large as Europe, to be sure. Yet it was growing and had manifest economic potential, many observed, if only its neighborhood could be stabilized. With China in the clutches of chaos and revolution and the rest of Asia either underdeveloped or laid waste by war, however, there was simply no alternative to Japan on the western Pacific Rim.

Most Japanese business and political leaders, whatever their differences as to rationale, concurred with their American counterparts on the concept of a postwar transpacific alliance. For Tokyo, after all, alliance meant independence restored, after nearly seven long years of occupation. And it also prospectively meant access to the massive American market—with more than twenty times the GDP of Japan.[4]

For intellectuals of both nations as well, a U.S.–Japan dialogue and broader partnership had distinct cross-cultural cachet. As John D. Rockefeller III and Edwin O. Reischauer agreed, echoing Nitobe Inazō, the alliance, in its broadest sense, represented a noble experiment. In a world traditionally beset by racism and balance of power strife, a Washington–Tokyo entente represented something distinctly transcendent—a potential oasis of tolerance, understanding, and forgiveness. It was to be a bridge over the troubled transcultural waters of the traditional Pacific relationship, as it had tempestuously evolved since the dawn of the twentieth century at least.

CHANGING TIMES

Times, to be sure, have changed. The Korean War is over, and indeed the Cold War also is staggering to a close. China has recovered from the excesses of revolution, and Southeast Asia, not to mention the four tigers,[5] has grown exponentially. America and Japan, amidst trade conflict and mutual recrimination, have found it difficult to achieve the meeting of the minds they had once hoped for. And many of their inspiring early postwar intellectual leaders, sadly, have passed away.

If times have changed so greatly since the days of Dulles and the inception of the Mutual Security Treaty, why then should the United States and Japan be so concerned for the relevance and fate of their now-venerable alliance? Why not just consign this three-generation-old relic to the dustbin of history? Why not simply celebrate its long and fruitful life and then let it quietly go?

THE ENDURING LOGIC OF THE ALLIANCE

Despite changing times, first of all, many of the underlying insights of Dulles and his Japanese colleagues about mutual benefit continue to be valid. For both countries, the alliance continues to play some enduring roles: (1) inhibiting serious conflict between the United States and Japan; (2) arresting the emergence of an unstable balance of power in Asia; (3) ensuring the one nation to have tragically experienced nuclear war at first hand against a repetition; and (4) preventing an antagonist to American and Japanese interests from dominating the western Pacific. As World War II recedes ever further into history and Pacific regional institutions and networks grow stronger, American consciousness of the first two points, and even the third, erodes, while a defensive "stop China" rationale grows more salient. Yet the fundamental logic of all four classic systemic arguments for the U.S.–Japan alliance remains, on both sides of the broad Pacific.

Cultural partnership is one final element of the classic San Francisco bargain that remains, in my view, a continuing argument for alliance—however frustrating the idealistic efforts to achieve it may have been in the past. The lingering shadow of Hiroshima and Pearl Harbor makes this doubly so. Both Rockefeller and Reischauer argued persistently, in the shadow of war, Occupation,

and beyond, for such cultural collaboration. They saw U.S.–Japan understanding not only in geopolitical terms, but also as a humanistic means for the
peoples of both nations to broaden and deepen themselves, so as to transcend
the rivalry and racism that had so tragically brought on the Pacific War. That
dialogue is an unfinished work, vitally essential to world peace, which their
generation has bequeathed to its successors.

For the United States, the logic of alliance on geopolitical grounds initially
may appear more problematic than for Japan. America is a preeminent world
power, accounting for almost half of global military spending. It can handle
most military contingencies without Japanese cooperation, if it disregards the
war cost of prospective conflict and the considerable time saved by transporting
troops and military equipment needed in a contingency from stateside rather
than from Japanese bases. In some specialized areas, such as minesweeping, the
alliance may have significant military utility for Washington, to be sure. Yet
these areas are distinctly limited and arguably not intrinsically worth the substantial prospective costs of the ambitious commitment which Pacific alliance
implies.

The alliance is important for the world as a whole because it represents a critical mass in the global system that, given its sheer scale, becomes a fundamental pillar of world stability. The United States and Japan, after all, are the two
largest economies on earth, with nearly 40 percent of global GDP between
them. In finance their ability to cooperate is especially important in global
terms: they are by far the largest debtors and creditors on earth, with Japan being close to a $2 trillion net creditor and the United States nearly a $2.5 trillion
net debtor.[6]

Japan contributes directly to U.S. military preeminence, both by providing
bases for U.S. forces and by supplying substantial levels of host-nation support—well over $4 billion annually.[7] Even more important, Tokyo quite con-
sistently supports the role of the U.S. dollar as a global reserve currency and
generally acts to stabilize its exchange-rate value. This "exorbitant privilege," as
Charles de Gaulle once put it, of providing the global key currency allows the
United States an autonomy from fiscal constraints on its military deployments
available to no other nation. It allowed the Reagan administration to accelerate
military spending in the 1980s, despite rising fiscal deficits, so as to force the
collapse of the Soviet Union. It also afforded George W. Bush the leeway two
decades later of flexibly pursuing the Iraq War.

The Japanese financial contribution to the bilateral alliance is, of course, a function of Tokyo's capital surpluses and capital exports. These began to accumulate in earnest during the early 1980s, with the relaxation of Japanese capital controls, and keep growing to this day. Japanese transactions within the United States in domestic and foreign securities swelled from $6.6 billion in 1980 to $130.6 billion in 1985 and to $1.1 trillion in 1989, before dropping by half in 1992. Japanese purchases picked back up, however, to $1.2 trillion in 2007.[8] Such flows continue to enhance American fiscal flexibility, including the critical strategic ability to raise military spending when circumstances demand. International foreign-exchange market instability, including a sharp revaluation of the yen or other foreign currencies, could obviously disrupt such flows and thus constrain American strategic flexibility.

For Japan, too, ongoing changes in the global political economy generate important new rationales for the transpacific alliance. Japan, after all, is a middle-range power, lacking strategic depth, which finds benefit in alignment with a larger power in world affairs. Japan is also an island nation, for whom alignment with a preeminent global naval power has particular attraction. That was the logic underlying the Anglo-Japanese naval treaty of 1902, and it still has some parallel relevance today. The United States and Japan are natural geostrategic allies, in the view of many.[9]

Apart from American military power—comparatively greater by far than that of any other nation, in the wake of the Soviet collapse—there is America's defense of the energy sea-lanes between Northeast Asia and the Persian Gulf. The strategic importance of the U.S. Navy was demonstrated painfully to Japan in the waning days of World War II, when American submarine warfare—rather than strategic bombing or island-hopping victories in the South Pacific—catalyzed Japan's World War II defeat, in the view of many experts.[10] American global naval preeminence continues to be vital to the security of Japan, an island nation that imports virtually all of its food and raw materials.

American global capabilities are also distinctly useful to Japan in two other key areas—intelligence and finance. Japan, as noted previously, still lacks a global intelligence network, despite its increasingly global political-economic interests, as the world's second largest economic power. The enormous sweep of American capabilities in that area is an attractive complement for Tokyo, although coordination problems remain, particularly given Japan's lack of effective espionage legislation and bureaucratic stovepiping within the Japanese government. In finance, the stability of the dollar remains fundamental to Japanese interests, given Tokyo's massive foreign-exchange reserves and the dollar's role as a global key currency. The U.S.–Japan alliance is thus highly important for Japan, as NATO is for Europe, in reinforcing the stability and credibility of delicate, often asymmetrical economic relationships.

Over the past half century, Japan has, to a remarkable degree, embedded its vital interests with those of the United States, under the assumption of indefinite American hegemony. This structural embeddedness gives Japan powerful reasons to cooperate with the United States in maintaining strong bilateral alliance ties. The Pacific alliance is thus highly important for Japan, as for Europe, in providing not only conventional military security, but also greater stability and credibility to delicate and often asymmetrical economic relationships, such as those in trade and finance, than would otherwise be true.

GLOBAL IMPLICATIONS

The U.S.–Japan bilateral alliance also makes considerable sense to the world as a whole. First of all, this solemn agreement between the United States and Japan, the two largest economies, not to confront one another militarily obviates the prospect of one major potential global disaster. Many other countries, including the European nations, have, like Japan, also embedded their interests in a U.S.-led global order, to varying degrees. Thus, erosion of the global order would seriously damage those countries as well, so the commitment of the two largest economic powers to cooperate and coordinate the alliance is vital.

Second, the alliance also generates the ability—flowing from pooled economic might—to provide important global public goods. For most of the last two decades, the two countries have been the largest providers of overseas development assistance on earth. In 1990, for example, the U.S. and Japan together provided 27 percent of the entire world's overseas development assistance, an impressive ratio that increased further, to 33 percent, by 2005.[11] In some nations, such as India and Indonesia, Tokyo and Washington have leveraged one another through pooled contributions. In others, such as China and Vietnam, they have complemented each other, with the Japanese ODA role in strategically supporting American foreign policy goals being particularly important.

The United States and Japan together make up, as is well known, nearly a third of the economic mass of the entire world. They import more than a third of the oil that moves in international trade and account for 80 percent of the green-technology innovations. On a broad range of issues, especially those relating to energy, the environment, telecommunications, and finance—all important correlates of security—their massive scale allows them to create bilateral models of best practice that can provide strong global pull.

Transcending the functional utility of the U.S.–Japan alliance, in any particular policy area, there is a simple but important structural argument in its favor: *it exists*. Both the military alliance and political-economic expressions like the massive flow of Japanese capital into American financial markets have a quiet stabilizing role. That role is embedded and would be sorely missed in the event of disruption by both the transpacific partners and the broader world. If American forces left Japan, for example, balance of power rivalries among Japan, China, and Korea would likely intensify. And if Japanese capital flows to America were diverted elsewhere, U.S. market interest rates would likely rise and financial markets could be sharply depressed. The global financial crisis provided a graphic illustration of the potential dangers to come.

There are thus numerous enduring arguments for both U.S.–Japan military alliance and corresponding bilateral political-economic coordination. Since the San Francisco Treaty of 1951, and even before, these elements have been intimately linked. Growing global economic interdependence makes them ever more closely intertwined. For Japan, the compelling part of the alliance was once the economic dimension, with the military aspect being more important to America; since the 1980s, with the rise of Japanese capital outflows and the parallel expansion of deficit-enabled U.S. military power, the incentive structure has arguably been reversed. Yet the interrelationship of the military and the economic dimensions continues. The U.S.–Japan alliance is decidedly a hybrid political-economic creature, and those who ignore that fundamental reality do so, as we shall see, at their peril.

EMERGING CHALLENGES

Despite the enduring importance of the U.S.–Japan alliance, recent sweeping global post–Cold War changes notwithstanding, the transpacific relationship is beset by problems not readily apparent to the casual eye. In the pages to follow, I detail the quiet ongoing crisis of the current alliance against the backdrop of its own history. I note, in particular, the importance of its economic, social, and cultural foundations and the silent yet serious erosion that those irreplaceable pillars have suffered in recent years.

However superficially strong the military dimensions of U.S.–Japan partnership may appear to be, atrophy in their political-economic correlates threatens serious consequences for the overall alliance relationship, as the bitter struggle in the fall of 2007 over Japan's Anti-Terrorism Special Measures Law and the decade-long controversy regarding the closing of the Futenma Marine Corps Air Station, for example, made clear. These political complications could grow even more serious as technical demands on the alliance for interoperability and precise coordination grow stronger, with the coming of missile defense, more integrated defense production, and complex political-military liaison far from Japanese shores.

Chapters 1 through 7 detail the deepening challenges that confront U.S.–Japan relations, centering on the political-economic and cultural dimensions, yet profoundly consequential for the military alliance as well. Following this historically oriented problematic, the book considers solutions. Chapter 8 outlines, in a search for clues, alternate foreign paradigms for dealing with the United States adopted by Britain, Germany, and China. Chapter 9 details, in conclusion, my prescriptions for making U.S.–Japan relations, quietly beset by deepening difficulties and the danger of irrelevance, whole and vital once again.

Chapter 1 The Quiet Crisis
of the Alliance

In April 2007 Japanese Prime Minister Abe Shinzō visited the White House with his wife, Akie, for a tête-à-tête dinner with George and Laura Bush. The next day the two principals helicoptered to Camp David, the president's private retreat, for a day of far-ranging talks as friends and allies. Their joint statement hailed a slew of fresh initiatives, elaborated at a high-profile joint news conference.

The *New York Times* published a panoramic photo of that august gathering the next day, with Secretary of State Condoleezza Rice and Minister of Foreign Affairs Asō Tarō, flanked by Ambassadors Katō Ryōzō and Thomas Schieffer, clearly in evidence in the front row. But it appeared only on page 6.[1] The policy pronouncements were totally ignored, both in the *Times* and in other mainstream U.S. media.

President Bush declared, as is standard at such occasions, that the transpacific relationship was sound, with historic progress being steadily made between Tokyo and Washington, emphasizing that "the alliance between Japan and the United States has never been stronger." Bush defined the relationship expansively as a "global alliance," while Abe termed it "irreplaceable."[2]

Yet in reality all was not well with Pacific affairs. Two weeks after Abe left Andrews Air Force Base for the Middle East, where 180 business leaders who had skipped the earlier Washington gatherings caught up with him,[3] the U.S. House of Representatives passed a sense of the Congress resolution advising Japan to admit to injustices against Asian "comfort women" engaged in servicing Japanese troops during World War II. That resolution also demanded an apology from Prime Minister Abe, despite the determined efforts of the Japanese embassy to forestall it. Back in Tokyo, Prime Minister Abe refused to oblige the Congress, although he reaffirmed past vague statements of national regret. In the Japanese Diet, legislation to fund ambitious military transformation proposals lay stalled, as Japan prepared to cut generous host-nation support (HNS) payments that for two decades had been a mainstay of American military support for continued forward deployment in Japan. More than eleven years after President Bill Clinton and Prime Minister Hashimoto Ryūtarō solemnly agreed at the Tokyo Summit of 1996 to close the Futenma Marine Corps Air Station and move it to northeastern Okinawa, not a single bulldozer had moved.

Meanwhile, in Beijing American negotiators were leading talks to cap and close North Korea's nuclear facilities at Yongbyon. The focus in these so-called six-party talks was almost exclusively nonproliferation issues. Japan's central concerns—its kidnapped citizens and mobile North Korean Nodong missiles capable of reaching Kansai—were not being addressed, although more than one hundred of the missiles were already operational. And in Japan itself, a debate had begun as to whether it might be appropriate for Tokyo to consider going nuclear.

Things did not get much better in the succeeding months. In September 2007 an exhausted Prime Minister Abe abruptly resigned, following a string of Cabinet scandals and a massive defeat in the triannual Upper House election. The following month, the newly emboldened opposition, controlling half of the Diet, forced the temporary recall of Marine Self-Defense Forces (MSDF) from the Indian Ocean, where they were deployed in support of U.S.-led anti-terrorist operations.

Early in 2008 a series of widely publicized crimes, ranging from murder and rape to theft and counterfeiting, were attributed to American servicemen in Okinawa and Yokosuka, leading to a strong popular backlash against U.S. bases. These bases, in addition to carrying out other strategically important tasks, sustain the only American aircraft carrier home-ported outside the United States, while also housing, in peacetime, one of the three worldwide

Marine Expeditionary Corps.[4] Prime Minister Fukuda Yasuo, Abe's successor, watched in frustration as the resurgent opposition in March 2008 rejected the $4 billion annual HNS agreement with the United States, threatening to reduce by half the total bilateral HNS funding that the U.S. military receives worldwide. The HNS budget was restored, over the opposition's heated objections, in May 2008. And four months later, Prime Minister Fukuda himself resigned, within a year of his installation, creating further uncertainties. The similarly unstable administration of Aso Tarō followed.

THE SEDUCTIVE DANGERS OF
SELF-CONGRATULATION

A senior State Department colleague once wryly advised me, during my four and a half years of U.S. embassy service in Tokyo, that "there has never been a U.S.–Japan summit or senior dialogue that did not succeed." His thin smile reflected the corrosive mixture of abject belief, smug security, and persistent cynicism that all too often pervades the professional handling of U.S.–Japan relations today. It adds up, in a word, to the antithesis of crisis consciousness. The United States and Japan, after all, *are* long-standing treaty allies, with a security relationship that has deepened measurably since 9/11. Indeed, many of their principal interlocutors have established ties of mutual trust that go back generations. And their summit meetings *have,* with the notable exception of a few in the early 1990s, gone remarkably smoothly.

The handlers of U.S.–Japan relations should be justifiably proud of such accomplishments, in a narrow technical sense. Certainly the senior policy meetings of late have been going smoothly. Yet those gatherings may amount to little more than rearranging the lounge chairs, in a composed, deliberate, and sophisticated fashion, on the main deck of the *Titanic.*

The institutional structures for managing U.S.–Japan relations today, especially those on the Japanese side, were born, as we shall see, almost without exception of Occupation and the early Cold War. They are based, as we shall also find, on an embedded bargain, forged at San Francisco in 1951, that was brilliantly conceived but is now arguably out of date. Japan's postwar constitution, together with the configuration of its labor unions, its agriculture, its political parties, and its mass media, not to mention its security ties with the United States, was profoundly shaped by developments of the first two post–World War II decades, the San Francisco settlement being the linchpin. So were the MSDF, the Defense Facilities Administration Agency (DFAA), the U.S.–Japan

Joint Security Consultative Committee, the Joint Committee on U.S.–Japan Security Relations, and many other institutions at the core of the Pacific alliance.

Yet the world, to reiterate, is changing. As we shall argue in coming pages, there are powerful forces building in the post–Cold War global political economy, not to mention the domestic systems of both nations, that quietly challenge the very fundamentals of transpacific partnership as well as the concept of bilateral alliance traditionally prevailing between Washington and Tokyo. In the broader world, China and a dynamic, growing Asia are attractive new magnets pulling both Washington and Tokyo away from their traditional focus on one another. And in domestic politics, changing ethnic equations and nativistic trends are diluting the primacy within Pacific affairs that U.S.–Japan relations have traditionally enjoyed.[5]

Dangerously, the institutions that the two nations have for dealing with these emerging challenges are inadequate to resolve them. These institutions are deficient either because the new challenges are painfully ensconced in a history of occupation and reconstruction now growing rapidly obsolete, or because they are so global that they do not address the unique problems that the United States and Japan mutually confront. There is a distinct need for change, even if the consciousness of that need is sorely lacking.

CRISIS AND INNOVATION

The most important deficiency, we shall argue, is ironically the fruit of recent apparent success. It is the lack of crisis consciousness—the perverse spirit of mutual self-congratulation—that pervades U.S.–Japan relations today. Historically, fear of future disruption—of radical departure from a fragile yet vital status quo—has been the force driving mutual accommodation between Washington and Tokyo as well as policy innovation in transpacific relations more generally. This fateful connection between crisis and innovation was, for example, graphically present in the crafting of the San Francisco Peace Treaty in 1951, amidst the Korean War; in the Kennedy–Reischauer years of the early 1960s, following the Security Treaty crisis; and in the Carter–Mansfield diplomatic era of the late 1970s, after the fall of Saigon. The Reagan–Shultz–Mansfield trio also successfully evoked it during the early 1980s to confront an expansionist Soviet Union after Afghanistan, with the strong cooperation of Prime Minister Nakasone Yasuhiro in Japan. So did the Clinton–Perry–Mondale team following the tragic Okinawa rape case in 1995, and the Bush–Armitage–

Howard Baker partnership, similarly aided by Prime Minister Koizumi Jun-ichirō, in the shadow of 9/11. For both Republican and Democratic adminis-trations in the United States, not to mention Japanese governments of every description, crisis has been the driving force of policy innovation, in both for-eign and domestic policy. Sadly, that dynamic engine of change still remains strangely silent today.

This book relies extensively on cross-national comparison to deepen and generalize my concrete observations about how U.S.–Japan bilateral relations themselves actually operate in the real world. We look at America's European alliances, both multilaterally within NATO and bilaterally, in particular with Britain, Germany, and Italy; U.S.–Asian alliances, especially with South Korea; and at the contrasting Sino-American relationship—an exception that intrigu-ingly demonstrates more general patterns configuring U.S.–Japan relations as well. In all these diverse cases, drawn from throughout the world, the impor-tance of crisis as the mother of innovation reveals itself, just as it does in transpacific ties between Washington and Tokyo.

THE PROBLEM FOR ANALYSIS

Measured against the standards of the past, the U.S.–Japan relationship of the past five years has in some ways undoubtedly functioned well. Ties of friend-ship and mutual esteem emanating from an unprecedented personal bond be-tween President George W. Bush and Prime Minister Koizumi Junichirō and extending to the parallel trust between U.S. Deputy Secretary of State Richard Armitage and Japanese Ambassador to the United States Katō Ryōzō led to some remarkable and historic deepening of transpacific security ties in the wake of 9/11. Trade frictions, endemic from the Nixon Shocks of 1971 until the auto-motive agreement of 1995, have abated remarkably.[6]

Yet the evanescent bonds of the recent past cannot cope with the pointed challenges of the future now emerging. As we shall see, those new challenges differ sharply from those of the past few years. And existing programs and in-stitutions, many dating back half a century, are not configured to address them well. It does not follow from the tranquil recent past of U.S.–Japan relations that benign patterns will continue, especially if the continually crucial catalyst to policy innovation that crisis consciousness provides does not prevail.

The problem for analysis here is thus threefold. First, this study profiles the unique and daunting, if surprisingly unobserved, longer-term policy chal-lenges that loom for U.S.–Japan relations, as their East Asian regional and domestic-political context steadily changes. Second, it inventories the institutional and interpersonal mechanisms for response that currently exist, comparing them with patterns prevailing in other comparable international relationships and accenting the distinctive, irreplaceable historical past from which they stem. Finally, after identifying the critical deficiencies, this work suggests how those gaps might be filled, so as to transform U.S.–Japan relations into the real pillar of stability in transpacific and global affairs that it has such rich potential to become.

Deepening Long-Term Challenges

The global context of the U.S.–Japan relationship in the twenty-first century, I argue, will be fundamentally different from that which has prevailed since the San Francisco Peace Treaty of 1951. As is well known, global economic interdependence is rapidly rising, most noticeably in such areas as direct investment and international finance. Global regimes to regulate rising transactions are forming in response, with all the attendant technical issues of multilateral coordination that such regimes necessarily involve. Those problems of coordination are intensified by the enormous potential volatility in markets and other political-economic parameters that the massive scale of global financial transactions and the lightning speed of Internet-related information flows mutually provoke.[7]

Third-Country Complications

U.S.–Japan relations, in that global context, are thus easily diluted and subordinated to broader concerns, as has proven true in cases ranging from Iran and Kashmir to North Korea. Traditional bilateral modes of resolution, which readily incorporate even nuanced Washington–Tokyo understandings of the past, are easily undermined and preempted. The potential problems for bilateral relations that this silent transition to globalism can generate were graphically illustrated in the remarkably bitter steel-trade controversies of 1998 and 2002. These flared up even after the traditional bilateral structures for resolution, such as trigger-price mechanisms and orderly marketing agreements (OMAs), were dismantled.[8] The subtle yet perilous frictions of a multilateral world were also apparent in the ongoing controversy over implementation of the Kyoto environmental protocol after 2001. There, once again, Japan and the Bush administration found agreement difficult, despite their continuing mutual declarations of alliance.

The regional context of U.S.–Japan relations is also changing, increasing the

Figure 1.1. Trade Relations: China Eclipses the Pacific Alliance Partners

A. American Trade   (unit = $ billion)

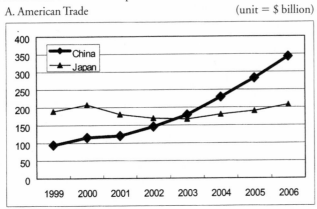

B. Japanese Trade   (unit = $ billion)

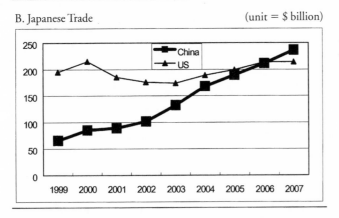

Source: (A) U.S. Department of Commerce; JETRO website: http://www.jetro.go.jp/.
(B) JETRO website: http://www.jetro.go.jp/.
Note: The figures are for total bilateral merchandise trade. In the case of China, the figures
do not include Hong Kong.

potential distraction to the alliance of third-party issues. Since 2001, America's
largest bilateral trade deficit has been not with Japan, but with China. Since
2002, Japan's largest source of imports has also shifted from the United States to
the PRC. Since 2003, as noted in figure 1.1, total U.S.–China trade has exceeded that between the United States and Japan by an increasing margin.[9]
And since 2007, Japan–China trade volume has eclipsed U.S.–Japan trade as
well.[10] Today U.S.–Japan trade is the most anemic link of what for most of the
past half century was an America-centric economic triangle among Japan,
China, and the United States.

More generally, intra-Asian trade is rising in importance, while transpacific trade is languishing, with future exchange-rate shifts likely to intensify this historic trend. A stronger yen, won, and RMB can only make the markets of Japan, Korea, and China collectively more attractive. The PRC, through its rapid growth, rising currency, and astute networking, is pulling both America and Japan into a tighter, if arguably more claustrophobic embrace with Beijing in subtle ways that are gradually coming to quietly challenge the bilateral U.S.–Japan relationship as well. China's priorities and definitions of desirable regional stability are growing more influential, as manifest in the six-party talks on North Korean issues. This subtle Chinese impact on U.S.–Japan relations is compounded by mainland China's growing political-economic ties with Taiwan, which have major geoeconomic implications for neighboring Japan also.[11]

Technology, especially defense technology, is likewise evolving in ways that create subtle, yet intensifying challenges for the U.S.–Japan relationship. Both North Korea and China appear to be increasing both the number and the accuracy of their missile systems. Chinese DF-11 and DF-15 short-range ballistic missiles (SRBMs) along the Taiwan Straits appear to have been increasing particularly rapidly.[12]

At present North Korea lacks missiles capable of reliably reaching the United States in any volume, and China remains far from strategic parity. Yet both have substantial and growing numbers of short-range missiles of increasing accuracy, capable of being targeted on Japan. North Korea now has well over one hundred mobile Nodong missiles operational, capable of reaching virtually any part of the Japanese archipelago. The DPRK has also been developing the multistage Taepodong 2, whose six-thousand-kilometer range would allow it to deliver warheads as far as Alaska and northern Australia.[13] The PRC has more than 725 SRBMs targeted on Taiwan and the Kansai area of Japan, plus over 35 intermediate-range ballistic missiles (IRBMs) capable of reaching any Japanese location, together with more than 50 intercontinental ballistic missiles (ICBMs), covering much of America's heartland.[14]

Domestic Sociopolitical Transformation

Domestic politics and society in both the United States and Japan are also slowly but surely changing, with fateful long-term implications for the Pacific alliance in its broadest sense. America, for its part, is becoming a more pluralistic society, with the number of non-Japanese Asian immigrants increasing rapidly and becoming a substantial part of local populations in California, the

Pacific Northwest, and the Northeast as well as Hawaii. Japanese-American populations, meanwhile, are growing far less rapidly and becoming progressively more assimilated in broader American society. They are also declining in political cohesiveness with the passage of time since the great unifying experiences of World War II, the relocation camps, and the subsequent redress movement.[15]

It is important, needless to say, to keep gradual changes in the ethnic configurations of America's population in proper perspective. Diversity has been one of America's great strengths throughout its history. And Japanese Americans, who were historically the most numerous group of Asian Americans for the first three-quarters of the twentieth century, share numerous interests with the rapidly growing groups of newcomers from elsewhere in Asia. Yet on issues of American Asia policy as well as historical interpretation, where their ancestral homelands are involved the changing demographics appear to be consequential, with Japanese voices increasingly overwhelmed, as the transpacific politics of the comfort-women controversy of 2007 graphically showed.

These new demographic trends are graphically evident in northern California, an area of major political importance in Democratic congressional politics owing to the presence there of several members of considerable seniority, including Speaker of the House of Representatives Nancy Pelosi. In San Jose in Silicon Valley, for example, the traditional home of many Japanese-American farmers for close to a century and still represented by *sansei* Congressman Michael Honda, the Chinese-American and Korean-American populations have been growing explosively in recent years.[16] As indicated in figure 1.2, there are now twelve times as many Chinese-Americans as Japanese-Americans in San Francisco. Even though the city has the oldest and what was for many years the largest Chinatown in the United States, the gap in Chinese-American and Japanese-American populations there has grown considerably, with the number of Chinese relative to Japanese Americans increasing from a 3.6 to 1 ratio in 1980. Meanwhile, in San Jose, whose overall Asian-American population today approaches 30 percent, the ratio of Chinese to Japanese Americans is 7 to 1, a sharp reversal of patterns prevailing until the 1980s.[17]

Developments in Washington, D.C., compound the impact of these recent demographic changes, so potentially unsettling for U.S.–Japan relations, in the broader nation. As Washington becomes more and more of a global political-economic locus in the post–Cold War era, foreign governmental and nongovernmental interests see increasing value in becoming systematic stakeholders within this Washington-centric New World Order.[18] The PRC, Taiwan,

Figure 1.2. Growing Non-Japanese Asian-American Populations in Major Northern California Cities

A. San Francisco   (unit = people)

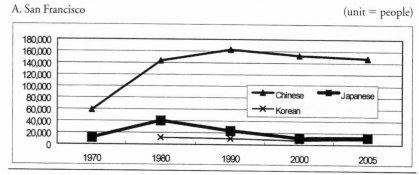

B. San Jose   (unit = people)

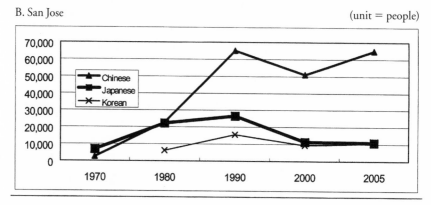

Source: U.S. Census Bureau, *American Community Survey* (2005 edition); U.S. Census Bureau, *Census of Population* (1990, 1980, and 1970 editions).

Note: (1) Figures are for distinct Asian-American population groups, with no provision for multiple nationality designations after 1990. (2) The category "Chinese" includes Taiwanese. (3) Figures are for individuals of a given ethnic background, determined by self-identification, without regard to immigration status or nationality.

India, and South Korea all have a complex of rising security and economic concerns that have driven them to rapidly expand their political representation in America's national capital over the past decade. By contrast, Japan's political-economic presence has been surprisingly static, reflecting the waning of traditional trade conflict and a historical concentration of U.S.–Japan economic and cultural activities in New York City.[19]

Falling prey to Japanese inattention and American indifference, the infra-structural base of U.S.–Japan relations in Washington has thus quietly yet dangerously eroded. Resident Japan specialists have disappeared from the staffs of the Brookings Institution and many other research centers, while such long-standing pillars of the Japanese presence in Washington as the Japan Economic Institute have closed their doors. In the capital's universities, as in major academic institutions throughout the United States, both the number of Japan courses and the proportion of students studying Japan and the Japanese language, relative to the shares studying other major Asian languages, have been steadily declining.

Driven by rising domestic income inequality, globalization, and changing participation patterns, American politics are growing increasingly volatile and polarized. Organized machine politics are decaying, Chicago being the only remaining major city where stable one-party patronage politics continue to prevail. At both the national and local levels, issue politics, influenced heavily by the mass media, are growing increasingly salient, while political parties capable of smoothly mediating and aggregating interests are decaying. Moderates in both major parties are increasingly endangered, as the political parties grow polarized: the Democratic Party is becoming increasingly populist, as the Republican base grows ever more neoconservative and fundamentalist.[20] Americans of "blue" and "red" persuasions find it increasingly difficult to pursue a serious grassroots dialogue with one another, however much their leaders may rhetorically implore it.

In Japan, meanwhile, society is also changing, in ways highly consequential to the stable long-term future of U.S.–Japan relations. Since 2005 Japan has become the oldest of the OECD nations in demographic terms, with a population that since 2004 has actually begun to decline, despite a slight increase in 2007. Gloomy yet widely credited forecasts suggest that Japan's population may well fall below one hundred million by 2055.[21]

With a shrinking workforce supporting a growing burden of elderly pensioners, Japan has fewer resources to devote to international commitments. Not surprisingly, Japanese foreign aid, once a mainstay of global cooperation with the United States, has been declining steadily since 2000. Japanese HNS for U.S. forces in Japan, traditionally the most generous in the world by a substantial margin, has been under domestic-political siege as well.

Politically, major pressures for change were unleashed in Tokyo by the electoral reforms of 1994.[22] These largely replaced Japan's traditional multimember district electoral system, which had previously created a strong policy bias toward distributive politics, with winner-take-all single-member districts.[23] This epic structural change both accelerated the collapse of smaller leftist and middle-of-the-road parties, on the one hand, and forced the largest, such as

Kōmeitō, into dependent coalition arrangements with the ruling Liberal Democratic Party. Combined with tactical mistakes by the Left, the electoral changes triggered a collapse of the Left in Japanese politics. This debacle reduced the combined Socialist/Communist share of the popular vote from over 8 percent in the general elections of 1996 to only 3 percent a decade later.[24]

While the Right has grown stronger in Japan, volatility has also risen. Disillusionment with the inability of conventional politics to deliver what the general public desires has decidedly increased, with only idiosyncratic politicians such as the former prime minister Koizumi Junichirō attracting much real following.[25] The Japanese general public has grown increasingly critical and issue-sensitive, while its propensity to consistently support any one political group has significantly declined.

Amidst their general disillusionment, the Japanese public appears to have grown increasingly interested in security policy. A Cabinet Office opinion poll in 2005 indicated that 67 percent of the Japanese people were interested in defense issues, an 8 percent increase in just three years.[26] Although traditionally the public has deferred on foreign affairs to the bureaucrats, that tendency is palpably declining, for several reasons. First, of course, Japan has become more directly engaged in global issues of war and peace, by sending MSDF, since 1992, variously to Cambodia, Mozambique, Rwanda, the Golan Heights, Afghanistan, the Indian Ocean, Kuwait, and Iraq, among other locations.[27] Generational transition has also made long-standing antiwar allergies less immediate than previously.

Politics, as mentioned, has shifted perceptibly to the right. Deepening Japanese offshore stakes in a turbulent Asia, combined with rising military capabilities in China and North Korea, have increased the perceived sense of geopolitical threat in Tokyo. And the upgrading in early 2007 of the Japan Defense Agency (JDA) into a Ministry of Defense has created a more powerful, prestigious advocate of national security priorities than at any time since 1945.

Although public sentiments concerning defense definitely appear to be moving to the right, however, disillusionment with the ability of the ruling conservatives to govern Japan has also increased. In the Upper House elections of July 2007, for example, the opposition Democratic Party of Japan (DPJ), representing a complex, contradictory coalition of right- and left-wing groups, won an overwhelming victory, growing from 81 to 109 seats and becoming for the first time ever the largest party in the Upper House.[28] With divided leadership in the two chambers of the Diet, the prospect of more serious and critical national security debate, fueled by partisan sentiment, is undeniably rising, although disputes risk focusing on details rather than on Japan's overall emerging security profile.

Increasing public attention to national security in Japan has spotlighted the distinctive, long-standing institutions with which U.S.–Japan relations are managed. Sensitively crafted in an era of Occupation by John Foster Dulles and his Japanophilic colleagues, many of these were admirably well suited for an early postwar era of hierarchical relations between Tokyo and Washington, when bilateral ties were managed quietly by the two nations' diplomats.[29] The Joint Committee on U.S.–Japan Security Relations and the DFAA, for example, together provided one of the best mechanisms for handling grassroots base-relations problems anywhere in the world, as long as such potentially explosive issues could be dealt with smoothly and bureaucratically.[30] But in high-profile cases in which it became necessary to explain the rationale for security-related actions and especially for the presence of American troops to a generally uncomprehending or unsympathetic public, these intricate compensation mechanisms were of far less use. In an era of increasingly partisan national security debate, they may be increasingly vulnerable in future, above all when facing scandals in the Ministry of Defense as well as crimes or accidents on the part of resident American troops.[31]

Beyond the conflict-resolution mechanisms themselves lie the fundamental structural realities of U.S.–Japan security relations: (1) the Japanese "no-war" constitution; (2) related constraints on Japanese offensive power-projection capabilities, including aircraft carriers, long-range missiles, and fighter-bombers; (3) the heavy American forward-deployed military presence in Japan; and (4) the unparalleled financial support Japan provides to back up the local U.S. military presence. Taken together, in an era of manifest global American political-military preeminence and a commitment to the stability of Asia that has continued since the Korean War, Japanese political military support has meaningfully complemented U.S. efforts to preserve East Asian regional stability, without strongly alarming or antagonizing Tokyo's neighbors. As nationalistic sentiments revive in Japan and across Asia, amidst economic prosperity, the passing of generations, and legislative transformation, however, both the political and the economic viability within Japan of the status quo are coming unavoidably into question.

Japan currently provides over $4.5 billion annually in HNS for U.S. forces in Japan—close to 60 percent of the entire bilateral HNS support that the American military receives worldwide.[32] At the same time, Tokyo devotes nearly a quarter of its national budget to social security expenditures and pensions.[33]

And that share, reflecting the historic graying of Japanese society, is steadily rising.

So are Japan's expenditures on its own offshore military activities. Since legislation to allow the Self-Defense Forces (SDF) as a whole to join UN peacekeeping operations was passed in 1992, Japan has engaged in substantial UN-related PKO activities abroad. In addition, since 2001, Tokyo has also funded extended deployments for its MSDF in the Indian Ocean, for the Ground Self-Defense Forces (GSDF) in Iraq (2004–06), and, more recently, for the Air Self-Defense Forces (ASDF) in Kuwait and Iraq (2003–08). Together, these deployments cost Japan more than ¥39 billion (about $330 million) annually during the 2004–06 period—money that must be diverted from other national spending programs, even as the pressure of demography on Japan's strained finances continues to rise.[34]

On top of this, Japan is also incurring major new expenditures in support of military transformation in the U.S.–Japan defense structure. The Japanese government has agreed, for example, to spend over $26 billion between 2007 and 2014 to close the Futenma Marine Corps Air Station; move its functions to a newly constructed base at Henoko on the northeastern coast of Okinawa; redeploy eight thousand Marines in Okinawa to Guam; move the headquarters of the U.S. Army's I Corps to Camp Zama; and relocate the SDF's Air Defense Command to Yokota Air Base.[35] Although these expenditures will be covered by special appropriations rather than through the annual defense budget, they impose an additional burden on Japanese governmental finances that must be ultimately borne by the Japanese people and approved by their national Diet.

The emerging world that U.S.–Japan relations confront, in sum, is sharply different from that of the past, along many dimensions: global, regional, financial, technological, and domestic-political. The new challenges are subtle and are becoming visible almost imperceptibly. Yet they are no less serious for their novelty. These pressures threaten to fundamentally change the prevailing status quo, in both its security and economic dimensions, and to thus plunge the overall transpacific relationship into turbulent, uncharted waters.

ADAPTIVE MECHANISMS FOR DEALING WITH
EMERGING CHALLENGES: STEADILY ERODING?

U.S.–Japan security relations, in their broadest sense, are thus beginning to confront a broadening set of major challenges. At the same time, their capacity to deal with these threats, many of them quite subtle, is steadily declining. This is the second, highly insidious element of this complex crisis, which we must now address.

To be sure, there are a few bright spots in the current institutional picture. Japan's Prime Minister's Office (*kantei*) has, under recent prime ministers, steadily assumed more substantial analytical and decision-making capabilities.[36] At the operational level, the U.S. and Japanese militaries are beginning to consolidate their response potential at Camp Zama and at Yokota Air Base, as noted above, preparing for an era of both active missile defense and dynamic joint responses to terrorism. Meanwhile, the two countries have also deployed PAC-3 and X-Band radar capabilities to help make joint missile defense a technical possibility.

These new cooperative developments themselves, however, highlight the embedded institutional obstacles that still remain to impede real bilateral cooperation. Japan has, to be sure, deployed X-band radar, a key element in missile-defense systems. Yet the ban on collective self-defense, through existing constitutional interpretation, makes questionable the constitutionality of Japanese support from Japanese bases against missile attacks directed either at the United States, over Japanese territory, or even against American bases on Japanese soil. And the process of constitutional reform that Japan has recently been considering is fraught with political minefields. Coping with the transpacific politics of revision will require both better-articulated rationales within Japan for national security and improved communication across the Pacific on such matters as well.

Sadly, the policy networks that during the early 1960s fostered excellent cultural and economic relations and in the early 1970s led to the graceful reversion of Okinawa to Japan have, over the past decade, begun to badly fray in many areas, despite the high-profile efforts of a few conciliators.[37] Generational change has been one key factor, as the Occupation-era specialists who knew Japan intimately during the early postwar years have steadily passed from the scene. Ambassador Edwin Reischauer passed away in 1990, Ambassador Mike Mansfield in 2001, Herbert Passin, one of the founders of the important Shimoda U.S.–Japan conference series, in 2003, and Bill Clark, longtime diplomat and Japan Society president, in 2008. On the other side of the Pacific, Ichimada Naoto, a prominent ex-governor of BOJ, who was also a founder of I-House and a powerful fund-raiser in the establishment of ICU, died in 1984. Ushiba Nobuhiko, the influential ambassador to Washington, also passed away in that year, while Matsumoto Shigeharu, founding director of I-House, died in 1989, and Kōsaka

Masataka, the Kyoto University professor and distinguished opinion leader, in 1996.

Legislative gridlock in the Japanese political world is a second, increasingly important roadblock to effective bilateral defense cooperation, as the bitter 2007–08 struggles over Indian Ocean deployments and HNS so dramatically demonstrated. The opposition's overwhelming victory in the Upper House elections of July 2007 created the possibility that Japan could have divided government until at least 2013, barring a major political realignment. And because of sharp differences between government and opposition with respect to defense policy, it is also quite conceivable that coherent U.S.–Japan alliance management could be a casualty of such a divided government.

A third problem has been the strong drift in the academic world, most notably in the United States, away from area studies and toward more abstract, comparative analysis involving less emphasis on cultivating networks, contacts, and country-specific knowledge of Japan.[38] Regrettably, it has become counterproductive professionally for first-rate American social scientists to seriously immerse themselves, on a continuing basis, in the details of Japanese domestic affairs. Globalization has also taken a toll, as U.S.–Japan specialists on both sides of the Pacific have diffused and diversified their geographical interests.

The stagnation of the Japanese economy for well over a decade following the bubble's burst in 1989–90, coupled with the related decline of Japanese investment in the United States, have both taken their toll. Those economic downdrafts have meant less institutional support for Japan studies in the United States and less interest on the part of both American students and professionals in studying Japan. At universities all across the United States enrollments in Japan studies courses are now less than half of what they once were, while the number of Japanese students in American universities has dropped by a full 25 percent over the past decade. Today more than three times as many Indians and nearly twice as many Koreans as Japanese college students study in the United States—a sharp reversal of patterns only a decade ago.[39]

The practical consequences of these sobering generational and economic changes for the fragile networks of transpacific interpersonal relations can be seen in three major areas. First, and perhaps most disturbing, from a long-term perspective, the number of students and teachers focusing on U.S.–Japan relations has been declining. Even in Washington, D.C., there are markedly fewer such specialists than a decade ago.

Second, and even more important, from a short-term political standpoint, the scale of parliamentary exchange between Washington and Tokyo has also been sharply declining. Twenty years ago there were a number of major congressional figures, such as Thomas Foley, later to serve as Speaker of the U.S. House of Representatives and ambassador to Japan, who were deeply involved in U.S.–Japan relations, either through formal parliamentary exchanges, or through NGO activities such as those of the Shimoda Conferences and the Trilateral Commission. Today those numbers, and their prominence, are sharply reduced.

A related problem has been the atrophying of NGOs striving to sustain U.S.–Japan interpersonal ties. Typical is the Shimoda Conference series. From its origins in 1967 until the mid-1990s it was highly active, involving such major figures as the former prime minister Nakasone Yasuhiro; several former ambassadors to Japan; and Donald Rumsfeld, the former defense secretary.[40] Unfortunately, however, the Shimoda Conference network has since become virtually defunct, most of its key members having left the policy arena.

The U.S.–Japan Parliamentary Exchange Program, founded in 1968, the year after the Shimoda Conference, also once involved most impressive participants. Over the years its members have included an extraordinary group of leaders in both countries: Howard Baker, U.S. ambassador to Japan, Senate majority leader, and White House chief of staff; Thomas Foley, U.S. ambassador to Japan and Speaker of the House of Representatives; Dennis Hastert, likewise Speaker of the House of Representatives; Richard Gephardt, minority leader of the House of Representatives; Al Gore, vice president; Dan Quayle, vice president; Donald Rumsfeld, secretary of defense; two Japanese prime ministers, Obuchi Keizō and Hata Tsutomu; Doi Takako, leader of the Social Democratic Party; and two LDP secretary generals, Katō Kōichi and Yamasaki Taku. The exchange continues in form, but the American delegates have not visited Japan since 2002, even though the Japanese counterparts still occasionally pass through Washington.[41] Only 39 American legislators visited Japan during 2000–05, many fewer than the 113 to China, 79 to India, and 68 to Taiwan.[42] And by 2007 the annual number visiting Japan under the auspices of this venerable and traditionally prestigious program had declined to 1.[43]

In 1973, the American Council of Young Political Leaders (ACYPL) and the Japan Center for International Exchange (JCIE) jointly launched the U.S.–Japan Young Political Leaders Exchange Program. The exchanges continue but with decidedly less frequency than before. Alumni include Elizabeth Dole, former senator from North Carolina; Wyche Fowler, former senator and ambassador to Saudi Arabia; Bill Graves, governor of Kansas; former prime minister Obuchi Keizō; Katō Kōichi, former defense minister and LDP secretary general; and former prime minister Hosokawa Morihiro.[44] Like the participants in the Parliamentary Exchange and the Shimoda Conferences, key past members of this program are steadily leaving the political scene and not being replaced.

The Trilateral Commission, originally proposed by David Rockefeller with the explicit aim of integrating Japan securely into the fabric of G-7 political-economic relations, was a major force in transpacific relations during the 1970s and 1980s. It played a significant role at a crucial stage in integrating Japan into the global community of nations. Recently it, too, faced with an aging membership and mounting financial difficulties, has become less active.

In the world of U.S.–Japan cultural exchange itself, narrowly conceived, economic frictions and Japan's economic downturn have taken their toll. Some Japan America Societies, like that in Washington, D.C., remain vigorous programmatically, but their funding and membership are suffering significant decline. The U.S.–Japan Business Council has also lost momentum, having nearly 10 percent fewer corporate members in 2007 than in 2004.[45] There is, to be sure, an important existing infrastructure of U.S.–Japan sister city relationships. Japan as of August 2008 had 437 such sets of transpacific ties with American counterparts, compared to only 326 for China and 120 for Korea.[46] Yet linkages with Korea and China appear to be growing much faster at the margin than those with Japan, reflecting the more rapid expansion of transpacific economic ties and immigrant populations in the latter two cases.

IMPERATIVES FOR THE FUTURE

The rest of this book focuses on how historical and comparative evidence can be summoned, in a practical, problem-oriented way, to address the quiet yet deepening crisis that U.S.–Japan relations today confronts. Concrete prescriptions will be presented in the concluding chapter. Yet let us briefly review, in the pages to come, the subtle challenges we have uncovered and the topics for future analysis that they urgently mandate.

We have identified emerging challenges for the transpacific relationship in five main areas. First of all, globalization is rapidly broadening both nations' range of political-economic associations. At the same time, it is also fostering a cosmopolitan new world society, in a still-volatile international system that demands increasingly sophisticated and sensitive global governance. In that newly globalized environment, which encourages fluid, cosmopolitan associations, what inclination will two countries as sharply distinct as the United States and Japan—in culture, history, and decision-making process—have to relate with one another? They demonstrably will need to do so smoothly, given their combined two-fifths of global GDP. Yet the coordination, as we have suggested, could well be difficult, and it may be neither eager nor well informed.

The second emerging challenge is regional. China is swelling rapidly in scale, to economic magnitudes of which Dulles never dreamed, although its relative size in such terms remains substantially smaller than Japan and will continue to be so for a decade or more. Chinese growth and the related disproportionate expansion of intra-Asian trade and investment relative to that across the Pacific create important new cross-pressures on U.S.–Japan relations which cannot be ignored.

These cross-pressures flowing from the rise of China have their correlates inside the domestic politics of both the United States and Japan. Chinese Americans are becoming much more numerous than Japanese Americans in many U.S. congressional districts, while the PRC's informal influence in Washington, like South Korea's, is rising as well. Both Japanese and American politics are growing more volatile and are evolving in different directions, the rightward drift of Japanese politics in tension with the increasing diversity and populism of its American counterpart. Transpacific elite political networks are decaying, while people-to-people understanding is becoming, in many areas, an increasingly complex proposition.

Technological change, especially in the defense sphere, also creates new challenges for U.S.–Japan cooperation. Even as the political systems of the two nations become more volatile internally as well as distant from one another, their operational needs for defense cooperation intensify. Missile defense and aerospace cooperation require intimate command and control liaison, implicit in the ambitious military transformation proposals of the Bush administration, for which the political basis remains to be fully established.

U.S.–Japan relations, finally, continue to be embedded in a set of Occupation-era institutions inherited from the past: the world of John Foster Dulles. Some of these institutions at the subnational level, such as the Joint Committee on U.S.–Japan Security Cooperation and the DFAA, appear to have been quite functional.[47] At times, however, as in the case of DFAA, this efficacy has come mixed with drawbacks that have generated separate problems of their own.[48] There are also enormous institutional problems of transition now impending in bilateral relations, as Japan and the United States confront an era of Japanese constitutional revision, not to mention changing mutual approaches to forward deployment and offshore force projection, amidst domestic political transition.

What do these subtle, looming challenges on the regional and global scenes imply for the future pattern of bilateral interaction between the United States and Japan? This question will be addressed in future chapters, sharpened through multifaceted historical and cross-national comparative analysis. Yet it is important to delineate a general road map here.

First, one must stress that the clear prospect of novel and deepening trans-pacific challenges does not necessarily imply the need for radical change in core bilateral institutions. Radical change, after all, can open dangerous new Pandora's boxes, and that appears highly likely in U.S.–Japan security relations. The U.S.–Japan alliance, together with the major American air and naval bases in Japan, in particular, are established elements, inherited from the past, that should be preserved, owing to the stabilizing impact they have on the broader transpacific political-economic structure as a whole.

The era of Cold War military containment of continental Asian powers such as China may well be drawing to a close, given the deep strands of interdependence, along the energy sea-lanes, for example, in the truly globalized world now dawning. Yet persisting delicacy in financial, political, and cultural relations—not to mention new strategic exigencies—gives continuing significance to Pacific alliance.[49] Nevertheless, in that global world now emerging, with economic and cultural relationships steadily growing more diverse, the viability of a meaningful U.S.–Japan alliance could still be problematic unless other changes in the software of the transpacific relationship are made. It is on those important yet neglected areas that the prescriptions in this book concentrate their focus.

An assessment of the challenges outlined above suggests four areas for prescriptive inquiry going forward. One, to be sure, is institutional: alliance consolidation. The demands of new defense technology, most visibly the rapid advance of communications, aerospace technology, and precision weaponry, mandate more intense alliance coordination—not only between the United States and Japan, but potentially with Asian allies and with NATO as well. Command and control, research and development, and defense production are all areas where consolidation and interoperability are issues of considerable importance for the future.

Two other areas for priority analysis and future innovation have to do with a softer yet no less significant issue—the configuration of interpersonal networks. U.S.–Japan networks have eroded dangerously, as has been noted, in several important spheres: parliamentary exchange, business dialogue, grassroots communication, and cultural-educational exchange. In an era of explosively rapid political-economic change, solid interpersonal networks, so essential to promoting mutual understanding across cultural gaps and so much more adept at managing change than rigid formal institutions, will be much more central in stabilizing the transpacific relationship than is often appreciated. Much of the analysis here therefore focuses on how to deepen and empower such human ties.

Strengthening Japan's presence in Washington, and America's converse standing in Tokyo, need to be subjects of the highest concern in the future. Even as nation-states may be waning in their ability to shape world affairs, national capitals and the interpersonal networks radiating out from them are arguably rising in importance. With the sociopolitical presence of China and Korea, in particular, simultaneously rising in both Washington and Tokyo, believers in the transcendent importance of the U.S.–Japan alliance must devote particular attention to how congenial interpersonal networks within and between their respective capitals can be reinforced and strengthened.

The Pacific alliance between Washington and Tokyo may appear at first glance to be principally a military artifact. Yet on closer inspection its broader, socioeconomic dimensions become clear. No such alliance can endure without deep grounding in the societies and the economic interests of its members: the contrasting failure of the Nazi–Soviet and the Warsaw Pacts, on the one hand, and the persistence of NATO, on the other, not to mention the remarkable, six-hundred-year-old Anglo-Portuguese alliance, make these broader imperatives clear.[50] A final subject of prescriptive research here will thus be how the U.S.–Japan alliance can be broadened and strengthened in its *nonmilitary* dimensions, so that it addresses the true needs and aspirations of citizens in both nations for *human security,* as well as the dimensions of military security central to national leaders on both sides of the Pacific.

In particular, this research will probe how the contrasting conceptions of national security prevailing in the United States and Japan can be bridged, so as to provide a deeper, more enduring bilateral sense of common purpose than has heretofore prevailed—one that can command public support in both nations during the challenging years ahead. While Americans conceive of security in generally military terms, Japanese tend to think more broadly, from a bottom-up perspective, using criteria approaching the classical definitions of human security. In this connection, energy, environment, transportation, and education are concerns that the general public of the two nations share and that should legitimately be considered relevant in definitions of common alliance goals, as long as the hard-security questions are also sufficiently addressed.

"Japan and the United States face each other, but across the broadest ocean of them all," as Edwin O. Reischauer pointed out in the opening lines of his classic study of U.S.–Japan relations.[51] To forge an enduring alliance across the overwhelming differences of culture and history that divide the United States and Japan, policymakers cannot ignore the differing conceptions of security that separate them. Only by addressing areas of mutual human concern and steadily broadening that effort toward areas of special geopolitical import, through the creation of new stabilizing institutions, can the two nations be bound in enduring fashion, and the quiet crisis of the alliance overcome. Understanding that complex process of binding and mutual understanding is the subtle yet vital task that we must now pursue.

Chapter 2 The World That
Dulles Built

Any human relationship is a becoming, with the past providing a continuing laboratory for the present and the future. So it is with the Pacific alliance. "Those who cannot remember the past," as George Santayana observed, "are condemned to repeat it."[1]

Two hundred years ago, there were few more contrasting nations on earth than Japan and the United States: one optimistic, self-righteous, and outward-bound; the other more subtle, introverted, and biased toward isolation. Both were inquisitive and clearly capable of dynamic dialogue. Yet they had little inkling of one another.

Underlying today's ties between Washington and Tokyo is the epic story of tutelage, growth, exclusion, and imperial rivalry that marked the first eight decades of U.S.–Japan relations. It could hardly be called alliance. Yet from the day that Matthew C. Perry's black ships first dropped anchor at Uraga in July 1853, the United States and Japan have been linked by a unique existential bond. It was America, after all, that pulled Japan from two centuries of isolation and then provided key advisors for its remarkable development. It was also America, however, that excluded Japanese immigrants in 1924 and embargoed Japanese oil and scrap metal supplies in 1941, as the two headed down the road to a savage intercultural conflict. There has been a faint hierarchical tinge to U.S.–Japan relations—mingled with a liberal dose of idealism—from the very inception.

Inevitably, a cataclysmic war, including both Pearl Harbor and Hiroshima as submerged elements of its bitter heritage, also looms in the background of the transpacific equation. More than three million Japanese and a quarter of a million Americans, after all, died in a struggle pitting these two deeply different nations as principal and deadly adversaries. Following that "war without mercy,"[2] Japan was occupied for over seven years, its domestic system and international environment both radically transformed, with the active cooperation, in the end, of the Japanese people. It was a process, however paradoxical, of "embracing defeat."[3]

THE SHADOW OF OCCUPATION (1952–60)

Founding experience can have fateful, long-term effects, by structuring institutions, networks, and ways of thinking. So it has been with U.S.–Japan relations. Occupation, however liberal and benign, was the starting point of the transpacific partnership as we know it today—profoundly influencing the tenor of both bilateral ties and the Japanese domestic political-economic system.

The current U.S.–Japan Mutual Security Treaty, which defines the Pacific alliance more than any other single document, was signed at the Golden Gate Club in San Francisco's Presidio district on September 8, 1951—only hours after the San Francisco Peace Treaty had been concluded at the Opera House across town. In the United States it was acclaimed as the signal handiwork of John Foster Dulles, advisor to Secretary of State Dean Acheson. Confidant of the Rockefellers at their Sullivan and Cromwell law firm, nephew of Robert Lansing, Wilson's secretary of state and soon to assume his uncle's weighty mantle under Dwight D. Eisenhower, Dulles was a scion of the Establishment and lauded for his accomplishments in deftly concluding a victorious peace in the Pacific.

In stark recognition of its ominous unpopularity in Tokyo, the historic document was signed on the Japanese side by Prime Minister Yoshida Shigeru alone. The peace and mutual security treaties were really a package: the peace treaty had no separate existence of its own, but rather was contingent upon

Japan's agreeing to a military alliance with America. It was, as John Dower succinctly put it, "magnanimity under lock and key."[4]

In the background of these highly asymmetric agreements crafted by Dulles were similarly unbalanced economic and political conditions, during the turbulent early 1950s, that rendered the asymmetric profile of the formal understandings finally arrived at almost preordained. Japan's economy, although stimulated by Korean War offshore procurements, suffered from substantial inflation and massive deficits on its trade account. In the wake of wartime destruction, it simply lacked the production capacity to supply exports and simultaneously meet fitfully rising postwar domestic demand.

Japan's trade deficits with the United States were especially massive and chronic owing to both the lingering effects of the Pacific conflict and the geopolitical shifts of the early postwar years. America took only 12 percent of the meager exports from a ruined Japan in 1947, for example, yet provided fully 92 percent of its total imports, largely on a concessionary basis. Before the war, Asia, especially the Northeast Asian colonial possessions—Korea, Taiwan, and Manchuria—had accounted for fully 53 percent of Japanese imports and 64 percent of exports; by 1947, however, trade with the former Co-Prosperity Sphere had shriveled to a marginal 6 percent of Japan's imports and only 4 percent of its exports.[5] Japan, in short, was effectively divorced from the Asian continent and consequently dependent on the United States for both markets and economic assistance.

Japan was also disarmed and divested of empire. In 1942 it had held sway over two-thirds of Asia's people and half the Pacific with one of the most powerful militaries in history. A decade later, as the Occupation ended, amidst the Korean War next door, it had only a small police reserve, dwarfed by the more than two hundred thousand American troops that still remained on its soil.[6] And Japan's peace constitution, coupled with lingering popular aversion to war, inhibited any prospect of major rearmament.

Politically, of course, Japan and especially its conservative ruling elite were in similarly vulnerable straits. The country, after all, had been under Occupation for well over six years, with no specified end in sight, when the peace settlement that structured future foreign relations was finally concluded. To be sure, a restive, radical public-sector labor movement had been crushed by the Reverse Course and the Red Purge. The Reverse Course was the Allied occupation's abrupt shift in policy toward Japan during 1948 from an emphasis on democratization to an accent on political-economic stability. The Red Purge (1948–51) was a series of arbitrary layoffs by government agencies and corporations aimed at eliminating from the workplace those unilaterally branded Red. Over twenty-seven thousand were ultimately purged.[7] Yet Japanese political leadership remained sandwiched between an Allied Occupation with unspecified yet absolute powers and an increasingly frustrated populace chafing for an end to that foreign dominance.

Many in Washington, especially in the Pentagon, wanted America's military presence to continue in straightforward fashion—even via an extended Occupation—given the seemingly dire security situation in Northeast Asia. Yet America, too, was constrained in its demands, by a parallel fear of the same instabilities and frustrations within Japan that concerned Japanese conservative leaders. As the Cold War deepened, compounded by the strains of hot war in Korea (1950–53), Acheson and his key advisor Dulles both feared that the Japanese, frustrated with an interminable Occupation and unstable economically, could easily fall to communism. They leaned increasingly toward concluding an early treaty of peace, ending the Occupation, defusing local nationalist resentment, and, amidst a deepening Cold War, encouraging an independent Japan to voluntarily join the Western bloc. Prime Minister Yoshida similarly pressed for a quick peace treaty and was willing to open idle ex-Imperial Army and Navy bases to American troops, to both reassure Washington of Japanese support and reinforce domestic stability in a Japan that was otherwise devoid of armed forces.

The idealistic concept propounded by the intellectuals, of concluding a peace treaty with all wartime belligerents, including the Soviet Union and the PRC, implied Japan's neutrality, no foreign bases, and no Japanese military. Neither of the Communist giants would have agreed to remilitarization or institutionalized alliance with an American superpower whose global condominium they opposed. The provisions demanded by Moscow and Beijing, however, were conversely unacceptable to the United States.

In the face of a palpable Communist threat, amidst the Korean War, Dulles insisted to Yoshida that Japan rearm itself when sovereignty was restored. SCAP tried to convince him to raise a military of three hundred thousand men to cope with Sino-Soviet and North Korean pressures. Yoshida, however, did not budge from his belief that the war-torn Japan could not afford such substantial military commitments, given the clear imperatives of economic recovery.[8] In the face of political imperatives to conclude a peace treaty that threatened to leave Northeast Asia without credible military protection, the United States compromised, with an agreement to forward-deploy its own forces at bases in

Japan and the Ryūkyūs—a settlement that even the Pentagon had not foreseen in the early postwar years.

The Asymmetric Cold War World
That Dulles Built

Influenced by the foregoing political-economic currents, both global and domestic, the post-Occupation Pacific alliance crafted by Dulles quickly assumed a form quite different from the more balanced American political-economic ties with Europe, as we shall see. The newborn San Francisco System, as it can appropriately be called, gave Japan broad trade access to the American market, aiding Japanese economic recovery, in return for intimate, if asymmetrical, transpacific security cooperation and Japan's acquiescence in isolating mainland China.[9] This evolution illustrates graphically the impact of sociopolitical contingency on institutional outcomes. It also shows clearly that general pronouncements about how grand strategy configures institutions such as global trading rules need serious qualification. The transpacific saga also illustrates the importance of critical junctures and domestic politics in shaping policy resultants, particularly subnational implementation.

The security treaty of 1951 itself provided that America would retain bases in Japan and Okinawa, in return for a vague promise from Washington to defend Japan. U.S. forces were also allowed, under the original treaty, to subdue internal riots and disturbances within Japan, at the request of the Japanese government. The operational rights of American troops within Japan, however, were handled discreetly in a separate executive agreement, not requiring Diet approval and hence avoiding the need for politicized legislative debate in Tokyo.

Although neither the peace treaty nor the security pact incorporated Washington's geostrategic designs for Asia explicitly, they did so indirectly, by omission. Most critically, neither mainland China nor the Soviet Union was signatory to the peace treaty.[10] Additionally, many postwar boundaries among successor states within the former Japanese Empire were left undefined. Territorial disputes between Japan and the Soviet Union over the so-called Northern Territories off Hokkaidō and between Japan and Korea over small islands in the Sea of Japan remained unresolved. The peace treaty also rejected the notion of reparations, a provision that many of Japan's wounded neighbors, such as the Philippines, had fervently and self-righteously demanded. Japan, in effect, was linked firmly to the United States in both military and economic terms but was left with ambiguous relations to its neighbors that could easily become the seeds of future conflict.[11] The peace treaty ratification process introduced further constraints on future Japanese relations with Asia, encouraged by Dulles. Less than a week after the treaty was signed in San Francisco, William Knowland (R-California), leader of the U.S. Senate's Taiwan-oriented China lobby, amassed the support of fifty-six senators—a clear majority of that critical body—to threaten rejection of the peace treaty unless Japan agreed unequivocally to support the Republic of China on Taiwan and to ostracize newly Communist mainland China.[12] Roughly six weeks later, Yoshida made controversial comments in the Upper House of the Diet indicating some interest in building relations with mainland China; the firestorm of protest in the U.S. Congress intensified.[13]

Dulles, accompanied by Senators John Sparkman and Alexander Smith of the Foreign Relations Committee, thereafter flew back to Tokyo to cajole Yoshida into accepting a conciliatory statement appeasing Knowland. In response, Japan's prime minister reluctantly signed what became known as the Yoshida letter, indicating that Japan had no intention of concluding a bilateral treaty with mainland China. It later became known that the Yoshida letter had actually been written by Dulles himself.[14]

America's political-military concerns, amidst the Korean War, coupled with Japan's economic vulnerability at the critical juncture of the Occupation's end, decisively influenced the configuration of the emerging Pacific alliance. Although the U.S.–Japan security relationship and its early interpretations favored Washington in highly asymmetrical terms, there was also a clear, if informal, economic corollary that advantaged Tokyo. To help put Japan back on its feet, the massive American market, close to 30 percent of global GDP in the early 1950s, was to be open to Japanese products.[15]

The reverse was not necessarily the case, as reciprocal access was not a primary objective of U.S. policy in the self-confident world that Dulles had made. Japan's bureaucracies selectively restrained a number of major American investments in Japan, and U.S. government objections were resoundingly moderate. The basic approach of the Japanese government was to permit inward direct investment and to progressively reduce barriers impeding such flows, but only after Japan Inc. grew strong enough to effectively confront its foreign counterparts.[16]

In March 1954, for example, three major American firms—Coca-Cola, Schaefer Pen, and Studebaker, the now-bankrupt auto producer—were stopped from investing in Japan.[17] U.S. Ambassador John Allison protested, but to no avail.[18] MITI's rationale was that "the firms involved were unable to positively assure that exports would actually develop, and therefore the proposals might constitute a drain on Japan's limited foreign-exchange holdings." The U.S. embassy in Tokyo understood MITI's stance, however, as opposition to foreign competition against domestic companies, coupled with fear of foreigner ownership and control.[19] The conflict did not escalate beyond the embassy.

Systematic inhibition of foreign investment across the early postwar years led to one of the striking structural distortions of the U.S.–Japan relationship to this day—the paucity of foreign investment in Japan. As will be discussed in chapter 4, direct foreign investment in Japan composes only 2.2 percent of Japanese GDP. That is only one-sixth of the share that foreign investment holds in the United States, and sharply less, relative to GDP, than that in any other major industrialized nation. Indeed, the absolute value of foreign investment in Japan is now only one-third that in China, although China's economy remains about three-fourths the size of Japan's in nominal terms.[20] This discrepancy appears to have considerable importance for the operation of the transpacific alliance in its political-economic dimensions, as we shall see.

After drafting the 1951 San Francisco Peace Treaty, Dulles served as chairman of the Japan Society (1952–53) and then U.S. secretary of state (1953–59). The 1950s were thus the Age of Dulles in U.S.–Japan relations. The key dimensions were all his handiwork: (1) a strong military alliance, involving U.S. forward deployment in Japan; (2) asymmetrical economic ties, involving an open American market; and (3) isolation of mainland China.

The events of the Dulles years powerfully influenced the long-term Pacific alliance relationship in four fateful ways, some good and some bad. Perhaps most important, as just illustrated, they failed to actively encourage foreign investment—giving birth to an unusual anomaly in Japan's relations with the broader world that has persisted to this day. The relative weakness of American corporate stakes in Japan, compared to those in Europe, Southeast Asia, and, in later years, China, naturally diluted the influence of the U.S.–Japan lobby in domestic American policy making—a subtle reality generating a potentially serious structural tendency toward "Japan passing" in Washington, D.C. That malady, from Japan's perspective, was to become more and more pronounced in later years, as China and South Korea, in particular, became ever more active in Pacific affairs.

Reinforcing the World That Dulles Built

The Dulles years also, however, fortunately enhanced the sophistication of cultural links between Japan and the United States, partially offsetting the sociopolitical impact of limited investment ties. Before World War II, of course, U.S.–Japan cultural relations had been limited, despite determined efforts by a handful of Japanese such as Okakura Tenshin, who wrote *The Book of Tea* and helped the Boston Museum of Fine Arts to accumulate the largest stock of *ukiyo-e* outside Japan (literally "pictures of floating world," ukiyo-e are a genre of Japanese woodblock prints produced since the seventeenth century and featuring motifs of landscapes, tales from history, the theater, and pleasure); Baron Kaneko Kentarō, a classmate of Theodore Roosevelt at Harvard, who privately gained the American president's support for his country during the Russo-Japanese War; and Nitobe Inazō, the author of *Bushidō: The Soul of Japan* and deputy secretary general of the League of Nations. There was also Shibusawa Eiichi, called a Japanese Morgan by the American media, who helped establish the Japanese-American Relations Committee (Nichibei Kankei Iinkai) in 1916. This group, through quiet collaboration with Elbert H. Gary, founder of U.S. Steel, succeeded in lifting the American ban on steel exports to Japan during World War I.

Yet these pre–World War II network ties paled in comparison with their postwar counterparts. The new postwar human connections were a welcome development, partially offsetting the deleterious lack of American direct investment in Japan on the overall U.S.–Japan relationship of the period. The weakness of bilateral transpacific networks, after all, had contributed dangerously to the misperceptions culminating in Pearl Harbor. During the fifteen years following World War II, however, there was a very substantial deepening and broadening of those invaluable human connections, providing key political and intellectual infrastructure for the major policy initiatives of later years.

There was, first of all, the GI presence, outlined in figure 2.1. It gave more Americans an authentic grassroots experience of Japan than at any time before or since. Immediately after World War II the Occupation brought as many as 500,000 Americans to Japan, and they were stationed in almost every village and town of the Japanese archipelago. After a major drawdown during the late 1940s, to 136,000 by early 1950, there was another surge in U.S. troop strength after North Korean troops surged across the 38th parallel in June 1950.[21] The Korean War, then, once again doubled the ranks of uniformed Americans in Japan from their prewar lows, to 250,000. Fully 190,000 remained in 1955, two years after war's end, although deployments began to fall not long thereafter, as the shadow of the early postwar world receded.

Reflecting this enhanced consciousness of Japan during the 1950s, as the Korean War–era GIs returned home, James Michener, whose wife was Japanese,

Figure 2.1. Declining American Military Deployments in Japan
(1950–2006)   (unit = people)

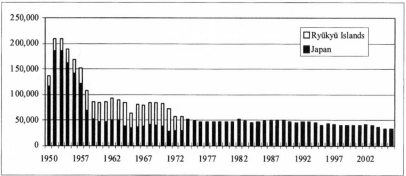

Source: U.S. Department of Defense, *Active Duty Military Personnel Strengths* (various editions).

Note: During 1950–56, the date of record was June 30, while for the succeeding years it was September 30. The Ryūkyū Islands were under American occupation from 1945 to 1972 but were returned to Japan in 1972. They continue to host major American bases, with around three-quarters of U.S. military forces in Japan currently stationed there. Figures for U.S. forces in Okinawa are included in those for Japan as a whole after 1972, following Okinawa's reversion in that year to Japan.

wrote *The Bridges at Toko-ri* and also *Sayonara.* In those pathbreaking novels, Japanese and Americans encountered each other as people rather than wartime stereotypes. When *Sayonara* was serialized in *Life* magazine during 1953, it reached an audience of five million people.[22] Even more spectacularly, the Godzilla movies, made in Japan, became major hits in the United States, although audiences who saw monsters attacking Japanese cities were typically ignorant that Godzilla was actually replaying the American bombings of those cities during World War II.[23]

Transpacific educational ties also intensified rapidly. Between 1950 and 1956, roughly 3,000 Japanese arrived to study in the United States. Around 250 a year of the best and the brightest belonged to the Fulbright Program, highly successful in early postwar Europe and extended to Japan in 1952.[24] This program experienced a golden era for the next fifteen years, with more than 300 Japanese and American students annually, on average, living and studying in each other's country for extended periods.[25] In Tokyo, International Christian University (ICU), collecting donations from both shores of the Pacific, opened in 1953 to show American encouragement of Christianity in Japan. Meanwhile, in Okinawa the University of the Ryūkyūs, established in 1950, promoted better trans-pacific cultural communication at that strategically important crossroads.

The Rockefeller Foundation, which had been active in Japan before World War II, returned to become a clearinghouse for the new cultural exchanges. Its driving force was Dr. Charles Burton Fahs, who had studied in Japan during the 1930s. After joining the Rockefeller Foundation in 1946, he wrote a confidential report criticizing the attempts of SCAP, led by MacArthur, to impose American textbooks and education principles on the Japanese.[26] With Rockefeller Foundation money he then began to send handpicked young Japanese journalists and broadcasters, many of whom played key roles in shaping Japan's media after 1952, to Columbia University for training.

John D. Rockefeller III, who first visited Japan in 1929 shortly after graduating from Princeton, was a longtime patron of Japanese art and culture and also played a catalytic role. Indeed, his activities at the Japan Society were highly synergistic with those of Fahs at the Rockefeller Foundation and of academics such as Edwin O. Reischauer, creating a powerful iron triangle (NGOs, foundations, and universities) of cultural exchange.[27] Returning to Japan after two decades in 1951 as a consultant on cultural matters to the Dulles Peace Settlement Mission, Rockefeller strengthened the ongoing work of the foundation, spearheaded by Fahs. He was also instrumental in erecting two of the central pillars of cultural communications across the Pacific. In 1952, he revived the Japan Society, in New York, which had been founded in 1907, by becoming its president. And in 1952 Rockefeller also helped establish the International House of Japan (Kokusai Bunka Kaikan) in Tokyo, thus forging an important new transpacific network (discussed more fully in chapter 5).

For good measure, Rockefeller also got his eldest son, Jay (John D. Rockefeller IV), interested in Japan. Jay concentrated in East Asian studies at Harvard as an undergraduate, under Reischauer's tutelage, and spent more than two years at ICU, just outside Tokyo. In later years he was to become, as an influential U.S. senator, one of the principal communicators in the American political world between the two countries.[28]

A third major development during the Dulles years of the 1950s, one that had a lasting impact on both U.S.–Japan relations and the global political economy as a whole, was Japan's admission to a series of major multilateral institutions. In 1955 it joined the General Agreement on Tariffs and Trade (GATT), which regulated the world trading system. The following year, after four successive vetoes by the Soviet Union, Japan was also finally admitted to the United Nations.

Looming in the background of U.S.–Japan relations across the Age of Dulles, finally, was a fourth continuing reality: the sharp separation of the socioeconomic and the military dimensions of the alliance, shaped by the shadows of the deepening Cold War. Within the socioeconomic realm, bilateral understanding, popular dialogue, and mutual interdependence were substantial and rising, as noted above. Political-military affairs, however, were a secret, separate, elite-dominated world, shaped by little public understanding or input, especially in Japan. Memories of Hiroshima, Okinawa, and Guadalcanal, after all, were still fresh on both sides of the Pacific. Elite understanding, rather than mutual public trust, became, perhaps inevitably, the foundation of the alliance—a standard reality that has continued to challenge its stability across the years.

With Japan's peace constitution and nuclear allergy in the background, the elites of both nations thus sought to limit discussion, debate, and even understanding of security issues. Their reticence helped in turn to render the transpacific world that Dulles so brilliantly crafted in diplomatic terms nevertheless a curiously incomplete partnership at the popular level, lacking a common mutual-security conception truly shared by the peoples of both nations.

The disjunction in transpacific popular sentiment, coupled with Cold War exigencies, gave rise to a cobweb of secret defense understandings that was at its height in the nuclear area. In 1960, for example, the confidential Fujiyama–MacArthur oral understanding provided that introduction of nuclear weapons would be an agenda for prior consultation between the two countries.[29] In 1963, the Reischauer–Ohira "grunt agreement" confirmed that visits of American warships to Japanese ports or passage of such vessels through Japanese territorial seas would not constitute nuclear introduction.[30] In 1969, a secret understanding between President Richard Nixon and Prime Minister Satō Eisaku provided that the United States could make major changes of military equipment in an emergency at American discretion, with prior consultation to Japan, although the related Okinawa reversion agreement did not, contrary to some speculation, involve secret special provisions allowing nuclear armament of U.S. forces in Okinawa.[31]

THE MUTUAL SECURITY TREATY CRISIS OF 1960

Few events have more fatefully shaped the profile and politics of the Pacific alliance than the 1960 U.S.–Japan Security Treaty crisis. To many among Japan's older generation, both liberal and conservative—and indeed, to many of their descendents, such as the former prime minister Abe Shinzō, the protagonist's grandson—that tumultuous watershed symbolizes, in all its complexity, the very essence of the Pacific alliance relationship itself. Aside from its lasting symbolic importance, the crisis also offered lessons for the future, while having a substantive impact on policy and institutions for stabilizing the alliance that endured long after the crisis itself was past.

The Security Treaty crisis was relatively short in chronological terms—it lasted from the time of Prime Minister Kishi Nobusuke's visit to Washington in January 1960 to sign the revised treaty until Ikeda Hayato's inauguration as his successor on July 19 of the same year. Yet the crisis was nevertheless a time of extraordinary turbulence and drama, fraught with historic importance. Amidst a stormy and prolonged Diet debate on the treaty beginning in February, the Soviets shot down an American U-2 spy plane on May 1 that had been photographing Soviet military facilities over Sverdlovsk. This led to abrupt cancellation of President Dwight D. Eisenhower's state visit to Moscow, exerting a fateful and perverse indirect impact on the politics within Japan of Eisenhower's projected Tokyo visit to commemorate ratification of the newly revised security treaty.[32]

Kishi rammed the treaty through the Diet on May 19–20 in a midnight snap vote, curtailing deliberations in the Lower House and intentionally avoiding the need to ratify the bill in the Upper House, through end of session passage. This approach, however, provoked over six million workers to strike because they viewed Kishi's tactics as disrespectful of democracy and popular consensus. White House Press Secretary James Hagerty, arriving at Haneda Airport on June 20 to prepare the way for Eisenhower's epochal visit, prospectively the first ever by an American president to Japan, was besieged by demonstrators for eighty minutes as he sat in his arrival limousine. This trauma led abruptly to cancellation of the Eisenhower visit itself, despite strong entreaties from U.S. Ambassador Douglas MacArthur II as well as the Kishi government not to do so.[33] On June 15, the radical Zengakuren student federation, together with labor movement protesters, invaded the Diet grounds, provoking a melee in which 482 students and 536 police were injured and a Tokyo University coed, Kamba Michiko, was trampled to death.[34]

Kamba's death escalated the crisis. On June 22, the largest mass protest in Japan's history exploded, with 6.2 million people demonstrating. The announcement on July 11 that U-2s would be withdrawn from Japan helped to ease political tensions, but on July 14 Prime Minister Kishi was stabbed at his residence by a right-wing fanatic. Only with Ikeda's succession to power and the installation of a sweeping set of new economic and social policies did the turmoil finally end.[35]

From the perspective of Japan's national security interests, narrowly defined, the crisis was paradoxical: the revised treaty signed by Kishi was markedly more favorable to Japan than the version it replaced. The revised 1960 treaty explicitly committed the United States to defend Japan and to consult with the Japanese before launching direct combat operations. Unlike the original San Francisco Mutual Security Treaty of 1951, its successor had a specified ten-year duration, so the agreement could be terminated at its completion by either party. The new version also eliminated the explicit right of American forces to intervene to suppress domestic disturbances within Japan.

The 1960 revisions, in short, effectively ended the "voluntary Occupation" that Dulles had seen Japan as having agreed to in San Francisco, initiating a new, more symmetrical era in bilateral relations. Yet the institutional fundamentals of the world that Dulles made—privileged roles for the American military and for Japan, coupled with liberal access to Japanese business in the United States—remained. So did the enforced isolation of mainland China, a central element of the world that Dulles made, whose erosion came to have such fateful implications for Pacific affairs in future years.

The crisis of 1960 had three enduring implications for the U.S.–Japan alliance, implications which have helped make that partnership distinctive in comparative perspective. First, the crisis created a strong disposition—one that has persisted to a remarkable degree—toward a limited, low-profile Japanese military. In particular, the crisis buried the issue of constitutional revision, vigorously debated throughout the 1950s, until the advent of the Koizumi cabinet nearly half a century later. It likewise inhibited increases in Japanese defense spending, which steadily declined as a share of GDP, until the mid-1980s, and which remain low in comparative perspective.[36] As a consequence of these rising constraints, much greater than Japan's counterparts in Europe or even Korea experienced, it became increasingly difficult, both fiscally and operationally speaking, for Japan to play a proactive military role within the Pacific alliance.

The new treaty, or *ampo,* as it was known in Japanese, also fundamentally transformed U.S.–Japan policy coordination processes, in directions sharply contrasting to other major U.S. alliances, including those with the ROK and with NATO. Ampo made Japanese bureaucrats more hesitant and equivocal in their handling of bilateral security questions, fearing complications from the political world or questioning at Diet sessions. Ampo intensified their penchant toward secrecy and a low profile on bilateral security questions. And the treaty consequently also made American officials loath to broach sensitive issues with Japan, unless absolutely necessary. It thus complicated both joint planning and the operational coordination basic to a classical alliance, while inhibiting efforts to generate broad popular understanding of security affairs in Japan and also undermining popular support for the Pacific alliance.

THE REISCHAUER YEARS (1961–66)

In the shadow of the Security Treaty crisis, Harvard professor Edwin O. Reischauer arrived in Tokyo as U.S. ambassador on April 19, 1961. The issue of the hour for the alliance was, as Reischauer himself had put it in a historic *Foreign Affairs* piece only months before, "the broken dialogue with Japan."[37] Reischauer proved to be a strong supporter of the military side of the alliance, personally taking the political lead in preparing for the visit of U.S. Navy nuclear submarine visits to Japanese ports, for example.[38] He also subscribed to the basic outlines of the Dulles–Yoshida bargain: economic opportunity for a recovering Japan in return for bases and broader Cold War diplomatic support.[39] In the emerging trade dispute of the early 1960s over textiles, for example, Reischauer pressed the State Department to design a trade policy flexible enough to accommodate Japan's domestic concerns, since "trade is so close to the problem [of] Japanese survival."[40] Reischauer also strongly opposed contentions of the Joint Chiefs of Staff chairman-designate Maxwell Taylor that bases in Japan were of marginal strategic importance, noting that Taylor failed to consider the valuable role of such bases in the defense of Japan itself as well as in enhancing the broader American geostrategic presence in the East Asian region.[41]

Reischauer will always be known best, however, for the steps he took to strengthen the nonmilitary dimension of U.S.–Japan relations and especially for his efforts to strengthen the intellectual and cultural dialogue between the two great allies of the Pacific. As Reischauer himself put it, "I was particularly anxious to have the Japanese stop thinking of the American military as being the real United States, and the relationship between the two countries as being primarily military rather than a matter of shared ideals and economic interests."[42] His conception of Pacific alliance was a broad and an interdisciplinary one, transcending the military realm to embrace cultural, social, and economic spheres as well.

The importance of Reischauer's fusion of the diplomatic, geopolitical, and cultural dimensions of U.S.–Japan relations is difficult to overstate. Reischauer, to a much greater degree than even Dulles, saw the importance of Japan to American global interests but realized that true alliance could rest only on much deeper mutual understanding than had previously prevailed. Before becoming ambassador, he had, as noted earlier, been at the center of the cultural iron triangle relationships among the Japan Society, Rockefeller Foundation, and academia that dominated U.S.–Japan private sector cultural exchange. Through his appointment, this powerful triangle was legitimated finally at the governmental level as well.

Traditionally the three top deputies of an American ambassador, following the deputy chief of mission, are minister-counselors for political, economic, and consular affairs. Among Reischauer's first personal initiatives, upon becoming ambassador, was to add a fourth, equally ranked with the more traditional ones: the position of minister-counselor for cultural affairs.[43] At the time the notion of cultural minister was an entirely new concept, unique in American diplomatic missions around the world. It continued throughout Reischauer's tenure, with Burton Fahs, previously director for the humanities at the Rockefeller Foundation, a fluent speaker of Japanese, and another key member of the cultural affairs iron triangle, as its incumbent. After Reischauer's departure, the position was abolished, although the Fahs appointment generated powerful public-private synergies in cultural relations during his tenure in Tokyo.

Some other institutional changes of the Reischauer years were more enduring. President John F. Kennedy himself had long supported Reischauer's notion of the "broken dialogue"—indeed, it had been on the basis of the landmark article developing that concept, it is said, that Kennedy first considered appointing Reischauer as ambassador. As a consequence, there was strong backing at the highest levels of the Kennedy administration for new institutional steps to broaden the dialogue with Japan.

In June 1961 Prime Minister Ikeda visited Washington for the first U.S.–Japan summit of the Reischauer era. At that meeting cabinet-level U.S.–Japan Joint Committees in three crucial areas were announced: (1) trade and economic affairs; (2) cultural and educational exchange; and (3) scientific cooperation. Each of these committees was to hold annual meetings, including a plenary in Japan within the following year.[44]

The first meeting of the U.S.–Japan Committee on Trade and Economic Affairs, agreed upon at the Kennedy–Ikeda summit in June 1961, was held in Hakone, on the slopes of Mt. Fuji, on November 2–4, 1961. Five members of the Kennedy cabinet, including Secretary of State Dean Rusk as well as Chairman of the Council of Economic Advisors Walter Heller, attended. Apart from the plenary sessions each cabinet member had long talks with his Japanese counterpart, and both sides got to know each other quite well. Apart from the personal understanding achieved, the talks also, as Reischauer pointed out, redirected the spotlight in U.S.–Japan relations from military to economic affairs, made a large group of prominent Americans more knowledgeable about Japan, and strengthened the spirit of "equal partnership," which President Kennedy had taken up as a hallmark expression of his concept of U.S.–Japan affairs.[45]

In mid-December 1961, the first joint U.S.–Japan science meeting was held, as agreed upon at the Kennedy–Ikeda summit six months before. The meeting dealt entirely with civilian questions and generated considerable enthusiasm among the specialists involved.[46] It produced a wide variety of specialized study groups, many of which continue in operation to this day.

In the same year, what was to become the principal private economic exchange body, the U.S.–Japan Business Conference (Nichibei Zaikaijin Kaigi), was inaugurated jointly by the Japan Federation of Economic Organizations (Keidanren), the Japan Chamber of Commerce and Industry, and the Japan Foreign Trade Council, in cooperation with the American Chamber of Commerce in Washington, D.C., in order to strengthen mutual understanding among business sectors. In 1971, the U.S. side established an Advisory Council on Japan–U.S. Economic Relations, chaired by Najeeb Halaby of Pan American World Airways, in order to deepen the bilateral dialogue with Japan and to advise the U.S. government. The Halaby group was renamed the U.S.–Japan Economic Council in 1985 and the U.S.–Japan Business Council, Inc (USJBC) in 1989. Reflecting a growing inclination in the U.S. business world to recognize the economic prominence of Japan, in 1971, the Keidanren, the Japan Chamber of Commerce and Industry, and the Japan Association of Corporate Executives institutionalized the organizing body of the USJBC as the Japan-U.S. Business Council, with an ongoing secretariat led by Iwasa Yoshizane, longtime chairman of Fuji Bank and the Japanese Bankers' Association. Iwasa was later succeeded by Sony CEO Morita Akio, Fuji Xerox CEO Kobayashi Yōtarō, and other prominent Japanese business leaders.[47] Though run by the private sector, the USJBC maintained close ties with government officials, especially on the Japanese side, and became initially a powerful agent for mutual understanding, involving annual consultations alternating between the United States and Japan.[48]

The third joint gathering of the bilateral committee initiated by Kennedy and Ikeda, dealing with intellectual and cultural exchange, convened in the last week of 1962. It also attracted a most distinguished group of participants from the American side, including the writer Robert Penn Warren and the composer Aaron Copland. Harvard historian Arthur Schlesinger, the putative chairman, was also involved, although he arrived late.[49] This meeting laid the foundations for a major new institution of U.S.–Japan relations, enthusiastically supported by Reischauer, that persists to this day: the U.S.–Japan Conference on Cultural and Educational Interchange (CULCON).

Apart from the foregoing, Reischauer also, later in his tenure, inaugurated a policy-planning conference between senior Japanese Foreign Ministry officials and the State Department Policy Planning staff, drawing upon his own personal academic network. The conference was held over the weekend of June 18–19, 1966, at Hakone, in the shadows of Fuji. It was chaired on the American side by Henry Owen, director of State Department Policy Planning, who had been a student in Reischauer's Chinese history course at Harvard before World War II, and provided a useful—and unusual, in historical perspective—working-level discussion forum.[50]

The United States and Japan thus created, during the early 1960s, a variety of new institutions for mediating their bilateral relationship that was virtually unprecedented in both its breadth and its depth, going far beyond anything developed in the Dulles years. The U.S.-Japan Committee on Trade and Economic Affairs, CULCON, and the U.S. embassy post of minister-counselor for cultural affairs were all new and important innovations. These entities exploited the influence of powerful private-sector NGOs and networks, such as those of John D. Rockefeller III and the Japan Society, to an unequaled degree, creating a balanced national effort in the United States to improve transpacific relations that will serve as a model for generations to come.

Beyond any institutional heritage, the Reischauer years created a hope—indeed, the kernel of an expectation—among many segments of the Japanese public that meaningful, person-to-person communication across the Pacific was a tangible possibility. Ambassador and Mrs. Reischauer themselves evoked much of this sentiment through their background and their actions. Ambassador Reischauer was born in Japan, the son of a missionary who had founded a school for the deaf, and was perfectly bilingual in Japanese. His wife Haru was the granddaughter of one of the most distinguished leaders of Meiji Japan, Matsukata Masayoshi.[51] The new ambassador—born in Japan and married to a Japanese—received an unprecedented welcome in Tokyo upon his arrival and investiture. His arrival statement, which he made both in English and in Japanese, was played live on the national television nightly news. The six-mile route from Haneda Airport to the U.S. embassy had been cleared of traffic, and po-licemen were stationed at every crossroad. The procedure was unprecedented for any ambassador and more nearly comparable to that accorded the arrival of a chief of state.[52]

Once established, the Reischauers were tireless in their personal diplomacy, meeting over fifty thousand Japanese from all walks of life during their five years at the U.S. embassy in Tokyo.[53] To their first Fourth of July reception in 1961 they invited fourteen hundred people, and more than seven hundred ac-tually came. Apparently more than two hundred others attempted to reach the ambassador's residence but were discouraged by the long receiving line and re-turned home.[54]

Soon after their arrival in Tokyo, the Reischauers resolved to visit every pre-fecture in Japan. They nearly succeeded in meeting this commitment, reaching all but seven of Japan's forty-six prefectures.[55] Ambassador Reischauer also vis-ited and spoke in Okinawa, although it was still under U.S. occupation at the time. He was one of the few ambassadors to speak formally there to a public au-dience—save a brief and curious appearance in 1967 by Alexis Johnson to ad-monish the Japanese to engage in more ardent defense efforts—until Ambas-sadors Walter Mondale and Thomas Foley resumed this tradition in the late 1990s.

Certainly the Reischauer years were not an unqualified success. Lingering re-sentment of the United States remained, as manifest in the attempt in 1964 to assassinate Reischauer, an attack in which he was badly injured. But after hav-ing a blood transfusion in Japan, the ambassador's comment that Japanese blood was now running through his body greatly pleased the Japanese and mit-igated much of the two-way suspicion and hostility that his stabbing had orig-inally elicited.

The later third of Reischauer's tenure was arguably less successful than the earlier portion because of delicate relations with President Lyndon Johnson, who succeeded Kennedy, and also because of broadening transpacific tensions over the Vietnam War. Yet in his emphasis on the crucial role of cultural and economic dialogue as the basis for strong U.S.–Japan relations and in his cre-ation of new institutions to support that effort, Reischauer perceptively ad-dressed bedrock fundamentals of the Pacific alliance.

YEARS OF CONFRONTATION (1966–77)

Classically, the test of an alliance has been solidarity in war, as it was when Dulles first crafted the Mutual Security Treaty. As the Korean War began, Japan was under occupation but nevertheless served as a foundry and arsenal for U.S. forces in Korea. Japanese also quietly and informally engaged in little-known direct support of American troops, such as the demining of Wonsan harbor in North Korea during the bitter, desperate winter of 1950, in an action that allowed the U.S. Marines to evacuate, in the face of a massive Chinese Peoples' Volunteers' offensive. In these operations, ordered by the United States, two Japanese ships were sunk, and a Japanese sailor killed.[56] Yet this relatively obscure episode—never publicized widely in Japan—was the extent of actual cooperation in armed conflict.

In February 1965 U.S. Marines came ashore in force at Danang, signaling a major escalation of American presence and the onset of the Vietnam War. This conflict was a rather different matter from Korea—further away from Japan, occurring in a more open and autonomous political context, and provoking a more complex Japanese response.[57] Tokyo's conservative elites supported the American intervention in diplomatic and logistical terms, also rendering substantial foreign aid to Saigon, while public opinion was much more skeptical. The contrasts between elite and popular responses to the war contributed to a growing tendency to avoid broad and realistic discussion of security matters as well as to a growing gap between form and reality in the functioning of the alliance.

Geopolitically, the dominant concern of Japanese diplomats and political leaders was, above all, the rising political-military power of mainland China. On October 16, 1964, the Chinese had exploded an atomic device as powerful as the weapon that destroyed Hiroshima. By mid-1966, they had detonated a bomb ten times larger. And in 1967 they exploded their first hydrogen bomb.[58] This rising Chinese nuclear capability clearly made American protection under the alliance more important to Japan.

Some were concerned about broader implications. When asked by U.S. Secretary of Defense Robert McNamara to estimate the impact on Japan if the United States lost South Vietnam, LDP Secretary General Fukuda Takeo reportedly replied that Japan's own Left would probably strengthen and protest more vigorously against U.S. bases.[59] The Japanese conservatives at the time, in short, feared domestic political transformation more than offshore geopolitical dangers and worried that sharply defying the critical sentiments of the broader public regarding the Vietnam War could dangerously increase the prospect of such a domestic transformation. The Pacific alliance was thus, for the conservatives, a double-edged sword. It could provide domestic legitimacy with the business world, on the one hand, and simultaneously arouse anti-American and antigovernmental sentiments among intellectuals and populist groups.

Japanese business—a more important force in determining the long-term configurations of the alliance than is often appreciated—saw stability in Southeast Asia as vitally important to Japan's future. That region, after all, had traditionally been one of Japan's largest markets and offered relatively few apparent political complications, in contrast to China. Beginning in the mid-1950s, the United States had strongly encouraged expanding Japanese involvement in Southeast Asia, under the Colombo Plan, United Nations Economic Commission for Asia and the Far East (ECAFE), and other arrangements.

Washington strongly encouraged large-scale Japanese ODA to the region, in place of reparations, as a means of consolidating those ties. The payment of well over $50 million in reparations and ODA provided Japan's framework for commerce with South Vietnam, for example. Between the end of World War II and the early 1970s, Japan was relatively uninterested in acquiring resources from the south, unlike the United States, but tremendously eager to open new markets there. In 1961, the peak year before the Vietnam War escalated, Japan sold goods worth $65.7 million to South Vietnam, while buying less than one-twentieth as much.[60]

Japanese popular support for the United States, meanwhile, did indeed sharply erode during the war. The share of Japanese with a positive view of the United States reportedly plummeted from 49 percent in 1964, when the war began, to only 18 percent in 1973, at its bitter end.[61] As Reischauer notes in his memoirs, most Japanese knew little about the details of the Vietnam situation but instinctively empathized with the North Vietnamese, identifying the American bombing of the north with the aerial attacks the Japanese themselves had suffered at American hands only two decades earlier.[62]

There was little appreciation in official Washington of the depth of feeling about the war in Japan, presaging an intensified transpacific communication gap that eroded the gains of the Reischauer years and became increasingly severe in the years to follow.[63] By 1969 only 12 percent of the Japanese people felt reassured by American nuclear guarantees, while 67 percent feared that the Pacific alliance could conversely drag them into war.[64] In October 1969 the antiwar Citizen's League for Peace in Vietnam (Beheiren) mobilized more than half a million protesters. Although no fatalities occurred, violence often erupted during the hundreds of street battles. During the 1965–70 period as a whole, more than 1.8 million Japanese joined in street demonstrations against the war.[65]

The overall impact of the Vietnam War on the alliance was mixed. Although the United States and Japan did not directly fight together in Vietnam, the conflict had a major indirect impact on their transpacific partnership, with significant implications for the future. Most important, it tragically complicated the cooperative human networks and the dynamic transpacific cultural dialogue that began in the Dulles–Rockefeller years and that Reischauer so energized and expanded. The war also dampened the vital flow of transpacific communication that had slowly begun to accelerate during Reischauer's tenure.

Reischauer himself resigned from his ambassadorial post and returned to the United States in mid-1966, principally out of quiet opposition to the war.[66] Many of the other major cultural dialogues he and others had started were disrupted or disbanded as a result of the conflict. The budget of the Fulbright program in fiscal 1969, for example, fell to half of the levels for the year before, while the number of grantees also declined sharply, from 196 in 1968 to only 82 in 1969.[67] Japanese government scholarships took up some of the slack but only partially.

The war also laid the bitter seeds of future economic conflict, threatening a central attraction—market access—of the political-economic structure that Dulles had built. Despite the fervent grassroots sentiment opposing it, the war, in the end, brought at least $1 billion a year to Japanese firms between 1966 and 1975.[68] Although war-related trade constituted no more than 7–8 percent of Japanese exports, it did prove to be particularly important for small firms. And the war-related expansion of demand in the United States created important new opportunities for American firms there, especially in the defense-electronics sector. Meanwhile, Japanese firms focused on the consumer markets that American companies like RCA abandoned to produce for the military in Vietnam, making major gains in areas from cassette recorders to television that led to later frictions.

In addition to the image of Japanese profiting as Americans were dying, which fueled popular resentment of Japan in the United States, the high levels of demand stimulated in the American domestic economy by the war led to rising U.S. imports from Japan and a steady deterioration of the American balance of payments. Bilaterally, the United States experienced its last trade sur-

Figure 2.2. The Widening U.S.–Japan Trade Deficit   (unit = $ billion)

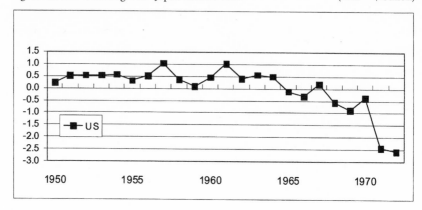

Source: Ministry of Internal Affairs and Communications Statistical Bureau website:
http://www.stat.go.jp/data/chouki/18.htm.
Note: The figures represent U.S.–Japan bilateral trade in merchandise and services.

plus with Japan in 1965, the year the war started. By 1970 the bilateral deficit across the Pacific had reached $1.2 billion. And by 1971 it soared nearly three-fold in a single year, to $2.6 billion, as suggested in figure 2.2.

The Nixon Years: Frontal Assault on the Dulles Heritage?

The San Clemente summit between President Richard Nixon and Prime Minister Satō Eisaku in 1969 achieved the one important success of the Nixon years in U.S.–Japan relations—but one which also sowed the seeds of future conflict. With the security treaty up for its periodic ten-year renewal, American officials, fearing a repeat amidst the Vietnam War of the violent Security Treaty crisis of 1960, resolved to defuse that prospect by returning Okinawa to Japan by 1972.[69] Above all, this agreement represented a triumph of career bureaucrats on both sides of the Pacific, providing a clear definition of a policy problem and working with a clear time deadline.[70] It was the tranquil exception, during the years of stormy confrontation across the 1960s and 1970s, that patently demonstrated the importance of sustained policy networks, with clear high-level support, to the efficient functioning of the U.S.–Japan alliance.

Of course, behind this agreement was the strong desire of Satō to achieve the return of Okinawa, even at the cost of making concessions to regulate the rising

Japanese textile exports to the United States that were of growing concern to Washington. For its part, the Johnson administration, under which the foundations for the accord were laid, feared repeating the treaty crisis of 1960 a decade later and tacitly understood that the United States could still effectively operate its military presence in Okinawa without a formal military occupation, under the same conditions as those prevailing at American bases in mainland Japan.

The American policymaker first proposing the return of Okinawa was actually Reischauer himself, toward the end of his tour as ambassador. President Johnson, in turn, was dubious about rewarding Japan in such a way because the action didn't contribute troops to the Vietnam War effort. And he was not fully impressed with Tokyo's contribution to establish the Asian Development Bank or with its $100 million aid proposal for the Southeast Asian countries either, for that matter, since the United States was providing twice as much financial assistance as Japan.

Secretary of Defense McNamara persuaded Johnson to listen to Japan during his meetings with Satō in 1967, stressing the long-term national security importance of impending issues. McNamara was more concerned with the ten-year extension of the alliance, to occur in 1970, than with the benefits of continued occupation of Okinawa, fearing instead a repeat of the 1960 crisis that could force the United States out of all its Japanese bases. McNamara also wanted to secure Japan's clear support for basic American Asia-Pacific security interests, including the provision of bases in Okinawa after reversion. In return for Tokyo's concessions on trade issues, Johnson's successor, Richard Nixon, finally agreed that Okinawa would be returned to Japan during 1972.[71]

Japanese leadership had never enjoyed an easy relationship with Nixon—most importantly because of his hawkishness and political realism. Those sharply etched traits contrasted sharply with dovish prevailing Japanese conceptions regarding the appropriate configuration of the U.S.–Japan alliance, especially those of the economics-first Yoshida School. In 1953, shortly after becoming vice president, Nixon had visited Japan, vigorously asserting that the "no war" Article IX of Japan's Constitution of 1947 was a mistake and that Tokyo should rearm. In 1967 he also argued, in a prominent *Foreign Affairs* article, that the United States could best avoid future Vietnams by allowing Asians to defend themselves.[72] Nixon maintained, in classic realist fashion, that Japan could most meaningfully mold Asia's future when it began a limited rearmament—a view sharply at variance with prevailing Japanese public opinion of the time, with its near-pacifist orientation.

Many of Nixon's early actions as president, including high-pressure demands for restraints on Japanese textile imports; threats to invoke the Trading with the Enemy Act of 1917; a soybean export embargo in 1973; and, most of all, the infamous Nixon Shocks exacerbated rising tensions between Washington and Tokyo. The first of these, on July 15, 1971, announced the completed secret visit of Henry Kissinger to Beijing, and the impending February 1972 PRC visit of President Richard Nixon, without forewarning Japan. The second shock, on August 15, 1971, involved a trade surcharge and suspension of U.S. dollar convertibility into gold. On July 15, 1971, Nixon announced—with virtually no prior consultation with Japan—Henry Kissinger's secret visit to China and his own forthcoming visit to Beijing. Just a month later, on V-J Day, no less, he announced a decision to suspend the convertibility of the dollar into gold and to impose a 10 percent surcharge on imports into the United States.

Both measures hit Japan hard and without warning. They sharply undermined the domestic political credibility of Prime Minister Satō and contributed to his untimely departure from office less than a year later, after a historic eight-year reign. Satō's successor was MITI Minister Tanaka Kakuei, by far the less pro-American of the two leading contenders.

What was the enduring impact of the Nixon Shocks and of Nixon's diplomacy more generally on the Pacific alliance? In very basic ways, they remodeled the Japan-centric Pacific edifice that Dulles had built, ushering the United States and Japan toward a new, more hard-nosed political-economic era. One clear consequence in Tokyo, flowing directly from the abrupt U.S. reversal on China policy, was greater distrust of American intentions, arguably leading to more assertive Japanese policies on issues ranging from China and the Middle East to delayed Japanese ratification of the Nuclear Non-Proliferation Treaty (NPT).

Japan signed the NPT in 1970. Yet it was 1976 before the treaty was finally ratified by the Diet. And that occurred only after the United States, through its ambassador in Korea, Philip Habib, had strong-armed Seoul into abandoning its own covert nuclear program also.[73]

A second impact of the Nixon Shocks was arguably to strengthen Japanese protectionism. The ill-fated American embargo of 1973 on the U.S. export of soybeans, fortunately never repeated, was especially disastrous in this regard. It has been cited ever since by protectionists in Japan as a strong reason Japan should retain agricultural self-sufficiency—to protect against the already demonstrated prospect that the United States might use its formidable competitive advantage in food production as a geopolitical weapon.

The Nixon Shocks also arguably exerted a substantial delayed impact across the generations. Japanese negotiators of the 1990s, raised with the Nixon Shocks as a formative experience, were markedly more confrontational personally with American diplomats than their predecessors had been. The shocks, after all, had suggested to them that in the absence of clear evidence to the contrary the United States respected and responded only to unambiguous power and to forceful personal presentation.

The most significant and visible short-run impact of Nixon's visit to China, however, was on the fragile and delicate coordination of China policy between the two countries. The sudden, unilateral announcement of the Kissinger and Nixon visits to China ignited a new fear in Tokyo of America choosing China in preference to Japan. As previously discussed, it was the United States that originally forced Japan to abandon recognizing the PRC in 1952, despite Tokyo's desire to resume traditional relations with mainland China, especially in the commercial realm. Over the years, as China steadily expanded, in both economic and political-military terms, this problem of trilateral coordination became more and more serious. It had, of course, been much less tangled in the days of Dulles, when China was marginalized both by its internal confusion and by American embargo policies.

In reality, Sino-Japanese trade was unofficially but substantially resumed during the 1950s. The Liao–Takasaki trade memorandum, signed in 1962, allowed a two-way trade that came to be valued at $80 million annually over the succeeding five years (1962–67). Against this backdrop, Nixon's visit sharply undermined the power base of Satō and his factional successor Fukuda Takeo, viewed as pro-Taiwan, and thereby contributed to the early ascent of Tanaka Kakuei, long considered pro-PRC, to the prime ministership.[74]

Less than eight months after Nixon's visit to Beijing and only three months after assuming the prime ministership, Tanaka triumphantly visited the Chinese leadership compound at Zhongnanhai. He not only normalized relations, as Nixon had done, but also formally recognized the PRC, after breaking a long and important, yet controversial, Japanese diplomatic relationship with Taiwan, forced on Tokyo at Occupation's end by Dulles. In 1978 Japan went forward with several Sino-Japanese long-term trading agreements, together with an "antihegemony" treaty with the PRC. These new Japanese steps went far beyond anything Nixon, Gerald Ford, or Jimmy Carter had concluded with China on Washington's behalf up to that time.

In 1979, the United States also recognized Beijing. Since then, as a consequence of different histories and political views as well as geopolitical and psychological distance, the United States has often irritated and concerned Japan on the China issue, as in the period following the Tiananmen massacre of June 4, 1989. Japan was, for its part, the first economic power to drop U.S.-led international sanctions against China, at a time when American opinion was still outraged by the events of June 4.

To be sure, the United States and Japan continue to share substantial interests and concerns regarding China. They have generally coordinated policies, as when China executed a series of nuclear tests before joining the Comprehensive Nuclear Test Ban Treaty in 1996, inciting strong criticism from both Tokyo and Washington. Yet as China steadily rises, the importance of policy coordination between Japan and the United States on China issues grows increasingly acute. And it grows increasingly difficult, given domestic political shifts in both nations, in ways virtually inconceivable in the Age of Dulles. This Pandora's box of the Pacific alliance was opened by Nixon and Kissinger and has never since been closed, making ever more urgent the discovery of new means of consolidating Washington-Tokyo alliance ties.

A second Nixon Shock, one that brought about the downfall of the Bretton Woods international financial order, marked the end of absolute American global economic superiority, provoking an erosion of U.S. lenience toward weaker economies that had been a hallmark of the early postwar years. This less tolerant—and more pragmatic—pattern of implicit reciprocity began taking shape during the 1980s, leading to rising trade frictions. Tokyo showed unmistakable ambivalence about this revisionist transformation of traditional trading practices, since Japanese business had enjoyed lucrative, asymmetrical access to the American market. Yet Japan slowly came to recognize its position as the second largest economic power on earth and to assume responsibility for its global standing, first in economic terms and later in the security area also, as we shall see.

Fortunately for the future of U.S.–Japan relations, the Nixon administration took a number of little-known and insufficiently appreciated steps, mainly in the political and military areas, to offset the disastrous potential impact of its trade unilateralism and China overtures on the Pacific alliance. First of all, as noted above, Washington agreed to return Okinawa to active Japanese sovereignty.[75] Additionally, President Nixon invited Emperor Hirohito of Japan to the United States. In late September 1971, only six weeks after the second of the Nixon Shocks, Nixon and his wife, Pat, flew to Anchorage, Alaska, to meet the emperor and his wife. This was the first time a sitting Japanese emperor and an active American president had ever met, in nearly 120 years of diplomatic relations stretching back to Commodore Matthew C. Perry and to the pioneer diplomat Townsend Harris.

Nixon's overtures to China, together with American downsizing in Vietnam, also provoked a providential reconfiguration of the U.S. military presence in Japan, which at least in part offset the other—for Tokyo highly disturbing—geostrategic changes. Following the Shanghai communiqué and Washington's related agreement to abandon military bases in Taiwan, the United States quietly approached Japan, in mid-1972, about home porting one of America's twelve aircraft carriers, the *Midway*, at the major Yokosuka American naval base, simultaneously the original home of the Japanese Imperial Navy. Tokyo agreed, and the *Midway* arrived at Yokosuka in mid-1973, two years before the U.S. Air Force evacuated Chiang Ching Kuo Airbase in Taiwan. The deployment of the *Midway* was a strategically important gesture of reassurance to Japan at a fateful moment when the abrupt Nixon–Kissinger overtures toward China might otherwise have provoked a stronger, more Gaullist response from Tokyo.[76]

As the *Midway* was arriving, the Nixon administration announced the Kantō Plain Consolidation Plan. This arrangement proposed to consolidate American bases in the Kantō plain around Tokyo and to redeploy a substantial portion of the forces in question to Okinawa, much closer to the Taiwan Straits. Although it left future flashpoints such as carrier aircraft based at Atsugi in Kanagawa Prefecture, which prompted considerable antagonism owing to their night-landing practice, the Kantō plan helped to substantially reduce anti-base sentiment around Japan's national capital, which could well otherwise have flared up strongly.

The final intended gesture by the Nixon administration was to conclude a state visit to Tokyo, around the spring of 1975. Nixon was apparently looking forward to the visit with special anticipation, as he had strong affection for historical firsts. It would, after all, have made him the first U.S. president to visit Japan, as he had also been the first to China and the Soviet Union.

Nixon's expectations were ultimately realized, of course, by Gerald Ford, not long after Nixon's abrupt resignation in August 1974 in connection with the Watergate scandal. Ford's Tokyo summit with Prime Minister Tanaka Kakuei in November 1974 highlighted the prospective future importance to the U.S.–Japan alliance of state visits, their action-forcing implications for policy, and the networks of mutual understanding they can potentially create. During this summit, defense cooperation between the two countries was reemphasized, boosting the momentum to discuss substance at the working-level U.S.–Japan Security Consultative Committee.

In 1978, defense guidelines for the alliance were agreed upon, articulating Japan's responsibility for more security "burden sharing." In 1981, in the course of a fateful state visit to Washington, D.C., Prime Minister Suzuki Zenkō agreed to the extension of Japan's maritime defense perimeter to one thousand nautical miles.[77] The previous year, the Maritime Self-Defense Forces (MSDF) had also for the first time participated in a multilateral RIMPAC military exercise, involving the United States, Canada, Australia, New Zealand, and five other nations as well as Japan. This new activity significantly broadened the geographical and diplomatic scope of Japan's emerging security role.[78]

THE MANSFIELD YEARS (1977–89)

In 1977 President Jimmy Carter named Senate majority leader Mike Mansfield as his new ambassador to Tokyo. No doubt neither of them dreamed that Mansfield would long outlast Carter in office, to become the longest-serving U.S. ambassador to Japan in history. Mansfield's tenure, coming at the end of a long period of turbulence in U.S.–Japan relations in which human networks across the Pacific had been badly frayed, provided a period of leadership stability at U.S. Embassy Tokyo. It helped substantially to rebuild the delicate human framework of the alliance, which had languished for more than a decade. It did less, however, to relieve the persistent economic tensions that were constantly challenging and threatening to corrode bilateral relations and to transform the collaborative U.S.–Japan framework Dulles had so subtly crafted.[79]

Mansfield's tenure started off on delicate ground. During his presidential campaign in 1976, Carter had promised to withdraw all U.S. forces from Korea, a proposal he was later forced to scale down from six thousand to thirty-four hundred because of fierce political and bureaucratic opposition in both Washington and Seoul.[80] Carter, taking office in the wake of the Vietnam War, felt bound to cut expenditures and reduce foreign commitments, a stance that immediately stirred consternation in Tokyo.

U.S.–Japan tensions flared further during the spring of 1977, when President Carter announced his opposition to Japanese nuclear-reprocessing programs, which would generate large plutonium stockpiles in Japan. He supported proposals within the U.S. government to force changes in Japan's Tōkaimura reprocessing plant that would take five years to realize, would delay exploitation of a major potential energy source as energy prices were rising, and would most likely provoke a confrontation with Japan on the delicate nuclear issue, just after Japan had ratified the NPT. Mansfield brokered a compromise on this fateful question, which had helped delay Japanese ratification of the NPT for six years during the early 1970s, as noted earlier, and persuaded Carter to accept it.[81]

As Senate majority leader, Mansfield had famously supported the downsizing of American forces in Europe during the Vietnam War, authoring the Mansfield amendment to that effect. He had also persistently opposed new, highly strategic U.S. military bases on Diego Garcia in the Indian Ocean.[82] Yet as ambassador to Japan Mansfield was a different person, working effectively to support and stabilize the U.S. military presence there. In October 1978, for example, he personally encouraged President Carter to beef up troop strength in Asia, helping to dilute and ultimately end Carter's attempts to reduce the U.S. military presence in Japan and Korea. During 1978–79, Mansfield also supported efforts by Kanemaru Shin, the director general of the Self-Defense Agency, to introduce a major HNS program of financial assistance to U.S. forces in Japan.[83] Today, that program provides over $4 billion annually in HNS for those troops—over half the total bilateral support of this kind that they receive worldwide.

Mansfield also showed the importance of an ambassador as a potential shock absorber in the case of delicate, politically sensitive accidents and incidents. In April 1981, not long after the defense hawk Ronald Reagan took office, a small Japanese fishing boat, the *Nisshō Maru*, was hit by a U.S. nuclear missile submarine, the *George Washington*, with loss of life. The submarine, under orders not to disclose its location, as an element in America's strategic force, disappeared after the hit-and-run accident, stirring up a political storm in Tokyo. That conflagration was resolved only when Mansfield offered an abject and heartfelt apology to Foreign Minister Sonoda Sunao.[84]

Mike Mansfield demonstrated to an extraordinary degree the multifaceted contribution that an ambassador can make to the U.S.–Japan alliance. There were four major reasons for his subtle success. Mansfield's Capitol Hill ties were a major aspect—his long-standing role as majority leader gave him legitimacy in pressing a particular viewpoint and also leverage that magnified his influence with his fellow policymakers, both in Tokyo and in Washington.

A second, related element of Mansfield's effectiveness was his direct personal ties to the presidents for whom he worked—first Jimmy Carter and later Ronald Reagan. Both chief executives respected him, despite their contrasting ideologies and party affiliations; both also encouraged direct personal contact on issues of importance, like Tōkaimura and troop withdrawals. Influential allies in both the executive and legislative branches, such as Secretary of State George Shultz during the Reagan administration, also reinforced this presidential access and the broader credibility it gave Mansfield's ambassadorial efforts.

Mansfield's long tenure in Tokyo also itself aided his effectiveness, especially in Japan. Since internal Japanese policy making often involves trade-offs over time, it is easier for Japanese to accommodate delicate or difficult problems flexibly if they can be confident that their foreign interlocutor understands reciprocity and that such reciprocity will continue to operate in future. Japanese leaders were able to deal this way with Mansfield because of their expectation, confirmed by his close relationship with presidents of different parties, that he would be around for an extended period and thus able to implement his side of prospective bargains.

Mansfield's fourth secret of success—especially relevant on the Japanese side—was his extraordinary human network and the sensitive way in which he went about creating and sustaining it. Mansfield forged close ties, for example, with Foreign Minister Sonoda Sunao, a hard-bitten former paratrooper widely perceived as being anti-American, through courtesy calls paid to him and flexible, consistent dealing.[85] He made an extraordinary and widely acclaimed gesture in accompanying the then crown prince and princess throughout their long visit to the United States in 1987.[86] And throughout his long tenure as ambassador, Mansfield carefully fostered his ties, in quintessentially Japanese fashion, with a small cohort of influential Japanese, including the chairman of Keidanren, Inayama Yoshihiro. This group was known as the Kibokai (literally, Association of Members Born in the Year of the Rabbit), which was Mansfield's birth year (1903).[87] Yet Mansfield did not forget the Japanese public and made friends by holding open office hours at seven on weekday mornings.

His network in both the United States and Japan helped energize the U.S.–Japan Wisemen's Group, founded in 1979 at the direction of President Carter and Prime Minister Ohira Masayoshi. It involved former ambassador to Japan Robert Ingersoll, Professor Hugh Patrick of Columbia University, and Ushiba Nobuhiko, former ambassador to the United States as well as five other members. This small, unofficial group was to immediately discuss any issues, ranging from trade in televisions to that in shoes, before they grew serious, as Jimmy Carter requested.[88] In January 1981, this aggregation presented American and Japanese leaders with a major report on opening NTT procurement markets, which had aggravated bilateral relations for the preceding three years.[89]

Soon after the Carter administration and the Wisemen's Group had gone, however, troublesome trade issues reemerged, producing mixed results that fell vaguely between "concessions and collusion." They included a series of "orderly-marketing arrangements" that regulated trade in products ranging from automobiles and steel to textiles. Japan voluntarily constrained auto exports during 1981–94 and created administered orange and beef markets in 1986, through an ostensible liberalization that allowed Japanese officials to manage import quotas. The United States and Japan signed a bilateral semiconductor agreement in 1986 after three American semiconductor companies had filed a dumping suit against Japanese semiconductor manufacturers; the agreement produced "results-oriented" trade, remarkably similar to the pattern in textiles, steel, and autos. The Reagan administration pressed Japan further with retaliatory tariffs on personal computers, color television sets, and electric tools under Super 301 in 1987, in an effort to further expand American market access. At the same time, Mansfield worked hard to prevent rising trade frictions from impairing the broader alliance relationship, although he was criticized sharply by trade hawks for needlessly placating Japan.[90]

Meanwhile, at the top level of the U.S.–Japan relationship, strong personal networks were emerging to complement the careful spadework of Mansfield and his interlocutors in Tokyo. Prime Minister Nakasone Yasuhiro, in particular, took important initiatives in strengthening the Pacific alliance that meshed closely with the priorities of President Reagan.[91] Nakasone came to office in 1982 just as Reagan was intensifying pressure on the USSR, calling it an "Evil Empire," and preparing ambitious Strategic Defense Initiative (SDI) plans. In his inaugural visit to Washington as prime minister in 1983, Nakasone announced Japan's departure from the three traditional principles of arms export, approving the transfer of purely military Japanese technology to the United States, and indicated readiness to undertake ambitious new strategic commitments that previous Japanese leaders had cautiously avoided. Japan would aim for "complete and full control of the transit straits" (Sōya, Tsushima, and Tsugaru) through its waters commanding the Sea of Japan "to constrain passage of Soviet submarines and other naval activities in time of emergency."[92] His statement was soon followed by a memorable description of Japan's role as "an unsinkable aircraft carrier" against Soviet backfire bombers. Nakasone even declared an end to taboos on revising Article IX of the Occupation-era peace constitution of 1947. His forthright pronouncements on the Pacific alliance naturally delighted the Reagan administration, inaugurating a warm relationship that continued throughout his tenure.[93]

Although the famous "Ron-Yasu" relationship was rooted partly in shared
strategic conceptions, the importance of supportive networks and the personal
dimension simply cannot be overestimated. Reagan and Nakasone had an invaluable asset in Mansfield and his Tokyo ties, as suggested above. Japan's ambassador in Washington, Okawara Yoshio, and his supportive staff were also
first-rate. And these diplomats, from both sides of the Pacific, worked unusually closely with Shultz and his close friend Foreign Minister Abe Shintarō, who
were personally very much committed to the alliance. Supportive institutions
may have been in slow decline during this period, but personal networks were
unusually strong, illustrating their continuing importance to the health of the
alliance as a whole.

YEARS OF TRANSITION: BEYOND THE
SAN FRANCISCO SYSTEM (1989–2001)

Mansfield returned to the United States at the end of 1988. By then, Japan was
nearing the height of a remarkable economic expansion that had propelled it
from Third World standing to the status of a global economic superpower, with
fully a sixth of global GDP. This expansion was clearly fueled by the supportive political-economic framework that Dulles, so obsessed with the danger of
Japan becoming an unstable Weimar Germany, had designed, although Japan
returned more to the United States, in political-economic terms, than is often
perceived.

Tokyo's capacity to quietly support major global geopolitical change congenial to American interests had been well demonstrated across the 1980s, as the
revision of its Foreign Exchange Law in December 1980 led to capital outflows
that crucially aided the United States in defeating the Soviet Union and accelerating its collapse.[94] The profound security importance of these capital flows
was tacitly recognized and subtly applauded by some of the most astute American diplomats and strategists.[95] Yet Japan's direct security role remained quite
limited.

The transition years—from an asymmetrical alliance between a superpower
and a self-evidently regional middle-range player to a partnership with at least
pretensions of equality—were difficult ones. They were set in motion felicitously, as noted above, through the tact, political skill, and cultural sensitivity,
in varying personal degrees, of players like Edwin O. Reischauer, Okawara
Yoshio, Ushiba Nobuhiko, and Mike Mansfield, at the working level; George
Shultz and Zbigniew Brzezinski as top-level advisors; and Jimmy Carter, Fu-

kuda Takeo, Ohira Masayoshi, Ronald Reagan, and Nakasone Yasuhiro at the summit. Yet the structural contradiction between the changing relative economic power of the United States and Japan, and their established, unvarying security roles and missions, together with the emergence of new players like China, naturally engendered tensions that would be difficult for any leader to manage. The world that Dulles made was changing profoundly; strong, trusting networks were a necessary precondition for effective management of the Pacific alliance, but even they could not be alone sufficient.

Shortly after taking office in January 1989, the George H. W. Bush administration confronted the bitter FSX controversy regarding Japan's procurement of its next-generation fighter and the degree of reliance Tokyo should place on American technology and equipment.[96] Over the ensuing years that Bush administration pursued the often-conflicting Structural Impediments Initiative (SII), which did address, in an integrated way and to an unprecedented degree, the macroeconomic, sectoral, and microeconomic problems implicit in the historic transition in transpacific economic relations.[97] This negotiation was facilitated by unusually strong supportive networks and attention to modalities of dialogue. This was followed, during the early Clinton administration, however, by the so-called Framework Talks, which involved substantial confrontation, including a rocky summit in February 1994 between Bill Clinton and Hosokawa Morihiro, as well as over a year of bitter subsequent automobile-trade talks during 1994–95. During this period less attention was naturally given to transpacific network and back-channel cultivation, with predictable results.[98]

The tensions between Japan's massive economic capabilities and its still-limited political-military institutions and political consciousness were something that Dulles, with his pessimistic view of Japan's prospects, would never have imagined. Those tensions showed up graphically in the Persian Gulf crisis of 1990–91, provoked by Saddam Hussein's invasion of Kuwait in 1990. Although Japanese firms flexibly mobilized car carriers to transport tanks to the Gulf and provided transistor radios to American troops, Japan could not muster a political consensus even to send noncombatant medical teams into the vicinity of a potential battlefield, not to mention onto one. Tokyo contributed $13 billion in support of the Allied effort in the Gulf War and was the only nation to raise taxes in that effort. Yet Japan was still criticized severely in American domestic politics for sending no direct military support. Its only material contribution of this kind was to supply minesweepers to remove mines from the Persian Gulf, and that only after the conflict was already over.

Japan did, amidst the pressures of the conflict, pass PKO legislation providing for the dispatch under UN auspices of peacekeeping forces to potential conflict zones in future. The first test of this new legislation was in Cambodia during 1992–93. Tokyo dispatched both an SDF engineering battalion and police observers. One of the observers was killed in the course of election monitoring, becoming the first Japanese killed in offshore peacekeeping duty since World War II. His death, however, touched off a storm of political controversy, evidence alike of the continuing delicacy of security issues in Japanese domestic politics and of the enduring domestic resistance within Japan to offshore deployments.

Japan did continue onward with increasingly substantial and demanding UN peacekeeping assignments. It sent forces to Mozambique (1993–95); Rwanda (1994); the Golan Heights (1996–); East Timor (1999–2000, 2002–05); Afghanistan (2001); Kuwait (2003–); and Iraq (2004–06).[99] Yet these were all pointedly within the purview of the UN-centric PKO legislation of 1992, rather than in the context of the U.S.–Japan alliance.

Although most of Japan's expanded security policy activity over the course of the 1990s was indeed under UN auspices, there was also, however, an understated but substantial reinforcement of the U.S.–Japan bilateral security relationship, during the latter half of the Clinton administration. In 1996, an Acquisition and Cross-Servicing Agreement (ACSA) was concluded to formalize procurement procedures for food, fuel, and transportation as well as medical, airport, seaport, and other military-related services.[100] Even more important, in 1997 the Defense Guidelines, originally introduced in 1978 to provide for U.S.–Japan cooperation in the defense of Japan itself, were updated to provide for operations during times of emergency in "areas surrounding Japan" (*shūhen jitai*), where Japanese political-economic stakes had expanded massively since 1985.[101] These changes, which substantially, if quietly, broadened U.S.–Japan operational coordination, formed the political-military basis for the more dramatic transformation in security policy—a transformation oriented toward the bilateral alliance—that began in the fall of 2001, following major terrorist attacks on the United States, which is covered in chapter 6.

It bears reiterating that the substantial recent reinforcement in the military underpinnings of the U.S.–Japan relationship began in the late 1990s, before the advent of the George W. Bush administration, and has consistently been a bipartisan venture in the United States. Neither the Democratic nor the Republican party can claim a monopoly on promoting strong security relations with Japan. The Democratic ambassadors to Japan Edwin O. Reischauer, Mike

Mansfield, Walter Mondale, and Thomas Foley did much to strengthen the military aspects of the U.S.–Japan alliance, as did their Republican colleagues.

The global circumstances, economic conditions, and sociocultural context surrounding U.S.–Japan relations all changed profoundly over the half century between the San Francisco Peace Treaty and the terrorist attacks of 9/11. The alliance began, as we have seen in this chapter, in the shadow of Occupation, with the Cold War deepening, and mainland China systematically excluded from diplomatic dealings with either nation. Japan was only beginning to recover from World War II destruction, under the economic stimulus of Korean War procurements. Yet the economic asymmetries with the United States, whose GDP remained over five times Japan's throughout the 1950s, were overwhelming.

The U.S.–Japan relationship early acquired, as we have seen, important economic and cultural dimensions, whose significance was enhanced by the distinctively asymmetrical and transcivilizational nature of the overall Pacific alliance. John Foster Dulles crafted the original outlines of this multidimensional partnership, although others, such as John D. Rockefeller III, significantly burnished its cultural and political-economic outlines. Security ties, Dulles and his confederates agreed, simply could not be sustained by guns, bombs, and bases alone, and their successors followed in a similar line. Indeed, it was arguably the strong human ties established during the Reischauer and Mansfield years, now nearly two generations distant, that fortified the Pacific alliance for days of controversy during the Vietnam War and beyond. What was once an exotic, marginal set of diplomatic ties, particularly for the United States, had become, by the end of the twentieth century, a complex, multifaceted, high-maintenance relationship whose component parts were intimately related and interlocking.

Much of the geopolitical logic within Asia of the U.S.–Japan relationship that Dulles built—to balance China while fostering positive political-economic ties between Washington and Tokyo—still no doubt remains. There are new technical imperatives, such as missile defense and the intensified terrorist challenge, although attempts to isolate China collapsed with Kissinger. There is the question of how Japan's enormous economic and financial power can be utilized beyond Asia to stabilize a broader world in which it is a much larger part than it was half a century ago.

Yet the human ties and the habits of consultation are not what they once were in U.S.–Japan relations. The passing of generations and the growing, fully global complexity of international relations have taken their toll. Many have come to question, as we shall see, whether the sobriquet of alliance truly characterizes what the relations between Washington and Tokyo, and between their peoples, have become.

Human networks would be critical in any transcultural relationship between East and West, as Dulles, Shultz, Reischauer, and Mansfield—to name but a few—so clearly saw. Yet they are particularly vital in U.S.–Japan relations today, as we shall see, given the new broadening of American relations with Asia since the Nixon–Kissinger initiatives with China in the early 1970s. What was once, in the Age of Dulles, a secure, stable, and hierarchical bilateral structure of Pacific affairs is now markedly more fluid and competitive, generating new imperatives that have yet to be seriously addressed.

The twists and turns of the U.S.–Japan relationship over the past three generations clearly show it to be a remarkably protean, enduring, yet paradoxical creature. It links two nations of vastly different cultural, economic, and political background, through ties that are potent strategically, yet which have never been tested in war, and which have multiple—indeed, arguably dominant—nonmilitary strands. This partnership, for all its manifest strengths, does look different from the U.S.–Britain, the U.S.–Germany, or, indeed, the U.S.–Korean relationships.

In what sense can the manifold links among Tokyo, Washington, and their peoples truly be called an alliance? What, indeed, is an alliance after all? And how does the U.S.–Japan relationship conform? It is to these classical questions of elemental definition that we now turn.

Chapter 3 The Notion of Alliance

The concept of alliance is among the most venerable in international relations theory, with a provenance going back two thousand years and more. Thucydides considered the notion in his classic *Peloponnesian Wars*.[1] So did Sun-Tze and other Chinese strategic theorists who were his rough contemporaries.[2]

Alliance has been a long-standing element of practice as well as theory. Indeed, it was the reality of nations banding together to forestall the inroads of adversaries in ancient Greece and China that gave rise to early theorizing. The Peloponnesian League, with Sparta as a hegemon, and the Delian League, centering on Athens, were among the earliest known alliances, dating from the sixth and fifth centuries BC, respectively; their interaction clearly inspired the theoretical works of Thucydides and others.

Throughout the eighth and the third centuries BC, when China was still balkanized into small kingdoms competing for hegemony, these units repeatedly formed alliances, waged wars, and then dissolved their fleeting coalitions. As the myriad kingdoms came gradually to be aggregated into seven, one prominent small-state strategist proposed an alliance with Qing, later to become the first dynasty to unite China, while another promoted a countervailing alliance of six kingdoms against Qing. The two groupings confronted one another, with individual sovereigns switching periodically between the two coalitions and provoking some of China's important early speculation about the notion of alliance itself.[3]

Despite its venerable roots in both theory and practice, the concept of alliance has been given surprisingly little attention in international relations literature, perhaps because it does not fit easily into the dyadic realms of conflict and cooperation with which analysts have been principally concerned.[4] Alliances are cooperative ventures in that their members direct efforts to the pursuit of some common goal. Yet that goal is the prosecution of conflict with a party external to the alliance coalition itself. National security specialists, a natural constituency for the study of alliances, focus more attention on the prosecution of conflict by such means as armaments, crises, and wars than on cooperative institutions like alliances, which are generally designed to deter such conflict.[5]

Another major reason that alliances are traditionally understudied may be that they are so difficult to disentangle from the broader political-economic context in which they are embedded. As George Liska pointed out, "It is impossible to speak of international relations without referring to alliances; the two often merge in all but name. For the same reason, it has always been difficult to say much that is peculiar to alliances on the plane of general analysis."[6]

THE SPARSE THEORETICAL LITERATURE
ON ALLIANCE

Alliance has long been a favorite topic of policy practitioners and practical analysts. This was especially true during the Cold War, when policymakers attached such central strategic importance to NATO and the Warsaw Pact. The U.S.–Japan alliance was also the focus of myriad policy studies.[7] With few exceptions, however, such works have been descriptive efforts, mostly edited, and focusing in detail on the bilateral relationship alone, without much of a comparative or theoretical dimension.

Apart from Liska's work, there have been only three or four serious attempts to create a comprehensive theory of alliance that transcends the voluminous body of literature describing and prescribing for particular variants of that genre. Ole Holsti, Terrence Hopmann, and John Sullivan published a useful behavioral study in 1973.[8] Stephen Walt followed this in 1987 with a volume destined to become a classic, exploring the origins of alliances and linking them to broader patterns in international affairs, particularly "balancing" and "bandwagoning."[9] Then, during the late 1990s, Glenn Snyder explored the dual problems of alliance formation and alliance management, using the concept of an "alliance security dilemma."[10]

There are also, as Snyder points out, several partial theories that focus on special aspects of alliance or approach it from a distinctive perspective.[11] The theory of collective goods has been applied to explain patterns of "burden-sharing" within alliances, concentrating a particular focus on NATO.[12] This analysis has not, however, been extensively applied to other alliances, especially of the pre–Cold War period, or to other aspects of alliance policy.[13]

Bureaucratic politics theory has also been applied to alliances, to explain failures in transnational coordination. Richard Neustadt, for example, examined select problems of alliance management between the United States and Britain, illustrating vividly how bureaucratic conflicts and "paranoid perceptions" flowing from them constrained the transatlantic relationship at the height of the Cold War. In presenting a counterintuitive picture showing the surprisingly severe difficulties that two close allies had in dealing with one another on matters of strategic importance in a time of major national security peril, he drew attention to the importance of subnational factors in alliance management.[14]

Statistically oriented scholars have also provided important insights into the notion of alliance. They have done so particularly by exploring broad relationships between alliance and other political-economic macro-variables. David Singer, for example, examined the quantitative relationship between alliance commitments and involvement in war, although this quantitative approach prevented him from examining in detail the political processes of alliance formation and maintenance.[15] Joanne Gowa similarly considered, through quantitative assessment, the broad historical relationship between alliance management and changing patterns in international trade.[16]

Most recently, broad historical and geopolitical analysis has been used, in specialized application, to draw attention to the counterintuitive nature of alliances themselves in the post–Cold War world. Rajan Menon, for example, has noted that alliances are a relatively unusual phenomenon in American history, limited largely to the post–World War II era of bipolar rivalry with the Soviet Union. He suggests that they have become superfluous with the collapse of the Soviet Union and raises the serious question of what substantial functions in global affairs alliances can continue to fill.[17]

CONCEPTUALIZING ALLIANCE

Modern international relations scholars, who tend to see alliances fundamentally in political-military terms, generally agree on three central elements in their definition of these basic units in international affairs: (1) the parties need to be nation-states; (2) the purpose of the relationship should be security enhancement, especially by pooling military strength against a common enemy; and (3) the target of the alliance should be states outside of the alliance itself.[18] Most modern theorists, including Gowa and Snyder, for example, argue additionally that an alliance should be based on formal agreement that specifies in general the circumstances under which it is operative.[19] Others, such as Walt, however, suggest a broader standard: that alliances can be based on tacit as well as explicit agreement.[20]

From a typological point of view, it is useful to distinguish between alliances themselves and "alignments," or "expectations of states about whether they will be supported or opposed by other states in further interactions."[21] Alliances are really a subset of alignments—those that flow from or are formalized by an explicit agreement, such as a mutual security treaty. This formalization adds specificity, obligation, and reciprocity that are lacking in informal alignments, thus engaging the international credibility of the contracting parties.[22]

Formal alliances can vary along several dimensions, thus providing a potentially useful basis of classification. With respect to size, first of all, alliances can be unilateral, bilateral, or multilateral. Most are bilateral or multilateral, involving reciprocal obligations on the part of the members. Yet unilateral guarantees are also conceptually possible and have at times been important in reality, as in the case of British guarantees for Poland and other east European nations on the eve of World War II in 1939.[23]

Alliances can also be differentiated in terms of their symmetry. Equal alliances—that is to say, between nations of relatively similar strength—usually generate symmetrical obligations and expectations. Conversely, alliances between strong and weak states are generally characterized by asymmetrical obligations and expectations. Such differences between the partners can generate distinctive frictions but can also at times be a source of unexpected strength.[24]

Alliances can also differ with respect to purpose. They can, of course, be either offensive or defensive in character. Defensive alliances can be further distinguished with respect to motive. The predominant motive is generally security against external attack, but augmenting a state's internal security or domestic political stability can at times be an important objective also.[25] A third possible motive could be to contain the implicit military potential of the ally and encourage its political evolution in a regionally stabilizing direction.[26] Alliances could also prospectively give an alliance partner entrée into the ally's decision making.[27]

The general presumption is that military alliances provide active military support, but that is conceptually not necessarily the case. At least one distinct type of alliance does not necessarily involve such support. That is the treaty of mutual alliance, which can involve a range of security commitments, such as agreements to stay neutral in disputes between the alliance partner and third parties, short of proactive military support. This arrangement involves nation-states as central parties, is intended to enhance security, and is directed at states outside the alliance, thus meeting the three critical conditions specified in the standard definition of alliance itself. A clear example is the Anglo-Japanese naval treaty of 1902.

Within the broad, three-point overall consensus definition of alliance outlined above, there is, to be sure, substantial variation in nuance and emphasis, as Holsti, Hopmann, Sullivan, and others point out.[28] Generally speaking, theorists are split into two camps. There are, first of all, the traditional realists, who view alliances rather narrowly, as a matter of expediency, and the nations that contract them as abstract, unified entities. The second camp, that of the "liberal institutionalists," sees nation-states as more complex entities composed of multiple interrelated institutions and publics, with their alliance ties to one another transcending narrow military relationships alone.[29] The basic logic of their position, as Walt points out, is that "as societies around the globe become enmeshed in a web of economic and social connections, the cost of disrupting those ties will effectively preclude unilateral state actions, especially the use of force."[30]

Hans Morgenthau and George Liska present the traditional realist position. Liska suggests, for example, that "alliances are *against,* and only derivatively *for,* someone or something."[31] Morgenthau, situating alliances within a balance of power framework operating in a multiple-state system, sees such institutions explicitly as a matter of expediency rather than principle, with national interest serving as the key criterion determining their ability to persist.[32] Neither of these theorists delves deeply into the subnational elements—bureaucratic, political, or sociological—that can potentially shape the contours of how an alliance actually operates.

A more recent school of thought takes a more complex, socially oriented approach that privileges subnational elements of analysis. Walt, as suggested above, relaxes the assumption of agreement on which alliances have classically been based, stressing the often tacit character of key elements of these alignments.[33] Friedman, Bladen, and Rosen stress that alliances are a narrow, specialized variety of international cooperation—distinct from multinational community building or economic partnership, for example, in that they presuppose the existence or prospect of enemies and contemplate the risk of war.[34]

These theorists also note, however, that alliances involve an intricate relationship between their military and nonmilitary functions and must hence be responsive to broader currents in the political economies and civil societies within which they are embedded. The planning and preparation for military action on which alliance credibility rests, for example, involves staff planning, mobilization of forces, disposition of weapons, and structures of command and control that are often deeply embedded in domestic political processes, it is argued.[35] If these domestic decision-making processes are not closely aligned—ideally through unified command and control systems—alliance decision making is held to be seriously impeded. On issues such as missile defense, such issues are sharply posed in the real world also.

Beyond the formal details of any alliance, there is usually a political penumbra, or "halo," which arguably activates the commitment to military assistance.[36] Allies expect their partners to support them on a range of issues short of war, in other words, even though there is nothing explicit in an alliance treaty requiring such behavior. Withholding such support, at least when it does not run sharply against the partner's own interests, is likely to weaken the overall solidarity of the alliance. Conversely, comprehensive cooperation—in cultural and economic matters as well as defense, narrowly conceived—can deepen security ties far beyond what could be achieved through technical interchange alone. Forging an alliance thus has important political and psychological dimensions that go far beyond the formal obligations of a mutual security treaty, as we shall see in the pages to follow. These nonmilitary aspects are crucial to the long-term health of any alliance and ultimately invest it with transcendent meaning.

ALLIANCE EQUITIES

As we shall see, there has been substantial variation over the centuries in the durability of alliances. Some, such as the Anglo-Portuguese alliance, have persisted for centuries. Most, until recently, lasted only a decade or two, if that. Since the Korean War, however, there has been a historically anomalous trend in the democratic industrial world toward enduring alliances. This pattern has continued even beyond the end of the Cold War and the collapse of global bipolarity and is a central analytical concern of this book, as noted in the introduction.

Before engaging in detailed historical consideration of particular alliances and their evolution, we want to introduce a concept that we believe sheds productive light on why alliances, once established, develop in the fashion that they do. That concept is the notion of alliance equities. Inspired by theories of constitutional governance, corporate accounting, and commonsense real estate concepts that most people use in calculating the value of their homes, the idea helps serve three important purposes: (1) to predict the future of alliances; (2) to project their internal configuration; and (3) to prescribe ways of making them more durable as well as more functional for the nations involved. It builds on the notion of "soft power" and accents the socioeconomic and cultural underpinnings of alliance.[37] Yet the notion of alliance equities can also potentially encompass political-military contributions by alliance partners and focuses conceptually on the magnitude of mutual investment in alliances themselves, rather than in factors promoting national power per se.

An alliance equity is defined here as a sunk investment by a national or subnational actor in the creation or persistence of a constitutional order between nation-states that is directed at security enhancement in relation to third parties outside the constitutional security arrangement itself. A broad range of economic, social, and political phenomena can be considered alliance equities, which heighten the stakes that a given actor has in maintaining the alliance itself.[38] Alliance equities could concretely include (1) military bases; (2) base-support arrangements, including host-nation support (HNS) and Status of Forces Agreements (SOFAs); (3) direct foreign investment; (4) ongoing portfolio capital flows; (5) institutionalized foreign trade arrangements, such as free-trade agreements (FTAs); (6) ongoing interpersonal networks, including policy networks; and (7) transnational cultural regard. Although there may occasionally be tensions and contradictions among various types of alliance equities, they are generally synergistic with one another. High levels of alliance equities promote alliance stability, independent of geopolitical circumstances, as well as a virtuous cycle of smoothly deepening political, social, and economic interdependence.

Alliance equities can be recognized as such only insofar as they influence the incentive structure of significant national and subnational participants in alliance politics. Shared democratic values, for example, could potentially affect alliance durability, if they make political actors within a given alliance more inclined to cooperate with one another. Yet that is not necessarily the case. Such shared democratic values did not prevent Gaullist France from pulling out of the NATO joint-command structure in 1966, at the height of the Cold War, for example. The impact of shared democratic values on alliance behavior is inevitably mediated through micropolitical incentives, including concrete social, economic, and cultural dimensions that must be considered when seriously evaluating such dangerously general rhetorical notions.

Alliance equities are not, of course, the only determinants of alliance stability. They do not repeal the laws of geopolitics or contravene global economic equations. Many alliances could potentially burst asunder in the twenty-first century or undergo severe trials, despite generally deepening levels of mutual alliance equity—just as they did with lower equity levels a century ago. Indeed, as we will see in chapter 7, dealing with the deepening global challenge, the international centrifugal pressures confronting alliances are steadily growing in an era of globalization, requiring ever-higher levels of alliance equities to allow such partnerships to retain their coherence and credibility.

THE ALLIANCE PHENOMENON ACROSS HISTORY

To fully understand the notion of alliance and to grasp the underlying dynamics that cause alliances to wax, to wane, and to persist, one needs to visit the laboratory of concrete historical experience. One must do so, however, with a prior conceptual framework in mind and a sense of how alliances relate concretely to the embedded political-economic context of their times. Despite the early classic applications of the alliance concept more than 2,500 years ago, and a few anomalous cases over the following two millennia, the evidence to support theoretical conceptions of alliance comes principally from the past 360 years of the history of international relations.

It was, after all, only following the Peace of Westphalia in 1648 that nation-states as we know them now—which modern theorists consider the irreducible constituent element of alliance—became the central components of the international system. These new, vulnerable nation-actors routinely banded together, in often shifting coalitions, to deter their neighbors and to otherwise secure state interests. Their dynamic interactions made the seventeenth, eighteenth, and nineteenth centuries in Europe the heyday of classical alliance.

The Grand Alliance of 1686, also known as the League of Augsburg, was among the first of these configurations. It formed to defend the Palatinate and other parts of western Germany from the expansionist France of Louis XIV. The members of the alliance, including Austria, Bavaria, Portugal, Spain, Sweden, and Britain, fought three wars together, in a union that persisted from 1686 until 1721.

A series of Quadruple Alliances were also prominent in this period. The first (1684) allied Spain, Brandenburg, the Netherlands, and the Holy Roman Empire in the context of the Franco-Dutch War. The second (1718) allied Austria, France, the Netherlands, and Great Britain in an attempt to revise, at Spain's expense, the verdict in the War of Spanish Succession. The third (1745) was directed at France in the War of the Austrian Succession, while the fourth (1814), among Britain, Austria, Prussia, and Russia, was aimed at upholding the settlement of the Napoleonic Wars. A fifth, used as an alternative term for the Central Powers of World War I, ensured the mutual security of Germany, Austria-Hungary, the Ottoman Empire, and Bulgaria.

Although alliances were thus central to classical European diplomacy, they were also conspicuously impermanent and unconstrained by socioeconomic context. Britain, in particular, was at one time or another allied with virtually every continental power, in shifting patterns, in accordance with its role as a "keeper of the balance." Britain has no permanent friends, only interests, it was said. The formal origin of this power-balance logic in British diplomacy is sometimes traced to William III's noted address to Parliament in 1701, in which he observed famously that "England *holds the balance of Europe.*"[39] The United Kingdom's powerful economic position at the vanguard of the Industrial Revolution, before the days of foreign investment, made this detached role in international affairs easier than it would have been for a less affluent nation.

Another distinctive trait of classical European alliances was their secretive nature, which made diplomatic dealings much easier politically than they were later to become. Many were never revealed to any but initiated diplomats. Until deep into the twentieth century, public opinion figured very little in the configuration of alliance patterns. Diplomats, in particular, faced few constraints from either public opinion or domestic politics in their alliance-defining behavior, despite the fitful advent of popular political involvement across the turbulent century following the French Revolution of 1789.

Evolving American Conceptions of Alliance

Although alliances were central to classical European diplomacy, American leaders rejected them defiantly and almost universally until well after World

War II. In a way this was paradoxical, as the Franco-American alliance of 1778, negotiated by Benjamin Franklin, was a crucial cornerstone of America's successful struggle for independence itself. Yet the key leaders of the fledgling Republic, including Alexander Hamilton and Thomas Jefferson as well as George Washington, nevertheless strongly opposed the principle of having their nation enmeshed in "entangling alliances" on any continuing basis.

The classic statement of this traditional American antialliance view was Washington's Farewell Address, which made six interrelated points concerning why alliances were bad practice, in his view, for the United States.[40] First of all, Washington feared that alliances would drag America, a new and better sort of state, back into a secretive, Machiavellian past it had firmly rejected. He also feared, in a related point, that alliances would entail a compromise of America's hard-won independence. Further, Washington was concerned that permanent alliances would be rigid, inevitably provoking the active enmity of those against whom they were directed. In addition to their perverse geopolitical implications, alliances would also give rise to special pleading by citizens whose personal interests were aligned more with those of the ally than with those of the home country itself, thus eroding domestic unity. Additionally, alliances would give rise to special pleading by citizens whose personal interests were aligned more with those of the ally than with those of the home country itself, thus eroding domestic unity. Additionally, alliances would give foreign allies privileged access to the institutions of government and public opinion, thus undermining national coherence within the fledgling American nation still further.

This deep skepticism of entangling alliances continued to dominate American thinking right down to the two world wars. During World War I Woodrow Wilson stubbornly tried to keep the United States out of war, hoping to use America's neutral position to mediate among the belligerents and then ultimately to orchestrate a postwar settlement that would replace the Continent's balance of power struggles and ephemeral secret alliances with a new order based on cooperation, collective security, and democracy.[41] Only German intransigence and U-boat warfare costing hundreds of American lives forced him, driven by public sentiment, reluctantly into the global conflict. And following the Armistice, America's Senate rejected not only any thought of entangling alliances but Wilson's collective security dream, embodied in the League of Nations, as well.

By the late 1930s President Franklin D. Roosevelt, to be sure, recognized Nazi Germany as a threat and realized that the United States could not stand aside and deny assistance to Britain and France in the event of conflict.[42] Yet neutralist sentiment remained strong, and Roosevelt did not press the American people headlong into war. When war finally did come, in the wake of Pearl

Harbor, and the United States inevitably moved into a position to shape the emerging postwar order, Roosevelt's grand design still had little room for alliance, other than a vague solidarity of values with the Anglo-Saxon world, as embodied in the Atlantic Charter. In place of alliance, Roosevelt stressed the collective role of the "Four Policemen" (the United States, Britain, the Soviet Union, and China), together with the United Nations itself, as the prospective guarantors of global order. Truman's views were relatively similar, until they were drastically altered by Cold War developments.

As late as 1948 the concept of alliance was making only minimal headway in American diplomacy. Even State Department Policy Planning Director George Kennan's celebrated doctrine of containment, embodied in the famed "X Telegram," proposed to arrest Soviet expansion not through military alliance, but through regional balance of power tactics, focusing on promoting the revival of Germany and Japan. It took a series of cataclysmic events and a related intellectual revolution in Washington to provoke the paradigm shift toward alliance that finally took place in American diplomacy during 1949–50.

Three traumatic events in the space of less than a year—a fleeting if turbulent interval suggesting to many the imminent outbreak of World War III—were the catalyst that finally gave birth and credibility to the notion of global containment based on alliance. First, in August 1949, the Soviet Union exploded its first atomic bomb, ending a U.S. nuclear monopoly that had persisted since before Hiroshima and Nagasaki in the summer of 1945. Then, in short order, the People's Liberation Army swarmed to triumph in the Chinese Revolution, highlighted by Mao's declaration of the People's Republic of China atop the Gate of Heavenly Peace in Beijing, on October 1, 1949. And finally, less than eight months later, North Korean forces burst across the 38th parallel, starting the Korean War, with Chinese Peoples' Volunteers soon thereafter entering the fray.

The sea change in official thinking was crystallized and accelerated by NSC-68, an assessment of Soviet motivations completed in February–March 1950.[43] This catalytic document was a clarion call for a military buildup that would provide the United States not only with the military might needed to counter Soviet inroads around the world, but also with a rationale for a gauntlet of encircling alliances.[44] These would in turn provide the political-military rationale for the establishment of a ring of bases surrounding the Soviet Union and China, across a vast geographic expanse much broader than Kennan's narrower concept of critical regions.[45]

The Washington-centric alliance structure that emerged during the Korean

War, both in Europe and in Asia, was revolutionary. It was sharply different from past patterns of American involvement in international affairs, which had not involved alliance in any fundamental way, as we have seen. The new alliance structure was also dramatically different from the shifting, ephemeral European alliance patterns of the previous three centuries.

Classical European alliance patterns had lacked substantial nonmilitary roots in the constituent nations—either in economic life or in civil society. They had lacked, in a word, enduring alliance equities. The new Cold War partnerships purported to grant those in copious degree. They supplied large-scale reconstruction aid to war-torn nations like Germany, Italy, France, Japan, and Korea through such programs as the Marshall Plan, Government Appropriations for Relief in Occupied Areas (GARIOA), Economic Rehabilitation in Occupied Areas (EROA), and the Colombo Plan. They also provided asymmetric economic access to the prosperous American market for these suffering allies. In return, the key alliances afforded American military forces access to bases in these nations, bases from which the United States could confront and contain what seemed to be steadily rising Sino-Soviet military power.[46]

With the coming of the Korean War and the felt imperative of global containment, alliances had thus, in unprecedented fashion, suddenly emerged as a central dimension of global security affairs. In a world where the recovery of war-torn nations in both Europe and Asia seemed crucial to the global fight against Communism, and where democracy held increasing sway, the economic and sociopolitical dimensions of alliance were becoming increasingly important as well, creating new imperatives for stable security ties that transcended geopolitics together with subtle new nonmilitary demands on emerging alliance ties. Despite the dangerous confrontation with Soviet might that was steadily emerging in the new nuclear age, managing the newly complex alliances of the Cold War was in no sense a simple proposition—either for the United States or for its new allies around the world.

Alliance from the Japanese Perspective

Like the United States, Japan was relatively slow to embrace and conceptualize the notion of alliance. It did, to be sure, have a deep traditional appreciation of Chinese classics, including Sun Tze, and of the tumultuous history within which China's own conception of alliance was born. Japan periodically applied these Chinese concepts to the turbulent reality of its own civil wars from the fourteenth through the sixteenth centuries, during which minor warlords fought and allied against one another, as in China during the Warring States Period.

Yet there was little original Japanese conceptualization, particularly regarding how Japan should relate to the broad, largely unknown world beyond its own shores.

For more than two centuries before the coming of Perry's black ships in 1853, Japan had stood in purposeful isolation and had little systematic involvement in international affairs to which alliance concepts could be meaningfully applied. Its first formal diplomatic commitment, the Anglo-Japanese alliance of 1902, was forged only after the bitter experience of the Triple Intervention of April 1895, by which Russia, France, and Germany forced Japan to cede some of the most important fruits of its earlier victory over Imperial China. That humiliating debacle made the need for systematic, cooperative ties with major Western powers, preeminently Britain, geopolitically clear to Tokyo.[47]

Over the ensuing century, the mainstream of Japanese policy-making opinion has embraced the notion of alliance, albeit often with substantial ambivalence and accompanied by extended internal debate. The general underlying rationale at the policy level has been a realist calculation: alliance with the preeminent global power of the day—particularly with the nation controlling the sea-lanes vital to the security and prosperity of Japan, an island trading-nation. Japan acquiesced in the termination of the Anglo-Japanese alliance in 1923, despite substantial domestic sentiment for its continuation in both Kasumigaseki and Whitehall, out of a desire—especially strong in the business world—not to offend the United States. Foreign Minister Matsuoka Yosuke assertively signed the Axis Pact in 1940, with strong Imperial Army support, albeit in the face of strong opposition from naval officers and some political leaders.[48] After a disastrous wartime defeat, Yoshida Shigeru in September 1951 signed the historic yet also controversial U.S.–Japan Security Treaty, which has continued in force to this day.

Contemporary Japanese views of alliance have been shaped since the late 1940s by the bitter experience of World War II and the exigencies of postwar reconstruction.[49] The fundamental lines of domestic division have centered, of course, on the propriety and utility of the existing U.S.–Japan alliance and have divided into three categories. On the positive side—favoring acceptance —there are both economic-utilitarian and political-realist streams. On the rejectionist side—powerfully influenced by the wartime experience—have been influential idealist intellectuals.

The economic-utilitarian argument sees the U.S.–Japan alliance as a useful vehicle for reducing the political risks associated with Japan's leveraged, export-oriented economic development, for gaining access to both global markets and the latest technology, and for allowing Japan to concentrate its attention on development-related tasks. Yoshida, the early postwar prime minister, forcefully espoused this line, and its adherents are thus commonly referred to as the Yoshida School.[50] Yoshida himself stressed that neutrality was useless for Japan, given its postwar lack of military power and its geographical location.[51] Over the years prominent members of the Yoshida School have included Amaya Naohiro, the former MITI vice minister for international affairs, and Kōsaka Masataka, of Kyoto University.[52] Kōsaka cautioned, in particular, that military reliance on the United States should be complemented by a proactive Japanese diplomacy, so as to neutralize the hegemonic implications that bilateral military asymmetries within the alliance could otherwise entail.[53]

There is, it should be noted, an important realist defense of the Yoshida School's view that Japan should cooperate pragmatically with the United States on diplomatic matters and even assent to the presence of American bases in Japan, dismissing the notion of neutrality between East and West as being totally unrealistic owing to the extraordinary military outlays required to make the policy strategically practical. That realist defense is epitomized in the work of Nagai Yōnosuke and in some respects that of Taoka Shunji and Funabashi Yōichi. Nagai argued that the need for friendly relations with the United States was a clear lesson of the Pacific War and that the existence of nuclear weapons compelled Japan to avail itself of Washington's nuclear umbrella, in the face of the Chinese threat. Otherwise Japan would have to substantially enhance its military capability and go nuclear, Nagai suggested.[54] Taoka adds that the U.S.–Japan alliance specifically is a useful vehicle for neutralizing potential anxieties that the United States might naturally have about Japan and also for forestalling pressures that might otherwise emerge within Japan for a rearmament that he views as likely to be both costly and counterproductive.[55] Funabashi agrees that the U.S.–Japan alliance can be considered marginally useful as a mutual deterrence and conflict prevention mechanism but cautions that too much reliance on it is unwise because of its floating, politically unstable character.[56]

An increasing number of Japanese realists both support the Pacific alliance and feel that Japan should play an increasingly substantial military role within it. Preeminent politically among them has long been Prime Minister Nakasone Yasuhiro (1982–87), who maintained that Japan should defend itself through its own efforts insofar as possible, with the U.S.–Japan alliance serving only to complement Japan's own forces in vital areas beyond Japan's existing capabilities.[57] Nakasone pressed, as director of the Self-Defense Agency in 1970, for the return of several U.S. military bases in the Tokyo area and for the notion of Japan defending the skies of Tokyo alone. As prime minister, he also led efforts to strengthen Japan's indigenous capacity to defend the Sea of Japan, so as to play a key alliance role in containing the Soviet navy.[58]

Okazaki Hisahiko, another prominent realist, argues that alliances with the Anglo-Saxon nations, which he views as having maintained global hegemony for the past four hundred years, are vital to assuring that Japan have access to strategic intelligence information, that its military safety be assured, and that it not be isolated from the mainstream of world affairs.[59] Yet he sharply criticizes the existing political framework in Japan for the way it handles alliance relations, especially constitutional constraints, for distorting Japanese security policy, and for depriving Japanese policies of any systematic relationship to strategy.[60]

Ozawa Ichirō, the leader of the Democratic Party of Japan, also views the U.S.–Japan alliance as desirable from a realist perspective, while arguing, like Okazaki, that it should be accompanied by significant Japanese military power. Ozawa argues that the alliance, ideally with three complementary dimensions, is needed to overcome major transpacific cultural and racial differences as well as a bitter, conflictual transpacific history, although he cautions against undue emotional attachment to reliance on the United States.[61] Using analogies with classical Venice to suggest that even trading nations need substantial military as well as economic power, Ozawa has argued for well over a decade that Japan must become a "normal nation" (*futsū no kuni*) that willingly shoulders international burdens, so as to secure international order.[62] Given the precedent of unbounded Japanese expansionism in the decade before World War II, Ozawa has long insisted that UN resolutions should be the prerequisite to Japan's sending its Self-Defense Forces overseas on peacekeeping missions. In this context, inspired also by domestic political calculations, Ozawa, as the leader of the opposing Democratic Party of Japan (DPJ), spearheaded the Diet's resistance in 2007 to MSDF deployments in the Indian Ocean, placing additional strains on the Pacific alliance.

Although believers in the concept of alliance, and specifically the prevailing U.S.–Japan manifestation of the notion, have dominated Japanese politics for well over half a century, rejectionists were long prominent in the Japanese academic world, particularly among the highly influential Marxist intellectuals. Both the intellectual and the existential roots of these rejectionists lay in World War II. Virtually all of the early leaders of the group experienced the war and were driven by the bitter "Never Again" sentiment, embodied in the activities of the Peace Problems Symposium (Heiwa Mondai Danwa Kai), founded in

1948.[63] The rejectionists included a broad range of Japan's most prominent scholars, including Maruyama Masao and Ōuchi Hyōe of Tokyo University; Shimizu Ikutarō and Abe Yoshishige of Gakushūin University; and Tsuru Shigeto of Hitotsubashi University, as well as many Socialist and Communist politicians.[64] All these rejectionists saw alliances as subversive of peace—both generally and, in the case of U.S.–Japan relations, specifically—since alliances impeded realization of the broad, impartial friendships with all nations that should ideally, in the rejectionist view, be Japan's overriding objective.

Many rejectionists pointed to the role of the Axis Pact in embroiling Japan in war during the early 1940s and feared that the U.S.–Japan alliance could similarly increase rather than reduce Japan's prospect of being involved in conflict. They frequently cited the Korean War and periodic confrontations with China to bolster their arguments. Many also held, on Marxist grounds, that Socialist nations were inherently peace loving, that alliances needlessly provoked international confrontation, and that global peace would be furthered by their dismantling as well as by the withdrawal of foreign (that is, American) forces from Japanese soil. Japan could, they maintained, most meaningfully influence world affairs through an unarmed neutrality (*hibusō chūritsu*) that, in the spirit of George Washington's America, rejected entangling alliances.[65]

The political culmination of the long rejectionist struggle against the U.S.–Japan alliance was the Security Treaty crisis of 1960. Rejectionism continued in vogue throughout the Vietnam War.[66] It became less prominent in Japanese thinking following the fall of Saigon in 1975, although Ishibashi Masashi, leader of the Japan Socialist Party (JSP), did sharply confront Prime Minister Nakasone's buildup of the early 1980s, arguing that the U.S.–Japan alliance of the day was nothing but a vehicle for dragging Japan into war.[67]

Following Socialist prime minister Murayama Tomiichi's acceptance of the security treaty in 1994, rejectionism declined still further in prominence, along with leftist political fortunes, damaged by the broad global repudiation of Communism at the end of the Cold War. Opposition to the Iraq War, accelerating sharply from around 2005, helped revive criticism within Japan of the Pacific alliance as a mechanism both depriving Japan of defense autonomy and simultaneously enmeshing Tokyo in aggressive American global designs. Saeki Keishi of Kyoto University, for example, argued strongly that the SDF dispatch to Iraq was wrong, but that Japan was nevertheless compelled to support it because of the inevitable strategic importance of the U.S.–Japan alliance in a Pacific regional defense system within which Japan had no autonomous ability to defend itself.[68]

The Paradoxical Post–Cold War Transition

The waning of the Cold War, with the fall of the Berlin Wall (1989) and the collapse of the Soviet Union (1991), presented a serious, if paradoxical, challenge to alliances established during that epic bipolar struggle: the loss of a common enemy. Significantly, however, both Washington and the leaders of U.S.-allied nations opted clearly to maintain the special relationships of the past—even agreeing, in most cases, to upgrade their ties from regional alliance to global partnership. With the substantial mitigation of the regional threats that had long obsessed America's transatlantic and transpacific partners, both European and Asian allies came to direct their cooperative activities increasingly to the global level. NATO, for example, dispatched troops first to Bosnia and Herzegovina, far southeast of its classic theater of operations, and has been operating in Afghanistan since 2001, much more supportively than during the Cold War. In 2003, American allies, including Britain, Japan, and Korea, dispatched forces to Iraq, while Japan (in 2001–07 and 2008) also refueled allied vessels in the Indian Ocean.

Modern alliances among the industrial democracies have thus proven remarkably durable in the post–Cold War world, despite the waning of bipolarity and the collapse of their principal mutual antagonist, the Soviet Union. This pattern of sustained alliance persistence in the face of waning military threats contrasts strikingly to classical experience in the earlier history of alliances, to the assumptions of realist theory in international relations, and to contemporary developments in Eastern Europe, where the Warsaw Pact alliance system abruptly collapsed in the wake of the Cold War. This G-7 anomaly poses a serious empirical puzzle—one of critical importance both to theory and to the practical future of international affairs—that clearly demands explanation.

Inherent Tensions in Alliance Relations

Post–Cold War developments do not repeal the deep, structurally rooted underlying tensions in alliance relations, which have classically made such alignments ephemeral in the past. The international system, as international relations theorists have tirelessly pointed out since Thomas Hobbes, is anarchic in its underlying character. There is, in short, no systematically prevailing authority structure—a reality that prevails among friends as well as foes. Even within formalized alliance relationships, as game theorists are quick to note, mutual national commitments are ultimately problematic, owing to the differing basic incentive structures of their participants.[69] Alliance members, like participants

in any prisoners' dilemma game, are often better off defaulting on their commitments, if others can be persuaded or forced to fulfill those obligations in
their stead. Smaller allies can be particularly tempted to engage in this sort of
free-riding behavior, which Olson calls "the exploitation of the great by the
small."[70] The leverage which the underlying incentive structure of alliances
gives to smaller players, coupled with their own often intense and embedded
domestic reasons to manipulate the terms of alliance, can cause alliance outcomes to be so skewed in their favor as to generate substantial "burden-sharing"
backlash in the larger-partner allied nation.[71]

Apart from classic free-rider problems, alliances can also potentially be
plagued by a wide range of other substantive tensions among the ostensible
partners. Incongruent objectives, if one potential enemy of an alliance partner
is not the enemy of the other, can cause serious problems of coordination and
cooperation, as have periodically occurred in Euro-American dealings with the
Middle East. Time after time, major European NATO allies of the United
States have denied American C-5As and C-130s overflight rights to resupply Israel, as during the Yom Kippur War of 1973. In that case only Portugal, through
its Lajes base in the Azores, agreed—among America's fourteen ostensible
NATO allies—to aid in Israel's resupply. Meanwhile, Spain and Britain, hosts
of other candidate bases for refueling (Torrejon and Mildenhall), turned down
the American requests.[72] In 1986, only Margaret Thatcher's Britain actively cooperated with the American strike on Libya, while Italy, Spain, and France,
among others, clearly declined to be involved.

Incompatibility in the social and political values of allying states, like divergence of strategic interest, can also generate intra-alliance tension, as occurred
between the West and the Soviet Union during and just after their mutual victory over Adolf Hitler in World War II.[73] Differences in national economic
structure, institutions, and domestic political climate can also generate important tensions among allies in the real world, as Putnam and Bayne point out.[74]
France and Britain have experienced perennial problems in alliance coordination over the years, despite their broadly parallel strategic interests, for example,
and domestic politics have arguably been largely at fault.

Why Alliances Endure

Given the prospective internal tensions that beset alliances and the underlying
divergence in the incentive structures of their participants, it is not intuitively
obvious why such cumbersome institutions endure at all, or why they vary so
much in their durability when they in fact do endure. The 1902 Anglo-Japanese

naval alliance, for example, lasted twenty-one years, which was relatively long for its day. Yet the post–World War II U.S.–Japan alliance has endured for well over half a century and continues to play a major role in global affairs.

Traditional realist theory has a ready-made answer for the twists and turns of alliance: national interest. Yet myriad leads, lags, ambiguities, and internal contradictions within this notion suggest that it is at best underpredictive. Some more refined concepts are required, especially to offer insights into why the new alliances of the Cold War period and beyond—embedded in both economic life and civil society in unprecedented ways—can endure, even outliving the initial purposes. A more interdisciplinary perspective is definitely required.

Liska suggests that ideologies and styles, alliance structure, and consultation processes—both routinized and ad hoc—influence the durability of alliance, in addition to basic considerations of national interest.[75] Walt echoes Liska's emphasis on consultation and shared political values, also stressing the importance of institutionalizing alliance relationships.[76] Putnam and Bayne add the importance of learning and other cognitive factors, domestic politics, and the structure of international regimes.[77] All these considerations, of course, are internal to an alliance, operating independently of whatever mutual cohesion among partners is introduced by external threat.

It is here that the notion of alliance equities, introduced above, becomes critical. Where mutual embedded stakes—economic and social as well as military—are high, alliances tend to be more stable, as among the post–Korean War G-7 nations. Where those stakes are lower, as in pre–World War II alliance relations and in the Cold War Warsaw Pact, alliance ties tend to be more fluid and ephemeral.

In the course of a detailed discussion of prospects for the NATO alliance, Walt presents socioeconomic preconditions for a strong, enduring alliance that echo the foregoing and that are useful in the comparative consideration of prospects for alliance cohesion, a major concern of this book. Walt suggests, first of all, the importance of the economic stakes that the preeminent partner (clearly the United States, in the case of NATO) holds in the relationship, especially in the form of direct foreign investment. He adds the vitality of transnational elite networks as a solidifying element in alliance cohesion.[78]

To understand the operation of alliance equities concretely, it is instructive, once again, to look to history and to the most venerable and long-lived bilateral defense partnership that has ever existed in the industrial world. The remarkable Anglo-Portuguese alliance, in operation for well over six hundred years, dates from the Treaty of Windsor, celebrated between Richard II of Britain and John I of Portugal on May 9, 1386.[79] A striking exception to the general rule of pre–World War II alliances being ephemeral, it helps us understand both why classical alliances were so fluid and why some of their postwar successors have better prospects of enduring.

Sealed by the marriage of Philippa of Lancaster to King John I in 1387, the bilateral Anglo-Portuguese alliance was distinctive early on for its dual security and economic dimensions and equally for the alliance equities they generated. Philippa provided royal patronage for English commercial interests that sought to meet the Portuguese desire for cod and cloth, in return for wine, cork, salt, and oil, shipped through English warehouses at Porto.[80] English merchants came to reside in significant numbers in Portugal, becoming a powerful constituency for the alliance over the centuries and thereby enhancing its durability.

On the security side, Portugal and Britain collaborated remarkably over the centuries, to the advantage of both. Britain was instrumental in the consolidation of Portugal's original independence from the Moors. The two nations were later close allies in the War of the Spanish Succession, the Seven Years' War, and the Napoleonic Wars. Indeed, Britain's contribution to preserving Portuguese as well as Spanish independence during the Peninsular Campaign of 1808–14 was its most important land contribution to the entire, tragically protracted Napoleonic conflict, up to Waterloo. And the British navy, in the wake of a French invasion of Portugal in 1807, provided invaluable evacuation for the Portuguese royal family to Brazil.

In the twentieth century, Britain and Portugal fought side by side in both world wars, British use of bases in the Azores being a crucial element of both anti-German submarine operations and the air bridge from America to Europe. Britain, to be sure, did little to aid Portugal in the face of India's occupation of Goa in 1961. Recently, most aspects of the ancient bilateral alliance have been subsumed within NATO, of which both nations have been members since 1949. Yet in a revival of venerable tradition, Portugal once again aided Britain bilaterally during the Falklands War of 1982, allowing Britain transshipment rights through the Azores during that short but sharp and bitter conflict.

Most classical European alliances, to reiterate, were ephemeral, often lasting for a matter of months and rarely as long as ten years. Yet they had few roots in the economy and society of the constituent nations, generating only very limited alliance equities. In that respect, the Anglo-Portuguese alliance is conspicuously and critically different. Indeed, its substantial cooperative economic dimension, most of it historically embedded between the fourteenth and the seventeenth centuries, appears to be the key to its longevity, together with the formidable elite interpersonal networks which that symbiotic economic relationship has fostered over the past six centuries and more.[81]

Three important developments shaped Anglo-Portuguese economic ties in ways that critically impacted on national security relations. First, as noted above, a substantial English merchant class was established early in Portugal, notably to manage the port wine trade of Oporto, which became in turn a significant domestic constituency within Portugal for liberal Anglo-Portuguese economic relations. This merchant constituency, in short, generated alliance equities that helped stabilize security ties and broaden them beyond the purely geopolitical realm. Second, King John IV of Portugal substantially reinforced the position of resident English merchants by granting them, in 1654, significant new commercial privileges in return for English help against Hapsburg Spain. This economic interdependence was reinforced by the deepening of elite interpersonal networks, through the marriage in 1662 of John's daughter Catherine of Braganza to King Charles II of Britain. Finally, the Methuen Treaty of 1703 guaranteed a Portuguese market for English woolens, in return for granting Portuguese wines privileged access to the English market. Throughout this process, alliance equities in the security and economic realms interacted with and reinforced one another, to generate an enduring alliance relationship in the fullest sense of the term.

On this basis, Portugal became a lucrative market for British investment, where the rate of return (14.3 percent) was more than double the overall average for British overseas operations.[82] This embedded liberalism helped to sustain the broader alliance over an eighteenth century during which Portuguese mercantilism under the fiercely protectionist marquis of Pombal, in particular, stirred severe British frustration that otherwise might well have disrupted broader alliance relations. Yet even the proliferation of Portuguese monopoly companies did not result in the blend of mercantilism and geopolitical conflict that prevailed in Britain's relations with such nations as Spain and Holland, and the absence of such a development was owing to the embedded liberal dimension and strong transnational elite interpersonal ties.

Economic interdependence helped to stabilize security relations between Britain and Portugal, including such dimensions as the customary use of Lisbon as a major port of call and de facto naval base for the Royal Navy. Causality also went the other way: the alliance had positive implications for the bilateral economic relationship that help produce a virtuous, reinforcing set of political-economic ties equipped to endure for centuries. In particular, the alliance helped to promote (1) open markets, through strategically motivated free-trade arrangements such as the Methuen Treaty of 1703; (2) credit access for Portugal to the advanced London capital markets, due to the predictability in political-economic relations that the alliance induced; (3) smooth transportation, especially maritime transport, due to the dominance of the Royal Navy in international sea-lanes, including those to Portugal's all-important colony Brazil; and (4) narrow trade specialization within Portugal, in commodities such as port wine. The last of these impacts was not positive for Portugal and forces a modification, to be sure, of the classic Ricardian claims about the utility of the division of labor achieved through international trade. Yet overall the Anglo-Portuguese alliance appears to have given rise to a felicitous, self-reinforcing dynamic of both positive security ties and stable economic interdependence. It thus generated alliance equities that bear important testimony, of surprising contemporary relevance, to the stabilizing, interrelated value of military alliance, interpersonal ties, and liberal trading relationships in the industrialized world today.

The notion of alliance, as we have seen, is a venerable one, with roots 2,500 years deep in the classic intellectual history of both Greece and China. The concept also has origins in the thinking of contemporary historians and philosophers such as Thucydides and Sun Tze, who graced that remarkable period. Yet the salience of alliance in political-economic history has varied greatly over time, there being long periods, especially during the first millennium of the Christian era, during which the concept bore little relevance.

Alliances appear to have been most salient in international relations within Western Europe and ultimately across the Atlantic, during the 360 years since the Treaty of Westphalia in 1648. Yet the alliances of the first three centuries—ephemeral and inaccessible in their details to the general public—were very different from what they have become since the Korean War. Contemporary alliances are much more deeply embedded in economic and social life than was traditionally the case, making consciousness of such nonmilitary dimensions crucial to understanding the well-being of military alliances as well. That economic and social penumbra of alliance generates many of the invaluable alliance equities that lend post–Korean War security partnerships across the industrialized world their remarkable stability.

Chapter 4 The Economic Basis
of National Security

America's leaders have traditionally understood that economics and national security are profoundly linked, both in configuring for security at home and in addressing international affairs. Even before the United States entered World War II, the Roosevelt administration prepared America to become an "arsenal of democracy," focusing intently on building an industrial base that might be needed in future years, one capable of supplying both friendly nations already fighting in the field and American forces as well. Providentially, this integrated economics and security approach proved crucial after Pearl Harbor in enabling the United States to mobilize rapidly for war and ultimately to defeat a mortal challenge with remarkable dispatch.

In planning for the postwar world, the United States also thought with foresight about how stable economic parameters, viewed as equitable by nations elsewhere, could consolidate America's central role in global security affairs as well.[1] In initiating global free-trading rules, together with the Bretton Woods system of open international finance, the United States moved simultaneously to promote economic prosperity for the war-ravaged world, to safeguard America's position in international affairs, and to economically rebut a mercantilist, static Soviet political-military challenge.[2] The creation of global economic bodies like the International Monetary Fund, the World Bank, and the General Agreement on Tariffs and Trade (GATT) reinforced this new, comprehensive global order.

AMERICAN POLITICAL-ECONOMIC CONSCIOUSNESS

With respect to the future of the Pacific, American policymakers also saw national security matters in political-economic terms from early on. To be sure, Treasury Secretary Henry Morgenthau, a confidant of President Franklin D. Roosevelt, together with a cohesive, activist group of New Deal reformers, prioritized demilitarization and democratization, as opposed to unrelated economic considerations, in planning the future of Japan, as they did with respect to Germany also.[3] Following the succession of the more pragmatic Harry Truman to the presidency in April 1945, however, the influence of these idealists began to wane. The stock of realists intent on economic stability and political continuity in Asia began, conversely, to soar.

The economic context of U.S.–Japan relations clearly shaped early U.S. government presurrender thinking about the future of Japan, even before the demise of Morgenthau. In March 1944, for example, the State Department's new Postwar Programs Committee (PWC), which together with the Army's Civil Affairs Division (CAD) had working-level responsibility for presurrender planning, reported that it favored a nearly exclusive American occupation, without zones such as those being designed for Germany. The PWC also recommended that the existing Japanese authority structure, including the emperor, be retained, at least temporarily, in the interest of stability.[4]

In April 1945, the PWC's successor organization, the Far Eastern Sub-Committee of the State-War National Coordinating Committee (SWNCC), argued strongly in its own "U.S. Initial Post-Surrender Policy" that stopping war production—a clear imperative to all presurrender planners—need not simultaneously imply wide-scale dismantling of heavy industry.[5] This moderate view was supported by the working-level Japan specialists, such as Hugh Borton, Robert Feary, and George Blakeslee. It contrasted strongly to the more draconian demilitarization and deindustrialization plans for Germany, especially those propounded by the Soviet Union.

With Truman's accession to the presidency, the pragmatic SWNCC line, with an economic point of departure integrating economic and political goals in prescribing for American policy, clearly became dominant. Among its pre-eminent supporters was Joseph Grew, the last pre–World War II U.S. ambassador to Japan and a cousin of John Pierpont Morgan. Grew served fortuitously as undersecretary of state at the end of the war, but in reality he assumed a much larger role. He actually ran the State Department at this critical juncture, since his immediate boss, Edward Stettinius, was inexperienced in diplomacy, especially with respect to the Far East, and was frequently away attending international conferences.[6]

Grew, together with other Asia hands, such as Eugene Dooman, Grew's pre-war counselor at the embassy in Tokyo; Walton Butterworth, who headed the Office of Far Eastern Affairs; and William Castle, another former ambassador to Japan who had been undersecretary of state under Herbert Hoover, stressed the overriding importance of stability in Japan.[7] They saw the Soviet Union as America's ultimate adversary in postwar Asia and viewed an economically recovered Japan as an essential bulwark for America's position in the Far East, given China's presumptive instability. Their geopolitical view, with its strong prescription of support for Japanese economic recovery, became the dominant line of American policy toward Japan from 1948 on, supported by such influential figures as George Kennan, director of policy planning at the State Department, and John Foster Dulles, author of the San Francisco Peace Treaty and ultimately secretary of state (1953–59). Indeed, it became the cornerstone of the world that Dulles made, as we saw in chapter 2.

The peace settlement with Japan embedded a profoundly political-economic understanding—it might be termed the San Francisco System—at the heart of U.S.–Japan relations.[8] To the United States, Japan provided forward military bases and the promise of defensive military cooperation. In return, America offered not only military guarantees, but also asymmetrically open access for Japanese firms to its massive domestic market, so as to promote an export-driven Japanese economic recovery. It simultaneously denied Japan's main prospective rival for Washington's favors, Communist mainland China, analogous favorable treatment through an economic embargo.

To be sure, Washington and Tokyo signed a Treaty of Friendship, Commerce and Navigation, providing reciprocal economic access rights, in 1953, not long after Japan's return to sovereignty. Yet in the interest of Japanese economic recovery, the United States did not insist on extensive trade and financial access to Japan, apart from limited involvement by major U.S. international banks and energy firms, which had operations almost everywhere else in the non-Communist world. Japan repaid this asymmetrical access with implicit fidelity in national security terms to American global designs.

CONTRASTING JAPANESE APPROACHES
TO POLITICAL ECONOMY

Japan, for its part, has also long recognized the economic basis of national security—indeed, even more explicitly and intensely than has the United States. After all, Japan emerged into the international system, opened by Perry's black ships in 1853, at the high noon of imperialism, when economic competitiveness was a critical determinant of national survival. Nations unable to modernize rapidly were being devoured politically and turned into either colonies or neocolonies, regardless of how brilliant their past civilizations had been. Vietnam, Korea, China, and the ancient principalities of India and Indochina soon learned this brutal new reality of the imperialist age.

Rapid and dynamic Japanese economic modernization, followed by military expansion against China, yielded additional resources, enabling Meiji leaders to modernize still further.[9] In a remarkably short time, Japan developed both a powerful military and a moderate-sized empire, vanquishing such major powers as China and Russia in war, while shrewdly allying with Great Britain, which boasted of the dominant navy of the day. Japan itself was able to avoid military subjugation until it fell into an endless war with China and then rashly attacked the United States in 1941. Yet through its continuing struggles, together with the study visits of its young leaders to the industrialized West, Tokyo gained an unshakable belief in economic strength as a cornerstone of national security. *Fukoku Kyōhei,* or "Rich Nation, Strong Army," was the rallying cry of Japanese modernizers throughout most of the pre-1945 period.[10]

HOW ECONOMICS AND SECURITY
ACTUALLY RELATE

Both the United States and Japan have traditionally had, as we have seen, a strong conviction that national security rests on a solid economic foundation and that economic interdependence generates valuable alliance equities. Yet because of its contrasting historical experience and economic realities, Tokyo's sense of the precise nature of interrelationships between economics and security has long differed from Washington's. These perceptual differences profoundly shape the two countries' expectations regarding the Pacific alliance and their incentives to cooperate with one another in maintaining it.

Contrasting Self-Conceptions: "People of Plenty" vs. "People of Scarcity"

Americans have traditionally seen themselves as a "people of plenty," most finding it difficult to even conceive of material scarcity or to existentially feel the need for resource conservation.[11] Japanese, by contrast, might be termed a "people of scarcity," who have historically been obsessed with their nation's lack of raw materials, their voracious appetite for the same, and their vulnerability in international competition for such valued commodities.

The strong Japanese sense of resource poverty—so deeply rooted by the late 1930s that it arguably became a casus belli in World War II[12]—has, however, only limited historical justification. Japan today, to be sure, is radically dependent on imports, across extended sea-lanes from the Middle East, Southeast Asia, and Latin America, for virtually every industrial raw material it consumes, including oil, iron ore, bauxite, and coal as well as most of its caloric intake. As shown in figure 4.1, Japan's actual energy self-sufficiency ratio was only a marginal 19 percent in 2005, compared to 87 percent in Britain and 70 percent in the United States, for example.[13]

Japan has not, however, always been so resource-poor. During the Edo Pe-

Figure 4.1. Japan's Low Energy Self-Sufficiency   (unit = percent)

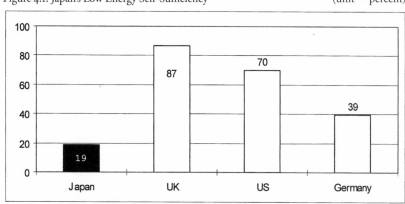

Source: World Bank, *World Development Indicators.*
Note: Figures are for 2005.

riod (1603–1867), predominantly an era of almost total isolation from the outside world, Japan was fully self-sufficient in raw materials. Indeed, for a country the size of California it was remarkably well endowed. Even as isolation ended and industrialization began, Japan exported brass, copper, and coal as late as 1902.[14]

Yet the building of a massive military-industrial machine on a relatively small geographical base, together with a doubling of population between 1850 and 1935, transformed Japan into a nation with a profound dependence for raw materials and food on the uncertain world beyond its shores.[15] That deepening and disturbing new reality of economic interdependence has grown to become a wellspring of Japanese national-security consciousness. In particular, deepening resource dependence has made Japanese of all persuasions and backgrounds—both strategists and the general public—conscious of the sea-lanes and their critical importance to national security, in the deepest personal sense.

From the early twentieth century, as the automotive age began in earnest, the energy sea-lanes feeding that ravenous new era became vitally important in strategic terms for Japan. Although it once possessed considerable domestic coal, Japan has never had any substantial local oil reserves, so its steady growth has meant deeper and deeper reliance on petroleum imports. It was across the seas, after all, that Tokyo obtained the kerosene, gasoline, and ultimately the aviation fuel that were increasingly crucial not only to feed its economy, but also to sustain its growing military machine.

Some of Japan's first strategic energy sea-lanes were across the Pacific, as the United States provided 80 percent of its immediate pre–World War II oil supply.[16] During the 1930s, Japan's semigovernmental Southern Manchurian Railway, among other firms, had synthesized artificial oil from coal and in 1937 moved to production.[17] Yet this did not substantially reduce Japan's vulnerability.

During wartime, oil supply shifted to Southeast Asia, and the ability of American submarines to throttle such sources was a major cause of Japan's wartime defeat. Since the early 1950s, the crucial energy sea-lanes have increasingly been those to the Middle East—even further away and even less subject to Japanese political-economic control—than the declining fields of Southeast Asia. Japan's dependence on the Middle East since the mid-1980s has steadily risen, as shown clearly in figure 4.2.

Japan to this day lacks substantial direct political-military relationships with most key Middle Eastern nations, and its military presence west of the Strait of Malacca, a fleeting one, dates only from 2001. Yet Tokyo's stakes in the energy

Figure 4.2. Japan's High and Rising Dependence on Middle Eastern Oil   (unit = percent)

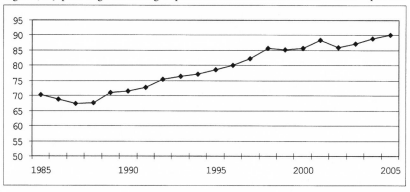

Source: Ministry of Economy, Trade, and Industry, *Energy White Paper* (2007 edition).

sea-lanes between Yokohama and the Persian Gulf are considerable and growing. Because of its low energy self-sufficiency Japan has been heavily dependent on the Middle East for energy resources since the 1950s. And that longtime, substantial dependence has actually been rising. In 1970 Japan got 84.6 percent of its crude oil imports from the Middle East,[18] a share that rose to more than 90 percent by 2005.[19] Japan now takes fully one quarter of all the oil exported from the Middle East,[20] making it by a substantial margin the largest customer in the world of the region's oil, especially that of the Persian Gulf. Indeed, Japan now imports one and half times as much oil from the Gulf as all of OECD Europe combined. The strategic importance of this striking new economic reality, which underlines the importance of the energy sea-lanes westward from East Asia to the Persian Gulf, can hardly be overstated, although it remains remarkably unknown to all but a handful of specialists. Sea-lane defense is thus a primary alliance equity for the United States in the overall U.S.–Japan relationship.

The sea-lanes to the gulf are relevant to the Pacific alliance, of course, for two major reasons. First, those long and vulnerable maritime lifelines are used increasingly by many nations of Asia, including China, South Korea, and India as well as Japan.[21] Second, the energy sea-lanes are dominated militarily by the U.S. Navy, the only real blue-water fleet on earth. To the extent that the United States perseveres in this sea-lane defense role and that other powers such as India, Australia, South Korea, or China do not emerge—singly or in combination—as an alternative, energy sea-lane defense will continue as a political-military cornerstone of the Pacific alliance.

The energy sea-lanes between Northeast Asia and the Persian Gulf are doubtless highly strategic—not only to the growing energy trade that is flowing across them, but also to the broader geopolitical stability of Northeast Asia itself. Chinese energy flows across these sea-lanes are also substantial and growing—indeed, net crude oil imports into the PRC have risen sharply in recent years, from zero as late as 1993 to 4.1 million barrels per day by 2007.[22] To the extent that the United States enjoys major political-military leverage over China through its dominance of the energy sea-lanes, China can be expected to be tacitly more moderate on delicate issues such as the stability of the status quo in the Taiwan Straits.

Despite the strategic importance of the sea-lanes to the Gulf—both for Northeast Asia as a whole and for the U.S.–Japan alliance more narrowly—the significance to the United States itself is only derivative. Those sea-lanes do not, after all, supply America directly, although Washington does incur substantial costs in their defense. Indian, Australian, and Japanese capabilities and interest in a sea-lane defense role are rising, and a more multilateral framework in the distant future, supplanting the role of bilateral alliances, cannot be excluded. Indeed, a Regional Maritime Security Initiative was advocated in 2004 by Admiral Thomas Fargo, the U.S. PACOM commander, to "develop partnership among willing regional nations with varying capabilities and capacities to identify, monitor, and intercept transnational maritime threats under existing international and domestic laws,"[23] with a special emphasis on the Strait of Malacca sea-lanes. Fargo's concept was transformed during 2007 into a Global Maritime Partnership initiative that sought a multilateral "approach to maritime security, promoting the rule of law by countering piracy, terrorism, weapons proliferation, drug trafficking, and other illicit activities."[24] Yet the central responsibility in energy sea-lane defense remains emphatically with the United States.

Changing Patterns of Foreign Trade

A second, related economic reality that influences national security ties between the United States and Japan is the contrasting relationship of the two nations to international markets. As previously mentioned, a sense of resource scarcity in Japan and converse resource availability in the United States has long distinguished the contrasting national consciousnesses of the two countries. While America has consistently viewed security primarily as a political-military matter, Japan has seen trade as a fundamental dimension of security also, ever since the Meiji period, because it has had to trade to live.

In the late nineteenth and early twentieth centuries, for example, Japan exported silk to the United States to earn hard currency. This silk trade in turn financed imports of raw materials and capital equipment, fueling further industrial expansion and facilitating a grading-up of Japan's industrial and production mix. Japanese light industry also exported cotton cloth to Southeast Asia and India. With the foreign currency gained thereby, Japan imported heavy industrial products and iron from the United Kingdom, thus nurturing its nascent machinery, shipbuilding, and armament sectors. Japanese heavy industrial products were then sold to China and Manchuria, the exporters capitalizing on price competitiveness as well as on imperial ties.[25]

For a half century after World War II, Japan's key markets were in the United States, providing a central rationale for intimate political, economic, and security ties with Washington. In the immediate aftermath of that conflict, with Europe and Japan in ruins, the gap in market scale between the United States and its putative Atlantic and Pacific allies was massive. Even in 1960, fifteen years after war's end, America alone accounted for nearly 40 percent of the entire global GDP, Japan for little more than 3 percent. By 2007 these ratios had shifted sharply, the American share declining to 25 percent of global GDP and Japan's nearly tripling to 8 percent.[26]

Reflecting changing economic magnitudes as well as globalization, the relative importance of U.S.–Japan trade for the two nations themselves has also been shifting. In 1952, at the end of the Occupation, trade with the United States made up more than 65 percent of Japan's exports and over 86 percent of its imports.[27] By 2007 those ratios had fallen sharply, to 20 and 11 percent, respectively, as indicated in figure 4.3.

Japanese foreign trade patterns have shifted strikingly over the past generation (see fig. 4.3). America's share of Japan's trade has fallen by roughly half. Asia's share has risen conversely by an even greater multiple, with China alone surpassing the United States as Japan's largest trading partner in 2007, as mentioned in chapter 1.[28] These trade trends must be seen in the context also of investment and technology flows, where the United States continues to be very important for Japan. Yet they clearly present an important, if indirect, long-term challenge to the traditional foundations of the Pacific alliance, which has involved U.S.-centric, rather than Asia-centric, Japanese foreign trade from its very inception.

To be sure, there are some market segments in which mutual interdependence between the United States and Japan, and mutual importance, is actually rising, representing exceptions to the broader trends described above. This ap-

Figure 4.3. Shifting Japanese Trading Patterns: Asia Rises as the United States Declines

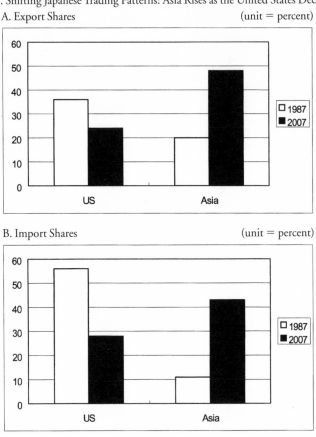

A. Export Shares   (unit = percent)

B. Import Shares   (unit = percent)

Source: Ministry of Internal Affairs and Communications Statistical Bureau website: http://www.stat.go.jp/data/chouki/18.htm; JETRO website: http://www.jetro.go.jp/jpn/ stats/trade/.

pears to be happening in finance. The Japanese financial assets market, holding custody over $1.3 trillion in gross savings during 2005, is by a substantial margin the second largest in the world, save only for the $1.7 trillion market in the United States. China's market, by comparison, was $1.1 trillion in size, as compared to $590 billion in Germany and $312 billion in Britain.[29]

American investment managers have by most accounts been the most dynamic and innovative in recent years. In fact, as described previously, virtually all major American financial institutions, including Citigroup, Goldman Sachs, AFLAC, and Prudential, have established significant positions in Japan, just as

Japanese financiers have in the United States. American-owned banks and private equity firms have played an important role in restructuring depressed sectors of Japanese industry, thus aiding long-overdue recovery from the collapse of the financial bubble of the 1980s and 1990s. Meanwhile, Japanese firms such as Nomura Securities and Mitsubishi UFJ Bank significantly helped stabilize the American financial structure following the collapse of Lehman Brothers in September 2008.[30] And American firms, which now handle nearly a quarter of the transactions on the Tokyo Stock Exchange, are the largest and most dynamic players in that globally important market.[31]

Automobiles are another sector in which transpacific interdependence has remained important. Auto trade volume rose rapidly before the 2008 financial crisis, growing by more than a third in only two years.[32] Direct investment, particularly from Japan to the United States, has also been substantial. Japanese auto firms produced more than three million autos[33] annually in the United States and employed over 613,600 workers until the 2008 downturn.[34]

Yet whether one or two dynamic sectors alone can sustain a healthy bilateral trade relationship, in the face of economic headwinds and broader overall national priorities elsewhere in the world, remains very much in question. U.S.–Japan economic relations, after all, take place in the context of an increasingly global economy, and a global economy is not deferential to bilateral relationships, no matter how important those may be in national security terms.

The issue of markets in the political economy of the U.S.–Japan relationship is by no means only a matter of magnitudes. One of the attractions for Japanese companies of involvement in the United States, for example, has been that the American market serves as a global standard-setter in terms of product quality. Once Japanese products are able to hold their own in the U.S. market, they are perceived within Japan as having reached world-standard quality levels, allowing such products to be sold in Europe, in Asia, and throughout the world.

The first Toyota cars shipped to the United States (in 1957), for example, did not sell at all. After establishing a clear goal of producing automobiles capable of being sold in the United States, Toyota improved its quality, to such a degree that by the mid-1960s its products were beginning to sell in the United States. With confidence, Toyota began expanding its sales area to the broader world.[35] Once Japan established itself as a producer of high-quality goods, however, this symbolic role of success in the American market as evidence of quality production began to wane in importance.

Markets are also important, from a political-economic point of view, in terms of the quality of commercial access they provide. During the 1950s and

1960s one of the great attractions for Japan of the bilateral relationship with the United States was that it gave Japanese firms asymmetrical access to the American market in two respects—both better than other prospective Asian competitors enjoyed in the United States and better than Americans had to the Japanese market. Strong relations with the United States, including security ties amidst the Cold War, also enlisted American support for Japanese access to Southeast Asia, providing another alliance equity of major interest to Japan at the time.[36]

The U.S.–Japan commercial bargain has rarely been as attractive, generally speaking, for American firms as for Japanese. Yet there have been some important exceptions. As we will see later, the profitability of U.S. firms established in Japan five years or more is extremely high by global standards. American service-sector firms, including insurance, private equity, software, and investment banking—as well, at times, as aircraft manufacturing—have done extremely well in the Japanese market and have clear alliance equities as a consequence.

With the passage of time and the emergence of an open global economy, the political-economic value of the U.S.–Japan alliance in generating alliance equities through preferential access has generally waned, even as the potential value of the alliance as a catalyst for broader international system stabilization has risen. Since the end of the U.S. strategic embargo against China in the early 1970s and the emergence of a broader Sino-American entente, trade discrimination in favor of Japan against China, due to Japan's alliance status, has steadily lessened, and with China's 2001 entry into the World Trade Organization (WTO) essentially disappeared. Almost all other Asian competitors are also meeting on a level playing field with Japan in an American market that is not nearly as large, in relative quantitative terms, as it has historically been. The weakening of the dollar against both the Euro and major Asian currencies is making the relative importance of the U.S. market smaller still. Yet as both Japanese and American firms go global, their need for a powerful advocate of stable global parameters—ideally a U.S.–Japan partnership—significantly increases.

Asymmetries in American and Japanese corporate access to one another's markets have also narrowed—to the benefit of equality, of course, but also to the relative disadvantage of Japanese firms, from Tokyo's perspective. And American support for Japanese economic interests in Southeast Asia—once substantial, in the shadow of the Vietnam War—has now become inconsequential. Rising Japanese political-economic power and the creation of global trade institutions like the WTO also allow Japan to pursue many economic policy objectives more independently of U.S. backing than was previously true. American support for Japanese market access elsewhere, in short, has deteriorated from a matter of substantial importance for Tokyo in the Age of Dulles, a matter that generated valuable Japanese alliance equities, to a question of lesser concern. Dynamic American global initiatives or gestures toward bilateral partnership on trade, energy, technology, and the environment could dramatically alter this equation, but they have yet to materialize.

Capital Flows

Capital flows are a third key aspect of the U.S.–Japan economics and security relationship, significantly linked to Pacific alliance for more than a century. Until the 1930s Japan was not an especially high-savings nation and borrowed extensively from abroad for its modernization. Foreign loans were directly crucial to national security at some critical junctures also, especially during the Russo-Japanese War in 1904–05, when the investment firm Kuhn Loeb, headed by Jacob Schiff, provided invaluable financial support to the struggle against czarist Russia.

Financial linkages to modernization and to national security broadly conceived were also present during the 1950s, and the Japanese business world expected they would continue to be so in the 1960s as well. Indeed, business expectations of financial flows from the United States were a key reason why the 1960 Security Treaty crisis and the related cancellation of President Dwight D. Eisenhower's Tokyo visit were so traumatic to the Japanese *zaikai*.[37] Confidence in the stability of Japan's political system was important to the continuation of those flows, particularly given the heavy debt loads that Japanese firms typically assumed. And the 1960 crisis temporarily called that stability into question.

Gradually Japan's economy became liquid enough not to require financial inflows from abroad. Yet capital flows remained important to the political economy of the Pacific alliance from a different perspective. By the early 1970s, Japan began to accumulate substantial balance of payments surpluses. And with the revision of its Foreign Exchange Law in December 1980—barely a month after the election of Ronald Reagan as president of the United States—those funds began flowing back overseas in significant amounts.

As indicated in figures 4.4A and 4.4B, Japanese investments began moving heavily into American long-term securities, particularly U.S. Treasury bonds, from the mid-1980s. Indeed, during the bubble economy period of the late 1980s T-bill purchases by the Japanese government, as well as by private Japa-

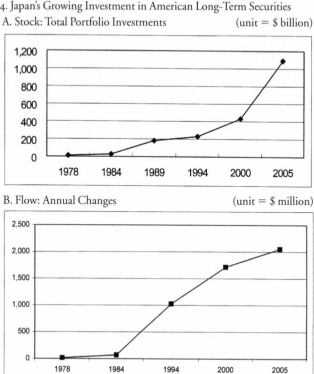

Figure 4.4. Japan's Growing Investment in American Long-Term Securities
A. Stock: Total Portfolio Investments   (unit = $ billion)

B. Flow: Annual Changes   (unit = $ million)

Source: U.S. Department of Treasury website: http://www.treas.gov/tic/fpis.shtml.

nese banks and life insurance companies (*seiho*), often totaled one-third to one-half of total Treasury security sales to the entire world, temporarily exceeding that level in 1989.[38] These heavy capital flows from Japan were a central factor in providing the Reagan administration with the macroeconomic flexibility to outpace the Soviets in defense spending and hence to win the Cold War.[39] After 9/11, parallel flows likewise allowed the George W. Bush administration to run massive fiscal and current account deficits to fund interventions in Afghanistan and Iraq, without inhibiting consumer demand or vitality in American domestic capital markets.

The consequence of such heavy transpacific financial borrowing, combined with substantial Japanese direct investment abroad, was a sharp deterioration in the net American asset position in the world, mirrored by a sharp improvement in Japan's standing. As indicated in figure 4.5, from the mid-1980s on, the United States became a massive debtor to the world, and Japan conversely a

Figure 4.5. Japan as Creditor and America as Debtor   (unit = $ billion)

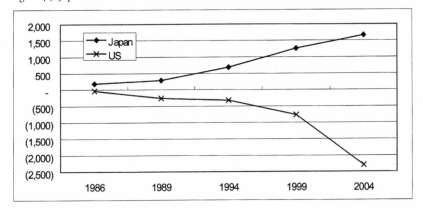

Source: Japan's Ministry of Finance website: http://www.mof.go.jp/bpoffice/bpdata/zandaka
.htm; U.S. Department of Commerce Bureau of Economic Analysis website: http://www
.bea.gov/international/index.htm#iip.
Note: Figures are for net liabilities, public and private.

huge creditor, with bilateral imbalances between them being the main cause of this globally important shift.

Japan's rising role as a massive creditor and America's converse role as a debtor had significant latent implications for the management of the Pacific alliance, inevitably linking financial coordination to the overall strategic calculus and magnifying the importance of the alliance itself in world affairs. This makes perfect sense, as a shift toward greater Japanese leverage in financial affairs would boost reciprocity, rather than intensify hierarchical dependence. Japan was providing something of tangible value to the United States (capital) in return for the security guarantees for sea-lanes, neighboring nations, and the Japanese homeland itself that Tokyo so clearly needs.

The Foreign Investment Challenge

There is a fourth dimension of economic life with enormous consequences for national security and ultimately for the functioning of the Pacific alliance: foreign investment. Despite the tangible, self-interested stakes that such investment creates in a host nation's stability and well-being, as well as the natural incentives it creates to prioritize the host nation's concerns, the importance of foreign investment in reinforcing alliance ties remains remarkably remote to both the American and the Japanese conceptions of national security.

Transnational capital flows to nations elsewhere in the world are, after all, a central means of linking local business communities with the United States. On-the-ground economic stakes abroad establish alliance equities, cemented by mutual economic interest, that make the American political and business worlds sensitive to political-economic concerns within the nation in question. These important political-economic forces are weaker in U.S.–Japan relations than in other major American bilateral relationships because of the distinctive patterns of foreign investment.

Foreign direct investment (FDI) in Japan is remarkably low relative to GDP—lower than in Europe, Latin America, China, or even South Korea. And that pattern has persisted throughout the post-Occupation period, with only marginal changes, despite the sharp expansion of FDI that has accompanied globalization elsewhere in the world. As shown in figure 4.6, Japan's stock of FDI in 2005 was only 2.2 percent of GDP, compared to 37.1 percent in Britain, 18 percent in Germany, and 13 percent in the United States.[40] Despite this low overall Japanese level, net FDI inflow to Japan remained only 0.1 percent of GDP, compared to 7.2 percent in Britain, 1.1 percent in Germany, 0.9 percent in the United States, and 3.5 percent in China.[41] The gap between Japanese inbound FDI levels and those elsewhere is thus widening.

American investment, to be sure, composes the largest share of foreign investment in Japan on a stock basis, at 43 percent of the overall total in 2005.[42] That investment also is relatively profitable in global comparative terms.[43] The average return on American investment in Japan across all industries during 2001–05 was 13 percent, while returns to Canadian, German, and British investment were 10 percent, 7 percent, and 5 percent, respectively.[44] Yet although it is relatively profitable, the asset value of that American investment in Japan, relative to local GDP, is lower than in any other major industrialized nation with which the United States has formal alliance relationships.

Major American investments in Japan are concentrated lately in the information technology (IT) industry and the financial sector. Among the most prominent are Shinsei Bank (Ripplewood), Aozora Bank (Cerberus), Nikko Citigroup Securities and Nikko Cordial (Citigroup), IBM Japan (IBM), Spansion Japan (Advanced Micro Devices), and Texas Instruments Japan (Texas Instruments). In terms of sales volume, however, information technology, petroleum, chemicals, and food products are most prominent. ExxonMobil, IBM, Wal-Mart, Xerox, and Pfizer were the top five American investments by this criterion during 2005.[45]

The major American defense contractors lack a substantial Japan presence today, in contrast to the current situation between the U.S. and European allies

Figure 4.6. Japan's Low Ratio of Inbound Foreign Direct
Investment to GDP   (unit = percent)

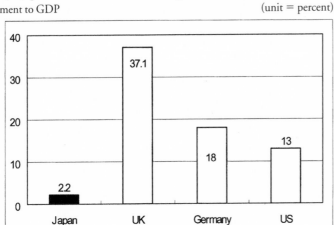

Source: UNCTAD, *World Investment Report* (2006 edition).
Note: Data are from national sources.

and to the prevalent pattern of the prewar Anglo-Japanese alliance. In industrial and technological relations of national security significance, what is striking about the U.S.–Japan relationship in Japan itself is how *marginal* defense-relevant industrial cooperation has traditionally been to the overall national security relationship of the two nations—especially in contrast to patterns in U.S. relations with major European nations and even with China. The static U.S.-Japan pattern could well change, however, should defense challenges in East Asia deepen and should the U.S.–Japan political relationship deepen.

Foreign investment has not always been so marginal in Japan. Between 1889, when a crucial amendment to the Commercial Law first allowed joint ventures with foreign capital, and 1930, Japan had relatively liberal foreign investment policies.[46] Such major firms as General Electric, Singer Sewing Machine, B. F. Goodrich, Ford, General Motors, and Otis Elevator established a significant local presence.[47] Indeed, by 1930 Ford and General Motors together controlled more than 95 percent of the Japanese domestic automobile market.[48] In 1929 Ford even bought a 9.2-acre site at Koyasu, near Yokohama, to build a modern auto plant and produce the Model A.[49]

Japan's mobilization for war during the 1930s and related government restrictions brought this vigorous early foreign investment presence in Japan to an end, thereby intensifying the prospect of conflict with the broader world. The military, in particular, was reluctant to see strategic industries such as automobiles and electronics dominated by foreign investment and pressured the government to discriminate strongly in favor of domestic competitors such as Ayukawa Gisuke's Nissan Group. Through a maze of foreign exchange and regulatory controls, the Japanese government increasingly made life so difficult for foreign firms that most of them, except for oil companies and joint ventures with powerful *zaibatsu* firms, had closed their doors by 1940.[50] And in January of that year, after the U.S.-initiated abrogation of the bilateral Commerce and Navigation Treaty, American investments in Japan lost the benefit of international legal protection. In July 1941 the remaining American assets in Japan, including those of twenty-nine individual companies, were formally frozen.[51]

In late 1945, at war's end, the frozen assets were returned to their original owners, and SCAP subsequently eased restrictions on American investment throughout the Occupation period (1945–52).[52] The Allied Occupation ended on April 28, 1952, and a new U.S.–Japan Treaty of Friendship, Commerce and Navigation became operative in the following year. That treaty guaranteed American investors national and most-favored-nation treatment in the Japanese market. It also bound Japan not to impose foreign exchange restrictions in an arbitrary manner, discriminatory to the competitive position of U.S. firms in Japan.[53]

Yet despite these commitments and despite the fundamental economic attractiveness of investment in a rapidly growing and increasingly advanced economy such as Japan, inbound foreign investment remained remarkably stagnant over the postwar decades, in contrast to patterns in Europe, thereby impairing the political-economic foundations in Washington of the Pacific alliance. Indeed, between 1951 and 1970 American direct manufacturing investment in Japan never exceeded $67 million in any single year, and the total value of such validations for the entire two decades in question came to less than $320 million. In 1950 American FDI in Japan, as a share of the stock of total U.S. investment worldwide, was only 0.2 percent. Yet despite Japan's extraordinary economic growth and underlying attractiveness, investment rose to only 0.8 percent of GDP in 1960, 2.0 percent in 1970,[54] and a meager 2.2 percent even in 2005.[55]

Government restrictions appear to have been the principal reason for the stagnation of foreign investment in Japan during this period, a pattern contrasting sharply to the expansion from the 1950s on of American investment in Europe. The two main obstacles were Japan's Foreign Investment Law (FIL) of 1950, and its restrictive foreign exchange legislation. Only the FIL could provide extended overseas remittance through official guarantees. Yet FIL approval, frequently determined in practice by the interests of Japanese industrial competitors, was extremely difficult to obtain. Failing such approval, prospective foreign investors had to confront the Foreign Exchange and Foreign Trade Control Law, which required explicit permission on a detailed case-by-case basis for almost every international business transaction related to foreign investment.[56]

In 1964, Japan formally altered its exclusionist stance toward FDI by adhering to the OECD Capital Liberalization Code when it joined that major association of advanced industrial nations. The government did so, however, only after the country had grown competitive enough to withstand major international competition.[57] And Japan implemented the new OECD commitments only gradually.

The complex institutional barriers implicit in the FIL thus inhibited foreign corporate entry into Japan long after rationales of infant-industry protection and current account deficit had ceased to be credible. Sweeping barriers limited investment, as suggested above, to only two areas: (1) nonstrategic consumer goods sectors, such as soft drink beverages, where Japanese firms had no substantial competitors; and (2) fields in which foreign firms like IBM, Texas Instruments, and Mobil Oil had such important technology or global resource access that the rationale for allowing them in was overwhelming. The result was both a very low general level of foreign investment in Japan and a pattern that was markedly skewed, generally speaking, away from the mainstream of firms that were influential in the American domestic political economy—particularly in its manufacturing sector.

To be sure, as shown in figure 4.7B, Japanese investment in the United States is substantial and rising. Such Japanese investments in the United States have consistently exceeded Japanese investments in all of the rest of Asia combined, in absolute volume across the past decade, in part owing to the sheer size of the U.S. economy. American investment in Japan, roughly two-thirds of the Japanese stake in the United States at book value, is slowly rising also, although the increases are discouragingly slow and little more substantial than in much smaller European economies, as shown in figure 4.7A. Recently both the United States and Japan are investing much more aggressively in other parts of Asia than in each other. During 2001–05, for example, Japanese direct investment in China more than doubled, from $10 billion to $24 billion, while that in the United States grew only marginally, from $141 billion to $149 billion.[58]

Figure 4.7. Comparative Trends in Transpacific Investment   (unit = $ million)

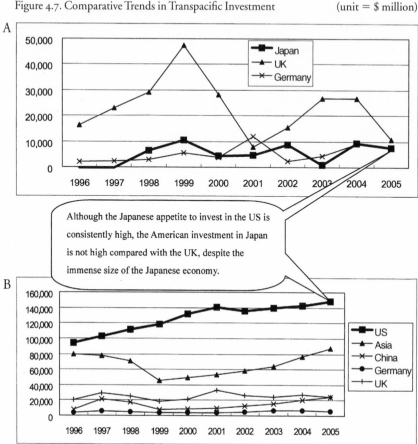

A. American Direct Investment in Japan and European Countries
B. Japanese Direct Investment in the United States and Asian Countries
Source: (A) U.S. Department of Commerce Bureau of Economic Analysis website: http://www.bea.gov/international/bp_web/list.cfm?anon=71&registered=0. (B) JETRO website: http://www.jetro.go.jp/jpn/stats/fdi/.
Note: (A) British GDP is roughly one-third the size of Japan's, while that of Germany is around one-half. (B) Asia, for the purpose of these statistics, includes China, Taiwan, Hong Kong, South Korea, Singapore, Thailand, Indonesia, Malaysia, Philippines, and India.

During 2005 and 2007, American investment in China, South Korea, and India tripled or more, compared with a doubling with respect to Japan.[59]

There have been a few spectacularly profitable American private equity projects, to be sure, such as the Ripplewood Group's acquisition in 2000 of the Long-Term Credit Bank of Japan.[60] The Group acquired that moribund bank for $1.15 billion in 2000, although with a supplementary $76 billion capital infusion from the Japanese government. In 2004 the bank was valued at more than $6 billion, nearly five times Ripplewood's initial investment. The Group floated a successful initial public offering involving 35 percent of its shares, priced at $2.1 billion, thus recouping double its original investment, while retaining two-thirds of Shinsei's equity.[61] Yet despite such success stories, foreign investment, despite a temporary upsurge during the late 1990s, has failed to emerge into the mainstream of the Japanese political economy to the degree that it has almost everywhere else in the industrialized world.[62] This structural anomaly could ultimately become an Achilles heel of the U.S.–Japan alliance and requires priority policy attention.

The perverse political-economic impact on the U.S.–Japan relationship of this limited American direct investment in Japan, coupled with stagnating converse Japanese investment in the United States, must not be underestimated. There is, of course, the deleterious impact on market incentives, innovation, and efficient resource allocation when vigorous international competitors are excluded. Restraining FDI also deprives Japan—and the U.S.–Japan alliance —of having mainstream advocates of the importance of the relationship itself within the American political process, people who would have been much more enthusiastic if investment ties had been more substantial or more dynamically growing. The negative effect is amplified by the contrasting patterns of dynamic American direct investment in China and elsewhere in Asia.

The political leverage effect of FDI has been discussed for a long time— longer, indeed, than large-scale capital flows themselves have prevailed. In the eighteenth-century *Spirit of the Laws,* for example, Montesquieu argued that "movable wealth" encourages peace between states, while also constraining the sovereign domestically.[63] Direct investment raises a nation's stake in maintaining linkages as well as creating incentives to strike deals, while providing a substitute method for resolving conflict.[64]

Because American stakes have been so limited and U.S. business relationships with the Japanese government so adversarial, mainstream American firms have not felt compelled to stand up for the importance of the U.S.–Japan relationship in Washington, D.C., as strongly as they have for ties with Europe or even China. Low foreign investment in Japan has thus contributed to the dangerous "bypass phenomenon," by which Japan is marginalized and sometimes ignored in American foreign policy processes, even as it is well represented in American state- and local-level decision making. The implications are potentially serious over the long term for the credibility of the U.S.–Japan alliance itself.

Figure 4.8. Japan's Heavy Technology Trade Deficit with
the United States   (unit = $ million)

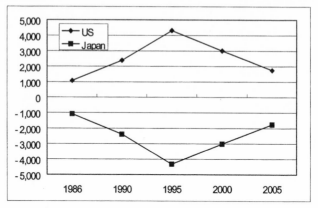

Source: U.S. Department of Commerce Bureau of Economic Analysis, *U.S. International Services: Cross-Border Trade, 1986–2006* and *Sales through Affiliates, 1986–2005,* at http://www.bea.gov/international/xls/tab4.xls.
Note: Figures are for total annual licensing fees and royalty payments between U.S. and Japanese public and private entities.

The problem is compounded by the structure by which the interests of American business in Japan are articulated in the U.S. and Japanese policy processes, as can be most clearly seen by comparison with patterns in Sino-American and transatlantic relations. In both of the latter cases, American business interests operate in both Washington, D.C., and local capitals through a single, integrated organization—the U.S.–China Business Council, for example, which has offices in Beijing, Shanghai, and Washington. In Japan, as in Korea and Southeast Asia, the local American Chamber of Commerce has no direct presence in the United States itself and operates through the headquarters of the American Chamber of Commerce in Washington, which has both different organizational interests and limited on-the-ground expertise in Japan. These organizational disjunctions in turn potentially undermine the effectiveness of American firms actually operating in Japan, especially newcomers, as they articulate their transpacific interests. They also impair the ability of such firms to convince Stateside top management as well as the American policymakers of the importance of Japan.

Technology

Finally, technology flows have been an economic variable influencing both the profile and the importance of the broader U.S.–Japan relationship. Japan, in particular, has traditionally viewed technology exchanges in national security terms, making positive flows from the United States a persuasive rationale in Tokyo for the Pacific alliance.[65] When Japan entered the modern industrial world during the 1850s, after 250 years of isolation, the technological gap with the West was enormous and threatened Japan's very independence as a nation. It lacked not only telephones, telegraphs, and railways, but also, even more consequentially for an island country, long-range artillery, not to mention oceangoing ships.

Following World War II, after a harrowing two decades during which Japan was almost totally divorced from the advanced industrial world by war and strategic embargo, transpacific technological gaps had once again grown substantial. As Tokyo attempted to redress this gap, Japan's technology imports rose nearly five-hundred-fold, from $2.6 million to $1.26 billion between 1960 and 1979, helping to stimulate the explosive economic growth of the 1950s, 1960s, and 1970s.[66] The introductions of the transistor from the United States into the Japanese electronics industry as well as the oxygen furnace from Austria into steel making are just two cases in point.

As suggested in figure 4.8, Japan's technology trade deficit with the United States has narrowed greatly in recent years. Globalization, coupled with the rise of alternative relationships with Europe, Korea, and to some degree China, is gradually giving both Tokyo and Washington more options with respect to one another, slowly weakening the originally exclusivist economic basis of the Pacific alliance. In 2005, the volume of bilateral U.S.–Japan technology trade was $8.5 billion, a declining share of Japan's total transactions, as Japan itself grows increasingly self-sufficient with respect to technology.[67]

BACK TO THE "BROKEN DIALOGUE"?

I have outlined five major dimensions of the U.S.–Japan economic relationship—natural resource endowments, trade patterns, capital flows, direct investment flows, and technology—that significantly impact the national security of the two nations and hence the health of their bilateral alliance itself. These are areas where alliance equities in the economic realm are generated. The broad publics of both countries are conscious of them all to a significant degree, although with differing intensity on the two shores of the Pacific.

Many of the economic foundations of the U.S.–Japan alliance, such as foreign investment, were precarious to begin with, when seen in comparative perspective. And the emergence of a nondiscriminatory global economy, while economically felicitous from a macroperspective, has badly compromised the more exclusivist traditional cornerstones of the alliance, which benefited from the benignly discriminatory world that Dulles built. However florid the diplomatic rhetoric about "the most important relationship in the world, bar none," the economic pillars of the Pacific alliance are quietly, yet steadily and surely, eroding. Vitally important alliance equities are steadily disappearing in this process, with subtle, yet potentially disastrous long-term implications for the national security of both nations.

This structural erosion matters because, as we shall see, it affects the mutual political-economic deference that both the United States and Japan accord to one another within the context of their broader alliance. When economic relations are vigorous and expanding, especially in their investment dimension, top-level attention is devoted to addressing the bilateral relationship, as is so clearly true with respect to Sino-American relations today. The elaborate Sino-American Structural Economic Dialogue of the later Bush years (2007–08) was no accident. When economic ties, however, are not growing, a bypass phenomenon begins to intensify, and the bypassed bilateral relationship tends to be consigned increasingly to the realm of rhetoric and benign neglect. This clearly happened during the latter stages of the Bush administration, its strong protestations and cosmetic steps, such as Koizumi's 2006 visit to Graceland, to the contrary. For the United States and Japan to spend two years (2004–06) with bovine spongiform encephalopathy (BSE), known as mad cow disease, and beef exports as the central items of their economic agenda, even as the United States and China attack much larger issues so dynamically, is testimony to the stagnation and marginalization of the Pacific alliance in its economic dimensions that have quietly set in.

There is a silver lining to this gloomy picture. The bypass phenomenon does not appear to have set in as strongly in American state and local dealings as in Washington, D.C. Vigorous Japanese investment in some sectors, such as autos, has slowed erosion in bilateral political-economic ties with Japan at the American grassroots, especially in the lower Midwest and Sunbelt states such as Mississippi and Texas. Yet the overall pattern, with a few exceptions, is bleak, especially with regard to American greenfield investment in Japan.

Sadly, remarkably little effort has recently been made to either understand or respond to these silent, yet strategically important developments in U.S.–Japan economic relations, from the perspective of the alliance as a whole. The focus since 9/11 has been almost exclusively on the alliance in its political-military dimensions. The economic agenda and its impact on alliance equities with

America's main strategic partner in the region have gotten remarkably little attention on the other side of the Pacific, despite its importance for the Pacific security structure in its broadest sense.

The depressing chronicle of erosion in U.S.–Japan bilateral economic dialogue, in the face of this quiet yet potentially dangerous deterioration of bilateral economic linkages, is a sobering one, ultimately subversive of the broader Pacific alliance itself. During the Reischauer years, the United States and Japan engaged in annual cabinet-level economic discussions in both Washington and Tokyo, analogous to the U.S.–China Strategic Economic Dialogue of the Bush–Paulson years. That experience, however, has never been repeated with Japan, a crucial ally, although it is being pursued zealously with Japan's neighbor China.

In the late 1970s, to be sure, President Jimmy Carter and Prime Minister Ōhira Masayoshi appointed the Wisemen's Group to inventory the economic relationship. During the late 1980s the United States and Japan engaged in the subcabinet MOSS talks, followed in the early 1990s, under the George H. W. Bush administration, by the so-called Structural Impediments Initiative (SII), and then the Framework Talks under the Clinton administration—all at the subcabinet level. These cross-sectoral talks were supplemented by a multitude of narrower sectorial discussions on topics ranging from textiles to steel to automobiles.

The George W. Bush administration also made some initial efforts. In June 2001, the first Bush–Koizumi summit at Camp David confirmed the U.S.–Japan Partnership for Further Growth, with six initial areas of emphasis: (1) subcabinet economic dialogue; (2) establishment of a private sector/government commission, to serve as a preparatory session for the subcabinet economic dialogue; (3) regulatory reform and competition policy initiative, focusing on communication, IT, energy, medical equipment, and medicine; (4) financial dialogue; (5) investment dialogue; and (6) establishment of a serious trade forum.[68] This was a most ambitious agenda. Yet remarkably little was achieved along any of these dimensions in the eight years to follow.

To be sure, 9/11 led to a dramatic and understandable short-term shift in national priorities. Yet the promising initial economic focus of the George W. Bush administration never returned. The U.S.–Japan alliance, however, can scarcely afford a continuing neglect of economic issues, given the rise of China and the quiet, yet fundamental and growing challenges of globalism to the broad coherence of transpacific political-economic ties.

Certainly the "trade wars" of the 1980s and early 1990s yielded remarkably little of concrete value to either American or Japanese firms, and their demise is hardly to be mourned. Yet the waning of bilateral trade conflict and the emergence of multilateral trade organizations such as the WTO do not obviate the need for a bilateral economic agenda, or the maintenance of bilateral economic policy dialogues. Whatever the utility in purely economic terms, there emphatically remains a powerful alliance rationale for bilateral economic dialogues and coordination between the United States and Japan, on a range of issues, including energy and environmental matters. New and vital alliance equities need to be forged in the Obama years. If the United States and China, potential adversaries, have reason for a Strategic Economic Dialogue—indeed, one that commands the total commitment of ten cabinet members for close to a week a year—it is far from clear why the United States and Japan, as major allies, with complementary economic strengths, cannot strengthen and broaden the much more meager bilateral economic-policy interaction in which they currently engage.

Since the coming of the WTO in 1995 these narrower bilateral sectoral discussions have virtually disappeared, leaving little more than beef, which hardly generates substantial alliance equities, as an atavistic residual. The broader analytical exercises, combining macroeconomic, microeconomic, and sectoral interchange, have also evaporated. U.S. and Japanese representatives, of course, interact frequently in a variety of multilateral settings, to be sure. But the bottom line, in the final analysis, must be the *Pacific alliance*. Whether it can survive in a vital form, with little attention to silent erosion of the alliance equities embedded in its economic realm, which have historically been so fundamental, is a question that both Washington and Tokyo need to debate more seriously in coming years.

Chapter 5 Networks: Sinews of the Future

We have seen, in the preceding pages, that transpacific relations have changed in fundamental ways, remarkably rapidly, since the dawn of this century. Indeed, the Washington–Tokyo alliance that we know today is remarkably different in military terms from what it was even a decade ago. By many technical standards, it may well be stronger. Thanks to the Internet and advanced telecommunications, the capacity for command and control in a purely technical sense is immeasurably strengthened. The alliance has also assumed important economic dimensions in an era of deepening global trade and financial and energy interdependence.

The key question for the U.S.–Japan partnership, however, amidst the euphoria on expanded cooperation, is, very simply: How enduring? The issues were dramatically posed in the anguished Diet debates of late 2007 over limiting Japan's Arabian Sea security role and in the confrontation during the spring of 2008 over host-nation support (HNS). At the everyday level, a steady procession of crimes, scandals, and nuisances is taking its silent toll.

Transpacific relations are beset today by a multitude of forces, social and economic as well as narrowly military. These introduce complex new un-certainties into what had been a comfortably predictable Cold War world. Many of these can have—as the acrimony of recent disputes has demon-strated—clear, hard-security consequences. To anticipate coming events, we must first understand the deeper forces, beyond guns, bombs, and even the economy, that determine future prospects. And we must perceive clearly the al-liance equities, calculated ultimately in human terms, that aid both resilience and cohesion in the face of storms impending.

Central among the vital social supports for the Pacific alliance are transna-tional, interpersonal networks. They enhance security both by improving com-munication—early warning, in particular—and by catalyzing action. Both functions are key in U.S.–Japan relations, given their distinctive, cross-cultural nature, which perpetuates a chronic information gap—and the unusual degree of institutional fragmentation that prevails in the relationship itself.

Alliances, as we saw in chapter 3, tend historically to be ephemeral. Before 1945 they were traditionally matters of convenience that came and went in what were, by modern standards, startlingly rapid periods of time. In August 1939, the Soviet Union and Nazi Germany were formally allied together for the in-vasion of Poland, only to be engaged in bitter, epic conflict with one another less than two years later. Across the eighteenth, nineteenth, and twentieth cen-turies, Britain allied at one time or another with virtually every power on the European continent, in an attempt to preserve the overall regional balance of power.

In recent years, however, the character of alliances has clearly changed, espe-cially in the advanced industrial nations. Since World War II, alliances have grown more enduring, around the world. They have assumed new functional roles in heightening economic prosperity and interdependence by reducing geopolitical risk, while also offering asymmetric trade and financial benefits to smaller allies. This stabilizing economic dimension has become an increasingly important aspect of alliance worldwide, contributing greatly to its durability, as we have seen, in cases ranging from East Asia to the "New Europe," just as it has for centuries between Britain and Portugal. Yet this new type of multifaceted political-economic alliance—like a fine race car—requires higher mainte-nance than its earlier, simpler, more pedestrian cousins.

A critical key to longevity for this New Alliance variant thus lies in human relations. The successful alliances of the postwar world—NATO not least among them—have had an interpersonal resilience and sophistication clearly enhancing their ability to overcome the varied challenges of a changing world.

At the heart of that resilience, so central to the meaning of alliance itself in a turbulent and unpredictable world, lie systematic social configurations that we will call "policy networks."[1] A policy network is a group of individuals engaged in ongoing, iterated transactions with one another, involving a substantial level of interpersonal trust, with the intention of shaping public policy.

Political-economic crisis has played an important but highly varied role, across sectors and nations, in defining both American policy networks and, through them, American relations with the broader world. These contrasting formative functions of policy networks have in turn helped fashion the contrasting profiles of various transnational relationships. The intermediate variable, in virtually all cases, has been human ties among key policy actors.

THE DEEPENING MALAISE OF U.S.–JAPAN
NETWORK RELATIONS

The genesis of American policy networks with Asia has profoundly influenced their long-term character and functioning. Broadly speaking, American policy networks with Europe and China emerged from an egalitarian process in which America had strong incentives of its own—initially strategic, but increasingly economic also—to conciliate these countries. First there was the desire for Cold War gains through NATO and through a "Golden Triangle" against the Soviet Union, followed by China's Four Modernizations and the steady emergence after 1979 of China as a major market and production base.[2] U.S.–Korea networks, like those linking the U.S. and Japan, arose from a contrasting history of occupation, sharply different from the evolution of postrevolutionary Sino–American ties. In the Korean case, however, as to some degree in Southeast Asia also, the hierarchical cast of the traditional bilateral relationship with the United States was mitigated by a mutual existential regard flowing from battle comradeship in both the Korean and the Vietnam wars.

U.S.–Japan networks confront arguably the most complex, historically rooted challenge to balanced network formation of any major American geopolitical relationship in the world. Despite close Bush–Koizumi ties at the top for several years, the network dimension of the U.S.–Japan alliance has fallen into a quiet crisis since around 2005, even as the need for intimate political-military coordination between Tokyo and Washington on a broad range of issues has deepened. This crisis exists on several levels: (1) declining Japanese-American political influence, as the Nikkei (Japanese-American) share of the Asian-American population falls; (2) declining mutual Japanese and American familiarity, due to limited travel and foreign study; (3) eroding elite cultural ties and institutions; and (4) the emergence for both nations of third-country alternatives, fueled by the rise of China. Encouraging trends in mass-cultural familiarity between the U.S. and Japan—new American fondness for sushi, anime, and Ichirō, for example[3]—cannot compensate for this quiet crisis in critical bilateral network relationships.

Quantitatively speaking, the shares of Japanese and Japanese Americans in the overall U.S. population are steadily falling, while those of Chinese and Koreans, Japan's prospective intra-Asian rivals for influence in Washington, are palpably rising, as noted in chapter 1. According to America's periodic tenth-year census, Japanese and Japanese Americans outnumbered their Chinese counterparts in the United States until 1980. In 1970 Japanese were nearly 50 percent more numerous, by nearly 3–2, while by 2000, following populous China's opening to the world, there were more than three times as many Chinese in the United States as Japanese.[4]

As shown in figure 5.1, the sizes of the Chinese and Korean communities in the United States in 2005—2.8 million and 1.2 million, respectively—were much larger than the Japanese figure of 800,000. By way of comparison, the populations of Americans of British and German ancestry were much larger still than those of Asians, totaling 29 million and 49 million people, respectively, in the same year, so the Japanese ethnic community looks quite small in comparative perspective. Conversely, in Japan, the share of Americans in the overall foreign population of Japan is steadily declining, albeit slowly, from 3 percent of total foreigners in Japan during 1997 to only 2.5 percent in 2006.[5]

Americans are also becoming a smaller and smaller share of total visitors to Japan. As indicated in figure 5.2, the share of Americans among total visitors to Japan fell sharply, from 14 to only 10 percent of the total, during just the 2002–06 period. Conversely, the share of Chinese and Koreans among total visitors was steadily rising during the same years.

Japanese students have traditionally studied in American universities in relatively large numbers. Indeed, in 1980 there were substantially more Japanese than Korean students in the United States. Since the mid-1990s, however, as figure 5.3 suggests, the number of Japanese enrolling in American universities has been stable or declining, with the total in 2007 nearly 10 percent lower than in 2001. Since 2000 it has been sharply exceeded by the number of Korean students, despite Korea's much smaller population.

Reflecting one relative bright spot in U.S.–Japan cultural relations, the number of American students studying at Japanese universities increased somewhat

Figure 5.1. Japanese-American Population Surpassed by Chinese and
Korean Counterparts   (unit = people)

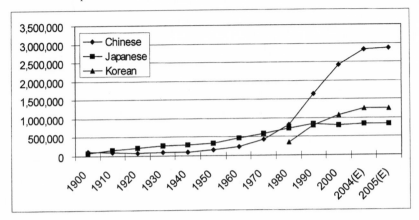

Source: U.S. Census Bureau, *American Community Survey* (2005 edition); U.S. Census
Bureau, *Census of Population* (1990, 1980, and 1970 editions).
Note: Figures are for Asian-American populations alone, not including more than one
ethnic group after 1990. The category "Chinese" includes Taiwanese.

Figure 5.2. America's Declining Share among Visitors to Japan   (unit = percent)

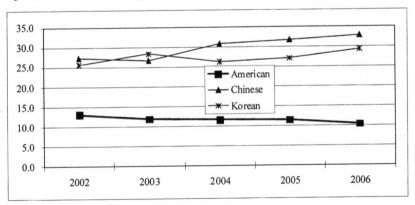

Source: Ministry of Justice Immigration Bureau website: http://www.immi-moj.go.jp/
index.html

Figure 5.3. The Crisis of U.S.–Japan Transpacific Study in
Comparative Context   (unit = people)

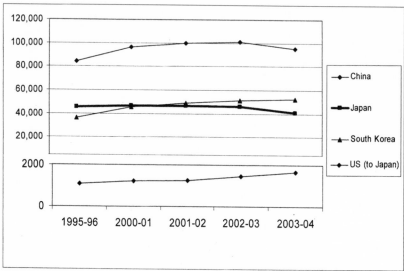

Source: U.S. Department of Education Institute of Education Sciences, *Digest of Education Statistics* (2007 edition); Ministry of Justice Immigration Bureau, *Zairyū Gaikokujin Tōkei* [Statistics of Foreigners in Japan] (various editions).

at the beginning of the twenty-first century, rising from around one thousand in 1999 to nearly eighteen hundred in 2005, as figure 5.3 also indicates. Much of this increase, however, was in short-term study programs conducted in the English language that did not provide in-depth exposure to Japanese culture itself. And the number of American students in Japan remains less than one-twentieth the number of Japanese students in the United States, as figure 5.3 also shows.

Although there are a modest number of students within Japan with interests in the American academic pipeline, the longer-term prospects are already disturbing. The number of U.S. college students taking Japanese increased slightly during 2003–06, according to a recent Japan Foundation study, but the number of primary and secondary school students studying the language fell by nearly 34 percent.[6] The number of teachers also fell by over 31 percent, to only 807 across the entire United States.[7]

Within American academia, there is little question that universities are producing significantly fewer Japan specialists—key to the U.S.–Japan policy networks of the future—than a decade or two ago. And there are, conversely, a rising number of Korean specialists being trained, with strong financial support for new academic positions from the Korea Foundation. This shift is especially pronounced in Washington, D.C. At the School of Advanced International Studies/Johns Hopkins University, for example, there are only half as many students in Japan studies courses, and one-third fewer courses, as there were in 1997, while a vigorous new Korea program has emerged. A similar pattern seems to prevail at other major schools in the area, including George Washington, Georgetown, and American universities. Conversely, far fewer Japanese than Koreans, relative to overall leadership population, have studied in the United States. And all too few Americans have studied in or traveled to Japan, as statistics in figures 5.2 and 5.3 clearly suggest.

Like the framework for educational exchange, the NGO network infrastructure of the U.S.–Japan relationship is also under siege. As indicated in chapter 1, the two countries can boast, to be sure, of well-established sister-city relationships. Japan had 437 sets of such sister-city ties with American counterparts, compared to 325 for China and 120 for Korea.[8] Meanwhile, American cities had 128 sets of ties with China, 44 with Korea, 78 with the United Kingdom, and 126 with Germany.[9]

For the past decade and more, however, membership in the nation's Japan-America Societies appears to have been going down. The corporate membership of the Japan-America Society of Washington, D.C., for example, declined from more than 100 in 1998 to only 70 over the past decade. This trend toward declining membership in American Japan-related NGOs has been especially pronounced among young people.

A disturbingly parallel trend on the other side of the Pacific is also apparent. Developments at the International House of Japan, a major focal point of U.S.–Japan cultural exchange in Tokyo, are a case in point. I-House membership dropped from 5,512 in 1992[10] to 3,955 in 2007,[11] with an inadequate inflow of young members replacing elderly counterparts accounting for much of the decline.

CONTRASTS TO THE "GOLDEN AGE"

Just as worrying as the quantitative trends, and their demographic expression, has been the erosion on the qualitative side of the U.S.–Japan network relationship and the disruption of important synergistic ties among its major support institutions. Neither institutions nor individuals working outside their respective governments are doing nearly as good a job of mediating tensions in transpacific relations as they used to do. This troubling erosion is most clearly seen by contrasting patterns of the 1950s and the 1970s with those of recent days. Ironically, those critical early years, when networks appear to have been strongest, were periods of transcendent perceived crisis—the typical catalyst worldwide for effective policy network creation and renewal, as we have so often seen.

Nineteen fifty-one, of course, was the year of the San Francisco Peace Treaty and also of the Mutual Security Treaty between the United States and Japan—both concluded in the throes of the Korean War and amidst domestic political turbulence in Japan as well.[12] Nineteen fifty-two was a landmark year for network formation and for institutional innovation in U.S.–Japan nongovernmental ties. Most important, as noted in chapter 2, John D. Rockefeller III was elected in that year as president of the Japan Society, with John Foster Dulles, the architect only months before of the historic peace treaty, as chairman.[13] The new board members also included such distinguished figures as Joseph Grew, U.S. ambassador to Japan at the time of Pearl Harbor; Yukawa Hideki, a Nobel Prize winner-to-be from Kyoto University; Winthrop Aldrich, Arthur Dean, Sir George Sansom, and Edwin O. Reischauer.[14] Amplifying the positive effects of the Japan Society's revival, Grew also established, in the same year, a namesake Joseph C. Grew Foundation to promote U.S.–Japan student exchange.[15]

Rockefeller, the new Japan Society president, was a long-standing friend of Matsumoto Shigeharu, formerly the Dōmei correspondent in Shanghai. Matsumoto had, in turn, become a confidant in wartime China of the Japanese diplomat Yoshida Shigeru, later to become a five-term prime minister and stalwart supporter of transpacific cultural exchange.[16] Together, Rockefeller and Matsumoto forged an important new transpacific network, linking the business, government, and cultural establishments of the two countries, with the Japan Society and the International House as institutional expressions. This combination had tremendous dynamism and influence, especially in its early days.

Typical of the new activities of the Japan Society–International House network alliance was the Intellectual Interchange Program, inaugurated in 1953.[17] Under its auspices, Japanese and American leaders from the worlds of art, literature, law, and political science visited each other's countries, met with their counterparts, and gave public lectures. Between 1953 and the late 1990s, when the program was discontinued, Intellectual Exchange Fellows included the former first lady Eleanor Roosevelt, who visited Japan in 1953; the theologian Paul Tillich; Robert Oppenheimer, president of the Institute for Advanced Study; and the distinguished diplomat George Kennan. Ichikawa Fusae, the moving spirit of the women's suffrage movement in Japan; Norman Cousins, editor of *Saturday Review;* former Japanese minister of education Nagai Michio; former U.S. Health and Human Services secretary Donna Shalala; novelists Saul Bellow and Endō Shūsaku; political commentator Garry Wills; and journalist Robert MacNeil also participated at one point or another.[18] The great majority of these prominent people, who gained an intimate personal sense of transpacific relations through their extended stays in the partner country, participated in the exchange program during the 1950s and early 1960s, with the general level of participation falling substantially in the program's later years.

Apart from its Intellectual Interchange Program, the International House pursued a vigorous research program on U.S.–Japan relations throughout the 1958–70 period. It was also involved in the Dartmouth Japanese-American Conferences of 1962–67, involving such prominent figures as Rōyama Masamichi of International Christian University, Tōhata Seiichi of JETRO's Institute of Developing Economies, and Walt Rostow, national security advisor to President Lyndon B. Johnson.[19]

Rockefeller served in all for twenty-six years at the head of the Japan Society—seventeen as president (1952–69) and nine more as chairman (1969–78). Only his tragic death in an automobile accident on July 10, 1978, ended his active involvement with the society and with U.S.–Japan intellectual exchange. Between 1945 and his untimely death, Rockefeller and his own charitable foundations contributed around $7 million to Japan-related projects.[20] Rockefeller's enormous wealth, extraordinary range of contacts, and deep personal interest in Japan allowed him to serve as a powerful catalyst for deepening the nongovernmental side of the U.S.–Japan relationship.

Among the major innovations at the Japan Society during Rockefeller's years at the helm, apart from the Intellectual Interchange Program, were an emergency fund and a scholarship fund for Japanese students (1953); a major film on the Japanese economy (1955), which was a hit in American schools and sold over 250 copies a year into the 1960s; support for Japan Societies across the United States, in such cities as Washington, Boston, Chicago, Los Angeles, Portland, Seattle, and San Francisco; student charter flights to Japan (1964); Japan Society Fellowships for artists and intellectuals (1965); the opening of Japan House, a new headquarters for the Japan Society on East 47th Street in New York City (1971); and the Parliamentary Exchange Program (1978). In addition, Rockefeller's involvement drew a succession of top-level speakers to the Japan Society annual dinners, including Secretary of State Dulles, previously president of the society, and a succession of Japanese prime ministers. The membership of the society grew from seventy-nine members in 1951, before Rockefeller became active, to over one thousand members in 1957, only six years later.[21] It has subsequently grown steadily to around three thousand, greatly outstripping Japan–America Societies elsewhere in the United States.[22]

Rockefeller's activities at the Japan Society in New York were complemented admirably by those of Matsumoto Shigeharu at the International House in Tokyo and by such academics as Edwin O. Reischauer and Marius Jansen at Ivy League educational institutions. Matsumoto served continuously as director of the International House until his death in 1989, providing a counterpart in Tokyo for a broad range of transpacific intellectual and cultural activities. Yamamoto Tadashi, director of the Japan Center for International Exchange (JCIE), founded in 1970, also played a long and significant second-generation role, becoming the Pacific Asia Director of the Trilateral Commission, another important international network involving both Japan and the United States, when it was founded—at Rockefeller's initiative—in 1973.

The rich U.S.–Japan cultural and policy networks of the 1950s and 1960s were thus centered on Rockefeller and the Ivy League, leveraged by the influential role that Ivy League universities played in American policy making during this period. Edwin O. Reischauer, Harvard's premier Japan specialist, was appointed by President John F. Kennedy as U.S. ambassador to Japan in 1961, the year that Marius Jansen, Reischauer's former student at Harvard and a professor at Princeton University, was appointed associate director of International House. Jansen, in his new capacity, inspired and helped organize the Hakone Conferences on Japanese Modernization—an attempt to arrive at a settled explanation for Japan's extraordinary socioeconomic transformation of the late nineteenth century and also to stimulate deeper dialogue between American and Japanese intellectuals, strongly supported from the embassy by Reischauer. In 1967, shortly after Reischauer had returned to Cambridge, Yamamoto inaugurated the Shimoda Conferences, a series of gatherings that networked Japanese and American political leaders as well as scholars and businesspeople. This important series continued until 1987. A frequent participant was House of Representatives majority leader and later Speaker Thomas Foley; Japanese and American specialists of a younger generation, such as Gerald Curtis and Nagai Yōnosuke, were also incubated.

Even after Rockefeller's untimely death in 1978, momentum continued for some years in the U.S.–Japan policy network relationship, with the major preestablished institutions continuing in place. The Japan Society Parliamentary Exchange Program, inaugurated just before Rockefeller's fatal accident, continued to be vigorous into the 1990s, with its 1988 session involving both House of Representatives majority leader Foley and minority leader Robert Michel. The appointment of three consecutive American political leaders as ambassadors to Japan—former vice president Walter Mondale, former House Speaker Foley, and former Senate majority leader Howard Baker—during the 1993–2005 period helped to maintain high-level network relationships, while also encouraging other prominent American political figures, including congressmen, to visit Tokyo. Under the JCIE's program to invite congressional members to Japan, in 1969 fourteen members visited Japan.[23] By 2006, only nine congressional members were visiting Japan, while twenty-two went to China.[24] In 2007 only a single member of Congress visited Japan under JCIE auspices—the lowest in many years, continuing a steady downward trend.[25]

EMERGENCE OF THE NETWORK GAP

Beneath the surface, however, the dynamic of U.S.–Japan network relations was changing, giving rise slowly to the insidious network gap and the quiet crisis that plague the bilateral relationship today, gravely threatening its future. With generational change, the architects of the dynamic bilateral alliance relationship of the early postwar years, who so brilliantly handled the delicate transition from war to peace over the first post–World War II decade, were slowly passing from the scene, on both sides of the Pacific. Yet the curious passions and myopia of the 1990s and beyond were inhibiting the recruitment of new, perceptive leaders to take their place.

Innovation and farsighted management in U.S.–Japan relations, as we have noted so often, have traditionally been stimulated by apprehensions of crisis. It was no doubt the fear of making Japan another Weimar Germany—victimized, isolated, and beleaguered—that drove Dulles and Rockefeller to devote so much creative and comprehensive attention to bilateral relations during the early 1950s. Similarly, it was the specter of Japan as a "fragile blossom"—vulnerable economically, however dynamic it seemed, and clearly misunderstood by the world—that drove the Rockefellers, in league with Zbigniew Brzezinski, Edwin O. Reischauer, and others, to found the Trilateral Commission and build new bridges to Japan following the Nixon Shocks of the early 1970s.[26]

From the Japanese side the same traumas led to the birth of the Japan Foundation in 1972, and $10 million in ensuing block grants to major American universities (the so-called Tanaka Ten) during 1973.[27] Parallel crisis sentiment also induced President Jimmy Carter, in cooperation with Prime Minister Ōhira Masayoshi, to create the U.S.–Japan Wisemen's Group in the late 1970s. Supported by a substantial research staff, it began searching systematically for ways to stabilize the bilateral relationship, as trade frictions were beginning to escalate.

By the mid-1980s, however, America's sense of crisis about Japan was being transformed. With Japanese growth continuing and Tokyo's global trade surpluses steadily rising, the challenge for policy in the United States was no longer perceived to be strengthening a weak and fragile Japan. Instead, Japan was increasingly seen as too strong and too unwilling to use its growing strength to stabilize the circumstances of those allies that had aided its rise across the years. America and Japan were, Clyde Prestowitz argued, "trading places," and many Americans perceived the mode of this transition to be unfair.[28] For their part, the Japanese, too, who had contributed so generously to the mutual relationship in the 1970s, were also developing siege consciousness and growing more skeptical of philanthropy.

Amidst this sea change in transpacific perceptions, the instinct of Dulles and Rockefeller to build and foster cooperative human networks with Japan began to look more and more antiquated. The changed sentiment was reflected in American behavior. The Rockefeller and Ford Foundations, which had been among the pillars of U.S.–Japan philanthropy during the 1950s and 1960s, phased down and ultimately terminated their grant programs.[29] Even groups like the U.S.–Japan Friendship Commission, charged with building bridges in the traditional style, began to pursue a more hardheaded, less fraternal approach.

As the 1990s progressed, there was less and less funding for collegial conferences and networking sessions, while basic area studies research grew scarcer. Conversely, there was more money for "hardheaded" trade studies. This transition complicated the traditional friendship networks and made it more difficult to recruit successors to a Rockefeller–Reischauer generation fundamentally sympathetic to Japan, and focused on its concerns, as the transition from Reischauer to Ezra Vogel at Harvard University, for example, made clear.[30]

Globalization, especially institutional manifestations like the World Trade Organization (WTO), also extracted its toll on U.S.–Japan network ties. Ever since the 1950s, bilateral trade relations between Washington and Tokyo had been an incongruous patchwork of free trade, nontariff barriers and "orderly

marketing agreements" that restrained Japanese exports without resort to unilateral restrictions contrary to the GATT. This informal regulatory structure,
which fielded numerous disputes over the years in such sectors as textiles, electronics, and automobiles, provoked continuing political friction. Yet it simultaneously fostered mutual consciousness of bilateral trade developments and
well-developed negotiating networks as well.

The establishment of the WTO in 1995 changed all this.[31] Its new, legalistic
procedures outlawed the old practice of bilateral orderly marketing agreements
and transferred resolution of trade disputes from government ministries to
multilateral dispute-resolution panels. This transition reduced the incentive of
ministries such as Japan's Ministry of Economics, Trade, and Industry (METI),
the traditional arbiter of most international trading arrangements, to closely
monitor trade patterns. Such lapses led to sudden trade surges and to political
backlash like the 1999 and 2002 steel trade sanctions against Japan. After the
coming of the WTO, no effective administrative procedures or negotiation
networks existed, especially on the Japanese side, to warn of, control, or nego-
tiate a national response to such unexpected and highly disruptive trade surges.

A final corrosive solvent for the constructive U.S.–Japan bilateral networks
previously built up under the San Francisco peace treaty system was simply benign neglect. Following the U.S.–Japan auto agreement of 1995, the last of the
great bilateral trade disputes before the coming of the WTO, an unprecedented
decade and more of near-total peace on the bilateral trade front transpired. Several traditionally contentious bilateral issues like the Eastman Kodak case that
had generated major bilateral trade frictions in the early 1990s virtually disappeared from the Washington and Tokyo agendas, consigned to the arcane
netherworld of Geneva dispute-resolution councils.

U.S.–Japan trade did not figure prominently in the U.S. presidential elections of 1996, 2000, 2004, or 2008, in contrast to several of the previous political cycles. To the extent that trade issues came to the fore in American politics,
the issues were largely with China, which by 2007 had a trade surplus with the
United States three times the size of that with Japan. A protracted U.S.–Japan
dispute over procedures for assuring BSE-free beef imports into Japan was the
glaring exception that illustrated the more general pattern of declining U.S.–
Japan trade conflict.

As the salience of trade issues on the U.S.–Japan policy agenda continued to
decline after 1995, however, the long-standing trade policy networks in the
United States and Japanese governments, in the Congress and the Diet, and in
the private sector all began to erode. These had provided much-needed positive

early-warning systems for the U.S. and Japanese bureaucracies, and their demise removed important shock absorbers. The decline of broader economic policy consultation networks compounded the emerging dangers.

The Reagan administration, for example, had pursued Market-Oriented Sector Selective talks (MOSS) with Japan. The George H. W. Bush administration had had the Structural Impediments Initiative (SII), a hybrid complex of sectoral, microeconomic, and macroeconomic negotiations, with associated policy networks. The Clinton administration had its Framework Talks, also a hybrid combination of micro and sectoral dialogues. Yet with the coming of the George W. Bush administration, this tradition of broad-based, multifaceted bilateral economic discussions between the United States and Japan, with their important role in reducing the network gap, was at an end, particularly after 9/11.

The United States and China have various vehicles for ongoing policy communication. One of the most prominent, under the George W. Bush administration, was a bilateral Strategic Economic Dialogue that typically occupied up to ten U.S. cabinet-level officials for two full days, and sent high-powered delegations to Beijing in 2006, 2007, and 2008.[32] The two countries also held a Global Issues Forum in 2005 to discuss sustainable development and energy policy, humanitarian assistance and development, and cooperation in law enforcement and public health;[33] and have periodically held a bilateral senior dialogue at the deputy secretary/vice foreign minister level since 2005.[34] Yet there was no remotely analogous set of bilateral discussions occurring between the United States and Japan, even at the subcabinet level, as had been common a decade earlier. How this atrophied structure of consultation could coordinate American and Japanese views in an increasingly volatile global political economy remained unclear.

On the security side, the United States and Japan have developed a Security Consultative Committee, also known as the 2+2. This body, established in 1960, originally included the Japanese foreign minister, the director of the Japan Defense Agency, the U.S. ambassador to Japan, and the commander in chief of the Pacific Command (PACOM).[35] It was upgraded to the current membership structure, consisting of foreign minister, defense minister, secretary of state, and secretary of defense, in 1990. The 2+2 is supported by the Security Subcommittee (SSC) at the working level (vice minister/assistant secretary level, in this case); the Subcommittee for Defense Cooperation (SDC) at the director-general/assistant secretary level; and the Japan–U.S. Joint Committee, which focuses on implementation of the SOFA, at the director-general/minister and counselor of U.S. embassy level.[36]

This security dialogue structure was further strengthened by President Clinton and Prime Minister Hashimoto Ryūtarō under their U.S.–Japan Declaration on Security (1996). Their efforts were followed by a review of the Guidelines for U.S.–Japan Defense Cooperation in 1997. Under the new guidelines, a comprehensive mechanism mainly for planning and a coordination mechanism that focuses on coordinating contingency responses to attacks against Japan or surrounding areas were created to facilitate security cooperation.[37] This relatively elaborate coordination structure is confined, however, to the operational military phase of prospective joint operations and does not concern itself with longer-term issues of strategic coordination or, of course, with economic matters.

ENHANCING ALLIANCE EQUITIES THROUGH POLICY NETWORKS

In the days when alliances were simply fleeting marriages of convenience, they had minimal need for structure, let alone supportive policy networks. Such configurations were little more than the product of a given moment in the ongoing international balance of power struggle. Their fate lay in the hands primarily of top-level strategists making case-by-case, top-down decisions.

As alliances have come to endure for longer periods, however, and to fill a broader range of specialized technical, political, and economic functions in an ever more volatile and uncertain world, they have grown to need infrastructure: secretariats, planning groups, and so on. All are increasingly crucial alliance equities. NATO, for example, has firmly institutionalized itself as an international organization, developing an extensive headquarters staff, Executive Management, a Division of Political Affairs and Security Policy, a Joint Forces Command, and other subdivisions for logistics, standardization, communication, and information systems.[38] Similarly, the United States and Korea have established, under the pressures of war and potentially imminent conflict, elaborate coordination structures like the Combined Forces Command (CFC).

In addition to their rising institutional sophistication, durable alliances have come, over time, to need supportive networks: ongoing relationships of human trust that allow the allies in question to communicate sensitively about delicate, often confidential matters. Where these shared equities and vehicles for communication exist, alliances prosper; where they are lacking, alliances erode. The roles of John D. Rockefeller III, Matsumoto Shigeharu, Edwin O. Reischauer, Ushiba Nobuhiko, Mike Mansfield, Nakasone Yasuhiro, and Miyazawa Kiichi, to name a few, in strengthening the cultural and political bases of the Pacific alliance, as well as Richard Armitage and Katō Ryōzō in the narrower security realm, show this pattern clearly.

Nowhere are transpacific networks more important than in dealing with crisis situations. Decisive action in fluid, delicate, high-stakes situations is much easier when taken in partnership with associates one knows and can trust than when carried out with unknown participants. Nowhere are crises in turn more important in fostering human networks, precisely owing to their necessity in that cross-cultural environment, than across the Pacific. Given the profound cultural divide that the Pacific Ocean represents, trusting interpersonal ties do not easily transcend its broad expanse, as the more than two centuries of remarkably intensive, if often misunderstood, interaction across that vast body of water since the days of the China Clipper ships clearly show.[39] It is only when events requiring immediate resolution unavoidably compel efforts in a common endeavor—cultural and racial differences notwithstanding—that enduring networks capable of bridging the East–West cultural gap begin seriously to form.

The salience of crisis in transpacific relations—the continuing importance of the struggles that have divided the nations of the region—has thus ironically become a major catalyst for those nations' reconciliation. To heighten the paradox, it has been the bitter struggles and the estrangement—war and culture conflict—that have in the end forged the sinews of cooperation. In the absence of bitter confrontation—or the prospect thereof—in the background, statesmen have only rarely been able to develop the relationships of trust—the true alliance equities—necessary to manage complex political-economic interdependence.[40]

Crises can also be useful in creating policy networks. When political actors are drawn existentially together and forced by crisis to cooperate, they tend to be bonded to one another and to associate in more routine contexts once the formative crisis that originally catalyzed their relationships has waned. World War II, for example, profoundly affected transpacific relations for nearly two generations after Pearl Harbor, through the living memory and associations of participants, while the impact of the Korean War remains with us today. Sino-American relations are likewise greatly affected by the residue of the 1972

Shanghai Communiqué, while U.S.–Japan relations continue to bear both MacArthur's and Reischauer's imprint a generation and more after they have gone.

Taken collectively, policy networks profoundly shape decision-making outcomes, facilitating transnational coordination. They do so in two major ways: by shaping information flows and by mediating resource transfers. Where networks are well developed and smoothly functioning, information flows freely and accurately, while misperception is minimized. Resources, such as government budget allocations, are also available to meet priority goals, like HNS in the national security realm. Where these conditions do not prevail, and the partners do not contribute to the common cause in a mutually acceptable way, relationships—including alliance ties—become much more dysfunctional.

Policy networks can be functionally differentiated into four basic types: (a) crisis networks; (b) agenda-setting networks; (c) implementation networks; and (d) sociopolitical networks. The first three have distinctive, self-evident roles directly related to policy making, while the last variety provides the general social infrastructure of a transnational relationship, within which policy issues are considered in a more general sense.

Crisis networks, the first and arguably most important type of network from a policy standpoint, are ongoing social relationships configured to monitor and manage discontinuous, high-impact developments invested with major political, economic, and security consequences. Such configurations can exist either at policy or technical levels, in either public or private sectors. The commonality, as noted above, is a focus on dealing collectively and cooperatively with unusual events.

Examples of crisis networks are not hard to find. The classic cases of the Cold War years were no doubt the NATO nuclear-planning groups. Since the 1970s the groups of Treasury officials and central bankers assembled to cope with sudden global financial developments should also qualify. So might, in the political arena, transition teams assembled to cope with the policy impact of assassination or sudden leadership incapacity. The functional commonality, in all cases, is the need to deal rapidly, on an efficient, confidential basis, with sudden, unanticipated developments.

Agenda-setting networks, or ongoing, patterned social relationships that generate issues for serious policy consideration, have a different functional role than crisis networks, although there is occasional empirical overlap.[41] Agenda-setting networks tend to be less secretive and often include a substantial concentration of academics and journalists, with a value bias toward openness. Examples include such groups as the Trilateral Commission, the antinuclear Committee of 1000, and, in U.S.–Japan relations, the Wisemen's Group appointed by Carter and Ōhira to develop policy suggestions for stabilizing the bilateral relationship.

Implementation networks are patterned social relations that transform policy ideas into policies themselves. Because of the character of such networks, most relevant members are government officials, although interest group representatives can also be involved. American and Japanese officials tasked to assure that the transformation agreement of 2006 for moving eight thousand Marines from Okinawa to Guam, together with members of the SSC, the SDC, and the Japan–U.S. Joint Committee are cases in point.

Sociopolitical networks, finally, are broad, multifunctional groups that operate for a variety of purposes. In transpacific relations, they are groups of people who have a general, nonspecific interest in deeper U.S.–Japan, U.S.–Korean, and Sino-American political and economic ties, for example. Institutional expressions include the Japan Society, Korea Society, and National Council on U.S.–China Relations.

Crisis networks such as the NATO nuclear-planning group and the International Monetary Fund financial contingency team need to deal rapidly with sudden, often momentous change. Yet such networks cannot readily be configured on the spot. Because trust, confidentiality, and mutual understanding are required, effective crisis networks, like other variants, need an existential history—particularly one of powerful, shared formative experience and common values. All three variants also need periodic nurturing and reinforcement. This is clearly true in current U.S.–Japan relations, where network maintenance and the related nurturing of alliance equities do not seem to be getting the attention they deserve.

Modern alliance relationships, as we have seen, are inevitably embedded in broader socioeconomic contexts that profoundly influence both their everyday functioning and their long-term viability. Rising global interdependence since the 1950s—accelerating over the past two decades—has embedded hard security in a much broader economic and social context than ever before. These changes have endowed the notion of alliance with a double-edged durability and vulnerability that policymakers around the world ignore at their peril.

Among the most important social influences on the operation of alliances, both in crises and in everyday situations, are interpersonal policy networks.

These can be distinguished, as we have seen, in terms of their functions. Crisis networks, agenda-setting networks, implementation networks, and general sociopolitical networks all play important and differentiated roles.

Nations vary substantially in the character and quality of their policy networks, with history profoundly shaping the institutional expression. Germany and Belgium, in particular, appear to maintain vigorously functioning interpersonal networks and network-support nongovernmental institutions that strongly support their transatlantic diplomacy within the NATO alliance, as Britain obviously also does. China has important nonalliance network ties across the Pacific that limit conflict within what otherwise could easily be a tense and highly conflictual relationship with the United States. Policy networks are also manifestly important for Seoul in its broad-based dealings with Washington.

U.S.–Japan policy networks continue to face unique, structurally embedded challenges that descend from a complex history of war and military occupation, amidst enduring cultural contrast. For many years, however, those networks effectively—indeed, remarkably—managed the U.S.–Japan economic and security relationships, periodic explosions like the Security Treaty crisis of 1960 notwithstanding. Among these many quiet achievements were the prevention of a second Security Treaty crisis in 1970, amidst the Vietnam War, and the smooth, peaceful reversion of Okinawa to Japan in 1972.[42] These discreet successes were in no small part due to the sophistication and credibility of the networks themselves, which included for many years such major figures as John D. Rockefeller III and Edwin O. Reischauer, longtime ambassador to Japan, in major roles within their membership, as we have seen.

Since the mid-1970s, however, a dangerously widening network gap has emerged between Washington and Tokyo, bringing with it declining interpersonal alliance equities as well. Several factors have been at fault: bilateral trade frictions, economic globalization, the coming of the WTO, and generational change, among others. Despite the expanding network gap, the demands on the Pacific alliance of technical coordination have been growing, in sectors ranging from missile defense to antiterrorism, as we shall see.

The network gap plays a key role in the quiet crisis of the alliance discussed in chapter 1. It urgently demands attention, especially given the new, twenty-first-century challenges now emerging. It is to those challenges, and to how the new Pacific alliance has so far addressed them, that we now turn.

Chapter 6 An Alliance Transformed: U.S.–Japan Relations since 2001

In 1970, when U.S. Secretary of Defense Melvin Laird suggested elliptically in an interview with the Japanese press that someday the Japanese Self-Defense Forces (SDF) might defend sea-lanes to the Strait of Malacca, there was a firestorm of protest and incredulity in Tokyo. In 1981, when Japanese Foreign Minister Itō Masayoshi suggested that Japan had a sea-lane defense responsibility only one thousand nautical miles from Japanese shores, he was fiercely criticized for what was then considered an overly ambitious commitment. Yet when, in the fall of 2001, the Maritime Self-Defense Forces (MSDF) were actually dispatched not just to Malacca, but also to the Arabian Sea three thousand kilometers beyond, there was hardly a word of protest.

Following the overwhelming opposition victory in the Upper House elections of July 2007, a different tide, to be sure, set in. By early November 2007, with the expiration of the Anti-Terrorism Special Measures Law authorizing their deployment, the MSDF warships deployed off Pakistan had been forced to return to their Japanese bases. Under separate legislation valid until December 2008, however, Japanese Air Self-Defense Forces (ASDF) remained in Kuwait, and public support for renewed global deployment of Japanese forces remained strong.[1] Indeed, by January 2008 the MSDF warships were back on station, although the ASDF aircraft were withdrawn from Kuwait at the end of 2008, and the MSDF offshore presence remained highly controversial.

Japanese security policies have thus sharply shifted over the past decade, and the working profile of the Pacific alliance along with them. The politics of the alliance have shifted as well, as the anguished profile of the Diet debate in the fall of 2007 over the Antiterrorism Law's renewal made clear, and the debate the following spring over HNS made clearer still. This chapter considers the profound military transformations that the U.S.–Japan alliance has undergone, the strategic challenges that it continues to confront, and the imposing sociopolitical foundations that the ambitious New Alliance flowing from the Bush–Koizumi years, with its intensified and globalized cooperation dimensions, will require. The implications of all these changes are substantial, for the peoples of both nations and for their future also, as we shall see.

THE SHADOW OF 9/11

On September 11, 2001, nearly three thousand Americans perished in terrorist attacks either in the World Trade Center, at the Pentagon, or fighting for their lives high above the fields of Pennsylvania. Yet there were victims of eleven other nations as well, including prominently Japan.[2] Indeed, some twenty Japanese firms, including Fuji Bank & Trust, Daiichi Kangyō Bank, and the Asahi Bank, had offices in the ill-fated World Trade Center.[3] And apart from the bloody World Trade Center attacks, which reportedly killed two dozen Japanese, another two Japanese citizens were passengers on the doomed planes, hijacked and used cynically as terrorist weapons.

Across Japan, as in much of the world, the impact of these dramatic and savage events was traumatic. Media coverage was intense. People donated for relief and recovery, and hundreds waited in an interminable yet empathetic line before the embassy in Moto-Akasaka, Tokyo, to sign the condolence book, to bring flowers, to donate thousands of paper cranes, a symbol of hope for recovery, and simply to express their sympathy. At a tasteful interval, the government of Japan donated $10 million to the relief effort as well. On September 23, an emotional ceremony in memory of the fallen was held in Tokyo, organized by the Japanese government and the Japan-America Society, with approximately two thousand Japanese people participating.[4]

A military response from the United States and its allies was expected and was soon forthcoming. Within a month, American Special Forces had established themselves at Kandahar, en route to fully vanquishing the Taliban. European NATO forces were present, in solidarity, at Kyrgyzstani bases, as they had been at Saudi bases after Saddam's tanks rolled into Kuwait on August 1, 1990. But what was different—and unprecedented—was Japan's participation.

During the Persian Gulf crisis of 1990–91, as noted, no Japanese forces set foot near the combat theater until the guns were still. Even noncombatant medical units went no closer to the fighting than Jordan. And the minesweepers explicitly authorized by PKO legislation never arrived until the conflict was long over.

In the shadow of 9/11, however, Japan's response was immeasurably faster, more sweeping, and more sustained. Only forty-five minutes after hearing of the attacks, Prime Minister Koizumi Junichirō established his own personal liaison facility at the government's Office of Crisis Management. He was among the first leaders to call George W. Bush personally and extend an offer of aid. By September 19, barely a week after the attacks, Japan had unveiled a coherent response to 9/11, including a historic proposal to dispatch the SDF overseas in support of American and other forces battling terrorism. On October 5 the government submitted the precedent-setting Anti-Terrorism Special Measures Law (ATSML) to the Diet. And by October 29, less than four weeks later, the normally languid Japanese Diet had passed the unprecedented bill into law. This novel legislation authorized the dispatch of the MSDF to undertake antiterrorist support activities within a sweeping area that included the whole of the Indian Ocean and the Arabian Sea, for a period of two years, potentially to be extended, with cabinet approval. Although historic in its own way, the dispatch of JSDF to the Indian Ocean was only part of a larger, decade-long movement toward globalization of Japan's security commitments, as indicated in figure 6.1.

The basic plan developed under the antiterrorism law was extended three times, bringing it up to October 2007, when it was briefly terminated,[5] before being renewed again in a dramatic, unprecedented special vote.[6] Under the basic plan, the JSDF's sphere of authorized action was specified as including not just the sea and airspace of the Indian Ocean itself, but also the land territory of the states located along the Indian Ocean littoral. It also included the supply lines of allied forces, stretching all the way back to Japan, Australia, and the United States.[7] MSDF flotillas, which included fuel supply and transport ships as well as two destroyers, together with ASDF transport aircraft were charged with providing refueling and logistical transport as well as medical and mainte-

Figure 6.1. Japan's Peacekeeping Goes Global (1992–)

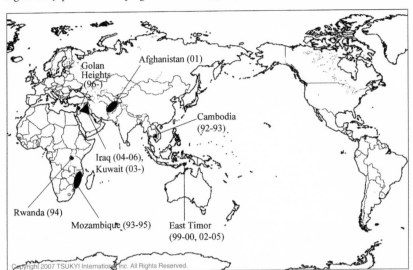

Source: Ministry of Defense, *Defense White Paper* (2007 edition).
Note: Figures in parentheses denote the years in which the Japan Self-Defense Forces were dispatched to the locations in question.

nance support to American and other military forces in both the Indian Ocean and the Arabian Sea. As of November 2007, five Japanese ships had supplied just over three million barrels of fuel to the allied fleet.[8]

The MSDF's original mission was to supply fuel to the American and British navies alone. From November 2002 onward, however, that mandate broadened sharply. Japan thereafter provided fuel to Germany, France, Italy, the Netherlands, Spain, Greece, and Pakistan as well as to the two major forces. It has also transported relief supplies for Afghan refugees through Karachi, Pakistan, and carried Thai army transport construction machinery to the Indian Ocean, to support the repair of American airfield facilities in Afghanistan. The ASDF have likewise flown supplies for the U.S. military from American bases in Japan to staging posts such as Guam. Under the basic plan, even the Ground Self-Defense Forces (GSDF) were given a potential role in Afghanistan—to provide medical treatment for refugees and American military personnel next door in Pakistan (they elected not to exercise the opportunity to perform these functions).[9]

Little more than a year later, in mid-January 2004, there were GSDF boots on the ground in Iraq. This was only at first a thirty-member advance team, but the main six-hundred-member contingent was deployed overland via Kuwait between late February and late March 2004. The GSDF constructed a fortified camp at Samawah, 175 miles southwest of Baghdad, and from March 2003 until July 2006 provided medical care, purified and distributed water, repaired water treatment facilities, and rebuilt public facilities such as schools and hospitals.[10]

During its mission in Iraq, the SDF hired more than a thousand local people a day, totaling nearly half a million, mainly in Samawah.[11] It thereby made another major contribution to a local community suffering from high unemployment. The GSDF even offered on-the-job training in the operation of construction machines. This economic-oriented approach helped elicit local information on potential terrorists' attacks, as those hired were sometimes friends and relatives of terrorists themselves, with incentives influenced by ongoing benefits to their local communities.

In addition to the carrot, there was also a bit of a stick, albeit one uniquely postwar Japanese in its hybrid adaptation to both Iraqi wartime conditions and Japanese domestic concerns. In addition to the GSDF's normal armament for overseas deployment of pistols, rifles, and machine guns, it was permitted to arm itself with recoilless rifles. GSDF troops likewise carried light antitank munitions and moved in wheeled armored personnel carriers and light armored vehicles, in order to counter the threat of suicide attacks by local insurgents. As a result of these precautions, combined with subtle Dutch, British, and Australian protection, the GSDF was able to accomplish its mission without any loss of life attributable to terrorist attacks.

Beginning in February 2004, around two hundred ASDF personnel became engaged in transporting humanitarian and reconstruction supplies via ASDF C-130s from Kuwait into Iraq. The ASDF's original mission statement under the basic plan included airlifting from Kuwait to Baghdad and other Iraqi urban centers. During the GSDF deployment in Samawah, the ASDF concentrated on supplying its GSDF colleagues, via air facilities in Nasiriyah and Basra, but that mission ultimately broadened to direct support of other allied forces after the GSDF's withdrawal from the country. As of September 10, 2008, the ASDF had transported 640 tons of equipment and supplies.[12]

The nominal rationale for the steady expansion of offshore SDF activities since 9/11 has been support for the "international community" in general, rather than explicit backing for the United States alone.[13] After the terrorist attacks on the World Trade Center and the Pentagon in 2001, there was some consideration given to framing Japan's response explicitly in terms of the recently revised U.S.–Japan Defense Guidelines. Yet this framework was considered overly restrictive of SDF activities, and political leaders in both Tokyo and Washington realized that it could be difficult politically to justify Indian Ocean operations, so far from Japan, on that basis, particularly given the "Far East clause" of the U.S.–Japan Security Treaty.[14]

Rather than relying on the guidelines, Japan based its response on relevant UN resolutions identifying the 9/11 attacks as a threat to international peace and calling on all UN members, including Japan, to combat terrorism. In the case of Iraq, Japan's legislation justifying the dispatch of troops (the Law Concerning Special Measures on Humanitarian and Reconstruction Assistance in Iraq) was based on UN Resolution 1483, appealing to member states to assist the people of Iraq in rebuilding their country.[15] It has been the domestic legitimacy in Tokyo of the United Nations—especially with politically pivotal swing groups such as the LDP's coalition partner Kōmeitō—that has provided the cover for this intensified and unprecedented overseas military activity.

Whatever the justification, the bulk of Japan's new offshore military activity since 9/11 has been in direct support of American geostrategic goals, in unprecedentedly concrete political-military ways, and undertaken in close operational cooperation with the U.S. military. The SDF, for example, has had a full-time liaison representative at the Tampa, Florida, headquarters of CENTCOM, which has been in operational control of the Afghan and Iraq wars—one of the few nations to do so. And the SDF's presence in Iraq, fully completed by the end of 2008, although noncombatant, was one of the largest and most enduring of any of America's allies, in a conflict increasingly criticized within the United States itself. The recent expansion of Japan's global military involvement has been remarkable from a historical perspective. Yet it was occurring, as became clear during late 2006 and thereafter, in what increasingly appeared to be a politically unsustainable domestic context.

Since 2001, to be sure, Japan's SDF has continued to pursue some broader, non-U.S.-related, multilateral peacekeeping activities, such as it has actively done since the UN PKO deployment of 1992 in Cambodia. It was involved, for example, in the East Timor UN peacekeeping operation of 2002–05, which did not actively involve the United States. It also continues to be deployed on the Golan Heights, in a noncombatant transportation function.

Yet the emphasis has markedly shifted. From 1992 until 2001, almost none of Japan's offshore military activities were U.S.-centric. Between 9/11 and the end of 2008, however, the vast majority of them were so. Japan's expanding offshore military involvement was increasingly tied operationally to the U.S.–Japan alliance, even if not technically sanctioned under the U.S.–Japan Mutual Security Treaty. The depth of bilateral U.S.–Japan coordination in relation to these third-country missions intensified substantially, albeit within a neglected political context that later proved to be both fragile and vital to the long-term continuity of alliance activities themselves.

Although bilateral military cooperation was unmistakably deepening, through Japan's involvement in Iraq and the Indian Ocean, the political-military benefits of such cooperation, for both nations, were less obvious. The utility and cost of the war in Iraq, in particular, came to be seriously questioned in both countries. And the diplomatic costs of involvement, particularly to Japan's traditionally credible relationships with Iran and other Persian Gulf states, became an increasing issue also, as was obvious in the case of American pressure on Japan throughout most of 2006–08 not to deal with Iran regarding the Azadegan oil field, where Impex, Japan's premiere oil development firm, held a promising concession.[16] Japan was thus more tightly linked to American global purposes than ever before, but whether this development was in Japan's strategic interest—or even in the fundamental interests of the alliance itself—remained an open question.

DEEPENING FORCES FOR CHANGE

Over the first five years of the twenty-first century, the U.S.–Japan alliance thus quietly became both a much more formidable military configuration—and one mandating much tighter tactical and strategic cooperation—than ever before in history. It literally became a New Alliance. What political, economic, and technological forces have been driving this historic transformation? How do they differ from the forces that had previously shaped this ever-changing bilateral alliance? And how enduring will these supportive forces be?

The Rise of China

One of the most important drivers for alliance consolidation, no doubt, has been the substantial change in Japan's strategic environment since 2001. A central element of the rising challenge, as is often remarked, is the rising political-military power of mainland China. Its GDP jumped from $1.2 trillion in 2001 to $3.4 trillion in 2007, and its military budget expanded from $17 billion to $46.7 billion in 2007, as indicated in figure 6.2.[17] The PRC's technological level was rising also. These trends have, not surprisingly, provoked Japan's *Defense White Paper* to express persistent concerns, dating back over a decade, re-

Figure 6.2. Rising Chinese GDP and Defense Budget Trends

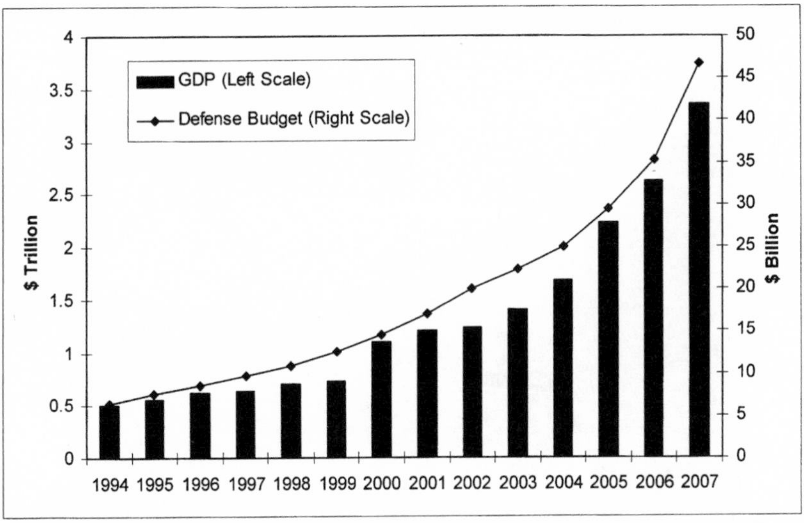

Source: IISS, *Military Balance* (various editions).

garding China's military buildup.[18] The 2007 edition, for example, noted that China's official defense budget growth rate has exceeded 10 percent annually for nineteen consecutive years, and that actual military expenditures extend far beyond the defense budget itself.[19]

The Shadows of Reunification

Also important have been the shadows of reunification across the Taiwan Strait.[20] Political-military relations there, to be sure, remain tense. Yet investment across the strait now totals well over $100 billion by most knowledgeable estimates, with over 60 percent of Taiwan's global foreign investment flow for 2007 going to mainland China.[21] The mainland is now also temporary home to nearly 5 percent of the entire Taiwanese population.[22]

Since 2002 the mainland has been a more substantial trading partner of Taiwan than the United States, and the gap is steadily widening, as indicated in figure 6.3. Four Taiwanese firms are now among the PRC's ten largest exporters. Lien Chan, then the leader of the Kuomintang (KMT) Party, which Chiang Kai Shek led in disarray to Taiwan at the end of 1949, in April 2005 visited his ancestral graves and the former Nationalist capital of Nanjing, while also meeting CCP General Secretary and Chinese President Hu Jintao. The KMT swept Taiwanese local elections in December 2005 and elected their leader, Ma Ying-

Figure 6.3. Taiwan's Deepening Cross-Straits Trade Relationships
(1995–2007)   (unit = $ billion)

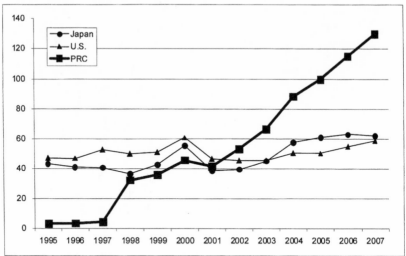

Source: Republic of China National Statistics Bureau website: http://eng.stat.gov.tw/;
Ministry of Economics Affairs Bureau of Foreign Trade website: http://eweb.trade.gov.tw/
mp.asp?mp=2.
Note: Figures for the PRC include Hong Kong after 1997.

jeou, as president of Taiwan in March 2008.[23] Ma's inauguration two months
later led rapidly to the intensification of cross-strait ties in transportation and
other dimensions.

Paradoxically, as Beijing and Taipei move closer economically, because of
complex factional politics on both sides of the Taiwan Strait, the level of military confrontation between them is escalating. The contradiction creates a
tense, ambiguous, and exceedingly dangerous situation, with serious corollary
implications for Japan as well. There are now well over seven hundred Chinese
short-range missiles, mostly CSS-6s and CSS-7s, as well as roughly twelve hundred fighters, sixty-two submarines, forty-six frigates, and two PLA army
groups deployed along the Taiwan Strait. Arrayed against these forces are nearly
three hundred fighters, of which half are F-16s, complemented by assorted tactical missiles.[24] One Japanese island at the end of the Ryūkyū chain, Yonaguni,
is less than forty miles from where Chinese missiles splashed down in the crisis
of 1996. And those missiles, now magnitudes more numerous than a decade
ago, have the range to easily reach mainland Japan.

Sino-Japanese Tensions

Beyond a classic security dilemma, intensified by growing Chinese economic power and the uncertainties of the Taiwan Strait competition, China and Japan confront other contentious questions that could interact with the Taiwan issue to catalyze conflict. Among the most pressing is their mutual thirst for energy. Japan is 99 percent dependent on imports for its oil and gas, while coastal China is similarly bereft. Offshore oil in the East China Sea is one of the few domestic development options available on either side.

The definitions of "domestic," however, conflict. And demarcation lines are dangerously ambiguous. China claims that the entire continental shelf of the East China Sea is a "natural prolongation" of the Chinese mainland, extending eastward all the way to Okinawa. On the other hand, Japan has drawn a hypothetical median line delimiting its territorial claims a full one hundred miles west of the Okinawa Trough, where the richest petroleum deposits in the area are believed to be concentrated.

The energy conflict has escalated ominously in recent years. In 2003, China began to develop the Chunxiao/Shirakaba gas fields, only four kilometers from the median line, provoking rising Japanese concern. Then in November 2004, a Chinese nuclear attack submarine intruded for over two hours into Japanese waters near Okinawa, ostensibly by accident. Meanwhile, a territorial dispute over Okinotorishima, a small yet strategic outcropping on approach routes from Guam to the Taiwan Strait, has periodically flared up owing to Chinese military marine-mapping activities in the vicinity.[25] In May 2005 the Ministry of Economy, Trade, and Industry (METI) authorized Japanese firms to explore in contested areas. And in September 2005, Chinese warships appeared at the now-active Chunxiao/Shirakaba gas fields, at the very edge of disputed waters, on the eve of Japanese national elections.

Tensions escalated steadily during 2005–06 on the political-military front. In May 2005 METI authorized Japanese energy firms to explore in contested areas. Both ruling and opposition parties prepared Diet bills to protect the operations of Japanese drillers and fishermen in those areas, while overflights by Chinese military surveillance aircraft in disputed airspace and research by Chinese military research ships rose to record levels. During April–September 2005, Japanese fighters scrambled thirty times to turn away Chinese planes approaching Japanese airspace, more than twice the comparable frequency during

2004.[26] In 2006, the Japanese Coast Guard detected seven Chinese warships in the vicinity of Japanese-claimed waters.[27]

The PRC seemingly grew more conciliatory after Abe Shinzō became Japanese prime minister in September 2006 and made his first overseas state visit to Beijing. The visits of Abe's successor Fukuda Yasuo to Beijing in December 2007 and of Hu Jintao to Tokyo in May 2008 gave further momentum to bilateral ties.[28] Fukuda also visited Beijing again to attend the opening ceremony of the 2008 Beijing Olympics, while Hu visited Tōyako, Japan, for the G-8 summit in the same year. Although bilateral relations remain to be seen, the two nations concluded in June 2008 that Japanese firms might take equity stakes in the Chinese firms operating near the median line dividing the East China Sea.

Potential frictions between China and Japan are not limited to energy issues and military capabilities. A further, more general point of contention is the redefinition of regional order implied by the rise of China. Amidst the Asian financial crisis, the proposal Japan made in 1996–97 for an Asian Monetary Fund faltered, in the face of opposition from both China and the United States.[29] While Japan has proposed open regionalism, as in Asia-Pacific Economic Cooperation (APEC), including the United States, Australia, and New Zealand, China has countered with narrower proposals for an East Asian summit excluding Japan's Anglo-Saxon allies, in an effort to circumscribe Japanese political influence in the region.

The North Korean WMD Threat and Ballistic Missile Defense

Since the Pyongyang summit of June 2000, intra-Korean trade has grown by 150 percent, tourism has boomed, and railway lines across the DMZ have been reconnected. An ROK-backed Special Economic Zone in the peninsula's ancient capital of Kaesong, now in North Korea, has steadily expanded. And agreements to close North Korea's most prominent nuclear facility at Yongbyon were achieved in February 2007, with some steps toward disablement taken during the summer of 2008, before foreign inspectors were banned from the site in September of that year.

North Korean military capacities remain substantial, with the security challenge to Japan rising even as tensions relax along Korea's DMZ. Since 1990 North Korea's missile threat, aimed primarily at Japan, has grown steadily more credible and has gained a clearer nuclear dimension since 2001, as noted. Totally apart from the DPRK's growing nuclear capacity, the North has numerous chemical and biological weapons as well as more than ninety operational

Nodong mobile missiles demonstrably capable of striking Japan, together with more than two hundred Scud missiles and a force of nearly ninety thousand special-purpose commandos, all of which pose a substantial added threat.[30] And the combined military forces of North and South Korea, whose rationale for intra-Korean conflict is declining, number close to ten times the total strength of Japan's SDF.

Defense Policy Response: Pressures for Systems Integration

Japan's reasons for intimate cooperation with the United States in the Northeast Asian region have thus strengthened over the past decade, regardless of what the argument for involvement in Iraq—clearly less persuasive from Japan's strategic viewpoint—might be. Consolidation of the bilateral U.S.–Japan military alliance is rapidly occurring in other areas as well, driven by both technological imperatives and political opportunity. Technologically, the driving force is the rising capability of North Korean and Chinese missile and nuclear capabilities, now demonstrably capable of delivering terror weapons into Japan's heavily populated Kantō plain and Kansai region and possibly capable of hitting some key American and SDF defense facilities as well. These capabilities, demonstrated unmistakably during the Taiwan missile crisis of 1996 and by the North Korean missile tests of 1998 and 2006 and suggested in reported advances of the North Korean WMD program, have accelerated the urgency, from Tokyo's standpoint, of introducing at least a modified ballistic missile defense (BMD) system.

In September 1993, following North Korea's provocative test launches of Nodong-1 missiles in May 1990 and May 1993, the United States and Japan established a Theater Missile Defense Working Group.[31] In 1994, the two countries undertook a major Bilateral Study on Ballistic Missile Defense (BSBMD) to investigate the technological feasibility of BMD systems. In 1999 Washington and Tokyo inaugurated a joint research program on four key BMD interceptor-missile technologies, including infrared seekers in missile nose cones; the protection of infrared seekers from heat generated in flight; a Kinetic Kill Vehicle for the destruction of ballistic missiles; and a second-stage rocket motor for the related interceptor missile.[32] These were all areas in which American and Japanese technical capabilities were well matched to the defense-industrial challenge at hand.[33]

Despite this vigorous bilateral research program, however, Japan was for some time hesitant to move toward implementation, even after 9/11. Indeed, in

December 2002, when JDA Director General Ishiba Shigeru noted, after meeting with U.S. Defense Secretary Donald Rumsfeld, an enthusiastic BMD proponent, that Japan was studying BMD "with a view of future development and deployment,"[34] he was sharply rebuked by both Prime Minister Koizumi and Chief Cabinet Secretary Fukuda for these comments.[35] It was only as the North Korean nuclear crisis began to deepen in 2003 that Japan decided to move more actively toward deployment.

In May 2003 Koizumi indicated that Japan might accelerate consideration of its participation in a joint BMD program with the United States. A few months later, in December 2003, Japan announced it would procure an off-the-shelf BMD system from the United States, while also continuing to study the joint development with the United States of future BMD technology. By June 2006 PAC-3 interceptors were deployed at Kadena Air Base in Okinawa to defend that key U.S. facility against opposing missiles.

Meanwhile, an X-band radar, a key element in BMD monitoring systems, was operationalized at the ASDF's Shariki base in Aomori Prefecture, near Misawa Air Base. In December 2006, the JDA announced plans to build a new joint-interceptor base at Sasebo in Kyūshū,[36] close to China and the Taiwan Strait, while in March 2007, PAC-3 interceptors became operational at Iruma Air Base north of Tokyo, in defense of the capital.[37] By December 2007, Japan had successfully demonstrated basic operational missile defense capabilities itself. In cooperation with the U.S. Missile Defense Agency the Japanese navy Aegis-equipped destroyer *Kongō* successfully destroyed a medium-range target missile with the general characteristics of North Korea's Taepo Dong I one hundred miles above the Pacific.[38]

In buying off-the-shelf technology, much of it likely to be black-boxed, Japan has apparently decided to deepen its technological reliance on the United States, and to integrate its strategies more decisively with Washington. By deploying a navy theaterwide mobile missile defense system highly dependent on information flows originating with the United States, Tokyo is also acquiring a weapon system that is dependent on American cooperation to function properly.[39] Its self-defense strategies are thus being intimately linked to the U.S.–Japan alliance in unprecedented ways.

Most important, the technological nature of BMD increasingly means that Japanese policymakers will no longer be able to employ the type of ambiguity found in the revised Defense Guidelines to obscure the full extent of their military support for the United States, as has often been true in the past. The short time frame—normally less than ten minutes—that is needed for a BMD system to respond to a missile launch means that there will be no time for Japan's political leaders to debate decisions on interceptor launches. They will need to devolve decisions increasingly on joint U.S.–Japan operational commands now being set up, as we shall see, expressly for this purpose. The best they can most probably do is to specify clear rules of engagement dealing with pre-planned scenarios for committing Japan to conflict.

BMD systems, like rapid-reaction antiterrorist arrangements, also have important implications for Japan's prohibition on the exercise of the right of collective self-defense, again in the spirit of the peace constitution. If strictly applied, Japan cannot legitimately defend American bases and troops in Japan. Despite the considerable operational complications that it generates for alliance with a foreign country, denial of collective self-defense has interestingly never surfaced, until recently, as a substantial political issue in U.S.–Japan security relations. The Mutual Security Treaty does not, after all, articulate Japan's duty to defend the United States, and Washington had never, prior to 9/11, asked Tokyo's help in defending the United States.

Given the fluid current international security environment, in which the United States has come to regard Japan as a "global partner," the collective self-defense issue has gradually emerged as a serious challenge to stable alliance relations, especially in connection with missile defense. In order to function effectively, BMD systems demand not only the free flow of sensor information from the American side but also reverse flows from the Japanese. It would be difficult to develop a transpacific missile defense architecture that avoids this problem. BMD will thus call the long-standing Japanese ban on the exercise of collective self-defense, under prevailing constitutional interpretations, into question. So could rapid-reaction responses to nuclear, chemical, or biological terrorism.[40]

All these considerations will necessitate increased Japanese planning for regional contingencies in much closer coordination with the United States than has heretofore been true. They will also require more clarification of prospective Japanese strategies. Such rules of engagement will also require some softening of the principle of civilian control over the military and provide Japanese commanders in the field with more latitude to support the United States than has previously been true.

Related to the accelerating implementation of BMD and preparing for new potential terrorist contingencies, the United States and Japan are integrating their military command and control systems in important new ways. The massive $26 billion military transformation proposals agreed to in October 2005

have been pivotal in this context. At the 2+2 foreign and defense ministers' bilateral meeting of May 2006, where those proposals were formalized, Japan
and the United States finalized the force-posture realignments involved in a
document entitled "The Japan–U.S. Roadmap for Realignment Implementation."[41] Inspired originally by the U.S. Department of Defense Global Posture
Review (GPR) of 2004, the United States and Japan have been setting institutions in place that will eventually make Japan a frontline American command
post for the Asia–Pacific region and even beyond, while also providing for ballistic missile defense.

The total number of American troops in Japan will ultimately decline
slightly under the 2006 transformation proposals because of the relocation of
eight thousand Marines from Okinawa back to Guam.[42] The carrier aircraft attached to the *George Washington,* the one U.S. Navy aircraft carrier home-
ported outside the United States, will also be redeployed from the heavily populated suburbs of Yokohama to sparsely populated Iwakuni, in western Japan,
reducing noise pollution and the inconvenience of night-landing practice in
the Tokyo area. Both the ground-troop reductions and the redeployments, coupled with the relocation of training sites from Okinawa to less populated areas
like Hokkaidō, are politically astute steps intended to reduce the negative impact of American bases on urban Japan. Yet their broader strategic objective,
like that of headquarters consolidation, is clear: to transform the U.S.–Japan
defense relationship into one that is much more unitary, operational, and ambitious than anything heretofore seen in the Pacific.

The details of the proposed roadmap suggest the imposing magnitude of the
logistical and political challenges—unavoidable, given the strategic and tech-
nological changes now under way—that systems integration within the U.S.–
Japan alliance will pose in coming years. The key changes will occur at Yokota
Air Base and at Camp Zama, the headquarters of the U.S. Air Force and the
U.S. Army in Japan, respectively.

Under the transformation plan, a Bilateral and Joint Operations Coordination Center (BJOCC) was established at Yokota Air Base to coordinate bilateral
actions relating to air defense and BMD, with Japan's ASDF Air Defense Command relocating to the base during fiscal 2010 (April 2010–March 2011). American personnel at Yokota returned portions of Yokota airspace, which they had
previously controlled, to Japanese authorities by September 2008, so that they
could concentrate on joint BMD-related coordination activities. Dual military
and civilian use of parts of Yokota Air Base are also being explored.[43]

Simultaneously, Camp Zama is also being transformed, in parallel fashion.

In December 2007 it became a joint task force headquarters, with the headquarters unit of the I Corps of the U.S. Army, an early deploying unit in the event of prospective military contingencies in the Pacific, being transferred from Fort Lewis, Washington. The consolidation of U.S. and Japanese headquarters units will enhance mobility and readiness, making the combined forces capable of playing an enhanced role in joint antiterrorist and disaster response activities. By FY 2012, the headquarters of the GSDF Central Readiness Force will also relocate to Camp Zama, so that I Corps and the GSDF can smoothly coordinate operational command activities in the event of a North Korean crisis or other contingency in the areas surrounding Japan.[44]

Importance of Political Context

The geopolitical imperatives, particularly in Northeast Asia, that have been rather smoothly driving the historic consolidation of the U.S.–Japan alliance since 2001 have an inevitable correlate: domestic politics. In both Japan and the United States, conservative governments had unusual power during 2001–06 and were working in the shadow of a major terrorist incident (9/11), which gave them further legitimacy. Neither the Bush nor the Koizumi-Abe administrations made much effort to elucidate a common political or ideological basis for the Pacific alliance. Yet they didn't really need to do so, as their underlying political constituencies could avail themselves of strong interpersonal networks for security policy coordination.

The year 2006 was a watershed. In Japan, electoral support for the Socialists and Communists fell from 14 to 3 percent during the 1996–2006 decade. Following Koizumi's electoral landslide in September 2005, the Communist and Social Democratic parties in the Diet held only 16 of 480 seats in the dominant Lower House. This collapse of the Left in Japanese parliamentary politics definitely aided consolidation of U.S.–Japan defense relations. So has the related impact of this collapse on the political balance within the ruling Liberal Democratic Party, where the weakness of leftist parties strengthened relatively conservative politicians within the party such as Abe. In the 1960s and 1970s, when the leftists were stronger, they would have had difficulty rising to leadership positions within the LDP as a whole.

In office, the conservatives undertook important administrative changes that laid the groundwork for the unusually decisive Japanese responses to 9/11, facilitating accelerated consolidation, between late 2001 and mid-2007, of the military dimensions of Pacific alliance. In 1998 the Office of Crisis Management, headed by a deputy chief cabinet secretary for crisis management, was created in the *kantei* (Prime Minister's Office) and charged with enhancing government coordination of responses to national disasters as well as domestic and international security crises. The revised Cabinet Law of 1999 clarified the prime minister's authority to propose key policies at cabinet meetings, thus strengthening his top-down leadership capabilities, while diluting the traditional bottom-up style of Japanese decision making.[45] It also reorganized the cabinet secretariat on horizontal lines, creating a single Office of Assistant Chief Cabinet Secretaries, to reduce ministerial sectionalism.

Prior to the reforms of 1999, the cabinet secretariat had been divided into three core policy offices. Headed by Ministry of Finance, MOFA, and JDA officials, these offices were plagued by bureaucratic infighting and stovepiping. The reformed post-1999 structure eased these organizational problems and was crucial in allowing Japan's unusually decisive response to 9/11, as outlined above.

At the level of national policy, the Abe administration took steps during 2006–07 to promote deeper integration as well. Shortly before Abe assumed the prime ministership, in August 2006, he announced plans for a U.S.-style National Security Council (NSC) at the Prime Minister's Office—relating his proposal explicitly to the need for closer operational defense cooperation with the United States. In April 2007, the ruling LDP approved a bill to create an NSC in Japan.[46] Abe also proposed the strengthening of Japanese intelligence capabilities and a streamlining of intelligence organization, in part to reinforce the functions of the prospective Japanese NSC. Yet neither he nor his LDP colleagues of the post-Koizumi period did much to strengthen the political foundations of the Pacific alliance or to enhance related alliance equities.

Those political foundations began to shake with a vengeance from 2006 on. In January 2007, a Democratic Party highly skeptical of Bush administration security initiatives, especially in Iraq, and with only limited contact with the ruling Japanese conservatives, took control of both the U.S. Senate and the U.S. House of Representatives.

In July 2007, the opposition won an overwhelming victory in the Japanese House of Counselors elections also, the DPJ becoming the first party other than the conservative LDP to dominate that Upper House of the Diet since the LDP's foundation in 1955. This group also had but limited transpacific security ties. The shifts in the tenor of Japanese security policy debate during the ensuing months showed clearly and painfully the importance of solid political foundations to alliance policy outcomes and the confusion potentially flowing from the lack thereof. The inability of the ruling party to renew the mandate of

MSDF in the Indian Ocean suggested at a minimum that supporters of the Pacific alliance needed to broaden their appeals and orchestrate a transparty consensus in order to enhance alliance equities and to assure the stability of the alliance itself. Amidst the transition first to a Democratic Congress in 2007 and then from the Bush to the Obama administration in early 2009, there was clearly a need for the same sort of broad, transparty consensus building in the United States as well, given the demanding coordination imperatives created by the military transformation package of 2006, which one might term the New Alliance.

THE NEW ALLIANCE: A VIABLE CONFIGURATION?

The New Alliance, involving intensified, globalized military cooperation on a fragile political-economic base, sharply enhanced its operational military capabilities and crisis-response mechanisms over the short five-year period between 2001 and 2006. The alliance now operates not only in Northeast Asia, but around the world, and prospectively in outer space as well, involving broad-based new liaison mechanisms. Linking Japan's strategic Northeast Asian location and massive economic and technological capacity more tightly to America's formidable military power than ever before, the New Alliance is fundamentally changing not only the Asian regional but also the global, geostrategic equation. Those are no mean accomplishments.

Yet those distinct military accomplishments inevitably stand on a more problematic political-economic foundation. Even as it so effectively appears to harness the military capacities of the two great North Pacific democracies, the ambitious New Alliance confronts imposing new challenges, both within the Japanese and American political systems and in international affairs more generally. Domestically, the problem in both nations, to be succinct, is political sustainability. Internationally, the issues are strategic coherence and resistance, from potential rivals and antagonists who understandably see the enhanced capacity of the alliance as something to be undermined rather than applauded.

The New Alliance, formidable as it may be militarily, thus has political and intellectual feet of clay. It requires, first of all, that the political authorities of its two member nations come to predetermined strategic understandings on such eventualities as how to respond to matters like a North Korean missile strike or a resumption of Chinese missile testing in the Taiwan Strait. It requires that they work out precisely what they would do and how they would coordinate with one another. Yet their decisions on such matters must inevitably rest on political and strategic premises that are, in all too many cases, unarticulated or unachievable, or often both.

The New Alliance ultimately also necessarily entrusts operational decisions on delicate matters of life and death to working-level officers of both countries that would, in democratic theory, be the responsibilities of leaders instead. These officers would, in a crisis, be working together in new forms of transnational interdependence heretofore unprecedented. Regional and local joint military commands, such as the Central Command (CENTCOM) and the Pacific Command (PACOM), now have an unprecedented importance that has not yet been publicly recognized.[47]

The New Alliance, for which terrorist incidents, missile attacks, and sudden natural disasters are major targets of concern, also confronts enormously increased demands for reliable, actionable intelligence. Obtaining the requisite information requires enormous new budgets and delicate intrusions into individual lives. It also requires reliance on another nation's information—often without knowing the full origins of that intelligence—and protection of both substance and origins, insofar as they are known.

The New Alliance, in short, requires a new level of common transpacific political understanding and consensus—on the meaning of national security, on national priorities, on confidentiality of sensitive intelligence, and ultimately on human values. The New Alliance also requires a political-economic mechanism to drive the two nations to concerted, coordinated action, more dynamically than has traditionally been the case. Without these broader political capabilities, whether the formidable but ultimately technical military capacities developed in recent years can effectively operate is open to question.

The New Alliance thus requires in the end something much more fundamental than just the ability to synchronize PAC-3 batteries with an X-band radar. It requires real communication and active, politically based coordination between Tokyo and Washington—in short, a tight, interactive Pacific alliance. Yet, as we have seen in the past several chapters, "communication and common understanding," as Reischauer once noted, "has been a chronic problem in U.S.–Japan relations across the years."[48]

The Nonmilitary Base of National Security: Deepening Vulnerabilities

The new, ambitious Pacific alliance that has emerged since 9/11, in short, appears formidably consolidated in operational military terms. Yet it remains dangerously underdeveloped in its cultural, political, and economic dimensions, as became clear in the Anti-Terrorism Law debates of late 2007, even though those aspects are crucial, in the long run, to stable and intimate transpacific security ties. Sporadically, there have been efforts to reduce this imbalance between the military and socioeconomic dimensions, as in the Reischauer years. Yet the tensions always seem to reemerge. How have the important economic and cultural dimensions of the alliance, to be concrete, evolved since 2001, as military interdependence has deepened so smoothly? Are the current alliance and its equities adequate to cope with emerging challenges?

The economic and cultural requisites of the alliance—to make it function smoothly enough on the political front that the peoples of the two nations can come to a common understanding on security matters—vary significantly between the United States and Japan. On the Japanese side, what is needed most is cultural understanding—a shared consciousness of national security and of global partnership with the United States. That understanding needs to be strong enough to support the security policy consensus building that is required, in the era of the New Alliance, to allow the emerging institutions for shared strategic decision to operate coherently. In the United States, by contrast, what is needed most are economic incentives and cultural publicity—something to make American influentials feel that allying with Japan is rewarding in the changing Asian regional context.

Institutional Atrophy

On the economic side of alliance relations, visible trade frictions have fortunately receded to levels much less delicate politically than during the 1980s and the 1990s. Yet the dangers of sudden explosions remain substantial because the mechanisms for monitoring and policy dialogue have dangerously atrophied. Virtually none of the bilateral mechanisms for economic conflict resolution that were operative even in 1990—not to mention the elaborate cabinet-level consultative structures of the 1960s—still exist today.

To be concrete, the Joint U.S.–Japan Economics and Trade Consultative Committee, inaugurated in 1961, has not met since 1966. The MOSS sectoral talks, which were active in the 1980s, have not been held since 1989. The Structural Impediment Initiative (SII) died in 1993. And the Framework Talks expired in 2001. In June 2001, the U.S.–Japan Partnership for Further Growth was inaugurated, as another partisan iteration, to expire in 2009.[49] Each U.S. administration from the 1960s has had its own bilateral economic dialogue with Japan, but none has continued into the term of another president.

Inadequate Investment

Even more than the specter of trade conflict, which is largely yesterday's problem in an era of widespread global cross-investment, the pressing structural economic issue for the alliance today in the United States is the paucity of American investment in Japan. The U.S.–Japan relationship is distinctive comparatively, as we have seen, in the low level of cross-investment that it involves, especially outbound from the United States to Japan. Japan itself has one of the lowest ratios of inbound direct investment to GDP in the industrialized world. FDI is crucial to the political economy of alliance because it creates vested stakes that encourage political leaders—in this case American political leaders—to commit to the stability of the bilateral relationship. Thus, a vigorous, rewarding investment dialogue will ultimately be important in security terms, owing to the enhanced stakes it could potentially give Americans in the future of the Japanese economy and hence in Japan's national security as well.

The Japanese Public's Ambivalence

For Tokyo, a key domestic difficulty in managing the overall U.S.–Japan relationship, in this era of the New Alliance, is the paucity of shared concepts of national security, especially at the popular level. Key Japanese leaders, it is clear, are committed to the alliance. Yet the commitment of the broader public—indeed, its understanding of the major national security issues involved—is much less apparent, the relatively high share of the Japanese public feeling familiar with the United States notwithstanding. The sharp declines in pro-U.S. sentiment during crises such as the Vietnam War illustrated this problem clearly. So did public disenchantment in Tokyo, during 2007–08, with American shifts in policy priority for Japanese abductees in U.S. dealings with North Korea, as the prospect of finally curbing the North's nuclear program came more demonstrably into view.

In January 2007, U.S. and North Korean officials met in Berlin, in contradiction of the Bush administration's long-standing policy of refusing direct discussions with North Korea. The following month they reached an agreement to disable the controversial Yongbyon nuclear facilities.[50] This agreement was concluded without extensive coordination with other Asian allies, and U.S. Ambassador to Japan Thomas Schieffer had to send an unusual private cable to President Bush warning that the pending nuclear deal with North Korea could harm relations with Japan.[51]

Since 2001 leaders in both the United States and Japan have worked quietly, taking skillful advantage of critical junctures like 9/11, the North Korean nuclear crisis of 2002, and the subsequent North Korean kidnapping revelations to consolidate key operational dimensions of their military alliance.[52] By 2007, however, in the wake of Upper House elections that decisively shifted the balance of Diet power toward opposition groups skeptical of expanded military cooperation, the conservative Bush and Abe/Fukuda governments appeared to have reached the limits of where elite cooperation alone could take them. And they faced still-deepening challenges from the broadening of national agendas in both nations and the simultaneous narrowing of mutual interdependence, as noted above. To overcome the resistance factor in third countries, as the domestic political requisites of the New Alliance become even more demanding at home, Tokyo and Washington in the Obama era will need to cooperatively develop and explain to their publics new, common concepts of national security that can provide the basis for true alliance.

The International Dimension

The New U.S.–Japan Alliance, as noted earlier, is becoming a potent phenomenon on the Asian and, indeed, on the global stage. Its geopolitical reach and technological scope naturally stir an ambivalent reaction among political realists in Beijing, Moscow, and to some extent even Seoul as well. On the one hand, the alliance is often welcomed in third-party capitals, to the extent that it preserves regional stability and checks the emergence of an unpredictable Japanese Gaullism. On the other, the manifest military capabilities of Tokyo's and Washington's new defense relationship are often greeted with trepidation in third countries, both for how much they leverage the United States and also for how much they strengthen Japan.

It is axiomatic in alliance relations that neither partner should let a third country outside the alliance dictate the terms of the mutual bilateral ties. Neither Japan nor the United States should thus allow China or any other third country to manipulate it. For China, however, driving a wedge between American opinion and Japan could well be its best strategy for defusing the threatening aspects of the U.S.–Japan military partnership.

Convincing Americans to privilege relations with China over the New Alliance could well be easier than most Japanese, or even American, decision-makers believe, or their rhetoric will allow them to admit. After all, Americans tend to forget or depreciate the political-economic dimension of international affairs. On that chessboard, dominated by trade opportunities and foreign investment, China is arguably much more attractive to American business than is

Japan. Beijing's market is growing faster and could well have more potential than Tokyo's, despite the massive scale of the Japanese economy, especially because local competition in China is less formidable.

Even if one depreciates the attractiveness of the PRC market, considering that China's economic potential has time and again failed across history to be realized, *investment* in China is growing far faster than in Japan, even though China's economy is significantly smaller than Japan's. Additionally, the PRC is adept at using American corporations to lobby Washington. And with over three times as many Chinese Americans as their Japanese-American counterparts, Beijing also has an ethnic card. Only the considerable geostrategic attractions of U.S.–Japan partnership hold the Tokyo–Washington relationship in place, in the face of all those formidable countervailing political-economic forces.

The threats to the New Alliance, then, are not purely military in their nature. The antagonists are not limited to terrorists or to the perils posed by a North Korean missile strike. Indeed, the challenges are much more subtle, extending broadly to the political, economic, and cultural realms so often neglected of late.

The New Alliance requires strong political and cultural foundations, to an even greater degree than its forebears across the years. Its political requirements are demanding because the New Alliance mandates unitary decision making— a tight consensus on values and on conceptions of national security, on top of common mutual technical understanding. Split-second decisions on unforeseeable scenarios regarding missile defense and antiterrorist response also necessarily require delegation—from political leaders, however cosmopolitan, to more provincial subordinates. And delegation requires forethought as to just who, concretely, should assume operating responsibility, and when. Proceeding in any other way is a recipe for chaos.

Domestically, the central challenges to the New Alliance appear to differ in Japan and in the United States. For Japan, and indeed for Americans concerned seriously with consolidating the U.S.–Japan alliance in the hearts and minds of the Japanese people, the issue is developing a common sense of transpacific security and partnership. For America itself, the issue is creating the incentives and understanding that cause key Americans to privilege the New Alliance, with all its geostrategic potential, over the clear temptation of powerful economic opportunities within China, including investment.

The dynamics of alliance, after all, are driven from Tokyo, constrained by its newly fluid and confrontational politics. Yet the details tend to be drafted in Washington, making it crucial for Americans of good will to help craft a common security agenda and shared alliance equities that resonate more with authentic Japanese concerns and values than has been typical in the past.

Internationally, the New Alliance so leverages Washington and Tokyo, because of its manifest military potency, that it inevitably will be challenged. It is to the collective advantage of the United States and Japan together to appreciate the power of their alliance and not to stimulate the paranoia of third parties unduly. At the same time, it is also crucial for the two transpacific partners not to let third parties manipulate the substance of something so fundamentally vital to both the American and Japanese peoples as their national security alliance, and to foster the needed alliance equities in both societies that will help their governments turn naturally—and consistently—to one another.

Chapter 7 The Global Challenge

Origins, as the economist Douglass North observed, can often set the course of the future, even when they have receded historically far into the past.[1] So it is with alliances. However much their authors desire them to respond to any eventuality as it arises, their origins configure them to react in preconditioned ways, regardless of dynamic, ongoing changes in their broader political, social, or technological surroundings.

The U.S.–Japan alliance, as we have seen, had its roots in war and occupation, well over half a century ago. Japan and the United States responded remarkably well, in partnership, to the multiple challenges of postwar reconstruction, the Korean War, and reintegrating Japan back into the family of nations following its traumatic wartime defeat. During the Reischauer years, at least, Tokyo and Washington made an ambitious start at broad bilateral cultural understanding also.

NESTLED WITHIN THE WORLD THAT
DULLES MADE

Behind the early successes of the United States and Japan in deepening their bilateral ties, despite the bitterness of the not-so-distant wartime past, was the mutually attractive, if highly asymmetrical, underlying structure of the Pacific alliance bargain. Through a maze of agreements during 1951–53, including the San Francisco Peace Treaty of September 1951 formally ending World War II, the U.S.–Japan Mutual Security Treaty, signed only a few hours later, and the Treaty of Commerce and Navigation of 1953, an asymmetrical yet remarkably stable and historic "security for economics" tradeoff arrangement was gradually forged. The complex framework both circumscribed the newly independent Japan and placed it squarely at the heart of Pacific affairs, devoid of burdensome reparations obligations. The United States gained a new and major military ally at precarious peace with its neighbors and basing rights in the Japanese home islands. It also secured administrative control of the strategic Ryūkyū Islands, including Okinawa, which lay just south of Japan and within much less than an hour's flying time by supersonic, nuclear-capable military jet of China's major political-economic centers. Such was the world, of both security and dependence for Japan, that John Foster Dulles, America's chief negotiator at San Francisco, laboriously struggled to create.

These asymmetric political-military advantages decisively established American strategic dominance in the North Pacific, while simultaneously inhibiting the prospect of Japanese military revival. In return, Tokyo received an extensive package of political-economic benefits, made especially attractive by the fact that they excluded key commercial rivals of Japan and required little actual economic reciprocity on Japan's part. Most important, Tokyo gained unfettered access to America's massive market for a broad range of Japanese manufactures as well as to Southeast Asian natural resources. Japan's major prospective competitor, mainland China, was explicitly embargoed from the United States for two long postwar decades.

During the mid-1950s that American market comprised nearly half of global GDP, so preferential access in the United States had enormous attractiveness for Japan.[2] Attraction was compounded for Tokyo by a critical de facto, informal reality: the United States did not insist on equivalent access for its own firms in Japan. And Cold War constraints on PRC access to the world did not unduly bother the Japanese, as the post-1980 system of offshore production for the world in low-labor-cost China had not yet emerged.

This comprehensive economics for security bargain, codified first in the San Francisco Peace Treaty of September 1951, can justly be called the San Francisco System.[3] It was literally the world that Dulles built. Owing to its mutually attractive features for key groups in both the United States and Japan—particularly manufacturers in Japan and the defense establishment of the United States—the system proved remarkably durable during the Cold War years (1952–89). Indeed, it became the cornerstone not only of U.S.–Japan relations, but also of the emerging Asia-Pacific regional security architecture as a whole.

The static, firmly bilateralist, and politically ordered character of the classic San Francisco System, including its economic correlates, was paramount—driven by Dulles's obsessive desire that Japan not be victimized by the peace settlement and transformed into an Oriental version of Weimar Germany. Japan was given privileged access to international markets, although it did not join GATT until 1955 or subscribe to the OECD Capital Liberalization Code until 1965, and thus initially was not subject to those constraints. Meanwhile, China was embargoed from the American market, as noted earlier, although Japan traded with the PRC on an informal basis, and the United States did not formally object.

There were, to be sure, important, if gradual, changes over the years in the content of the original economics for security bilateralist bargain, driven by Japan's remarkable economic growth. Most conspicuously, during the 1980s Japan, as it grew increasingly affluent, expanded its support for American strategic aims, which had originally centered on passively providing bases for U.S. troops, and sustaining a democratic-capitalist developmental model. Following a fateful revision of the Foreign Exchange Law in December 1980, implemented a month before Ronald Reagan's inauguration as president of the United States, Japan gradually became a massive capital exporter to America during the late 1980s, buying at times nearly one-half of all the Treasury bills issued by the U.S. government.[4]

Japan also steadily expanded its ODA spending, to the highest levels on earth, and directed it increasingly to nations of strategic interest to the United States, such as China, Indonesia, the Philippines, and the Caribbean. Japanese ODA to China started in 1979, for example, just as Washington was recognizing the PRC and enlisting it as a tacit Cold War ally.[5] Tokyo's ODA to Beijing then jumped three-hundred-fold, from $2.6 million in the initial year to $832 million in 1989, only a decade later. Meanwhile, aid to Indonesia, the Philippines, and Mexico more than doubled during the mid-1980s alone.[6]

Bilateral alliance cooperation worked smoothly within the San Francisco

System, across the 1980s, for three basic reasons: the viability of the U.S.–Japan economics for security bargain; the continuation of the Cold War; and the generally ordered nature of international affairs at the time. The asymmetrical economics for security bargain forged at San Francisco in 1951 still held, despite Henry Kissinger's subversive efforts, even as it frayed steadily around the edges. The bargain retained its coherence because Japan got special economic privileges in both the United States and its own home market, together with defense of its energy sea-lanes to the Persian Gulf, while supplying Washington with military bases and substantial capital outflows that allowed the U.S. flexibility in its own defense spending. The Cold War, which sealed the common interest of the two incongruous allies, masked the gradual emergence of new political-economic poles like China and their gradual intrusion into the integrated political-economic benefits package that was the U.S.–Japan alliance in its classic incarnation.

THE CHANGING CONFIGURATION OF THE
GLOBAL POLITICAL-ECONOMIC SYSTEM

Meanwhile, globalization quietly began transforming the international political economy along lines of fateful long-term importance to the U.S.–Japan alliance, disrupting the comfortable, static Pacific world that Dulles made and paving the way for volatilities and uncertainties to come. From the mid-1980s, the information revolution began to gain force, fueled by advances in aerospace technology as well as by telecommunications deregulation in the Anglo-Saxon world. Global capital flows also began to intensify, stimulated by London's Big Bang, America's rising fiscal deficits, and the substantial Japanese capital outflows mentioned earlier.

Together with the broadened flow of capital around the world, multinational corporations (MNCs) began to expand their international operations, both in manufacturing and in services. From a traditional transatlantic and Western hemispheric focus, the MNCs began to outsource production more broadly, across the 1980s and 1990s, to China, Southeast Asia, and other parts of the developing world.[7] From the late 1990s on, they began to outsource services as well, ranging from accounting and drug testing to credit card debt collection, with a special focus on English-speaking nations with strong legal traditions, like India. Major multinationals like IBM, Toyota, General Electric, Shell, and Nestlé were becoming truly global firms, with few areas on earth beyond their business ambit.

After the fall of the Berlin Wall in 1989, global political-economic change began to accelerate still faster. The intellectual force of Cold War logic began to wane in Europe, especially after the collapse of the Soviet Union at the end of 1991. With the integration of Russia, Eastern Europe, and Central Asia into the global system for the first time in the post–World War II era, a unified world seemed to be emerging economically, complicating Cold War–configured diplomacy and politics in its wake. Historic reforms in India during 1991 and after, together with the glimmerings of information industry outsourcing, began expanding the ambit of that global system to South Asia also.

With the waning of the Cold War, institutions of global governance were geopolitically easier to configure and began fitfully to emerge, steadily eroding bilateralism. The G-7 summits of advanced industrial nations were broadened, with the admission, first, of Russia in 1997 and then the partial participation of China and India since 2003. This new broadening was complemented by the growing influence and vigor of informal global business-government networks, such as the Davos World Economic Forum. Initiated in 1971, Davos had, by the 1990s, become an influential, if informal, agenda-setting forum on a diverse range of political-economic issues, ranging from the Israeli–Palestinian dispute to global trade liberalization. By the late 1990s, invited global leaders had begun using Davos as a major forum for floating important global initiatives on subjects ranging from poverty reduction in Africa to global climate change.[8]

New institutions of global trade and finance also began to evolve, to accommodate the emerging "one-world" international economy. Most conspicuous was the World Trade Organization, founded in 1995 to replace the GATT and to more comprehensively regulate world trade. It has steadily expanded to include the large newly emerging economies, with China joining in 2001. As of July 2008, the membership had doubled from the original 76 to 153, plus 30 observer governments. Despite a proliferation of often-discriminatory bilateral trading arrangements, a distinct new system of global trade governance, one less dependent than heretofore on state-to-state regulation, has also begun to emerge, making typically bilateral orderly marketing agreements (OMAs) increasingly a thing of the past.

In the new global political economy, nations with low-cost factors of production—be they land, labor, or capital—have had particular competitive advantage and have begun growing much more dynamically than ever before. This situation has especially benefited Brazil, Russia, India, and China (the BRICs). They have notably generous, low-cost endowments of labor, in the case of China and India, and resources, in the case of Russia and Brazil. Expanding new opportunities for global commerce have allowed these large nations to grow rapidly, at rates ranging from 5 to 10 percent annually in recent years, and to steadily increase their share of global product. From 7.5 percent in 1990, the BRICs' share of global GDP rose by more than half, to 11.6 percent in 2006, although growth was tempered by the 2008 global financial crisis.[9]

Rising Pressures on U.S.–Japan Alliance Relations

The classic San Francisco System of the 1950s and 1960s, as noted, was a brilliant geopolitical conception. Yet the world that Dulles built was encumbered by economic correlates that became less and less realistic over time. The system assumed a small, fragile, and vulnerable Japanese economy, a system in need of asymmetric access to a massive, buoyant American market, to prevent the sort of economically linked sociopolitical disruption that Germany had suffered in the 1920s and 1930s. It also assumed Cold War constraints that estranged China and Russia economically as well as politically from the Western world.

The sparkling recovery of the Japanese economy between the Korean War and the oil shock of 1973, together with the waning of Cold War tensions with China across the 1970s, undermined both of these key assumptions. Japan's recovery introduced, in its wake, new fluidity and tension into the complex, interrelated parameters of Japanese political and economic relations with the world. Tokyo could afford significant military enhancement to match its rising economic power, even as the United States lost its earlier tolerance of protectionism in Japanese domestic markets. Both countries vied to shape the emerging pattern of Chinese integration into global markets and became less concerned with one another.

Meanwhile, globalization was steadily advancing. Apart from the substantive political-economic changes and the institutional adaptations it fostered, globalization was intensifying uncertainty, volatility, and fluidity—both in world affairs as a whole and in the human relationships of those managing global developments. Under the classic San Francisco System key American and Japanese officials could deal with one another bilaterally in stable and predictable fashion, drawing on personal and institutional alliance equities accumulated from the past. Yet during the late 1980s and the 1990s also, as the ordered world that Dulles built began to crumble, such person-to-person fine-tuning became ever more difficult.

This transition was a particular hardship in U.S.–Japan relations, for two major reasons. On the American side, primary negotiating responsibility slipped away from Washington's Japan specialists and their Japanese friends to unconnected trade negotiators with little knowledge of Tokyo, leaving the Japan specialists frequently isolated from top-level decision making in the White House and on Capitol Hill. Meanwhile, in Tokyo the range of players brought into the decision-making process was proliferating, as long-standing LDP and bureaucratic dominance simultaneously eroded, making transpacific consensus building ever more time consuming and difficult.

Apart from the procedural complications it creates for handling important bilateral relations in an increasingly volatile and multicornered world, globalization has shaped U.S.–Japan alliance equities in three other important ways. First of all, it has fatefully eroded the notably discriminatory provisions of the original San Francisco System, such as preferential access to the American market for the manufactures of U.S. Asian allies. It was on such favorable provisions that much of the economic attractiveness for Japanese business of the Pacific alliance originally rested.

Japanese firms, of course, have grown vastly more globally competitive and rely much less on preferential support than they did in the early postwar decades. Their incentive structure has shifted to more global concerns.

A second impact of globalization on U.S.–Japan alliance equities is that it has intensified economic competition among American Pacific allies, including Japan and South Korea, even as it has also increased the volatility of financial flows and exchange rates, making intra-alliance economic ties ever more difficult to manage. Globalization has clearly undermined bilateral approaches to transpacific economic affairs, such as OMAs, contributing to a general atrophy of bilateral policy networks and bilateral policy focus among U.S. allies in the Pacific. Third, globalization has helped propel dramatic political-economic changes in Japan's neighborhood, including the rise of China and India. Because of the rising resource prices they have provoked, these changes have increased the salience of energy and resource security issues in world politics. And they have also rendered the "bypass phenomenon," whereby Japanese concerns are overlooked in favor of the emerging Asian giants, an increasingly important question for the U.S.–Japan alliance itself. None of these new challenges born of globalization were present in the safe and stable world—so congenial for Japan—that Dulles built half a century ago.

Newly Emerging Global Security Imperatives

During the Cold War era, there were two central dimensions of global security that the U.S.–Japan alliance was committed to provide: military deterrence and political-economic stability. Formal, preexisting commitments, including credible operational preparations for honoring them, were the essence of security itself. And the nation-state was clearly the definitive actor for meeting such commitments, especially as it had few capable rivals in the global system of the day.

With changes in the world political economy of the past two decades, seven increasingly serious post–Cold War security imperatives have emerged that are of major concern to all global powers, regardless of their geographical location—and preeminently the United States and Japan. In this section we propose to outline these imperatives. Then we will consider implications for how the United States and Japan should appropriately deal with this pressing new global agenda.

To begin with, the stability of the Middle East and particularly the Persian Gulf must rank high on any list of shared global concerns. Three countries there—Saudi Arabia, Iraq, and Iran—possess nearly two-thirds of world oil reserves, while the region as a whole likely holds three-quarters of the global total. Fully a quarter of the world's natural gas supplies also likely lie beneath the Persian Gulf and its littoral nations.

Just as important for the U.S.–Japan relationship, Japan is overwhelmingly dependent on the Gulf for its oil and, to a lesser degree, for its gas supplies. It gets 90 percent of its oil and slightly more than 20 percent of its gas from that volatile region.[10] Those ratios are among the highest on earth and have been steadily rising over the past decade. The United States is much less dependent, getting only 21 percent of its oil in 2007 and virtually none of its gas from the Persian Gulf.[11]

Washington has, to be sure, crucial interests in the stability of the broader global energy regime and also in the security of Israel. These strategic concerns transcend its narrower national energy stakes and provide a crucial rationale for some sort of continuing American geopolitical involvement in the region. Japan, by contrast, clearly has a strong energy and economic interest in the stability of the Middle East, especially the Gulf, and few political-military means to assure it. This transpacific asymmetry regarding Middle East affairs—entering on the stability of the Gulf and access to it—provides one of the most important political-economic rationales for the U.S.–Japan alliance, especially from the Japanese side.

Russia also figures importantly in the Middle Eastern stability equation, especially in its geopolitical dimensions. It is a neighbor to the Middle East, as shown in figure 7.1, bordering both Iran and Turkey to the north. This geographical propinquity is a matter of utmost importance in global terms, especially when viewed in conjunction with the energy equation.

Figure 7.1. Strategic Neighbors: The Middle East and Russia

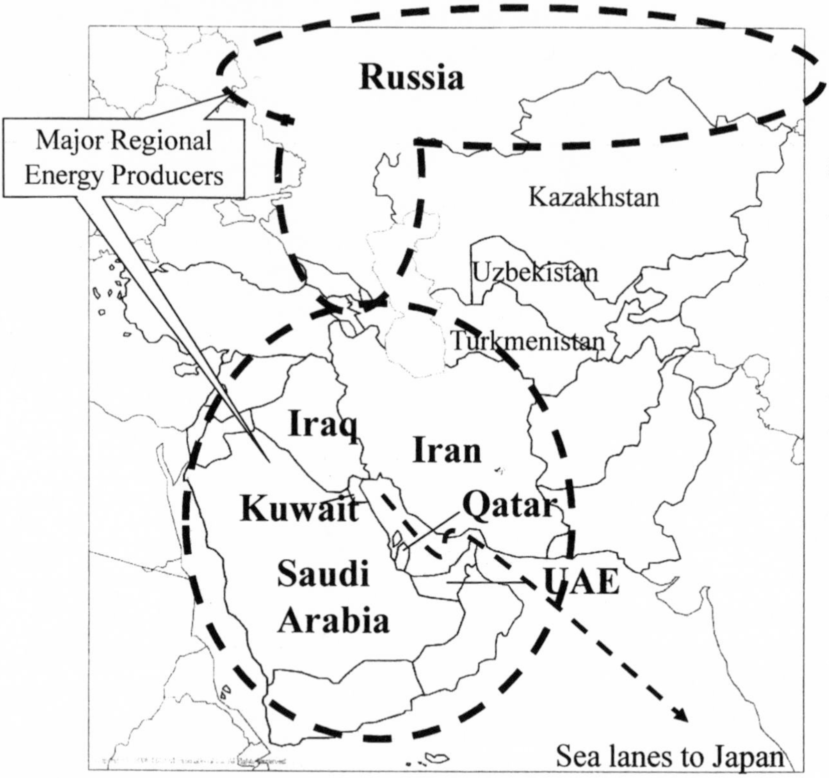

Note: The map has been adapted.

Russia is also a strong complement to the Persian Gulf in the world of energy, with roughly one-third of proven world gas reserves and another 10 percent of global oil. Russia and the Middle East together thus hold around 70 percent of proven world oil reserves and 67 percent of global gas, as indicated in figure 7.2. Together, they have the potential to exercise a controlling influence on a resource of vital importance to both the United States and Japan, which are the two largest energy importers in the world. The former Soviet "near abroad"—primarily Central Asian states over whose energy access to the broader world Russia continues to hold substantial sway—contributes another 6 percent to the world gas and 4 percent to the world oil equation, thus compounding Central Eurasian dominance with respect to global energy supply.[12]

Several of the most crucial emerging security issues that confront the United

Figure 7.2. Energy Reservoirs: The Middle East and Russia

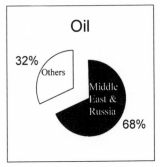
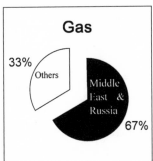

Source: British Petroleum, *Statistical Review of World Energy* (2007 edition).
Note: Figures represent percentage shares of global reserves.

States and Japan in the unitary global political economy now emerging thus relate to stability in the Persian Gulf and surrounding regions. There is, first of all, the question of political-economic stability in the countries concerned. This is a crucial question with respect to Iran, the largest of the nations bordering the Persian Gulf, and also Saudi Arabia, which holds a quarter of the world's oil reserves, not to mention Iraq. These countries face enormous looming demographic and employment challenges and joblessness over 10 percent in some Persian Gulf countries. Yet the GDP of all the Gulf Cooperation Council (GCC)[13] nations combined—oil wealth notwithstanding—remains less than that of Spain alone.[14]

Apart from this stability issue, there is the pressing question of how Russia and the Middle East, immediate neighbors that they are, will relate to one another politically and diplomatically in future years. Confrontation and enflamed relations between Russia and the world of Islam are not, in the post–Cold War era, in the interest of either the United States or Japan, as they could exacerbate the already delicate and volatile ethnic balance of the region. Yet neither has intimate and plausible understandings with the other, especially with respect to energy pricing and supply.

Russia and the Middle East in combination have extraordinary market power in both oil and gas, which could be especially threatening to deficit nations like Japan that lack their own energy supplies. There is a geopolitical dimension here of which the United States too must be aware, with the U.S.–Japan alliance, Japan's vulnerability, and recent Russian efforts to use energy as a geopolitical tool magnifying that imperative of understanding. Supported by the leverage provided by high oil prices, the Russian state is consolidating control of the domestic energy production under national companies, while shifting its pro-American policy toward confrontation over the Iraq war and Iran,[15] while inviting non-Western investment to develop the East Siberian oil fields.[16]

Deeply linked to the fateful questions of Middle East stability and Russia–Middle Eastern collusion is the critical issue of the energy sea-lanes. These delicate avenues of commerce are growing steadily more important, especially for Japan, which has by far the highest dependency on Persian Gulf energy supplies of any major nation on earth. The energy sea-lanes are also growing ever more contested, as the volume of oil and liquefied natural gas passing along them rises inexorably, to a broadening panoply of nations.[17] In 2006, eleven million barrels of oil passed daily through the Strait of Malacca and its environs.[18] Fifteen years ago the vast bulk of this Strait of Malacca transit oil was going to Japan. Yet now Japan must share this vital commerce, and the strategic energy sea-lane across the Indian Ocean to the Persian Gulf, with China, Korea, India, and ASEAN as well.

Relating closely to the question of Middle East stability is the burning issue of terrorism. This is not, of course, solely an Islamic question, as those who remember the KAL airliner and the Rangoon bombing incidents perpetrated in the 1980s by North Korea will vividly recognize. Yet in recent years terrorism has been primarily linked to the Muslim world. Most terrorist suicide bombers, after all, including those attacking the World Trade Center and the Pentagon on 9/11, have been Islamic fundamentalists, and most have hailed from the Middle East.

Given the present and prospective future turbulence of the Middle East, under virtually any scenario, as well as that volatile region's linkages to a troubled but energy-rich and increasingly assertive Russia, the availability of alternatives to Middle Eastern and Russian energy is patently a deepening global-security imperative. As Thomas Friedman points out, the United States, through its extravagant energy consumption, is placing itself in the thrall of a host of unsavory dictators, while also laying waste to the global environment.[19] Accelerated conservation and alternative energy programs—areas in which Japan is a global leader—are definitely needed. Promoting clean coal technology (CCT) is one such initiative. During the decade 1996–2005, Japan conducted nearly six hundred CCT transfer projects in developing countries, which was an important step forward.[20]

There is a growing international consensus that global warming is inexorable, threatens to precipitate major natural disasters, and needs to be a central human security priority. The United Nations Environment Program (UNEP) report (2007) indicates that 40 percent of the world's population could be adversely affected by a loss of snow and glaciers on the mountains of Asia. Even a 20 percent melting of the Greenland ice cap and a 5 percent reduction of its Antarctic counterpart would provoke a four- to five-meter rise in sea levels around the world. A mere one-meter rise in sea level would, unless preventive steps are taken, expose more than 145 million people to flooding, Asia being the continent most disastrously affected.[21]

Globalization has provoked historic shifts in the international distribution of economic resources. It has produced deepening growth differentials and income inequalities worldwide, burdening particularly the poorest of the poor.[22] Between 1973 and 2000, economic output doubled in the OECD nations, tripled in the Asian NIEs, yet nevertheless dropped 10 percent in 168 other faltering nations of the world that are home to fully one-third of the entire global population.[23] By 2000 the richest 1 percent of the world's people were earning considerably more than the poorest half, the combined wealth of the world's two hundred richest individuals amounting to over $1 trillion.[24] This concentration was far more extreme than even a decade or two before.

Viewed from a geographical perspective, globalization appears, in particular, to have left Africa, with its eight hundred million people but only 3 percent of world output, largely outside the charmed circle of world prosperity. The income of its poorest forty-three nations dropped 25 percent in the last two decades of the twentieth century, giving the entire continent, by the year 2000, an economy smaller than that of either Italy or California.[25] South Asia was similarly disadvantaged, although growth on the subcontinent began to accelerate somewhat from the mid-1990s.

The plight of the nonbeneficiaries of globalization was deplorable. At the beginning of the twenty-first century, between one-third and one-half of South Asian and sub-Saharan African children, or nearly 150 million children in all, were malnourished. Half of the two regions' women and one-third of their men could not read. Nearly 30 million Africans were infected with HIV, while twelve million had died of AIDS during the previous decade.[26]

Remarkable telecommunications advances have made us graphically aware of such human tragedies, so long obscured from human view. The Darfur genocide since 2003 in western Sudan, in which over 200,000 people have been killed and thousands of displaced refugees have starved to death, would likely never have emerged as a global issue before the era of the Internet. And the dramatic Myanmar monks' rebellion in 2007, which gained such worldwide prominence, would have been known merely through rumor and hearsay. World opinion creates ever-stronger pressures for such injustices to be addressed.

Globalization also, however, produces other historic economic shifts that are more heartening. It has, in particular, reduced the relative wealth concentrated among the G-7 nations, whose share of world GDP dropped from 62 percent in 1990 to 60 percent in 2005. Simultaneously, it has increased the global GDP share of the BRIC nations sharply, from 7.5 percent in 1990 to 11.6 percent in 2006.[27]

Apart from the Middle East, the other world region whose stability is of transcendent worldwide security significance in the post–Cold War world is clearly East Asia. That dynamic region, the fastest growing on earth, now has nearly a quarter of global GDP, 30 percent of international savings, and two-thirds of worldwide foreign exchange reserves, and it imports roughly a third more oil than North America. With the recent acceleration of growth in India, adding onto explosive ongoing trends in China and ASEAN, and considering the latent potential for expansion in continental Northeast Asia should a North Korean nuclear settlement be achieved, the prospect is that East Asia will grow ever more important in world affairs.

Yet Asia's stability is far from assured. Globalization, as suggested above, is affecting its key nations differently, accelerating the rise of China and India while contributing to Japan's relative stagnation. These historic shifts in relative growth patterns naturally generate geopolitical tension. And incipient Sino-Japanese rivalries, combined with the uncertainties of transition both on the Korean peninsula and across the Taiwan Strait, make U.S.–Japan security cooperation as well as Japanese economic revival increasingly critical for global stability.

The deepening security challenges in East Asia, it should be stressed, are qualitatively different from the conventional Cold War threats the United States and Japan confronted two decades ago. There is, to be sure, still a subtle deterrent dimension, especially along the Taiwan Strait. In that volatile quarter both Japan and the United States are committed diplomatically to one-China policies, although their peoples strongly insist that any resolution to the Taiwan question be peaceful. Yet many of the emerging regional issues, including Chinese and North Korean missile threats, terrorism, nuclear proliferation, drugs, and the dangers of disorder owing to transnational migration, are largely new and may require different mechanisms for resolution than have been considered in the past.

In sum, globalization has broadened and transformed the agenda between the United States and Japan, as illustrated in figure 7.3.

Figure 7.3. Challenges of Globalization in U.S.–Japan Relations

1950s: Security for Economics Bargain
• Basing Rights
• Administrative Control of Ryūkyūs

• Access to the Markets in the West
(Tolerant to Protective Japanese Markets)
• Security Functions

1980s: Altered Security for Economics Equation
• Basing Rights
• Capital Inflow, ODA to Strategic Allies of the U.S.

• Access to the Markets in the West
• Security Functions, including Sea Lanes

2000–: Globalization Broadens Agenda and Interests of the Two Allies

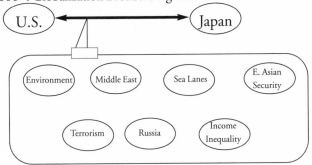

THE PRESSURES OF GLOBALIZATION:
IMPLICATIONS FOR U.S.–JAPAN RELATIONS

Before considering substantively the merits of emerging global issues, and how the United States and Japan might cooperate in addressing them, it is important to look back and reflect. The world today is dramatically different from the world that Dulles built, which privileged a devastated Japan and within which it rested secure. One needs to recognize how profoundly globalization has transformed the underlying logic of the U.S.–Japan alliance, the utility of accumulated alliance equities, and the effectiveness of traditional ways of realizing alliance goals. The impact has been especially pronounced on the economic side of the bilateral relationship. That has gotten comparatively little attention in recent years.

As we have noted throughout, starting with the very first pages of this book, the U.S.–Japan alliance has never been a purely military conception, even though recent myopic rhetoric has often treated it as such. To the contrary, the alliance has been an economics for security bargain since its very inception at the hands of Dulles and was clearly recognized as such until the 1970s. The terms of the bargain as well as its underlying logic may have changed profoundly of late, yet the political and the economic dimensions of the U.S.–Japan partnership remain intimately related, as they have always been.

Globalization, the most dynamic economic factor currently impacting on the Pacific alliance, has undermined the attractiveness for Japan of the economic dimensions of the underlying asymmetric bargain implicit in the San Francisco System. Through that arrangement the United States tacitly acquiesced for many years in Japanese protectionism within the Japanese domestic market. This behavior was often inconsistent with Japan's formal obligations of reciprocity under the Treaty of Friendship, Commerce and Navigation, but American authorities failed to press the issue very hard until the late 1960s and thereafter. Since the Nixon Shocks, of course, matters have changed, and globalization has further eroded the classic dividends for Tokyo, as we have seen.

For America, too, the original San Francisco bargain has been fraying at the edges, under the impact of deepening globalization. Perhaps most important, prolonged stagnation in the Japanese economy, following the collapse of the bubble of the late 1980s, exacerbated by the sustained outflow of Japanese capital and the depreciation of the Japanese yen, has forced Tokyo to cut its ODA, which has fallen by a third since 1999, and also its defense spending.[28]

The waning of the Cold War and the advent of the information revolution, both also ultimately driven by globalization, have also arguably undermined U.S. security dividends implicitly contained in the Dulles San Francisco bargain. A major attraction for the United States of that bilateralist arrangement, after all, had classically been the availability of military bases in Japan, including Okinawa. The attractiveness of Okinawa basing was long enhanced by administrative control of the Ryūkyū Islands as well. That allowed the American military much more operational flexibility than it would have enjoyed in a mainland Japan inhibited by the constraints of its "no war" constitution.

The political-military benefits for Washington were first eroded in 1972, when the United States returned the Ryūkyūs to Japan. They were further undermined by technological change. That allowed satellite reconnaissance, for example, to assume surveillance functions traditionally filled by ground stations and regionally based reconnaissance aircraft. Although the floating bases concept advocated in the mid-1990s proved too costly at Henoko in Okinawa, it was technologically feasible and loomed as another potential alternative to traditional bases in Japan, should the political and economic costs of alternative traditional facilities prove exorbitant.

There have always been, to be sure, significant nonintelligence strategic benefits to the United States of basing in Japan, especially in Okinawa, owing to its proximity to the major political-economic centers of a rising, potentially hostile China. Those security benefits have been eroded recently by the development of long-range strike aircraft such as the B-2 bomber, which can carry out global missions from Guam and even from the continental United States. At the same time, the prospective security costs to America of forward deployment have risen. Although Japan has provided generous HNS in financial terms, defraying three-quarters of nonsalary local stationing costs, the potential human costs of deployment in Japan have risen owing to the rising range and accuracy of Chinese and North Korean missiles.[29]

Globalization has, finally, seriously undermined the traditional U.S.–Japan security bargain that Dulles struck by fueling the rise of rival third parties, particularly China, India, and South Korea. As noted, all these nations have proved to hold a dynamic global economic vision and to boast of a rapidly rising share of world GDP. These countries have an increasing strategic significance as prospective collaborators of the United States or even allies, especially in a post-9/11 world chronically divided between the ordered and the politically ungoverned parts of the globe, where terrorism is a salient security concern.[30] At a minimum, the emerging transregional role of these rising rival Asian powers, fueled by a globalization that privileges them because of their relatively efficient yet low-cost labor, raises important new questions about the very meaning of the traditional concept of a Tokyo/Washington–centric Pacific alliance.

Were the quintessentially bilateralist U.S.–Japan partnership to remain static, encapsulated in the traditional mold within which Dulles cast it, the fissiparous pressures implied by globalization could well destroy the Pacific alliance or render it irrelevant in world affairs. Globalization, however, also fortunately generates new opportunities, albeit often in the form of new dangers to be addressed. Challenges such as antiterrorism, the potential threat of a rising, global China, and the imperative of stabilizing the Middle East have already impelled the United States and Japan to cooperate with one another far beyond the original terms of the Mutual Security Treaty they signed at San Francisco's Presidio well over half a century ago. Global issues like these became catalysts for Japan to assume more responsibility on matters of worldwide security, as can be seen by the dispatch of SDF contingents to Iraq and the Indian Ocean; and of regional security, as can be seen by deepening U.S.–Japan cooperation on missile defense. Cooperation between Tokyo and Washington is clearly not enough to resolve transcendent global questions, but it can potentially serve as an important catalyst for broader global solutions, given the weighty mass of this partnership in international economic and financial affairs.

In that cooperative process, Tokyo needs to advise Washington, and vice versa, building on its expertise in the important nonmilitary dimensions of alliance. The most urgent substantive global challenges to policy, to summarize the preceding discussion, thus center on stabilizing the Middle East and on dealing with the environmental and energy-security problems that its instabilities, combined with the global overconsumption of resources, inevitably create. These challenges must be dealt with in a global system in which, as never before in world affairs, communication is faster, there is a greater variety of power resources, decision making is more complex, and active players in the international system are more numerous.[31] The United States and Japan are not alone in the system and must consider the interests of third parties, while preserving enough of a core trust, communication, and predictability between each other to justify the notion of alliance itself.

The original San Francisco bargain between the United States and Japan that Dulles and Yoshida forged may well now be outdated after half a century, even as the formal institutions and rhetoric remain. If this is the case, how should the U.S.–Japan alliance be recast, in all its multifaceted dimensions to retain relevance in the new global age now dawning? The following chapter will provide concrete policy prescriptions, based on the comparative and historical research offered in this volume. But first let us outline the general conceptual approach that we feel the very different and yet complementary strengths of the United States and Japan in world affairs suggest for meeting the global challenges now impending.

TOWARD A TRUE U.S.–JAPAN GLOBAL PARTNERSHIP

The U.S.–Japan alliance of the postwar years, as we saw in chapter 2, was distinctive in emerging from seven years of occupation, following a long and bitter Pacific War. In this sense it was similar to the U.S.–German postwar relationship. Yet it was sharply different from the Anglo-American alliance, the Anglo-Japanese alliance, or post-1972 U.S.–China relations.

Over the years the Pacific alliance between Tokyo and Washington has gradually shed the hierarchic flavor of its Occupation origins, to be sure. Yet any balanced global partnership of the future must fully eradicate the last traces thereof, which still remain. Such a partnership needs to exploit the contrasting yet complementary strengths of the two sides, building on those traits themselves, rather than on some hierarchical division of roles and responsibilities, however venerable it might be.

Meeting the global challenge must effectively utilize the awesome, near-hegemonic powers of the United States, to be sure. But that needs to be done by first recognizing those distinctive strengths of Japan that have broad international significance. It must consider the unique transcultural, democratic character of the Pacific alliance as well, together with the complex, dynamic character of the post–Cold War international system, described above.

Japan brings three crucial traits that resonate far beyond its shores to a potential U.S.–Japan global partnership: its triple character, as non-Western, democratic, and advanced industrial. Unlike that of Europe and America, Japan's culture does not flow from the Judeo-Christian heritage. Indeed, it gained broad, sustained exposure to that tradition little more than one hundred fifty years ago.

Yet despite its non-Western origins, Japan today is pluralist democratic, with periodic competitive elections and a free press. Since the early post–World War II period this pattern has been evident, but its roots are much deeper. Indeed, starting in the 1870s there was prolonged popular struggle, led by ex-samurais and wealthy local farmers, for broader suffrage, combined with public campaigns to force the government to both abide by the existing constitution and accept party politics. This struggle eventually led to universal manhood suffrage, the resignation of the last nonparty premier, Katsura Tarō, and the advent of Taishō democracy during the 1920s.[32]

Japan is internationally distinctive, finally, for its advanced industrial character. For a century and more, it was unique globally in being the only non-Western nation that was industrially advanced. Since the late 1980s South Korea has also joined that club as well as the league of democratic nations, with China and much of Southeast Asia now arguably following behind, at least in the industrial dimension. Yet Japan remains the most industrially advanced and the most mature.

The U.S.–Japan partnership is also unique in being one of the very few transcultural and transracial alliances between democracies in the entire world. As such, it has both a special advantage and a special challenge, in an era of globalization. The advantage is that the alliance can, through a more explicit division of labor between its partners than has been identifiable heretofore, reach out and thus help bridge the gap between the Western and the non-Western world. The challenge is the obverse of this strength: the Pacific alliance between Washington and Tokyo has a special problem of mutual understanding and internal cohesion that is greater than that facing any of the other partnerships that we consider here, except possibly the early twentieth-century Anglo-Japanese alliance, which ultimately collapsed.

These general considerations suggest a distinctive approach to the Pacific alliance and to U.S.–Japan global partnership (on which we shall elaborate in the concluding chapter). My approach is designed first to stabilize the alliance itself, in a turbulent world of deepening economic interdependence in which stability requires intimate transnational cooperation. It is also designed to enhance the global utility of the U.S.–Japan partnership, so that it functionally benefits those beyond the North Pacific itself.

Such an approach would have three basic components. First, it needs to reach out to the non-Western world. On this matter Japan, as a non-Western nation, and the world's second-largest economic power, should take the lead, with a special focus on the Middle East, India, and China. Energy and environmental ODA needs to be one major dimension. Medical assistance, including work addressing the human costs of nuclear weapons, such as the hospital that Japan built in Semipalatinsk, Kazakhstan, former Soviet nuclear-testing sites, should also be a part.[33] Islamic and pariah nations that do not deal directly with the United States—such as Iran under certain conditions—as well as more directly cooperative partners like the Gulf Cooperation Council, Jordan, and possibly Iraq in future, could be a part of such an initiative.

In addition to reaching out to the developing world, the Pacific alliance also naturally needs to reach out to constituencies at home. Historically, flowing from its Occupation roots and the difficulty of explaining political-military issues in a nation like Japan with a peace constitution, neither Japanese nor

American officials have done so very intensively. It has been far more convenient, and easier politically, to give the alliance a low domestic profile, despite the fundamentally democratic character of the two allied nations. The only time that most Japanese heard about the alliance was when there was an accident or other incident involving resident American military forces.

The days when the U.S.–Japan alliance can successfully keep a low profile, particularly concerning base relations, are effectively over. With the erosion of ruling Liberal Democratic Party dominance and the related escalation of political competition in Japan, both the media and the public are growing more inquiring. Information on heretofore arcane and delicate subjects like defense is diffusing ever more rapidly via the Internet. Meanwhile, a new generation of Japanese with no recollection of the early postwar era of American benevolence and no clear understanding of either Japan's enormous economic scale or the commensurate responsibilities it entails grows increasingly irreverent, self-interested, and uninterested in alliance equities. This group tends to judge the alliance more and more clinically, in terms of the concrete benefits it provides, without a perception of the perverse global consequences of such a narrow, overly pragmatic approach.

Meanwhile, in the United States, weariness with global commitments is rising, in the wake of an Iraq War that early in 2007 passed America's entire World War II involvement in duration and an Afghan conflict that has continued even longer. As in Japan, the question increasingly rises in American minds as to what utility the U.S.–Japan alliance—or any alliance, for that matter—actually has. In a post–Cold War world of rapidly proliferating interests and connections, Americans, like Japanese, are growing more skeptical of the abstract value of particular international relationships and more prone to judge them individually on their concrete merits.

To be credible in the increasingly important domestic politics of the United States and Japan, in short, as alternate rival allegiances proliferate in a globalizing world, the Pacific alliance needs increasingly to appeal to both the personal interests and the idealism of citizens in both nations. It needs to appeal to their cultural concerns, to resonate with their personal networks, and to complement their economic interests. These broader dimensions of the transpacific relationship, in short, are what generate real alliance equities, and they are becoming increasingly important in determining the viability of the narrower military partnership itself. Their role as the true foundation of alliance is growing increasingly clear, and it is strengthening the social foundations, and not only the military superstructure, that we address in the chapters to come.

Chapter 8 Alternative Paradigms

The U.S.–Japan alliance, as we have seen, is a remarkable yet fragile relationship, viewed in historical perspective. One of the first major ongoing international security partnerships to bridge oceans and cultures and arguably the most enduring, it has its origins in war and occupation. It has had unusual economic, social, and cultural challenges with which to contend. Yet it has evolved, nevertheless, since the late 1990s, into a remarkably potent, if unbalanced, military configuration, making substantial positive contributions to the national security of both nations and to global stability.

The challenge for the future is to stabilize, deepen, and legitimate this remarkable artifact of international affairs while correcting distortions in its underlying structure. The challenge, in short, is nothing less than achieving a renaissance of the Pacific alliance. A reasoned response to that imposing task necessarily involves two aspects: understanding and prescription. My approach has been to address both dimensions through the powerful, and yet still strangely underutilized, tool of comparison.

In previous chapters we have struggled to understand the current

challenges confronting the alliance through comparison with other developments in the U.S.–Japan relationship's own past. They have shown that success
in managing the alliance has been frustratingly uneven. Yet they have also
demonstrated that success correlates strongly with the development of alliance
equities—particularly supportive policy networks attached to top-level leaders, together with comprehensive attention to the economic, cultural, and social as well as military dimensions of the transpacific relationship.

The challenge for the future is to constructively prescribe. In doing so, we
look internationally at four alternate bilateral paradigms:

1. The Anglo–Japanese alliance (1902–23);[1]
2. The Anglo–American alliance (since 1941);[2]
3. The U.S.–PRC relationship (since 1971);[3]
4. The U.S.–German partnership (since 1955).[4]

Each provides, in a unique way, kernels of insight to edify the search for ways to
enhance and strengthen the U.S.–Japan alliance as it exists today.

PARADIGM 1: THE ANGLO–JAPANESE ALLIANCE
(1902–23)

Consummated formally as the Anglo–Japanese Naval Treaty of January 30,
1902, this alliance was Japan's first major formal security commitment, at once
global and geostrategically conscious. Originally inspired by Germany's efforts
to divert Russian attention from Europe toward Asia, this historic cross-cultural partnership was a central element during its early years in the global
strategic game of power balancing. It was designed to contain Russian ambi-
tions in Asia at the turn of the twentieth century and to help maintain the
global strategic status quo, not only in the Pacific, but also in Europe, by blunt-
ing the late nineteenth-century rise of czarist power.

In the East Asian regional diplomacy of the day, as on the global stage, the
Anglo–Japanese Naval Treaty also figured importantly. For Japan, it cleared the
way for further advances in Korea, which Tokyo ultimately annexed in 1910.
The treaty also forestalled the prospect of further Triple Interventions in
Northeast Asia that might rob Japan of its conquests and began to integrate
the powerful British navy with Japan's fleet in war planning across the western
Pacific.[5]

For Britain, the alliance also had considerable strategic utility across the pre–
World War I decade, in global as well as regional terms. It foreclosed the possi-

bility of a Japan–Germany deal, otherwise uncomfortably plausible for White-hall, in view of the considerable pro-German sentiment in Tokyo, especially in the ranks of the army, which had been trained by the Prussians. This agreement reduced the need for retaining large naval forces in the Far East, allowing the Royal Navy to recall them home to weigh in the scales of the deepening, fin de siècle Anglo–German naval rivalry.[6] By forcing the Russians to preoccupy themselves with Northeast Asia, the alliance also relieved czarist pressures against Afghanistan and India, where British strategic interest was strong.

Less than two years after concluding the Anglo–Japanese treaty, Japan had attacked the Russians at Port Arthur. And within a year thereafter it had de-feated the czarists in a historic naval victory at Tsushima and established a pro-tectorate over Korea. Tokyo thus rapidly and actively exploited the strategic benefits of alliance, even as Whitehall enjoyed them in more passive ways, through increased latent defense capabilities against the kaiser's rising navy.

Japan's Proactive Alliance Role

At the onset of World War I, Japan dutifully declared war on Germany and oc-cupied Tsingtao as well as German mandates in the South Pacific. It thereby manifested an aggressiveness which Britain did not particularly welcome—es-pecially the Twenty-One Demands of 1915, which Japan forced China to swal-low without the full consultation of its British ally. Still, Japan filled its global alliance role by patrolling in the Indian Ocean at Britain's request and sending cruisers and destroyers to the Mediterranean, primarily for troop transports and antisubmarine operations, in accordance with the treaty.[7] This global ac-tivism far beyond Asia contrasted sharply with Japan's pronounced post–World War II quietism in worldwide security affairs.

In the early years of the Anglo–Japanese treaty, especially under President Theodore Roosevelt, the United States was seen to be a tacit supporter, quietly encouraging the Japanese and the British to cooperate in balancing an expan-sionist czar. Yet a decade and more later, with the United States also a rising Pa-cific power and with the Russian Revolution having eliminated the czarist geopolitical threat, many in Washington came to view the Anglo–Japanese treaty as a cover for aggressive and needless Japanese actions in the Far East that could adversely affect U.S. interests. Many Americans also saw it as a relic of the nefarious prewar era of secret bloc diplomacy that had ultimately provoked World War I.

As Britain and Japan began discussions on treaty renewal in the fall of 1920, the outgoing administration of Woodrow Wilson seemed willing to accept its continuation, with some modifications. The incoming American secretary of state, Charles Evans Hughes, however, was adamant. Pointing to growing Japanese military power and World War I activism in China, he insisted that any renewal would only encourage Japanese imperialism, which already seemed to be rearing its head.[8]

Key groups in London and Tokyo well appreciated the diplomatic leverage that the now-venerable bilateral agreement gave them. For some in Whitehall, it was an especially attractive vehicle for maintaining imperial influence in the Far East, even as Britain's financial ability to sustain global commitments declined.[9] Tokyo was generally supportive too, although the business world, led by large *zaibatsu* such as Mitsubishi, did not want to persist at the cost of alienating the United States.

During the Washington Naval Conference of 1921, a deal was finally struck. The Anglo–Japanese naval alliance was formally abolished, and an amorphous Four-Power Treaty—signed by the United States, Britain, France, and Japan and binding the signatories only to consult in the event of a Pacific crisis, with no action provisions—took its place. The death of the alliance, contrary to the desires of diplomats and military leaders in both Tokyo and London, came about through informal cooperation between Secretary of State Hughes and Japanese business interests, represented by Japanese Vice Foreign Minister Shidehara Kijūrō, the son-in-law of the Mitsubishi Group founder, Iwasaki Yatarō.[10] Thus, in the 1920s, as in postwar years, did economic pragmatism trump geopolitical ambition in the Japanese foreign policy process.

Strengths and Weaknesses of the Alliance

Looking at the experience of the Anglo–Japanese naval alliance in comparative perspective, one notes that three elements present in combination a provocative alternative paradigm to U.S.–Japan alliance politics today. First, the earlier alliance facilitated dynamic, proactive political-military initiatives on the part of Japan, such as the Port Arthur attack in 1904. Late-Meiji Japan was, in short, by no means a "reactive state."[11] To the contrary, Japan used the alliance as leverage for an extremely proactive diplomacy, especially under Foreign Minister Komura Jutarō, in the fateful years before Port Arthur. Its successful attack on czarist Russia (1904), its declaration of a protectorate (1905) and then annexation of Korea (1910), and its actions against German colonies in the Pacific (1914–15) were all enabled by the alliance. Japan did not hesitate to take advantage of the fresh opportunities for expansion that tacit British support provided, without any external prodding at all.

Second, the Anglo–Japanese alliance had a weaker economic dimension than its postwar U.S.–Japan counterpart. The two countries did, to be sure, make provisions in the earlier case for some limited preferential Japanese access to British markets, and vice versa.[12] The scale of tariff concessions, however, was small by post–World War II standards. Although Britain provided Japan with significant loans and diplomatic support for railway concessions in China during the period of the alliance, the share of bilateral trade in the two countries' global trade actually declined during the alliance's duration.[13]

An exception to the relatively weak linkage of economics and security was the arms trade. Japan's Imperial Navy imported British naval vessels in bulk, with the inventory of British-made Japanese naval tonnage peaking around the time of the Russo-Japanese War. Indeed, Britain's share of major new ship orders from the Japanese navy rose from 57 percent during 1878–95 to 82 percent of Japan's total during 1896–1906, before dropping precipitously to only 6.2 percent during 1907–21.

Partly to reinforce the Anglo–Japanese alliance, British defense firms such as W. G. Armstrong Whitworth, as well as Vickers Limited, invested in Japan to establish two joint-venture companies, Japan Steel Works and Japan Explosives, both of which in turn licensed British technology. Armstrong relied on the Japanese navy for around 30 percent of its sales during the period 1880–1910. Meanwhile, the six major British arms exporters to Japan accounted for around 20 percent of Japan's naval procurements on average during 1890–1900. It would not be hard to imagine these companies being, like the British Admiralty, ardent supporters of the Anglo–Japanese alliance. Their arms trade began to dwindle, however, as Japan gradually developed the capability to produce weapons independently after 1910, falling to a mere 4 percent by 1920.[14]

Despite the lack of formal economic provisions, common financial and humanitarian interests—including, although not limited to, "common values"—linked Britain and Japan, especially in the early years of the alliance, giving their partnership more durability than would otherwise have been the case. In April 1904, for example, after the Japanese Treasury failed to float large loans to fund the Russo-Japanese War, Jacob Schiff, the powerful CEO of the Kuhn Loeb investment banking firm, worked with his friend Baron Walter Rothschild to block Russian loans in London and Paris. Then Schiff put together the first major flotation of foreign securities ever successfully offered in New York City, on behalf of Imperial Japan. In total, Schiff helped Japan float four bond issues, for a total of $350 million, which funded almost half of the entire cost of the war for Tokyo.[15] This all would likely not have occurred had it not been for the legitimacy conferred on Japan in London financial markets by the Anglo–Japanese Naval Treaty, combined with the opprobrium visited on the Russians by the vicious pogroms occurring simultaneously in their homeland.

Financial interests again shaped the profile of alliance toward the end of the war. To further its economic development and to ensure the option of further autonomous political-military action beyond the Russo–Japanese War, Tokyo strongly aspired to secure an indemnity from Russia at the end of the conflict. This was the one result it was unable to achieve, stirring tremendous popular backlash in Tokyo. The financial constraints flowing from failure to secure an indemnity, however, no doubt inhibited the prospect of further Japanese imperial adventures in Asia, at least until the onset of World War I. The leverage that the Anglo–Japanese alliance provided Japan in proactive intra-Asian diplomacy was thus heavily contingent on its ability to borrow from Western investment banks.

Finance was important again, nearly two decades later, in provoking the demise of the Anglo–Japanese Naval Treaty. Much of the opposition to the treaty in the early 1920s came from American investment bankers like Thomas Lamont of JP Morgan, who saw the pact as destabilizing in Asian regional affairs. And the crucial concessions within Japan that provoked Tokyo ultimately to acquiesce in the treaty's demise came from influential bankers and businessmen, such as Shibusawa Eiichi and the Mitsubishi group, who presciently feared the destabilizing impact for Japanese foreign policy of confrontation with the United States.

A third consequence of the Anglo–Japanese alliance was to forge and deepen interpersonal networks, with major political-economic implications over time. Many Japanese naval officers, including Admiral Tōgō Heihachirō, hero of the Russo–Japanese War, studied in allied Britain. Promising businessmen such as Katō Takaaki, later to be the son-in-law of Mitsubishi's founder, Iwasaki Yatarō, were also dispatched to London. In strategic discussions of the Anglo–Japanese alliance, thoughtful Japanese leaders such as Admiral Yamamoto Gonbei consistently emphasized the value of educational and cultural exchange, in reinforcing long-term Anglo–Japanese ties.[16]

This priority in Tokyo on cultural familiarity with Britain, however, did not survive, succumbing to a deepening alienation, as the alliance itself eroded in the aftermath of World War I. Yamamoto Isoroku, the brilliant architect of Japan's Pearl Harbor attack in 1941, belonged to the generation succeeding Tōgō and failed to follow Tōgō's academic passage to England. Ironically, he became a special student at Harvard instead. In the business world, Mori Tsutomu, a prominent Mitsui alumnus later to serve as vice foreign minister under Prime Minister/Foreign Minister Tanaka Giichi during 1927–29, similarly lacked experience in the United Kingdom. The number of Japanese naval officers studying in Britain dropped sharply, from 457 during 1868–1923 to only 172 during 1923–41, between the termination of the Anglo–Japanese Naval Treaty and the outbreak of World War II.[17]

As in Japan, so also in early twentieth-century Britain the navy had a strong say in Asia policy. The voices of Admiral David Beatty, Admiral Ernle Chatfield, and other senior advisors who had worked with the Japanese since the 1900 Boxer siege of foreign legations in Beijing a generation earlier were highly valued. Such leaders were impressed by the integrity and efficiency of the Japanese military and contributed their positive, legitimating sentiments in London to the creation of the Anglo–Japanese alliance. Japan's contribution in the Mediterranean during World War I also deeply impressed the influential naval minister Winston Churchill, which was another personal factor reinforcing the alliance in Whitehall.[18]

Under pressure from a severe German U-boat challenge that threatened its naval supremacy, Britain in 1917 asked Japan to dispatch a cruiser and twelve destroyers to the Mediterranean—a crucial link in the imperial sea route to India. Japan accepted, on condition that Britain support both the Japanese occupation of German Pacific colonial territories north of the equator and its position in Shantung. The U.K.'s reaction was lukewarm.

Despite Tokyo's dissatisfaction with Whitehall's response, the Japanese imperial fleet was ordered to support the Royal Navy: escorting of British troops across the Mediterranean would enhance the Japanese image. The Japanese Imperial Navy ultimately escorted 788 British vessels and 700,000 Allied troops on 348 occasions, losing in the process several hundred sailors and a destroyer. Fully satisfying the British requests, the monthly mobilization rate of the Japanese ships, indicating the percentage of vessels being pressed into service at any point in time, was 72 percent, compared with a British level of 60 percent and French/Italian ratios of 45 percent. The Japanese also frequently risked lives to save passengers fleeing from torpedoed vessels, prompting the *London Times* to praise them for "speedy arrival and seamanlike ship handling" as well as "good seamanship and great rapidity of action." In 1917, the British Parliament adopted a resolution of thanks to the Imperial Navy, while King George V invited Chinda Sutemi, the Japanese ambassador, to Windsor Palace to personally express his nation's gratitude.[19]

It was not only the uniformed military that deepened Anglo–Japanese rela-

tions. State visits by the respective royal families and nobility of the two countries also contributed to strong alliance ties. In 1902, for example, Prince Komatsu, a distant cousin of Emperor Meiji, was invited to the coronation of Edward VII, though the ceremony was ultimately postponed because of the king's
appendicitis (he subsequently suffered a heart attack).[20] Nevertheless, the
prince was warmly welcomed to London. Similarly, from the British side,
Prince Arthur of Connaught, for whom many Japanese of the period came to
have great regard and affection, visited Japan three times and presented the Order of the Garter to Emperor Meiji in 1906. The next year, Prince Fushimi was
sent as a messenger of appreciation to London, and he visited there again in
1910, sadly attending the funeral of the suddenly deceased Edward VII. In 1911,
Prince Higashi Fushimi, an uncle of the earlier imperial envoy, attended the
coronation of George V, accompanied by the Russo-Japanese War heroes Tōgō
Heihachirō and Nogi Maresuke, while the next year Prince Arthur of Connaught visited Japan once again for the funeral of Emperor Meiji.

In 1918, King George V conferred on Emperor Taishō the title of Marshal of
England, and Japan reciprocally presented George V with an analogous rank.
These warm exchanges of royal visits and honors ended, however, in a remarkable degree of coincidence, with the expiration of the Naval Treaty in 1921. The
Prince of Wales (the future Edward VIII) visited Japan the following year, making a positive impression on the Japanese people, but his journey was the last of
the high-level reciprocal visits. The evolution of royal networks and alliance relationships, in short, covaried closely with one another, the end of the alliance
in 1923 precipitating a broader chill in bilateral Anglo–Japanese elite relations.[21]

To be sure, some nostalgia and residual respect remained. Emperor Shōwa,
who reigned across more than six decades of war, occupation, and, finally, the
democratic rebirth in Japan (1926–89), wrote to his brother Chichibu, who
was studying in England, that he had learned "freedom as a human being" for
the first time while in the United Kingdom.[22] These liberalizing voices and
personal relations, however, quietly died out for a generation and more with
the rupture of the Anglo–Japanese alliance and the perverse changes in the international environment that sadly followed in its wake.

PARADIGM 2: THE ANGLO–AMERICAN
ALLIANCE (SINCE 1941)

In recent years, influential American policymakers have suggested that the Anglo–American relationship is the most appropriate paradigm for future U.S.–Japan relations. Richard Armitage was particularly enthusiastic about this concept. An influential blueprint for his tenure as deputy secretary of state during the first George W. Bush administration (2001–05) maintained that "we see the special relationship between the United States and Great Britain as a model for the alliance."[23] Armitage personally echoed this sentiment on many occasions thereafter.

This ambitious contention merits serious scholarly analysis in three dimensions. It requires, first of all, examining the Anglo–American relationship of the twentieth century itself, to determine how substantial and effective that partnership as a whole actually was and how consequential it proved to be in global affairs. Second, it also requires disaggregating Anglo–American relations and identifying subnational practices and institutions that have proved especially useful and those that have not. And it involves, finally, an effort to determine what in that intimate Anglo–American partnership is readily transferable to a U.S.–Japan setting. The cultural and historical context of the two bilateral alliances is obviously sharply different, the United States and Britain being ethnic relatives who fought side by side in several major conflicts across the twentieth century, while the United States and Japan lack both cultural familiarity and the powerful existential experience of battle comradeship.

To highlight the cultural and historical differences between Anglo–American relations, on the one hand, and U.S.–Japan ties, on the other, is not, however, to deny the serious possibility of identifying Anglo–American practices that could constructively be employed in strengthening the U.S.–Japan alliance, broadly defined. To the contrary, I argue here that there are important points of relevance in Anglo–American relations, just as in German–U.S. or Sino–American ties, that can be studied with profit by those desiring to strengthen and deepen the U.S.–Japan alliance. These are, however, mainly at the subnational level, and their identification requires more thoughtful analysis than is commonly employed by the pundits and policymakers who indulge routinely in broad, rhetorical generalizations.

**Key Elements of the British Approach to the
United States**

In trying to uncover relevant, cross-nationally transferable elements in Anglo–
American relations, it is useful to start with the British approach to the United
States. Britain, after all, is a middle-range power in political-economic terms,
one that is trying to influence the global American superpower. Its situation is
to that extent similar, as Walt points out, to that of many other nations in the
post–Cold War international system, including Japan.[24]

The Anglo–American relationship is not currently, nor has it ever been,
America's preeminent trading relationship, and rarely in the past century has it
been the most consequential in geopolitical terms. In 2007, Britain's GDP, for
example, was 5 percent of the global total, compared to 8 percent for Japan,
while Anglo–American trade was only $107 billion, or 51 percent of that be-
tween the United States and Japan in 2007.[25] Britain's military budget today is
only one-tenth that of America.[26]

Yet ever since the early days of World War II, Britain has persistently characterized its ties with Washington as a special relationship and found considerable
resonance among American policymakers in that contention. Despite substantial British political-economic decline since then and the steady ascent of
American global superpower, and despite recurring "paranoid perceptions,"[27]
the Anglo–American "special relationship" has had a "Lazarus-like quality" of
persistently rising from the dead.[28] It thus has had a remarkable intensity and
resilience that can be studied with profit from a comparative public policy perspective.

Over the past three generations, there have been seven central elements of
the British approach to Anglo–American relations:

1. A preoccupation with steering American policy, rather than balancing American power
       The fundamental approach was laid out in a classified British Foreign Office
   paper of March 21, 1944, entitled "The Essentials of an American Policy."[29] It
   argued farsightedly that the traditional policy of balancing British power
   against that of the United States was no longer appropriate, given American
   preeminence, and that the United Kingdom's objective should instead be to
   single-handedly harness American power to British ends. The report stated, "If
   we go about our business in the right way, we can help steer this great unwieldy
   barge, the United States of America, into the right harbor. If we don't it is likely
   to continue to wallow in the ocean, an isolated menace to navigation."[30]

2. A belief that it is best to steer the "unwieldy American barge" from onboard rather than from the "surrounding oceans"

Britain has, from the days of Churchill, generally operated on the assumption that it could retain credibility with American policymakers only if it were willing to reflexively back U.S. policy once it was conclusively decided in Washington, even at the cost of national sacrifice. As the British ambassador to the United States Sir Robin Renwick put it in 1996, a prime British objective should arguably be to "help ensure that the United States is not left alone to respond to crises in which the interests of the West generally are engaged."[31] To this end, Britain sent its troops to fight alongside American soldiers in Korea (1950–53); provided strategic bases for nuclear-armed American aircraft and submarines throughout the Cold War; and backed the United States again militarily in the Gulf War (1991), in Afghanistan (2001–), and in Iraq (2003–). The one case in which Britain did not do so— the Vietnam War—demonstrated to many British eyes the pitfalls of non-cooperation, because personal ties between President Lyndon Johnson and Prime Minister Harold Wilson suffered substantially as a consequence.

3. Developing an intimate style of Anglo–American consultation and collaboration

This tradition, a hallmark of the "special relationship," was grounded in the close cooperation during World War II that led General George Marshall, chairman of the U.S. Joint Chiefs of Staff during that conflict, to claim in 1945 that the Anglo–American partnership represented "the most complete unification of military effort ever achieved by two allied states" in the history of warfare.[32] Beginning with the Arcadia summit conference of December 1941–January 1942, the two countries had frequent, highly personalized leadership meetings at many levels. They also created a series of Combined Boards that played a crucial role in the direction and coordination of the Allied war effort.

Long after the end of the war and the death of his wartime counterpart Franklin D. Roosevelt, Churchill, whose mother was American, adamantly promoted this intimate, highly personalized style of Anglo–American consultation. In preparation for his January 1952 Korean War consultations with President Harry Truman, for example, Churchill insisted on "a few informal meetings or meals" rather than an agenda meeting and was adamant that "it would not be worth while going unless we were 'a deux.'"[33] He also insisted on meeting old acquaintances such as General George Marshall individually and on seeing other key officials like Defense Secretary Robert Lovett one on one rather than jointly with larger groups of subordinates.[34] This pattern of informal consultation continued over the years, particularly during the administrations of Ronald Reagan and Margaret Thatcher; Bill Clinton and Tony Blair; and George W. Bush and Tony Blair.

4. Getting involved in American thinking at an earlier stage than other nations

British decision makers have long understood that Washington policy making is typically a complex process with a long gestation period and that early access is consequently critical to shaping ultimate policy outcomes.[35] They have made a point of seeking out meetings with American leaders so frequently that they are invariably able to uncover budding initiatives at an early stage of decision. As Henry Kissinger pointed out, reflecting on his personal experience, "it became psychologically impossible in American policymaking to ignore British views . . . given meetings so regular that autonomous American action somehow came to seem to violate club rules."[36]

5. Intimate and extensive defense and intelligence cooperation

In the final analysis, the core of the Anglo–American special relationship is an extraordinary level of security cooperation, including joint air force planning, intelligence coordination, and even collaboration on nuclear warhead design. Both nations, to begin with, are nuclear powers and cooperate intimately in that realm. Their intelligence services, including America's Central Intelligence Agency (CIA) and Britain's MI6, also reportedly engage in flexible, ongoing confidential information exchange, as do their Treasuries and central banks. Both the United States and Britain have global intelligence and financial intervention capabilities as well as subtly different perspectives that complement one another, thus making collaboration particularly attractive in such areas.

6. Joint public diplomacy

British and American leaders have often emphasized their close personal relationships, as epitomized during the administrations of Churchill and Roosevelt, as well as Thatcher and Reagan, and have often appeared together on symbolic occasions. In many cases, they literally stand together, for example, in formal photographs at G-7/G-8 summit meetings. When President George W. Bush addressed a joint session of Congress on September 20, 2001, in the shadow of 9/11, Prime Minister Tony Blair was present in the gallery, in another typical gesture of support.

7. Using "common history" and "shared values" as a rationale for justifying and perpetuating early, privileged entrée into American decision making

Again, it was Churchill who established and perpetuated this pattern. In his classic Fulton, Missouri, Iron Curtain speech of March 5, 1946, Churchill referred repeatedly to "fraternal association" and "mutual understanding" between two "kindred systems of society" as the basis for an Anglo–American "special relationship" that was urgently needed to confront a Communist order with dramatically different values. Over time, Churchill's strong commitment to Anglo–American partnership and his wartime collaboration with the United States became a reinforcing symbol evoked by other leaders. In November 1995, for example, Bill Clinton announced to a joint session of the two British Houses of Parliament that one of the newest and most powerful American surface ships, the thirty-first Arleigh Burke–class guided missile destroyer, would be christened the *Winston Churchill;*[37] similarly, on the eve of Bush's first presidential visit to the United Kingdom in July 2001, British Ambassador Sir Christopher Meyer presented the president with a fifty-five-year-old bust of Churchill. Evocations of Churchill and the wartime partnership have frequently—and successfully—been used by the British, in particular, to reenforce their traditional early access to American decision making.

Atlantic defense cooperation was firmly established during World War II. Between 1940 and 1942 so many Joint Chiefs of Staff meetings and other working-level meetings were established that in early 1942 it was said that "it was as though the British government was functioning in duplicate on both sides of the Atlantic."[38] Preliminary nuclear cooperation started in 1940, the two countries formally agreeing to share technology in 1943.[39] In the area of intelligence cooperation, British authorities provided the United States with substantial intelligence on Germany and, by 1944, had agreed even to complete American participation in ULTRA, the sophisticated, top secret British effort to break German military codes.

With war's end, the honeymoon abruptly ended. In 1945, President Truman suddenly suspended the Lend-Lease Act, which had greatly aided Britain, while working-level officials debated reimbursement prices of wartime Lend-Lease supplies and began dissolving the numerous joint wartime coordination mechanisms. In 1946, the McMahon Act, which prohibited the sharing of nuclear secrets with foreign countries, including the U.K., passed the U.S. Congress, ironically encouraging London to foster its own independent nuclear base.

The Berlin Blockade of June 1948, however, prompted the U.S. and the U.K. to cooperatively develop a draft of the North Atlantic Treaty Organization (NATO) to be signed in April 1949. Britain hosted ninety American B29s by

September 1948, showing strong political commitment to the delicate notion that the United Kingdom was a vulnerable potential front in the event of war with the Soviet Union. During 1948–50, the Burns–Templer Agreements, a series of bilateral landmark security understandings, were signed, which allowed for unlimited information sharing between the two allies in the area of guided missile technology. Britain sent 15,700 troops to fight in Korea (1950–53) and announced a £4.7 billion rearmament plan, to which the United States added £7 billion as military aid.[40] This support from Washington helped Britain to maintain its status as a global power for some time, albeit precariously. Firmly determined to focus American post–Korean War attention on Europe, Foreign Minister Anthony Eden succeeded in uniting Western Europe in support of German rearmament within NATO, with the British military steadfastly maintaining its forces in Germany after the German sovereignty agreement of 1955.

As the head of the Commonwealth, however, Britain was displeased to be excluded from ANZUS in 1951, fearing a decline in British influence in the Pacific as a potential consequence. American leadership in the United Nations' Korean War effort also illustrated London's dwindling power in Asian security affairs.

Along with the success of Britain's first nuclear experiment, at Trimoulle Island off northwestern Australia in 1952, the return of Churchill to 10 Downing Street in 1951 and the elevation of his wartime comrade Eisenhower to the White House in 1953 brought a further deepening of the Anglo–American alliance, particularly in the strategic and nuclear dimensions. Since the passage of the U.S. Atomic Energy Act of July 1958, Britain has received preferential information on the design and production of nuclear warheads and fissile material. In late 1962, Britain also acquired the Polaris submarine-launched missile at a bargain price.

In the 1970s the Labour government's secret Chevaline program to update Polaris renewed the Anglo–American nuclear partnership, especially in testing, fissile materials, and technology exchange.[41] In 1982 Britain secured the highly sensitive Trident II missile system from the United States and in 1984 agreed to the politically controversial deployment of cruise missiles in Britain. Throughout the postwar period, Britain has hosted highly sensitive American Strategic Air Command (SAC) bases, at which nuclear weapons are routinely deployed, as well as advanced early-warning systems.[42]

The cooperative spirit so well developed in the strategic and nuclear areas from the dark early days of World War II spilled over into other fields as well. In 1957, for example, in the wake of Sputnik, Eisenhower offered to deploy Intermediate Range Ballistic Missiles (IRBMs) to Britain. The United States and Britain also undertook coordinated military interventions in the Middle East during 1957–58, when U.S. Marines landed in Lebanon and British paratroops deployed to Jordan at the request of the respective national leaders, President Camille Chamoun and King Hussein. Working in tandem, Britain supported the U.S. Navy in the Mediterranean and provided access to its Cyprus bases, while the Americans furnished air transportation and logistical support for British troops in Jordan.

Despite the two countries' extensive cooperation, the Anglo–American relationship confronted two serious shocks during the early 1960s: the Cuban missile crisis and the Skybolt missile controversy. In the Cuban missile crisis of 1962, the British were disturbed by the cold reality that the major decisions shaping their security future were made entirely on the U.S. side, the British being reduced to "hapless bystanders."[43] The second blow, "a bolt out of the sky," came in the same year when U.S. Secretary of Defense Robert McNamara announced Washington's unilateral decision to abandon the joint Anglo–American Skybolt missile program. The news came after Britain's decision in 1960 to stop the producing of its own Blue Streak missiles so as to switch to the projected Skybolt.[44] Mistrust and anti-American sentiment spread in the United Kingdom, and the United States was compelled to supply alternative Polaris missiles at a very low price.

The mid-1960s brought "admirable working relations" between McNamara and British Defence Minister Denis Healey, especially in achieving defense spending economies.[45] At this time the United States was allowed access to naval facilities on the strategic British Indian Ocean Territory island of Diego Garcia, which by 1971 had emerged as one of the most important power-projection bases in the world.[46]

The Anglo–American partnership was clearly complicated by the British refusal to dispatch troops to Vietnam during the Vietnam War. Anglo–American relations were further worsened in 1967, when Britain announced its intention to withdraw its troops from east of Suez, a declaration that Washington vigorously protested. The British bias toward isolationism under Wilson was demonstrated again in 1971, when Britain announced the end of its role as the protector of the Middle East and summarily withdrew its troops from the Persian Gulf, once again disappointing Washington. This was followed by London's decision to significantly reduce its military deployments in Singapore, Malaysia, Hong Kong, Cyprus, Mauritius, and the Mediterranean, including Malta.

Anglo–American relations were dampened even further by differences over the Indo–Pakistani War of 1971 and the Yom Kippur conflict in 1973.

Britain's sweeping military retrenchment coincided with crucial U.S.–Soviet arms control negotiations, culminating in the 1972 SALT I treaty and the follow-on SALT II treaty of 1979. These important strategic talks were concluded without the United Kingdom, demonstrating further the steady decline of Britain as a world power. They also graphically confirmed exclusive American preeminence within the alliance on global issues and an inclination to limit consultation with London on such matters.

By 1974, however, Anglo–American atmospherics were beginning to turn for the better, owing to deepening transatlantic concerns about the Soviet Union's continuing military buildup. The United States and Britain resolved to help strengthen NATO by standardizing their military equipment within NATO and encouraging broader collaboration in arms procurement.

This defense cooperation was not just a "one-way" transfer from the United States to Europe; it was reciprocal. In 1970–71, for example, the United States imported British-made Harrier vertical/short takeoff and landing (VSTOL) aircraft for use by the U.S. Marines in Vietnam. This represented the first arms imports by the American military since World War I.

During the 1980s, the close personal friendship between Thatcher and Reagan helped to further consolidate the Anglo–American alliance. Despite its important ties to Latin America, the United States provided Britain with access to important military and diplomatic intelligence during the 1982 Falklands War. Britain reciprocated with involvement in the Lebanon intervention of the early 1980s and with support for the 1986 American air operation against Muammar Ghadaffi's Libya. Britain proved to be the only European country allowing local-base access for U.S. attack fighter-bombers. During the first Gulf War (1991), Thatcher also strongly supported the United States, deploying more than thirty thousand British troops in the conflict. Britain also backed America in Operation Desert Fox (1998) as well as in the invasions of Afghanistan (2001) and Iraq (2003).[47]

Drawbacks in the Special Relationship

The special relationship has involved substantial costs and dangers for Britain. First, it has arguably narrowed the options available to British diplomacy. As Ambassador Renwick pointed out, "The price of consultation has always been presence and participation."[48] Close British involvement with Washington limited Whitehall's European options during the 1960s, especially with France, for example. And it similarly intensified both domestic British and broader European criticism of Tony Blair nearly two generations later.

The special relationship with Washington has arguably also given London an exaggerated view of its potential role and capabilities. It has made the United Kingdom feel that it is the consort of a superpower, appropriately revolving with the United States and, for many years, the Soviet Union in the preeminent realms of diplomacy, even as in political-economic terms it was, over the 1960s and 1970s, steadily descending into middle-power status. This disjunction between Britain's continuing role in the rarified realms of high-octane global diplomacy and its modest actual power resources opened the prospect of sudden shocks, such as the Suez and Skybolt disappointments and related "paranoid perceptions," as it justifiably feared a repeat of such demeaning shocks at some random, unexpected time.[49]

Lessons for Japan?

Several crucial differences between Anglo–American and U.S.–Japan relations naturally limit the relevance of the special relationship between Washington and London for America's allies in Tokyo. Ethnic ties across the Atlantic are much stronger, and there are intimate nuclear dimensions to the Anglo–American partnership against which many in Tokyo would recoil. For U.S.–Japan military-intelligence coordination to achieve the intimacy it has reached between Britain and the United States, there would have to be fundamental changes in Japanese official secrets legislation and in informal political practice, changes which many in Tokyo would reject. And as for transatlantic-style financial cooperation, there would need to be a more transparent Japanese bureaucracy, greater freedom for senior officials from political constraints, and a more decisive and internationally responsive Japanese policy process.[50]

Yet despite the caveats—which make the Armitage paradigm of Anglo–American relations as the appropriate model for the U.S.–Japan alliance ultimately unrealistic and inappropriate—there are certainly elements of the Anglo–American partnership that students of U.S.–Japan relations can study with profit. Most crucial, the political importance of frequent, informal consultation at the early stages of policy formation is clear. So is the need for a clear rationale for such consultation and appropriate tactics for bringing it about.

Unlike Britain and the United States, Tokyo and Washington have no history of shared battle comradeship to rationalize frequent and intimate consultation. Indeed, the nuclear dimension of international relations divides rather than unifies them, in contrast to the Anglo–American pattern. Neither do Japan and the United States have iconic leaders from their shared past to play the kind of unifying role that Churchill does for the Anglo–American partnership. Nor can they make a really persuasive argument about common values, except in relation to China.

The shared foundations of the U.S.–Japan relationship will need to be different from those of the United States and Britain. Yet they will need parallel forms of consultation and parallel rationales for intimate partnership. The U.S.–British partnership shows, in its intimate consultation processes, the sort of relationship that the United States and Japan need to have, although it unfortunately does not provide a road map for getting there.

PARADIGM 3: U.S.–CHINA RELATIONS (SINCE 1972)

My principal concern in this book is understanding the dynamics of alliance relations. The United States and China are not formal allies or even strategic partners in any but a highly rhetorical sense. Yet it is naïve to deny that they have substantial and indeed growing rapport with one another, as evidenced by the vigor with which both nations pursued a Strategic Economic Dialogue, involving the bulk of their respective national cabinets, at a series of international meetings in 2006–08. The vigor of their relationship—despite the lack of alliance ties—is a useful point of reference for considering both the deficiencies of the U.S.–Japan relationship as it currently stands and also how it might be deepened and strengthened as it confronts a challenging future.

The Puzzle of Sino–American Relations

Empirical puzzles are a classic point of departure for theory building, and U.S.–China relations pose some intriguing paradoxes from a comparative standpoint. China, after all, is a Communist nation, one that fought the United States in the Korean War, and it has sharply contested fundamental American security policies for most of the three generations since. Washington and Beijing have sharp policy differences over Taiwan, Cuba, human rights, arms exports to the Middle East, energy, foreign investment criteria, and a wide variety of other questions. In 1999 U.S. war planes bombed the Chinese embassy in Belgrade, costing the lives of three Chinese journalists and triggering fierce protests from China. Beijing refused to accept the repeated apologies and detailed explanations from Washington and NATO.[51] And as recently as the spring of 2001, a Chinese fighter collided with an American EP-3 reconnaissance plane as it attempted to stop the U.S. aircraft's surveillance activities, killing a Chinese pilot and forcing the American plane to make an emergency landing on Hainan island. China released the crew eleven days later and the plane three months after that, only after the United States reluctantly issued a letter of the two "very sorries."[52]

Despite their substantial areas of disagreement and geopolitical rivalry, however, the United States and China have developed a remarkable ability to cooperate. The EP-3 confrontation, as threatening as it appeared while under way, was ultimately resolved and has not been repeated. Their substantial differences notwithstanding, the United States and China agreed on terms for China's accession to the WTO: Beijing entered that global body in 2001, with American support, after fifteen years of effort.[53] More recently, the United States has endured massive bilateral trade deficits with China—well over $200 billion annually—with relative equanimity. Those imbalances are more than three times the size of the deficits with Japan that generated far more political heat in Washington only a decade ago.

A second puzzle regarding Sino–American relations—one which may help unravel the first—is the pronounced and repetitive cyclical pattern in political tensions between the two countries. Since the advent of the Nixon administration, now four decades ago, the first two years of American presidencies have typically been periods of pronounced tension between the United States and China. Following the midterm elections of a president's first term, however, Sino–American relations invariably improve and persistently continue on positive terms until the next presidential campaign season. The presidencies of Nixon, Reagan, Clinton, and George W. Bush—all the reelected presidents in recent American history—show this pattern very clearly.

Economic Context: The Importance of Investment

Among the most striking features of the remarkably adaptive U.S.–China relationship is the importance of investment, especially inbound to China. Since 1993, except for the 1999–2001 aftermath of the Asian financial crisis, China has consistently been one of the top five foreign investment destinations on earth.[54] The PRC's combination of a large, rapidly growing domestic market, low labor costs, and good infrastructure makes it a primary destination for multinationals throughout the world. Yet comparative cost advantage alone does not necessarily assure active multinational involvement in the local economy of any given nation, as the long experience of India before the mid-1990s or Africa even today suggests.

The key reality for our purposes is that China has actively encouraged foreign direct investment (FDI), despite (or perhaps because of) its standing as a socialist country. Tax rates are reasonably low. Infrastructure is good. Membership in the WTO since 2001 also encouraged foreign investment—not least from Taiwan, where China's WTO commitments help clarify the otherwise highly ambiguous political-economic situation that Taiwanese firms face.

Five major factors appear to be working, at the national level, to give FDI considerable utility for China. First, China has massive developmental requirements, which support a felt need for continuous flows of capital, despite China's high domestic savings rate. Second, at the microeconomic level, FDI plays an important *functional* role in effectively privatizing and rationalizing the Chinese economy, which makes it attractive to modernizers in Beijing.[55] Third, FDI is extremely important in promoting Chinese exports, more than half of those exports being generated by foreign firms. Fourth, for certain groups in China that might otherwise be hostile to multinationals on noneconomic grounds, including potentially certain elements of the military, FDI is useful in creating political-economic hostages on the Taiwan question as well as in providing strategic technology needed for economic and military modernization.[56] Finally, during periods when Chinese political elites have been domestically vulnerable—notably following the Tiananmen incident of 1989—foreign investment has provided domestic political reinforcement and legitimization through its role in producing local prosperity and in intensifying the popular sense of China being accepted by and in constructive interaction with the broader world.

Responding to the positive incentives and building on economic logic, American firms have flocked to China. Motorola, Goldman Sachs, GM, AIG, Eastman Kodak, and Wal-Mart, for example, have all invested heavily and made China a cornerstone of their global strategies.[57] These commitments, and the PRC's willingness to accommodate them, in turn enhance their disposition to help underwrite a stable U.S.–China relationship, one that looms large in the overall architecture of American foreign policy.

The Key Intermediaries: Institutions and Networks

U.S. and Chinese economic interests, in short, are aligned in such a way as to create a positive environment for broader diplomatic relations, despite the absence of any security treaties—indeed, in the face of a fundamentally adversar-ial security relationship. Yet parallel interests do not automatically translate into cooperative policy outcomes. Also critically important to an understand-ing of *why* the United States and China get along so well—in spite of the geopolitical differences that realists would so readily identify—are the distinc-tive institutions and interpersonal networks that translate interests into policy.

Some of the institutions that contribute to the remarkable resilience of U.S.–China relations are fundamental pillars of the democratic political process. Congress and state governments, in particular, play generally support-ive roles that dampen the tensions arising from geostrategic friction. During the 1980s and early 1990s these pillars of grassroots democracy in America were oriented strongly toward Taiwan—indeed, it was Congress that passed the Tai-wan Relations Act in 1979, which to this day constitutes the legal basis for America's discreet, continuing informal relationship with Taiwan. Los Angeles, under Mayor Tom Bradley, flew the Taiwanese flag outside its city hall as re-cently as 1993. But since 1995, as mainland China's economy has gained mo-mentum and as Beijing has grown more pragmatic in its own political approach to the U.S. policy process, Congress as well as state and local governments have all grown ever more strongly oriented toward the PRC.

The Chinese government has skillfully used the deepening economic inter-est of America's grassroots in relations with China to strengthen political ties that might otherwise be quite precarious. Indeed, the PRC's recent political strategy has been the reverse of Japan's—grassroots rather than White House–oriented. It has often prioritized meetings with local business leaders, gover-nors, mayors, and congressmen over inside-the-Beltway activism.

Hu Jintao's visit to the United States in April 2006—in contrast to that of Koizumi in July 2006—is a good case in point. Hu spent four days in the United States, of which only a day and half were in Washington, D.C. He started with a visit to Washington State, the home of Microsoft and Starbucks and a major center for Boeing; Hu's short stay included a friendly visit with the governor. He included visits to facilities of Boeing and Microsoft, both of which have substantial business interests in China, and had dinner with Bill Gates, chairman of Microsoft, at his home.[58] Henry Kissinger, a key figure in engineering the U.S.–China rapprochement of the early 1970s, attended two meals with Hu in Seattle and introduced him at another dinner. Hu also held extensive informal meetings with business and civic leaders all over America.

The White House did, to be sure, embarrass Hu when a Falun Gong demon-strator intruded into the White House South Lawn welcoming ceremony for

Hu and when a White House announcer confused the official name of the PRC with that of Taiwan at the reception in his honor. The White House decided early on not to call his trip a state visit and denied the Chinese leader valued symbolic perquisites like a state dinner.[59] Indeed, Hu was accorded only salmon for lunch by President Bush, compared with the steak that Koizumi was served at a state dinner. Yet Hu's visit was arguably far more substantive, both with business and at the grassroots, than Koizumi's high-level escorted trip to Elvis Presley's residence in Memphis, Tennessee. The night before Hu left Washington, nine hundred people attended a farewell dinner in his honor sponsored by the U.S.–China Business Council and numerous other influential organizations in the nation's capital.[60]

China has also used procurement decisions effectively, to the same end of strengthening a bilateral relationship that would otherwise be under siege because of geopolitical pressures. Its cultivation of Boeing is instructive in this regard. China's aviation sector is growing explosively, air travel there having quadrupled since 1990.[61] Many of its existing aircraft are of ancient, unsafe Soviet vintage. Yet China has alternatives to Boeing, notably Airbus, and it has been shrewdly promoting competition to obtain the best terms for itself. It has kept Boeing apprehensive and has increased the company's incentive to use its considerable political influence in Washington on behalf of China, the world's fastest growing aircraft market. "We have the potential of a 100-fold increase in travel per person in a country of 1.2 billion people, and that's a huge market," Philip M. Condit, Boeing's chairman and chief executive, noted in 2000.[62]

Boeing undoubtedly has influence to wield. Producer of the B-29 bomber during World War II, it has a long and distinguished history as a defense producer and venerable ties and credibility with Capitol Hill flowing from that. It also has one of the most widely distributed domestic production networks of any American firm: some 10,000 suppliers scattered across 420 of the nation's 435 congressional districts.[63]

Capitalizing on Boeing's credibility with Capitol Hill and its immense network at America's grassroots, China has been strategic but generous in its contracting with Boeing. During President Hu's visit to the United States, he pointedly noted that Chinese airlines were expected to buy as many as two thousand planes over the next fifteen years, many of which would be built by Boeing.[64] As of late 2006, Boeing had contracts for about one hundred aircraft with various airlines in China and was importing parts worth $600 million from the PRC. Major Chinese-made parts could be found in roughly 34 percent of the twelve thousand Boeing planes in service around the world.[65] This symbiotic pattern could well persist far into the future, providing an important political-economic firebreak for geopolitical frictions in Sino–American relations.

While China itself generally keeps a low profile in most cases, it certainly does not discourage American business groups with which it has common commercial interests—led by Boeing, General Motors, AIG, Eastman Kodak, and Motorola—from speaking for themselves. Although the PRC is not among the top ten countries formally lobbying in Washington, behind the scenes Beijing quietly wields the stick of trade retaliation and the carrot of a vast domestic market to encourage American firms to do its bidding.

This strategy of indirection works well for Beijing and is one that other nations might seriously consider. Informal Chinese lobbying power helped, for example, to win repeated renewal of Most Favored Nation trading status for China each year throughout the 1990s. In 1995, Boeing took the lead in organizing the China Commercial Normalization Initiative, a long-term grassroots campaign now active in thirty states that was aimed at winning China permanent Most Favored Nation status as well as entry to the WTO. Under the initiative, Boeing and other firms acted as so-called state captains responsible for winning over congressional delegations. Boeing handled Washington and Kansas, where it had major factories producing for the Chinese market, while Motorola took Illinois and Texas, for similar reasons.[66]

Part of the formidable effectiveness that the China lobby still exhibits on Capitol Hill is no doubt historically embedded. The Taiwan lobby was among Washington's most powerful for three generations, from the 1930s until the mid-1990s, though with a partial hiatus during the 1970s, when the United States and the PRC were moving to normalize their relations.[67]

Taiwan's lobbying also complicated U.S.–PRC–Taiwan relations in ways that provoked Beijing to become more proactive and well versed in Washington. The announcement of Taiwanese President Lee Teng-hui's visit to the United States in 1995 badly shocked Beijing. China's initial response was to recall its ambassador, and demand that Taiwan suspend its lobbying campaign as a condition for improving relations.[68] Through such bitter experiences, however, the PRC also came to appreciate the importance of the role played by Congress, which had traditionally backed Taiwan, in American foreign policy. In late 1995, for example, China's Politburo organized a high-level Central Leading Working Group to study and understand the U.S. Congress. The Chinese embassy also began asking many American lobbying firms for advice on how to conduct public relations campaigns in the United States.[69]

The contrast to the U.S.–Japan dimension of Boeing's transpacific activities is instructive in suggesting options for the future of U.S.–Japan relations as well. For more than twenty years Japan has been Boeing's largest foreign customer and continues to be its most consistent one. Japan Air Lines (JAL) and All Nippon Airways (ANA), Japan's two largest carriers (and two of the largest in the world), fly Boeing aircraft exclusively, something few Chinese airlines do. ANA is the largest and most loyal customer for Boeing 747s, and, despite influential Airbus lobbying representation in Tokyo, Japanese carriers are not buying any Airbus A380s.[70] Boeing has 80 percent and 75 percent market shares, respectively, in Japan and Korea.[71]

Yet Japan seems not to get the political mileage with Congress for its strong support of Boeing that China does, even though China's backing is far more equivocal. From the congressional perspective, America's transpacific aviation alliance seems to be with China, not with Japan, notwithstanding the manifest loyalty of Japanese airlines to American brands. In crucial dimensions, the Chinese aviation lobby is both better organized and more assertive than that of Japan, although market conditions are clearly also a factor.[72]

In addition to the distinctive role of Congress and local governments in supporting stable U.S.–China relations, other specialized private bodies work actively to the same end. Indeed, U.S.–China relations probably have the largest network of support organizations in Washington of any American bilateral relationship, apart from cases in which strong ethnic ties prevail, such as U.S–Israel, U.S.–Greece, U.S.–Italy, and U.S.–Poland relations. Among the most important of these supportive intermediaries is the U.S.–China Business Council (USCBC).

A paired comparison of the USCBC to its counterpart in economic relations with Japan is highly instructive, helping to explain the remarkable resilience of U.S.–China relations in the face of the persistent geopolitical challenges that confront it. Founded in 1973, just as the United States and China were reestablishing economic ties after a long Cold War hiatus, USCBC has more than 250 member firms, including most of the major American multinationals dealing with China. The U.S.–Japan Business Council (USJBC), by contrast, has only 49 members, despite a history stretching back to 1948. The USCBC is also a unitary organization, operating not only in Washington but also in branch offices in Beijing and Shanghai.

The USJBC, by contrast, has no branch offices in Japan. Instead, it relies upon a local Amcham, the American Chamber of Commerce in Japan (ACCJ), for liaison with Japanese government and business as well as with American representatives in Japan. The ACCJ, dominated by businesspeople with long-standing experience in Japan, has subtly different incentives from those of the USJBC. In contrast to the situation in U.S.–China relations, the Tokyo-based ACCJ—with its own local ties and incentives "inside the castle"—is the more active interlocutor with the Japanese government. The Washington-based USJBC thus finds it complex and at times difficult to engage in systematic, concrete, and ongoing dialogue across the Pacific.

Once again, this situation contrasts sharply with the dynamic in U.S.–China relations. For embedded historical reasons—the need, between Nixon's visit to China in 1972 and U.S.–China normalization in 1979, for a credible semiofficial entity to coordinate bilateral trade relations—the USCBC is often accorded clear semigovernmental status within China. Its president, for example, who often travels to China, is typically given informal vice ministerial ranking at bilateral U.S.–China meetings. As noted, the USCBC also has, in contrast to its U.S.–Japan counterpart, small but effective local offices in Beijing and Shanghai. These offices directly support frequent high-level corporate visits from the United States and also provide a broad range of consulting and informational services, relying on their extensive and proactive policy networks in China.

U.S.–China relations also involve a host of other semiofficial support organizations that do not exist in U.S.–Japan relations, including the National Committee on U.S.–China Relations (NCUSCR), the China Institute, the U.S.–China Policy Foundation (USCPF), and the Committee on Scholarly Communications with China (CSCC). All are endowed with both tacit public support and semigovernmental functions.[73] The NCUSCR mainly supports informal discussions among intellectuals and former officials in the United States and China, building on its historic role as sponsor of the table tennis visit that preceded the historic Nixon–Kissinger visits of 1971–72.[74] The USCPF is another organization involving congressmen and intellectuals that promotes mutual understanding between the two countries.[75] CSCC, part of the American Council of Learned Societies, rather than pursuing political objectives like the other two organizations, plays a role as a catalyst of interactions among academics in the two countries.[76] The China Institute, a venerable body with highly contemporary functions, fosters U.S.–China networks and sociocultural understanding through activities ranging from an executive summit and varied elite social events to study-travel programs for teachers and artists as well as children's after-school workshops and summer camps.[77] Since 2006 it has been assisted in its efforts to enhance American understanding of China by the

Chinese government's support of a growing number of centers for cultural and language study, called Confucius Institutes.[78]

As a group, these bodies collectively perform several invaluable functions that have crucially helped to stabilize U.S.–China relations, including agenda setting, early warning, and public education as well as informal lobbying. They also help to accord U.S.–China ties special legitimacy and priority in the American policy process, despite or perhaps because of the mixed conflict and cooperation structure of relations between Beijing and Washington, D.C. While these mediating NGOs have some analogue in U.S. relations with NATO and, to a lesser degree, in American ties with Korea, they have no good parallel in U.S.–Japan relations, for a variety of historical reasons.

Most important, these private bodies with public functions help to *legitimate* the bilateral U.S.–China relationship—with the general American public and with U.S. policy elites. That has been a formidable task, considering the broad American public hostility toward mainland China during the Korean War, in which most of the thirty-seven thousand Americans killed there died at Chinese hands; during the McCarthy years; and across the ensuing generation.[79] Yet these groups, led by the National Council on U.S.–China Relations, have performed their conciliatory functions remarkably well.

How far the National Council and its sister organizations have legitimized postrevolutionary Sino–American relations, compared to the McCarthyite era, was manifest concretely in December 2003, when Chinese Premier Wen Jiabao visited the United States. The NCUSCR hosted an enormous dinner in his honor at the elegant Ritz Carlton Hotel in Washington, D.C. Attended by six hundred guests, the affair was cosponsored by eight influential local organizations: the U.S.–China Business Council, the America-China Forum, the Asia Society, the Center for Strategic and International Studies, the Committee of 100, the Council on Foreign Relations, the U.S. Chamber of Commerce, and the U.S.–China Policy Foundation.[80] Such massive supportive events held to welcome Chinese leaders and organized by wholly American sponsors are not unusual in U.S.–China relations. In striking contrast, U.S.–Japan events in Washington are typically government-centric, with a limited private sector involvement that contrasts sharply to the U.S.–China pattern. Many of the most important U.S.–Japan social events are held in New York, far from the Washington political process.

This important supportive infrastructure in U.S.–China relations, distinctive for its political-economic sensitivity, was the product of a critical juncture: it grew up during the seven crucial years (1972–1979) when the United States had a new and dynamic strategic relationship with the PRC, crucial in the Cold War with the Soviet Union, that was devoid of formal diplomatic relations. The United States was politically constrained by the Taiwan issue from moving toward the sort of formal bilateral embrace that mainland China fundamentally desired. Yet Washington nevertheless wanted to deepen strategic ties and pull the PRC out of the xenophobic isolation into which it had fallen during the Cultural Revolution. China, for its part, was willing to reciprocate on a track two basis. As a consequence, an intricate shadow framework of quasi-official NGOs grew up and, as we have seen, continued to play an important stabilizing role in the overall U.S.–China relationship even after full normalization.

The important intermediary institutions of U.S.–China relations have been synergistically reinforced by and have given encouragement to the other key supportive dimension of U.S.–China relations: its elite interpersonal networks. Interpersonal networks have considerable importance generally in transpacific relations for three reasons: (1) East Asian societies themselves are traditionally relationship-based; (2) transpacific information flows and political understandings are often highly imperfect; and (3) the configuration of problems as well as policy mechanisms for resolving them are highly fragmented, on both sides of the Pacific. Integrative networks are especially important in U.S.–China relations today, owing both to the unusual prominence of the intermediaries involved and to the way in which Chinese policy making has encouraged and perpetuated the continuing involvement of these intermediaries in the bilateral relationship with the United States.

By examining the dominant policy networks in U.S.–China relations and contrasting them with their U.S.–Japan counterparts one can better understand the paradox of the persistently positive relations the United States has enjoyed with the PRC in recent years, geopolitical rivalry notwithstanding. Indeed, the embedded history of interpersonal networks between the United States and the two major powers of Northeast Asia explains much of the paradox in positive U.S.–China relations, and it does so far better than realist theory or domestic structure arguments might. In particular, informal networks play a decisive role in the consistent improvement in Sino–American relations over time that has occurred in the course of virtually every U.S. presidential administration since Nixon in the late 1960s.

The key informal Sino–American policy networks were forged during a period when U.S. relations with China were uncertain, relatively egalitarian, and perceived to be fatefully important to America's future: the so-called Golden Age of U.S.–China–Japan relations.[81] This period lasted roughly from the beginning of Kissinger's normalization efforts with China during 1970–71 until the Tiananmen massacre of 1989. During those euphoric years, China was perceived as a key strategic partner of the United States against the Soviet Union. Interpersonal networking and information exchange became so intense that in December 1980 the CIA began a decade-long tradition of sending its Director of Central Intelligence (DCI) on obligatory liaison trips to Beijing.[82]

During the Golden Age of strategic cooperation, America's highest-level White House national security advisors, including Kissinger, Brzezinski, Haig, and Scowcroft, were also drawn into intense personal interaction with China. And they related to their Chinese counterparts as peers rather than as superiors (the latter attitude was prevalent in America's more formal alliance relationships).[83] Kissinger and Haig, for example, were principals in secretive early trips that opened the way for Nixon's visit to Beijing in 1972; they interacted with high-level Chinese officials like Huang Hua and Qian Qichen. Brzezinski negotiated much of the normalization agreement at the end of 1979 with similarly influential Chinese.[84]

The relatively balanced, intensely personal interactions of all these people with China, involving all the powerful existential trappings that such exclusive and exotic experiences could convey, contrasted with their more hierarchical, distant, and often frustrating dealings with Japan. The national standing of these key figures, coupled with the self-interest of American corporations doing business with China, has continued to shape the tenor of U.S.–China relations to this day. It has biased those ties in a more egalitarian fashion than is typical of a U.S.–Japan relationship that emerged from wartime Occupation. Indeed, high-level networks involving prominent national security advisors have given U.S.–China ties a unique and somewhat paradoxical legitimacy, given the underlying strategic tensions, which Washington–Tokyo relations under the Pacific alliance have often failed to enjoy.

Think tank activities and business interests, as suggested above, leverage the impact of national security advisors on policy networks and ultimately on policy making itself. Henry Kissinger, for example, played a key role, together with David Abshire, Zbigniew Brzezinski, Harold Brown, and others, in the development of the Center for Strategic and International Studies (CSIS) in Washington, D.C., serving for many years as head of its International Counselors group, from the late 1970s. CSIS in turn became a major informal stabilizer and mediator in U.S.–China and in cross-strait relations, supported by AIG, Boeing, and other major firms with a strong commercial interest in stabilizing U.S.–China and cross-strait ties.

The experience of negotiating with the United States in the Korean War armistice talks at Panmunjom also gave birth to influential networks for mediating U.S.–China relations, as did the informal Warsaw talks of the 1960s and 1970s and the normalization negotiations of 1978–79.[85] As Harry Harding and Yuan Ming have noted, "Despite the hostility and bitterness engendered by the Chinese Revolution and the Korean War, the immediate legacy of the period was a productive mixture of Chinese flexibility and American restraint that opened a channel for dialogue between the two countries in Geneva and Warsaw, and that helped somewhat to moderate their military confrontation in the Taiwan Straits."[86] Interestingly Kissinger's interaction with the PRC appears *not* to have had much enduring impact on transpacific networks on the Chinese side, despite its historic diplomatic role and the enduring importance of Kissinger-related networks in the United States. This anomaly may be due to Kissinger's personal negotiating style, which was so secretive and high level that it involved little of the Chinese government apparatus beyond very senior leaders who are now long gone.

Summit conferences, as a form of intense, if relatively routine, interaction, have also been a positive formative experience for Sino–American networks—not only for top leaders in question, but also for their bureaucracies and related interest groups. In some periods, especially the Nixon, Carter, and Clinton years, these gatherings were an important bonding experience for officials on both sides. They reinforced networks that continued long after government service, although they were probably not quite so important as the dynamic networking that the early, pre-1979 relationship stimulated. In the evolution of U.S.–China relations across the Clinton years, a relatively mature stage of the bilateral relationship, summits may have been especially important, as they provided a catalyst for the broad-based intergovernmental dialogues that became increasingly important as Sino–American economic interdependence deepened.

The Clinton years were a period of flux, following the end of the Cold War, during which the traditional strategic rationale for cooperative U.S.–China relations was undermined by the collapse of the Soviet Union. Sino–American relations were delicate throughout the first three years of the administration, culminating in Lee Teng-hui's visit to Cornell in 1995 and the Taiwan missile crisis of 1996. Yet an exchange of state visits (Jiang to Washington in 1997, and Clinton to Beijing in 1998), as well as the related invigoration of working-level ties, led to a sharp intensification of network interaction and bilateral policy communication. In recent years, two new high-level U.S.–China dialogues have been initiated: the U.S.–China Senior Dialogue under the auspices of the State Department; and the U.S.–China Strategic Economic Dialogue under the auspices of the Treasury Department. Each is intended to meet twice annually so that cabinet-level officials of the two countries can hold regular talks on key issues. Apart from these two major U.S.–China dialogues, at least eight more, including the Global Issues Forum, were previously established and are continuing.[87]

PARADIGM 4: THE U.S.–GERMAN RELATIONSHIP (SINCE 1955)

In each of the preceding three case studies there are elements that can be applied to strengthen the U.S.–Japan partnership in its fullest sense. Yet in U.S.–German relations—not in analogies to Britain, as some would maintain—one finds the most realistic and constructive overall paradigm; the strikingly similar strategic and political problems the two former adversaries faced in building their postwar bilateral relationship account for this. Germany's ties with America, like those of Japan, had their roots in wartime defeat and in Occupation. Like Japan, Germany had to transcend cultural barriers, linguistic differences, and lingering wartime hatred. Also like Japan, Germany loomed large in its region's geostrategic equation, providing an attractive proxy for American power if its delicate relations with wary, injured neighbors could be stabilized.[88] Germany, like Japan, was thus an attractive cornerstone of a "dual containment" strategy for American global dominance.

The early postwar U.S.–German relationship began from a point of much deeper subjugation and penetration by international forces than was true of U.S.–Japan relations.[89] In contrast to Japan, Germany was almost totally occupied by foreign military forces, physically speaking, before war's end, and much of it was occupied by a deeply embittered Red Army intent on total subjugation and economic dismantling. West and East Germany were subsequently integrated into incompatible and opposing economic and security frameworks, unlike Japan.

Yet the fundamental domestic political-military manifestations of the victor-vanquished postwar partnership, such as American troops on local soil, supported economically by the host government, and favored by Status of Forces Agreements (SOFAs), were similar.[90] So were patterns of defense technology cooperation, although those have evolved more fully in the U.S.–German case than in that of U.S.–Japan.[91] The two cases—one transatlantic and one transpacific—are thus similar enough to be comparable.

Considering the reunification of Germany, the sharp waning of East–West tensions since 1989, and important foreign policy differences between Berlin and Washington on major issues like the Iraq War, U.S.–German alliance relations have been remarkably stable and productive in recent years. They have involved a striking two-way flow of ideas that has significantly shaped American policy toward the Caucasus, Ukraine, Turkey, and other areas of common interest, without provoking superpower resentment. This mutuality stands in striking contrast to U.S.–Japan relations, where Washington has been frequently unresponsive, or sometimes even negative, toward Japanese efforts to engage on third-country questions ranging from Kashmir and Iran to the configuration of the UN Security Council and the recent concept of a Corridor for Peace and Prosperity linking Israel and Jordan.

Germany and the United States have also—both bilaterally and through broader transatlantic institutions—had a much more vigorous mutual economic dialogue than the United States and Japan. Their business leaders meet more often and have a more complex, realistic agenda.[92] This comity has helped deepen security relations by providing a supportive environment for defense-industrial cooperation and interoperability.[93]

The Sources of U.S.–German Synergy

Balanced economic interdependence is a cornerstone of the broader U.S.–German alliance. To be sure, trade interdependence between the United States and Germany is not nearly as deep as that between the United States and Japan overall. In 2006, for example, American trade with Japan reached $207 billion, while that with Germany was only $130 billion.[94] Yet transatlantic trade tends to be more balanced, with cyclical fluctuations in surpluses and deficits and without continuing, chronic asymmetries. U.S.–German direct investment interdependence is also much greater than in U.S.–Japan relations.

A few statistics are illustrative here. The stock of foreign investment as a share of German GDP was 18 percent in 2005, as compared to 2.2 percent in Japan.[95] And American investment in Germany included a much broader portfolio of industries—including major auto firms like GM and Ford—that are largely absent in Japan. These investment interests, which have created around seven hundred thousand jobs in Germany, are active participants in bilateral chambers of commerce and contribute significantly to the vigor of transatlantic business diplomacy.[96]

German–U.S. cultural and academic relations are also an established policy priority on both sides of the Atlantic, reflecting a conscious effort by both parties to address and move beyond painful historical issues between them. The German-American Fulbright program, funded jointly by the governments of the two nations, for example, is the largest in the world.[97] Each year an average of seven hundred U.S. and German students, scholars, teachers, administrators, and journalists take part.

Another striking area of difference concerns the relative configuration and vigor of bilateral policy institutions, especially those operating in Washington, D.C. Both Germany and Japan, to be sure, have substantial, well-staffed embassies, and official information centers. The critical difference comes in the nongovernmental and semigovernmental dimensions.

The heart of Germany's powerful nongovernmental presence in Washington is the German Marshall Fund (GMF), announced by German Chancellor Willy Brandt at the Harvard commencement in 1972, as a return gift in appreciation of George Marshall's original Marshall Fund proposal of 1947. Funded by the German government and German corporations and administered solely by American citizens, the GMF in 2007 had an endowment of $254 million, much of it provided by the German private sector, supplemented by American donors. The fund is currently managed by an exclusively American board of directors, giving it special legitimacy in domestic U.S. politics.[98] Over the past quarter century it has played, as we have seen, a remarkable role as an agenda-setter and sponsor of cultural exchanges in transtlantic relations, accenting the key role of Germany within that broader transnational dialogue. On some questions of major foreign policy interest to Germany, such as the future of Ukraine and the Caucasus, the GMF has played a highly strategic role in supporting underlying German interests, even though it involves no direct German supervision or personal leadership.

The Marshall Fund, energized by its huge endowment and deep integration with American society, engages extensively in grant making, particularly to journalists and NGOs. The GMF has also increasingly engaged in proactive research and agenda setting of its own. It has played an especially influential role in shaping the approach of both the United States and Germany to emerging democracies, particularly in Eastern Europe and the Middle East.

Germany's informal Washington presence goes far beyond the GMF.

Among other major manifestations are the Goethe Institute, a nonofficial cultural body with governmental support; the American Council on Germany; the American Institute for Contemporary German Studies; and the offices of six major political party foundations. These unique institutions are especially important in reinforcing the bilateral relationship.

In order to invigorate and deepen the political debate within Germany on matters of foreign policy, German government agencies like the Foreign Ministry provide substantial subsidies to foundations associated with political parties to maintain overseas offices.[99] All six major institutes have offices in Washington: (1) Friedrich Ebert Stiftung (SPD); (2) Konrad Adenauer Stiftung (CDU); (3) Hans Seidel Stiftung (CSU, the CDU's Bavarian counterpart); (4) Friedrich Naumann Stiftung (FDP); (5) Heinrich Boll Stiftung (Greens); and (6) Rosa Luxemburg Stiftung (Left Party). These bodies are especially active in liaison with Capitol Hill, taking advantage of their unofficial yet legislatively related standing to network on a flexible, egalitarian basis with members of Congress and their staffs. Their legislative connection and NGO standing give them special legitimacy and immunity from grassroots aversion to "junketing" in arranging dialogues and conferences—often overseas—between German and American legislators.

The Importance of Networks

Personalistic policy networks are as important in the Pacific as in the Atlantic, if not more so. One key reason is that personal relations are so salient in East Asian decision making. In both Japan and China as well as Korea and Southeast Asia strategic information flows are often subterranean and regulatory decisions commonly particularistic. In the view of most Asian policymakers, one perpetuates and enhances one's influence and understands where events are moving by cultivating crucial human networks. Miyakawa Tadao of Hitotsubashi University illustrated this point by likening the Japanese public decision-making system to "Political-Bureaucracy-Business Circle (i.e. Network) Building," in which the edifice has a foundation consisting of a network of school alumni and fellow citizens.[100]

Both Asian and American political economies are changing, with Asia's rising strength provoking special tensions with embedded hierarchical transpacific structures—the "basement of the system," in Miyakawa's parlance. Ongoing communication and policy networks are crucial in today's volatile world, and they are not invariably present when they are needed. Their gestation period is long. And formative experiences that do not occur every day, from comradeship in battle to old-school ties, are indispensable in building them.

Policy networks are crucial to effective alliance functioning everywhere in the world, as comparative analysis shows. In some places—notably in transatlantic relations, including U.S. relations with Britain, Germany, and the Benelux nations—the network infrastructure is well developed, continuing, and conducive to positive alliance ties, as we will see. In other cases, as in U.S.–South Korean relations, positive networks are long-standing, yet have been so tied to conservative domestic politics in the ROK that they have functioned only intermittently when opposing groups have held power. In Sino–American relations, ironically, positive networks have evolved outside of an alliance framework, mitigating geopolitical tensions that could otherwise generate a strong adversarial relationship. U.S.–Japan relations, as we will see, present a challenging case prospectively similar to that of South Korea.

Policy networks in transatlantic relations have an underlying cultural basis, of course. For the first three decades after World War II, when the NATO alliance functioned most dynamically, key leaders also shared profoundly meaningful experiences of solidarity in war and postwar reconstruction.[101] Paul-Henri Spaak is a typical case in point. Spaak's extraordinary career illustrates the existential network-building process at the interpersonal level that gave such strength and dynamism to transatlantic relations in later years.[102]

Born into a distinguished Belgian political family, Spaak was a German prisoner of war for two years during World War I. He served as prime minister of Belgium on the eve of World War II (the first of four occasions) and as foreign minister in exile throughout the war itself. While living for over four years in London as a prime symbol of continental European resistance to the Nazis, he forged deep ties with both British and American leaders in the common struggle against fascism.

In 1946 Spaak was elected chairman of the first General Assembly of the United Nations. Thereafter, he also played a formative role in European integration as the author of the so-called Spaak Report (1955), which proposed the customs-union framework culminating in the Treaty of Rome (1957). From 1957 to 1961 Spaak also served as secretary general of NATO, until being called once again (1961–66) to become Belgian foreign minister one last time.

Spaak, in short, served as Belgium's face to the world for three full decades. He forged profound ties to a broad range of top European and American leaders in the course of World War II and in leading the effort for transatlantic unity once peace had returned. Spaak, together with Eisenhower, Churchill, Jean Monnet, Allen Dulles, James Galvin, Bernard Baruch, and others who had lived together through the turbulence of World War II and its aftermath, imparted a stability, flexibility, and camaraderie to transatlantic ties in the uncertain shadow of war that infused that international relationship with enormous creativity in the early postwar years.

Complementing the longtime strength of trans-Atlantic policy networks at the interpersonal level has been their rising strength since the 1970s in more institutionalized form as well. This pattern has been well demonstrated over the past three decades by the multifaceted networking activities of the Federal Republic of Germany in Washington, D.C. Rather than pursuing the conventional Washington route of funding lobbyists to present the German position through formal consultations with expensive law firms, the German government, supported strongly by the German private sector, has created and systematically fostered a powerful NGO network. That network keeps Germany effectively informed of fast-moving developments in the United States and, by means of effective tools like the GMF, subtly helps to set American agendas in ways conducive to German interests.

The Trilateral Commission, originally proposed by John D. Rockefeller III with the explicit aim of integrating Japan securely into the fabric of G-7 political-economic relations, was a major force in transpacific relations during the 1970s and the 1980s. It played a significant role at a crucial stage in integrating Japan into the global community of nations. But in recent years, as its membership has aged and its financial difficulties have mounted, it too has become less active.

Another element of German networking is cultural exchange. The heart of this effort is the Goethe Institute, an independent cultural organization since 1976, although most of its funding comes from German Foreign Office and German Press Office grants. This body, which operates in eighty-three countries around the world, including North Korea, not only offers German language courses, but also sponsors extensive cultural programs that afford important U.S.–German networking opportunities. In 2006, for example, the New York office organized a film series; lectures on literature; classical, jazz, and rock music concerts; art exhibitions; dance performances; film screenings; and theater productions.[103]

Germany undertakes a number of specific programs in the United States that Japan does not pursue to a comparable degree but might constructively reference. The Marshall Memorial Fellowship Program, for example, is much larger than any counterparts in the Pacific, having over one hundred recipients annually and close to fifteen hundred alumni since the program began in 1982.[104] This program also operates, through the GMF, several active legislative exchange programs, including the Congress-Bundestag Forum; the APSA Congressional Fellowships (giving Germans an opportunity to work in congressional offices); and congressional staff study tours to Germany. The GMF also operates extensive journalist exchanges, public opinion survey programs, cooperative research efforts on topics like immigration, and defense policy study seminars for young leaders. Japanese counterparts have undertaken relatively few such activities in the context of U.S.–Japan relations.[105]

Few pairs of nations, in the rapidly globalizing world of the twenty-first century, face a more delicate, more complex challenge in maintaining alliance relations than the United States and Japan. The two nations are poles apart in cultural terms. After forming a fateful teacher-pupil relationship a century and a half ago, in the wake of Japan's opening by Perry's black ships, the United States and Japan had little historical interaction to speak of—apart from geopolitical rivalry, racial exclusion, and war—until little more than half a century ago. And many of the factors that bridge cultural and historical animosity in other contexts—direct foreign investment and elite social networks, for example— are underdeveloped in the U.S.–Japan relationship.

In the face of daunting challenges, U.S.–Japan relations since World War II have been remarkably smooth and placid. Yet they have narrowed, especially since 9/11, and focused on the military dimension. We have shown that there need to be other dimensions of alliance—a broader and deeper social and economic foundation, in particular—but we have also noted that those conditions remain ominously unfulfilled, even as competitive alternatives emerge.

Much, in short, can usefully be changed in U.S.–Japan relations, despite the seeming solidity of the alliance and the surfeit of congratulatory rhetoric about its soundness. To gauge what those changes might entail, I have turned to international comparison for alternative paradigms in this chapter. What have these revealed?

Clearly no other national pattern fully suits either Japan's or America's requirements. The two nations are too unique in their own character, America being the world's lone superpower and Japan the culturally unique, leading modernizer of Asia. Yet a hybrid model that draws on the best of several nations' qualities and points the way to a renaissance in the U.S.–Japan relationship is very much in order.

The U.S.–German model, while far from perfect in some dimensions, holds the largest share of relevant lessons for U.S.–Japan relations of any case examined. This is in a way natural because the challenges that the U.S.–German relationship has historically confronted are probably most similar to those of the U.S.–Japan alliance. Both Germany and Japan were occupied nations after being defeated in a world war; they recovered to become major allies of the United States, with substantial numbers of American troops remaining on their soil. Both needed to overcome historical memories and develop subtle lobbying capabilities to restore their traditional political leverage and credibility with the crucially important American ally.

Germany has accomplished these tasks—neutralizing historical suspicions and restoring its ability to help shape policy agendas in Washington—to a remarkable degree. The secret appears to have been its effective use of nongovernment institutions such as political party think tanks and the German Marshall Fund to both foster interpersonal policy networks and shape policy agendas. Support for American foreign investment and for the American troop presence in Germany has also had a positive impact on bilateral relations and, through them, on the alliance.

The Anglo–American alliance is an admirable institution, one involving strong military ties reinforced by extensive cross-investment and intimate cultural relations. It appears, however, to be far less relevant to the U.S.–Japan relationship than its German counterpart, as we have seen. This is true because the Anglo–American partnership—a league between cousins, after all—has never faced the challenges of overcoming language barriers and differences of perception flowing from such traumas as defeat in world war, as the U.S.–German relationship has done.

U.S.–China relations offer some surprisingly useful lessons for the U.S.–Japan alliance, even though no formal alliance is involved in the Chinese case. Those lessons relate particularly to the effective political use of FDI, at which the Chinese are masters, and the importance of social and economic networks unrelated to formal lobbying. Over the past decade the Chinese have far outpaced their Japanese counterparts along these dimensions, thereby becoming most effective operators in Washington, and there are concrete counterintuitive lessons to be learned.

The Anglo–Japanese alliance of prewar years, finally, also presents important reference points for its post–World War II U.S.–Japan counterpart. The global approach and geostrategically conscious character of ties a century ago between Tokyo and Whitehall contrast sharply with the more regionally specific and asymmetrical character of postwar U.S.–Japan relations. Yet those earlier features also no doubt usefully prefigure where the U.S.–Japan alliance in a globalizing world needs to be headed today—and tomorrow.

Based on these general prescriptions—the need for balanced economic and cultural dimensions to alliance, in addition to the military—it is useful to speculate more concretely about the future. The U.S.–Japan alliance faces a dramatically different world from that which either Americans or Japanese have encountered before. The challenge of confronting that uncertain world is deepening, and the people of both nations need to think long and hard together about how it might be overcome.

Chapter 9 Prescriptions for the Future

As has become clear across the past eight chapters, my method in this volume has been comparative—to cast the net as widely across both history and geography as possible in search of broad and relevant generalization. And my overriding objective has been prescriptive—to discover when and why alliances endure and then to identify best practices worldwide for sustaining them. The ultimate purpose has been to strengthen and deepen a U.S.–Japan partnership that Mike Mansfield justly called "the most important relationship in the world, bar none."[1]

THE POWERFUL RATIONALE FOR CONTINUING ALLIANCE

Some would question the importance of formal alliances in the more fluid world that has emerged since the collapse of the Soviet Union at the end of 1991. My analysis has suggested once again the importance of looking at the specific details of the U.S.–Japan case, which generate imperatives that are somewhat different from those that may prevail elsewhere. Whatever may be said generally about the strategic logic of alliance in the post–Cold War world, for Japan and the United States specifically the continuing rationale, we have found, is compelling.

As we have noted previously, the alliance continues to play some enduring roles in both countries: (1) inhibiting serious conflict between the United States and Japan; (2) arresting the emergence of an unstable balance of power world in Asia; (3) providing a nuclear guarantee to Japan; and (4) preventing an antagonist to American and Japanese interests from dominating the western Pacific. As World War II recedes ever further into history and as Pacific regional institutions and networks grow stronger, American consciousness of the first two points, and even arguably the third, erodes, and a defensive "stop China" rationale grows more salient. Yet the fundamental logic of all four classic systemic arguments for the U.S.–Japan alliance remains, for both partners.

The Chinese challenge is compounded, in Japan's case, by deepening political-economic interrelationships across the Taiwan Strait and by parallel ties between Pyongyang and Seoul, even as North Korea increases its chemical, biological, and nuclear capabilities in the wake of actual nuclear tests, and enhances its military delivery systems. Alliances matter for Japan, in particular, because of its relatively modest scale in geostrategic terms; the dangers of an arms race with a nearby rising China; North Korea's emerging WMD capabilities; the need for defense of energy sea-lanes to the Middle East; and the imperative of assuring stable relations with the United States. Alliance with America, in particular, is attractive owing to Washington's geopolitical preeminence, its global intelligence-gathering capabilities, and its importance in helping stabilize global finance and trade systems crucial to Japanese well-being.

For the United States, Japan is the inevitable strategic pillar of America's position in the North Pacific. It controls naval access to major Russian Far East, Korean, and North Chinese ports and lies directly adjacent to the Russian SLBM bastion in the Sea of Okhotsk. Japan also has sophisticated communications facilities, technologically advanced air and naval forces, and a powerful military-industrial base as well as one-eleventh of global GDP[2] and $1.3 trillion in gross savings.[3] It hosts the only American aircraft carrier home-ported outside the United States, the largest U.S. overseas air force base, and America's largest Marine Corps rapid-deployment force outside the Middle East, while providing $4 billion annually in HNS to sustain U.S. facilities financially. These assets, along with Japanese diplomatic cooperation, continue to weigh substantially in the scales of global affairs, despite the waning of the Cold War.

Since the early 1980s, Japan has also grown steadily more important to the

United States in political-economic terms, as we have seen. As the largest creditor in the world, it has neutralized the short-term financial and macroeconomic implications of America's massive current-account deficit—perhaps the only nation willing and able to do so. Without capital flows from Japan, American interest rates would undoubtedly be much higher, and American fiscal flexibility to pursue an active global foreign policy much more constrained than has historically been the case.

Japan, unlike India, China, the EU, or Russia, is not a vast continental power with a large population and numerous men under arms. Consequently, unilateral initiatives are, in principle, more difficult for Tokyo, and the value of allying with major powers commensurately greater. The strategic incentives for Japan to engage in cooperative action are strengthened by a domestic-political reality—the fragmented and consensus-driven character of Japanese decision making. This makes unilateral initiatives slower and more difficult than in many major nations. Tokyo, in short, benefits for many reasons from being shielded by a sturdy umbrella, given the heavy weather in its neighborhood. That indispensable umbrella is the U.S.–Japan alliance.

THE CHANGING POLITICAL-ECONOMIC CONTEXT

Although the strategic logic of transpacific alliance between the United States and Japan clearly continues, the political-economic context has shifted sharply over the past half century, creating a dramatically new set of political imperatives that remain dangerously unpursued. As we saw in chapter 2, the world that Dulles built in the early 1950s assumed a Japan alone with the United States in the North Pacific—weak and vulnerable, yet strategically important, and meriting indulgent, preferential treatment. Within both American and Japanese politics, there were few dissenters to this view.

The world of the early twenty-first century is dramatically different. China is massively larger, rapidly growing, interdependent economically with both the United States and Japan, and increasingly influential in both Japanese and especially American domestic politics. South Korea is also more active and influential in the Pacific. Both Tokyo and Washington have active competitors for their alliance partner's affections, and a "bypass phenomenon" is a real danger, in political-economic relations, especially for Japan. These new developments need to be the basis for realistic thinking about the bilateral U.S.–Japan future.

LESSONS LEARNED

As the strategic rationale for the Pacific alliance is so compelling, even as the political-economic context changes, we need to direct special attention to how the alliance can be realistically maintained and strengthened. Now it is time to review what we have learned regarding the fine art of sustaining vital partnerships like that between Washington and Tokyo. Then we will distill the implications for policy at this critical juncture in transpacific relations.

From our comparative and theoretical studies, we have come to see, first of all, that truly fruitful, well-functioning, and durable alliances are a rare breed. Alliances themselves have existed across history in various forms, to be sure, since at least the days of the Peloponnesian Wars, nearly twenty-five hundred years ago. There have also been a few long-standing alignments that predate the post-1945 era, such as the Anglo-Portuguese alliance, which has endured for a remarkable six centuries without interruption.

Yet such enduring partnerships have been distinctly unusual. Until recently, alliances were creatures of diplomatic and political-military convenience that typically lasted no more than a decade or two, if that. Naturally, strenuous efforts are needed to keep them vital and smoothly functioning.

A second, related discovery has been the deepening political-economic functions of alliances since the Korean War. Alliances have become, over the past half century, a vehicle for securing economic prosperity as well as military security, through mechanisms such as the Marshall Plan and the San Francisco System. Both of these provided economic assistance while opening American markets on an asymmetrical, selective basis to allies in Europe and Asia who agreed to host American bases and cooperate with U.S. strategic goals. In the most smoothly functioning alliances, the partners served both military and economic functions for one another, in balanced and mutually reinforcing fashion.

A third insight flowing from comparative analysis concerns the utility of the alliance equities concept. Where security alliances exist between highly interdependent democratic nations, the concrete socioeconomic stakes of subnational actors are an important determinant of alliance health and long-term viability. The concept of alliance equities captures that complex reality and is a useful barometer for tracking the domestic political health of alliances as well as for prescribing means of assuring their persistence.

A fourth, related insight is that when either the military or the economic dimension of an alliance fails to deliver substantial returns for the partners on a "win-win" basis, the alliance itself is in danger. Failure to deliver economic returns was arguably a principal reason for the ephemeral character of alliances in the prewar period, for example, while the persistent health of the economic dimension conversely contributed to the remarkable longevity of the Anglo-Portuguese alliance. On the other side of the coin, the decline of strategic bipolarity in the post–Cold War world has been a source of tensions for America's alliances across both the Atlantic and the Pacific, with some analysts even predicting "the end of alliance."[4]

A fifth observation is that political and cultural sensitivity, as well as trust, is crucial to sustaining both military and economic relations. They are crucial shock absorbers. This is particularly true under conditions of substantial economic or military interdependence. In such circumstances the destabilizing impact of intrusion into the partner's domestic sociopolitical fabric can be especially high, even as the imperative of stability in the relationship grows more substantial. And instantaneous communication via mass media and the Internet can magnify the impact of possible missteps still further.

HOW THE U.S.–JAPAN ALLIANCE CAN BE STRENGTHENED

Stable, win-win elements—in both political-military and economic dimensions—are the first and most domestic foundation for sustaining the U.S.–Japan alliance. The military side of the partnership, historically the weaker aspect, has deepened markedly over the past decade, in the shadow of the North Korean threat and the rise of China. There are important remaining tasks with respect to military transformation and missile defense, to be sure. Yet the technical military side of the Pacific alliance is in relatively good shape.

(1) Implementing Military Transformation Agreements

Between 1996 and 2006, the United States and Japan concluded an ambitious series of new agreements fundamentally deepening and transforming their alliance, as noted in chapter 6. While most of these have been implemented, the 2006 military-transformation package includes sweeping, transnational elements, some of which are not scheduled to be fully implemented until 2014. The package includes, for example, coordinated bilateral support for the relocation of eight thousand U.S. Marines and over five thousand dependents from

Okinawa to Guam, as well as the construction in Guam of related housing and other infrastructure.

The complex, interrelated pieces of the $26 billion transformation package depend on a timely resolution of the controversial Futenma Marine Corps Air Station (MCAS) relocation to Henoko in northeastern Okinawa. That move was agreed at the Clinton–Hashimoto summit of March 1996 but had not yet been implemented by late 2008.[5] Actual, on-the-ground progress on the Futenma issue is urgent because the redeployment of Marines to Guam cannot be undertaken until the Futenma redeployment occurs, and that movement is in turn related to larger, longer-term DOD planning and budgeting regarding the future profile of the U.S. military presence in the western Pacific, a matter of considerable political and national security salience in Washington.

For the sake of alliance credibility, some mutually acceptable plan for Futenma relocation is urgently needed. A clear-cut vision for how current military facilities at Futenma might be used after reversion to Japan could also help resolve the controversy and move relocation forward. History suggests that effective communication between the United States and Japanese national governments, on the one hand, and all key local Okinawa parties is vital. Ultimately implementation of the ambitious 2006 transformation package will be a key test of the U.S.–Japan alliance over the coming decade, regardless of political administration.

(2) Joint Defense Production

From a comparative standpoint, the unfinished tasks of the U.S.–Japan alliance in its military dimensions would seem to lie in the area of joint defense production. There are enormous complementarities between the American and the Japanese defense-industrial bases, reflecting the broader U.S. strength in service industries like software and telecommunications, and the contrasting Japanese strengths in precision manufacturing. These respective skills, however, took some time to develop. Under the original Mutual Defense Assistance Agreement between Japan and the United States, signed in 1954, Japan stood in a subordinate, receiver position with regard to technology, as in other dimensions of bilateral military relations, relying until 1967 on the Military Assistance Program.

U.S.–Japan defense-industrial cooperation has deepened steadily over the past three decades, although the process of integration has been slow and politically complex. Gradually accumulating advanced military technology through licensed production, Japanese defense firms during the 1970s and early 1980s came to excel in some fields dominated by dual-use applications, making cooperation with them attractive to the Pentagon. In 1980, the U.S.–Japan System and Technology Forum started as an unofficial body linking the two governments; its aim was to facilitate information exchange regarding defense systems and technology as well as licensing. Following an official request in 1981 by U.S. Defense Secretary Caspar Weinberger, Japan agreed to raise its level of defense technology transfer to NATO standards. Two years later, the two allies started a Joint Military Technology Commission (JMTC) to facilitate defense technology transfer. This mechanism allowed Japan to join the Reagan administration's SDI program in 1986 and to participate in the joint development of the FSX fighter from 1987. During the 1990s, Washington and Tokyo agreed to jointly develop ducted rocket engines, missile target seekers, and submarine degaussing.[6]

Today, Japanese manufacturers produce a broad range of strategic components for both American military and civilian aerospace systems, although almost exclusively in a subcontracting role, with production concentrated at their U.S. plants. Japanese manufacturers, for example, produce ceramic packaging and opto-electronic components for Tomahawk missiles, including guidance cameras, while U.S. firms provide propulsion systems, munitions, and software. On the civilian side, Boeing and such Japanese firms as Mitsubishi Heavy Industries and Kawasaki Heavy Industries have cooperated on major civilian projects like the Boeing 777 intermediate-range jetliner, for which Japanese firms produce over 75 percent of the fuselage.

U.S.–Japan military coproduction however, has not even approached the level of analogous cooperation within NATO, in part owing to the lack of emphasis on state-of-the-art technology development. The mindset of the Japanese side tends to focus instead on quick benefits from access to the latest technology and on its efficient dissemination among Japanese producers.[7] Joint R&D, as well as coproduction of major military systems involving technology transfer mutually beneficial to both sides, could be further enhanced.

Standards-policy coordination is one important key to broader transpacific defense-industrial cooperation. Levels of interoperability between America and Japan have simply not developed to the degree that they have between the United States and its NATO allies. This is an area to which both government and industry may need to devote increased attention, especially in an era of rapidly deepening common requirements, as with respect to missile defense.

To facilitate closer transpacific defense-industrial cooperation, new bilateral consultation mechanisms may be in order. The basic institutional framework for such cooperation is now over a quarter century old, dating from initiatives like the Systems and Technology Forum launched late in the Carter administration, Recent U.S.–German defense-industrial cooperation could provide some useful benchmarks for reform.[8] Whatever new consultative mechanisms are established, they should capitalize on the formidable transpacific synergies between Japan's strengths in precision manufacturing, on the one hand, and American creativity in producing both technological breakthroughs and new approaches to concrete business problems, on the other.

(3) Foreign Direct Investment

A second priority area for U.S.–Japan economic cooperation is in achieving more symmetrical direct foreign investment patterns. As we have seen, Japan has the lowest levels of inbound direct foreign investment relative to GDP of any OECD nation—much lower than in Western Europe, the United States, or even South Korea. This pattern needs to be changed. The relative lack of foreign investment in Japan lowers local levels of competition, employment, and technology diffusion from abroad, contributing to economic stagnation in the globalized world of the twenty-first century. Just as important, however, Japan's low levels of inbound foreign investment erode the political constituency overseas—not least in Washington—that promotes an understanding and appreciation of Japan and its importance abroad. The substantial role of American multinationals in promoting stable and amicable Sino–American relations—a product of their heavy stakes in China—is a useful reference note for Tokyo in this regard.

Important advances were made during the late 1990s in enhancing the role of foreign investment in Japan. U.S. banks and investment firms, in particular, gained strategic new roles in the Japanese banking and securities industries following the Asian financial crisis. Indeed, foreign investors now account for roughly half of trading volume on equity transactions at major Japanese stock exchanges.[9] Anglo-American investors account for nearly two-thirds of this total.[10] This new foreign role is catalyzing pressures for further change in Japanese corporate governance, which will likely be a priority topic for U.S.–Japan economic dialogue in coming years, together with issues of adequate and appropriate financial oversight.

In 2001, Prime Minister Koizumi Junichirō announced Japan's intention to help stimulate Japan's economic revival by doubling foreign investment into Japan within five years. To support this goal, Japanese commercial law was revised to facilitate cross-border mergers and acquisitions, while also enhancing the transparency and reliability of corporate information. Japan also introduced an "angel tax" system, reducing taxes on investment in IT and R&D by new ventures. Meanwhile, it also reviewed rules to allow foreign lawyers to have joint offices with Japanese law firms and authorized triangular mergers in which the foreign partner has an active subsidiary incorporated in Japan. In 2007 foreign firms were allowed to pay for new acquisitions in cash or in shares of the foreign parent company.[11]

Unfortunately, Japan's ambitious plans for accelerated inbound foreign investment have met with distinctly mixed success. The total stock of foreign direct investment in Japan did in fact rise between fiscal 2001 and 2006, from roughly $65 billion to $101 billion. The latter amount, however, still represented only 2.2 percent of Japan's overall GDP, compared to 16.4 percent for FDI in the United States and an average of 22.3 percent for the world as a whole.[12] The FDI share in Japan also fell more than 22 percent short of Koizumi's declared five-year goal, although his successor, Abe Shinzō, promptly reiterated his predecessor's pledge of doubling the FDI ratio in GDP to 5 percent, this time by 2010.[13] Abe's successor, Fukuda Yasuo, however, soon after making a speech at the Davos World Economic Forum welcoming foreign investment into Japan, proved more equivocal, abolishing the Japan Investment Council and imposing regulations on foreign investment in Tokyo's Haneda Airport.

Looking to the future, it is important from a geostrategic perspective that expanding Japanese trade relations with Asian nations such as China, so natural from an economic standpoint, be complemented by deeper U.S.–Japan economic interdependence as well, where such mutual reliance also has its own natural economic logic. Technology, health care, and finance—particularly in their service-sector dimensions—are prime areas for greater U.S.–Japan interdependence and should be given particular attention by both the private and the public sectors. In an era of aging (*kōreika*), American pension fund management, pharmaceuticals, and insurance-related expertise have particular value to the Japanese people in helping to raise rates of return and in providing better services to local consumers in a wide range of economic sectors.

American investment in education, including MBA and other business-related programs, likewise has a place. Several American academic institutions, such as Temple University and Minnesota State University, have campuses in Japan. Other universities and colleges have business alliances with Japanese counterparts or, like Stanford, band together with like-minded institutions to form consortia.[14] Such efforts need to be expanded and strengthened.

(4) Strengthened Bilateral Institutions

Technology is unavoidably driving the U.S.–Japan alliance, in its political-military dimensions, toward institutions for closer, almost instantaneous emergency communication and cooperation, especially with respect to problems like terrorism and missile defense. The needed technical institutions, such as the Bilateral Joint Operations Coordination Center (BJOCC), are steadily evolving, at places like Yokota Air Base and Camp Zama, near Tokyo. Yet despite these important new political-military developments, institutions for addressing the political-economic dimensions of the bilateral relationship still leave much to be desired.

Throughout most of the post-Occupation period, Tokyo and Washington have had well-developed bilateral mechanisms for exploring and negotiating economic issues, be they macroeconomic, structural, or sectoral. Perhaps the most sophisticated were the institutions of the late 1980s and the early 1990s, in the days of the Structural Impediments Initiative (SII), which featured elements that addressed all three sorts of issue.[15] Since then, however, economic globalization, together with the coming of the WTO and the demise of traditional bilateral orderly marketing arrangements (OMAs), has sharply reduced both private sector and governmental interest in bilateral coordination mechanisms.

Important substantive problems of bilateral economic coordination between the United States and Japan still remain, however, due to lingering embedded structural differences between the political economies of the two nations. As became graphically clear amidst the steel crisis of 1999 and subsequent bilateral tensions over steel and beef across the ensuing decade, systematic bilateral economic dialogues between the United States and Japan are still very much needed. Yet the ongoing infrastructure to sustain such dialogues is clearly insufficient, as previously active subcabinet dialogues and internal consultation processes within the respective governments have atrophied.

The pronounced "organization gap" that has emerged in transpacific economic dealings since the birth of the WTO in 1995 contrasts strongly with developments in the security realm, which have fostered and enhanced the bilateral Security Consultative Committee, also known as 2+2. This body was established in 1960, to include the Japanese foreign minister, director general of the Japan Defense Agency, the American ambassador to Japan, and the commander in chief of the Pacific Command (CINCPAC).[16] It was upgraded in 1990 to its current membership structure, including the Japanese foreign minister and defense minister, together with the U.S. secretary of state and secretary of defense, and supplemented by an unusually cohesive transpacific working-level network.[17]

In U.S.–Japan relations, the critical imperative of fostering policy networks is creating a parallel need, finally, for dynamic analytical and agenda-setting institutions. President Jimmy Carter and Prime Minister Ōhira Masayoshi resolved in 1979 to create a U.S.–Japan Wisemen's Group, composed of prominent businesspeople, academics, and former statesmen, to deliberate on the long-term future of the bilateral relationship. Although the group disbanded after two years, at the end of the Carter administration, and was never reconstituted, it produced important, academically respectable research; shedding valuable light on long-neglected structural problems in the bilateral relationship that also generated thoughtful policy proposals.[18] The bilateral character of the group and its formal commissioning by the heads of government in both nations made it more credible than the unilateralist and self-appointed, albeit relatively substantial, Armitage Reports of 2000 and 2007 and was an analytical exercise well worth repeating.

Improved data-support infrastructure needs to be a central element of any new bilateral analytical effort. Although highly sophisticated time-series data exist on virtually all aspects of bilateral economic and political relations, it is much poorer with respect to cultural and social affairs. Neither country, for example, has detailed information on why so few students choose Japan as a study destination, or why the number of Japanese students in American universities declined by a full 17 percent in 2005 from its peak in 2000, as shown in figure 5.3. Enhanced efforts also need to be made to digitize historical materials, making them broadly available to the publics of both nations.

Together with ad hoc bodies such as periodic U.S.–Japan Wisemen's Groups, there is also a strong need for a new, financially secure Trans-Pacific Partnership Fund, based in the United States.[19] The model should be the large, innovative, and American-administered German Marshall Fund (GMF), discussed in chapter 8. Although the GMF is effective and well run, U.S.–Japan bilateral interests would be best served by a new, independent institution, focused explicitly on transpacific issues.[20]

(5) Political-Economic Network Building

Comparative analysis in chapter 8 showed emphatically the importance of informal political-economic networks in strengthening U.S. relations with Britain, Germany, and China, especially at the critical early stages of decision making, when many American policies are actually formulated. Historical analysis has also shown us that U.S.–Japan informal elite ties were once stronger than they are today.

In the final analysis, many of the pressing problems in U.S.–Japan relations flow from a disturbing atrophy in bilateral policy networks. Many unexpected bilateral trade frictions, as in both steel and beef, have in recent years been clearly attributable to inadequate policy networks. Inadequate policy networks have also contributed to such U.S.–Japan defense confrontations as the 2007 disputes between U.S. Embassy Tokyo and the opposition Democratic Party of Japan over the details of Maritime Self-Defense Force refueling operations in the Indian Ocean. Troubling evidence of a resurgent "broken dialogue" problem similar to that of the 1950s and 1960s and flowing from inadequate transpacific policy networks is steadily increasing.

U.S.–Japan bilateral policy networks appear to have seriously eroded over the past decade for three major reasons. First, as noted above, global institutions such as the WTO have emerged, institutions that deceptively appear to render the bilateral networks that were so important in the era of bilateral OMAs suddenly irrelevant. Second, bilateral trade conflict has waned, with (1) the apparent passing of Japan's economic challenge to the United States, (2) the stabilization of bilateral trade imbalances, and (3) the rise of an apparently more serious set of transpacific trade challenges from China. And third, the quiet passing of the Occupation generation of U.S.–Japan specialists, with their deep, if parochial, mutual interest in relations between Tokyo and Washington, has deprived the two countries of an invaluable resource for stabilizing ties that is not being replenished.

These bilateral policy networks, which could productively enhance the political and social sensitivity of both countries to one another, are eroding at precisely the least opportune time: when their importance is quietly, yet imperceptibly, rising. In the economic/financial area, revived policy networks are desperately needed to develop new strategies for reinvigorating policies and setting agendas in key areas: corporate governance; expanded markets access; increased interdependence in technology, health care, education, and services; and the appropriate configuration of the future of the international financial system. In the defense area, enhanced policy networks are especially crucial both (1) to coordinate reenergized public diplomacy aimed at increasing Japanese public support for security cooperation; and (2) to provide the enhanced technical coordination that innovations such as missile defense require.

SEVEN-POINT PROGRAM FOR U.S.–JAPAN POLICY NETWORK DEVELOPMENT

Clearly, the enhancement of policy networks is a pressing priority for the U.S.–Japan partnership, in its broadest and most important sense. Without such innovation, the danger is that Tokyo and Washington's bilateral alliance will, despite its strategic importance, grow ever more irrelevant to the increasingly global realities of world affairs. An effective emphasis on policy networks, however, can both reinvigorate the Pacific alliance and also help it assume its rightful role at the center of global political-economic discourse.

The first imperative is to build on existing strength by exploiting the expertise on Japan in the United States that flows from the Japan Exchange and Teaching (JET) program.[21] Over the two decades since 1987, nearly 90,000 foreigners from forty-four countries have worked in Japan under this program, normally for a period of two years and mainly with local governments and high schools across the country. In the past five years 2,826 Americans annually, on average, have been invited to Japan, many more than from any other nation.[22] Better means need to be found to exploit the knowledge and skills of former JET program members, including assistance in finding meaningful Japan-related jobs.

Tokyo and Washington also need to think about expanding and deepening the Mansfield Fellows Program, another rare success in the crucial area of U.S.–Japan policy network relations. Every year since 1994 this program has placed up to ten American government officials annually in midlevel internship positions with various branches of the Japanese government. It has given both sides enhanced familiarity with the policy problems that their counterparts face, while simultaneously helping bureaucrats on both sides to develop a transpacific network for confronting common challenges. The program is widely recognized as a success and is one that could usefully be enhanced by making it reciprocal. In other words, Japanese government officials could be selectively dispatched to the U.S. executive branch, in areas where stronger personnel contacts are viewed as mutually beneficial by both sides, or could engage in more systematic informal consultation with U.S. counterparts on topics of mutual concern.[23]

The JET and Mansfield programs have given large numbers of American teachers and government officials invaluable enhanced familiarity with Japan. This collaborative concept, configured to enhance alliance equities in a balanced way, needs to be extended to the journalistic sphere. Given the political importance of the mass media in the U.S.–Japan relationship, especially in security relations, and the monumental distortions and misunderstandings that are conveyed through the media, a systematic, well-funded media-exchange program extending in both directions across the Pacific ought to be a strong bilateral priority. In addition to exposing the American media more systematically to Japanese society, press club systems that restrict nonmembers' access to news from the central government, local authorities, and corporate bodies should be revised to allow more international media involvement. Influential Japanese TV networks, such as NHK, could broadcast more English-language programs that target Americans, addressing concerns that are not necessarily answered by watching ordinary, often parochial Japanese TV programs.[24] The era when there was merit in being an invisible, silent superpower has passed.

A dynamic media-exchange program should have follow-up dimensions that help American journalists to continue accessing information and contacts on Japan, even after their stay in Japan is over. For Japanese journalists, a reciprocal effort might be coordinated with the U.S. State Department's International Visitors' Program and possibly with university activities as well, to help provide the journalists with ongoing access to American media, government, and academic sources. Not only human exchanges but also more exchanges of media viewpoints and interpretations should be encouraged.[25]

A fourth dimension of policy networks relates to international conferences. China, with its annual Boao Forum on Hainan Island, and South Korea, with its biannual Jeju Forum on its own southern island of Jeju, have already learned the importance of such gatherings as a vehicle for helping national leaders in various spheres to create and maintain personal transnational policy networks. Japan should do the same, perhaps patterning its own international conference after regional elements of the Davos World Economic Forum series and situating the conference in a picturesque part of the country that is representative of Japanese culture and natural beauty.

U.S.–Japan relations also badly need a forum for young people, who are not yet candidates for the full-blown senior gatherings. They, after all, must play a key role in enhancing alliance equities over the long term. The U.S.–Japan Foundation's Leadership Program, which annually brings together about twenty rising stars in their thirties and forties from each country, specializing in politics, business, academics, and the arts, for two substantive weeklong conferences over two years, has made a good start. Such gatherings need to be held more frequently and to be supported by an ongoing and frequently updated website.

(6) Agenda Setting

The policy research- and agenda-setting processes of U.S.–Japan relations are traditionally bureaucratized and linked to action-forcing events. Since the Security Treaty crisis of 1960 and especially since the advent of routine yet high-level bilateral and G-7 multilateral leaders' meetings in the mid-1970s, summit conferences have come to play a key agenda-setting role for the formal, intragovernmental deliberations that are naturally the heart of policy making itself. Yet these formal processes need continual supplementation and invigoration, as technology, the nature of domestic politics, and the structure of the international community themselves continuously change.

Thanks to the coming of the Internet, entertaining broader inputs can now be a more dynamic process than heretofore, especially at the civil society periphery of agenda setting. Wikipedia, the online reference service that can be freely revised online by members of the general public, is one partial, albeit arguably extreme, model. U.S.–Japan relations could well use one or more portal websites, also possibly used as chat rooms, where policy issues in the bilateral relationship could be aired in a systematic way. A U.S.–Japan alliance web portal is one concrete notion whose time has come.

To give further momentum and incisiveness to what is fundamentally a competitive process of agenda setting, a variety of prize competitions for essays and policy proposals on U.S.–Japan relations could be inaugurated, with a special focus on ideas from younger people. Simultaneously, more effort should also be put, especially within Japan, into project monitoring and the eliciting of feedback from knowledgeable observers. Japanese have recently begun to be much more involved than previously in international outreach activities, with universities and think tanks being strongly encouraged by the government to develop external contacts. Yet there is still insufficient feedback and monitoring regarding just how effective these new projects have been.

Innovative forms of outreach and networking emphatically need to come to terms with advances in technology. Internet websites, as suggested earlier, can be part of that process. So can video conferencing, which is creating new potential for bringing Americans and Japanese into direct virtual contact with one another across the broad expanse of the Pacific. In late 2007, the SAIS Reischauer Center for East Asian Studies, in collaboration with Tokyo Foundation and the Temple University Institute of Contemporary Japan Studies, started a real-time, online, transpacific discussion group on the U.S.–Japan relationship as well as on regional Asian issues of security and foreign policy; the group includes government officials, academics, and researchers in their thirties and forties.

(7) Deepened Cultural Communication

Elite understanding, rather than public trust, has traditionally been the foundation of the U.S.–Japan alliance. Professional diplomats and military personnel have communicated relatively well with one another, but the peoples they represent have typically remained much more isolated from one another than their leaders. This pattern is not viable in the long run, particularly given the substantial prospect of increased political volatility in both countries.

As technology advances, creating more and more opportunities for rapid, direct personal contact, it is cultural misunderstanding that could easily come to have greater impact on transpacific politics and on policy context. International communicators, often naïve about the culture of one another's country, are suddenly thrust into direct dialogue or have their domestically oriented remarks reported internationally. Such disjuncts can create all manner of frustrations and frictions, as transpired following the racially oriented remarks concerning American blacks by the Japanese politicians Nakasone Yasuhiro and Watanabe Michio in 1986 and 1988, respectively. Remarks involving the "comfort women" issue by former prime minister Abe Shinzō and various conservative Japanese political commentators created similar transpacific turmoil during the spring of 2007, a full generation later.

Improved cultural communication is a vital yet complex imperative. One element, no doubt, is education, particularly that directed against cultural stereotypes. Broader and more effective language education is another important dimension. Heritage education for Japanese Americans and bicultural citizens as well as teacher exchanges should be expanded and supported by public-spirited corporations and civic groups. At the policy level, the U.S. government should support Japanese-language study under the National Defense Foreign Language (NDFL) program. The other two major languages of Northeast Asia—Chinese and Korean—are given NDFL support, and there is no good reason that Japanese—the little-spoken tongue of a strategically important ally—should not receive such backing also.

Another, less well recognized imperative is mutual, transpacific affirmation of distinctive national symbols. For Americans, Japanese recognition of major

league baseball and the emergence of such widely admired Japanese stars as
Nomo Hideo, Suzuki Ichirō, Sasaki Kazuhiro, Matsui Hideki, and Matsui
Kazuo in America's national pastime increases familiarity and the ability to
communicate in a positive way.[26] Similarly, American recognition of Japanese
tea ceremonies, with their positive message of peace and reconciliation, elicits
conciliatory Japanese sentiments in an era when such positive mutual rein-
forcements are urgently needed. The experience of the SAIS/Johns Hopkins
University Reischauer Center in cosponsoring major tea offerings with the
Urasenke Foundation at the National Cathedral, on Capitol Hill, and at the
U.S. Naval Academy during 2006–08 has certainly been that innovative forms
of cultural diplomacy, by reaffirming national symbols, help to deepen mutual
understanding.

(8) Stronger Reciprocal Partner Presence in National Capitals

Despite the strategic importance of the transpacific alliance to both the U.S.
and Japanese governments, partner-nation presence is remarkably limited in
both capitals, particularly outside government channels. In Tokyo, the local
ACCJ is often vigorous and knowledgeable, yet underfunded, while foreign investment is distinctly limited, outside a few key sectors like finance. Language
and cultural barriers are a continuing difficulty for many expatriate Americans,
who are greatly outnumbered by Chinese and Koreans with a much deeper
sense of Japanese ways. The local U.S. military presence in Japan is substantial,
but controversial and based well outside Tokyo.

America's physical presence in Tokyo, in short, is limited and remains outside the mainstream of Japanese society, despite the considerable importance of
the transpacific alliance to Japan. Americans clearly need to engage more vigorously in Tokyo. Yet the heart of the current capital-city problem for the alliance
is in Washington, D.C., where Japan cannot avoid competing with East Asian
neighbors for influence, given America's dominant position in world affairs.

For most Asian nations, including China and Korea, in particular, Washington, D.C., is the focal point of their presence—cultural, social, and economic
as well as political—in the United States as a whole. Most of these Asian nations, together with their European counterparts, have devoted considerable
effort to strengthening private sector NGOs dedicated to promoting their interests in the American capital. This Washington-centric pattern is much less
pronounced in the case of Japan.

For a wide range of legitimate historical reasons, the focal point of Japanese unofficial relations with the United States is New York City rather than Washington. The headquarters of virtually all major Japanese firms operating in the United States are there, and fifty thousand Japanese live in the vicinity.[27] The Japan Society, by far the most important—and the wealthiest—NGO in the United States promoting interest in Japan, is based there and boasts a distinguished, century-long history. Washington, by contrast, has fewer than five thousand Japanese citizens, a Japan-America Society only half the age of its New York counterpart, and markedly weaker Japan-oriented NGOs, apart from traditional lobbyist firms.[28]

This marked Japanese orientation toward New York did not matter much even half a decade ago. Third-country issues were not salient in U.S.–Japan relations, and powerful lobbyists could handle Japanese corporate needs in the nation's capital. Since 2005, however, rising competition from China and Korea, intensified by their rising economic scale, their affluence, and their strength in ethnic politics as well as their vigorous efforts in Washington, has created a different equation. Trends in the American domestic political economy, including the rising federal regulatory role in finance impelled by the crisis of late 2008, strengthen this growing importance of the nations' capital in U.S.–Japan relations.[29] The Japanese government, including both bureaucracy and political parties, as well as Japanese firms need to seriously contemplate a stronger Washington presence. Germany, which relies heavily on NGOs, including many run by Americans, and on subtle, selective information dissemination rather than traditional lobbying, is a possible model.

(9) Rapid-Reaction Mechanisms

Technology is also intensifying the need for rapid reactions in transpacific crisis management. A graphic example was the *Ehime Maru* case of early 2001, in which the Japanese coast guard training ship of that name was cut in half by a resurfacing U.S. Navy attack submarine off Honolulu. The accident was publicized on the Internet all over Japan within hours, necessitating a much more rapid and decisive reaction on the part of U.S. Embassy Tokyo and other American interlocutors than had ever previously been true. Such experiences show the need for real-time monitoring and update of critical websites as well as sensitive, timely electronic crisis-response mechanisms. The emergence of blogs, YouTube, and other Internet derivatives intensifies this rapid-response imperative.

Close consultation and collaboration between the two countries in the case of unfortunate incidents are necessary for speedy damage control. Preparatory arrangements should be carefully examined, including lists of advisory contacts and contingency operating procedures. Maintaining active, ongoing personal networks with relevant NGOs and political parties in peaceful times can aid effective management in time of crisis.

BENCHMARKS FOR THE FUTURE

U.S.–Japan relations are in some respects sui generis, as by far America's most substantial cross-cultural alliance relationship. Yet in many more ways, they present challenges that are echoed in other bilateral interactions, both across the world and across history. The responses of others to such challenges can in turn cast light on how the United States and Japan should cooperate with one another. In this chapter we have detailed some specific lessons emerging from our comparative approach and some concrete policy innovations that seem in order. Yet as we conclude, it is also important to reflect more philosophically on what sorts of alternative national paradigms provide the best benchmarks for the emerging Japan and a changing United States as they struggle to relate to one another across the enormous dual divides of culture and geography.

Richard Armitage has suggested Britain and the Anglo-American alliance as the most appropriate benchmark for the future of U.S.–Japan relations. On close inspection, this appears to be an inappropriate macroscopic model. The United States and Japan have sharp cultural contrasts and deep historical differences regarding nuclear weapons technology, in particular, that differentiate their bilateral ties from those of the United States and Britain. Their embedded relationships with neighboring continental powers are also markedly different for fateful historical reasons. Japan could, to be sure, emulate with profit the subtle tactics that the British have employed ever since Churchill in cultivating their special relationship with Washington. U.S.–Japan relations should indeed be special to both partners, as Anglo-American ties clearly are. Yet Tokyo and Washington need to conceptualize their underlying relationship somewhat differently than London and Washington.

What, then, is the best national benchmark for Tokyo and Washington to use in conceptualizing the future of their common partnership? Britain, South Korea, China, and even Japan's early twentieth-century alliance with Victorian Britain offer important, underlying insights, as we saw in chapter 8. The best overall fit, however, is with U.S.–German relations.

Like Japan, Germany is the largest economic power in its region. It was a defeated, non-English-speaking aggressor in World War II, newly revived in economic, yet not in political, terms. Like Japan, it needed first to reassure its neighbors, while subtly manipulating Washington's imperial preconceptions, before it could credibly begin to manage alliance relations themselves. Germany's underlying strategic and political challenge in approaching Washington was very similar to Japan's, whereas Britain's was arguably much less demanding.

Germany's diffident postwar response to American power and preconceptions is also one that Japan can ponder with profit. That response involved a substantial element of self-reflection, stressing German appreciation of the enormity of Nazi crimes and clear resolve to part from its dark, destructive previous course.[30] Japanese observers are entirely correct in stressing the differences in the scale of German and Japanese war crimes and the absence of a Japanese Hitler. Yet the corollary they often draw, that of dismissing Japanese responsibility for the war, is one that does not sit well overseas, not least in an ethnically changing America, where Chinese and Korean Americans are assuming steadily more important economic and political roles. The dismissal of war responsibility provokes a persistent and politically incendiary critique that Japan does not recognize basic human values in the same way as the industrialized West.

Because of the Germans' clear-cut self-reflection, their extensive agenda-setting institutions in Washington, and their willingness to assume when necessary an activist role in international security coalitions from Afghanistan to Bosnia, Berlin is politically able to play a much more active and effective role in setting American policy agendas from the inside than is Tokyo, despite the larger economic scale of Japan. Why Germany is so effective and what tactics it uses to influence American policy are topics that Japan could study with profit.

There are also limited areas in which Tokyo can learn from its own past and seriously reference the experience of its Asian neighbors, particularly China and South Korea. Obviously the Japanese and Chinese political systems are significantly different: China's authoritarian capitalism gives its authorities more discretion than their Japanese counterparts could ever enjoy. Yet the PRC has been remarkably effective in dealing with multinational firms and enlisting their support, either overt or tacit, for its own geopolitical purposes, in ways that Japan could reference with profit. The U.S.–China Business Council, composed of around 250 American multinational firms that deal with China, is one of the most effective lobbies in Washington. And its economic incentives are significantly shaped by Beijing, in ways that the Japanese government could, once again, study with profit.

Tokyo could also learn, lately, from Seoul with respect to national public relations. We have shown here that the activities of Japanese diplomats abroad have at times been oriented heavily toward servicing the requests from Tokyo of politicians and others of significance, even at the expense of paying attention to the broader outside environment in the host country. This inner-directed approach, which can easily lead to dangerous diplomatic myopia, contrasts to the more other-directed Korean diplomatic strategy, for example, which is also more intensively focused than Tokyo's approach on Washington, D.C. The cross-national contrast is further amplified by Korean reliance on semigovernmental or private institutions for promoting national perspectives—examples are the Korea Economic Institute (KEI), the Korea Foundation, and the KORUS House—to a much greater degree than is typical of Japan.

Japanese business diplomacy, to be sure, is generally dynamic, pragmatic, and conscious of its local social role, as symbolized by the 2007 congressional resolution draft commending Kikkōman Foods on its half century of operations in the United States.[31] It tends to operate largely at the state and local levels, however, and should, like American business, consider broader national strategies focused on Washington to help strengthen the U.S.–Japan relationship as a whole. Other nations are targeting Washington with increasing intensity, and multinational business—influential as it is, both within Japan and on the global stage—needs to be a central part of Japan's overall national response, regardless of how salient trade and investment issues themselves may be on the policy agenda at any given point in time.

In charting its future course with the United States in the Obama years and beyond, Japan can also, finally, benchmark its own past with some profit. Japan used the Anglo–Japanese alliance of 1902, for example, quite astutely to contain czarist Russia, so as to make it geopolitically possible to successfully wage war against that major European military power for more than a year. That classic alliance also proved a useful vehicle for advancing against Germany, in both China and the South Pacific, at the onset of World War I, and ultimately for securing new territories for the Japanese Empire. Japan's willingness, in return, to send naval forces to the Mediterranean to confront Austria-Hungary and to assure the safety of British convoys, there and in the Indian Ocean, also showed the benefits to Japan of a global geopolitical presence and of pragmatic, flexible military deployments. Those venerable instances of global activism, now close to a century old, are highly relevant lessons to both Japan and its allies, in the fluid, turbulent world that began emerging in the shadow of 9/11.

TOWARD A ROBUST AND RESPECTED ALLIANCE

The U.S.–Japan alliance, like all successful, enduring security partnerships of the past, rests on three pillars: military strength, economic interdependence, and cultural-political communication. If any of these three elements is lacking in substantial measure, the Pacific alliance would be, like a three-legged stool with uneven legs, presumptively unstable and prone to collapse. Military power alone, while important, cannot carry the day.

Over the past decade, both before and after 9/11, substantial innovation has taken place in the military structure of the alliance and in the deployment of Japanese forces abroad. Some elements of this emerging profile, including Indian Ocean deployments, were temporarily reversed in the fall of 2007, but the long-term secular evolution remains substantial. Even though the Japanese Self-Defense Forces temporarily withdrew from west of Malacca in November 2007, they gained valuable operating experience from their seven years there, for their refueling craft, their air-logistics operations, their Aegis cruisers, and their ground forces also. This concrete experience will stand Japanese Self-Defense Force personnel in good stead in the future.

Important changes are also afoot in the alliance with respect to basing structure, command, and control. Driven by the technical imperatives of missile defense as well as the struggle against terrorism, the army and air force command structures of the two nations at Camp Zama and Yokota Air Base are being steadily integrated with one another. As communications technology proceeds, the potential for integrating Japan-based military capabilities with those elsewhere in the world is growing also.

The escalating challenge lies in achieving the sort of intimate coordination in the economic, political, and cultural realms toward which the United States and Japan have been moving so steadily in the military sphere. That is not an easy task, as the raging debate in the fall of 2007 over Japan's Indian Ocean deployments and the separate struggle six months later over HNS for U.S. forces in Japan made dramatically manifest. At the heart of the matter is the still-unresolved question in Japanese politics of just what constitutes national security, and just what the underlying needs of the Japanese people ought to be.

For most of the past six decades, the publics of the United States and Japan have been engaged in a dialogue of the deaf regarding the operational meaning of national security. They have been talking past one another in terms that have no clear, existentially rooted common definition. This monumental transpacific communication gap is not surprising, as the principals—unique among America's major security partnerships—have never fought together in war.[32] For the Japanese public, security has a "food and resources" cast, while for the American public, security is more a matter of responding militarily to terrorist and geopolitical challenges to American international preeminence.

The consequence has been the sort of ambiguous debate that U.S. Ambassador Thomas Schieffer had with the leader of the Democratic Party of Japan, Ozawa Ichirō, in early August 2007. Schieffer appealed for support in the allegedly common "war on terrorism." Ozawa objected on procedural grounds, arguing that American intervention in Afghanistan had taken place without formal UN sanction, so Japan could not support it, the World Trade Center bombings notwithstanding. Reflecting this procedural logic and oblivious to Schieffer's strongly felt appeal, Japan's opposition parties rejected reauthorization of Japan's six-year Indian Ocean role, forcing Japanese forces to return temporarily home in November 2007.

For the sake of the long-term U.S.–Japan relationship—alliance in the fullest sense of the term—the two countries have an urgent need to develop a common conception of national defense—at least, one with enough overlap that they can agree on some common strategic imperatives. This research suggests that energy, as well as broader resource security and environmental protection, lies at the heart of that common conception. The energy sea-lanes between Yokohama and the Persian Gulf, after all, are critical to Japan's ability to supply itself with oil, and they need to be defended, as has been increasingly true of late, through common effort. Defense of the energy sea-lanes is an enterprise that should generate popular support within both countries over the long run. The military dimension of cooperative Pacific defense beyond Japanese shores should be grounded in that mutually accepted core.

"Japan and the United States face each other," as Edwin O. Reischauer pointed out, "but across the broadest ocean of them all." They are of different cultures, creeds, and histories, replete with embedded institutions that coexist only uneasily across that vast expanse of both water and misunderstanding that is the Pacific. Yet the challenge of coordination that the two sharply different nations face is of consequence for all the world. Together, they give new meaning to the concept of alliance, and they must not fail.

Notes

INTRODUCTION

1. Mike Mansfield, "Sharing Our Destinies," *Foreign Affairs* 68, no. 2 (Spring 1989): 3–15.
2. On the perceptions and domestic politics behind the San Francisco Peace Treaty of 1951 and the regional political-economic order it created, see Calder, "Securing Security through Prosperity."
3. On these transwar details, see Roberts, *Mitsui.*
4. This comparative figure is for 1955. The U.S. statistics are from the U.S. Department of Commerce Bureau of Economic Analysis website, at http://www .bea.gov/. The Japanese figures are from the Statistical Bureau website of Japan's Ministry of Internal Affairs and Communications: http://www.stat .go.jp/data/chouki/o3.htm.
5. The four tigers are Korea, Taiwan, Hong Kong, and Singapore.
6. In 2006 the United States was a $2.5 trillion net debtor and Japan a $1.8 trillion net creditor. The U.S. figures for 2006 are preliminary. They come from the U.S. Department of Commerce Bureau of Economic Analysis website: http://www.bea.gov/. The corresponding Japanese figures are from the Japanese Ministry of Finance website: http://www.mof.go.jp/.
7. Japan provided more than $4.5 billion in 2007. Japan traditionally provides well over half of the bilateral HNS received by U.S. military forces worldwide. See U.S. Department of Defense, *Report on Allied Contributions,* annual.

8. U.S. Department of Treasury website: http://www.treas.gov/tic/s1_42609.txt.

9. See, for example, Yoshida Shigeru, *Kaisō Jūnen* 3:115–23.

10. With the fall of Saipan in 1944, making it virtually impossible for Japan to expect oil supplies from Southeast Asia, Kishi Nobusuke, previously munitions minister and then prime minister-to-be (1957–60), confronted Tōjō Hideki to demand the end of the Pacific War, triggering Tōjō's resignation as prime minister. See Blair, *Silent Victory;* and Hara, *Kishi Nobusuke,* 96.

11. OECD DAC online website: http://stats.oecd.org/.

CHAPTER 1. THE QUIET CRISIS OF THE ALLIANCE

1. Reuters, "World Briefing Asia: North Korea: U.S. and Japan Press for Disarmament," *New York Times,* 2 May 2007.

2. Substantively, there were joint statements on energy security, clean development, and climate change, but no formal summit communiqué. See White House website: http://www.whitehouse.gov/news/releases/2007/04/20070427–6.html.

3. Hiroyuki Nakamura and Wakako Takeuchi, "Abe Focuses on Resource Diplomacy; Middle East Tour with Business Leaders Aimed at Remedying Slow Start on Energy," *Daily Yomiuri,* 1 May 2007.

4. The III MEF, based in Okinawa and partly in Hawaii during peacetime, represents the only rapid deployment combat capability of the U.S. Marine Corps permanently based outside the United States. I Marine expeditionary force (I MEF) is based in southern California and Arizona; and II Marine expeditionary force (II MEF) is based in North and South Carolina. See GlobalSecurity website: http://www.globalsecurity.org/military/agency/usmc/mef.htm.

5. Not least among these domestic trends is the declining relative role of Japanese Americans in transpacific ethnic politics, as we shall see.

6. This epic transition began to occur during the mid-1990s, in the latter half of the Democratic Clinton administration, and was far from being the achievement of George W. Bush and his policy advisors alone.

7. Global foreign exchange markets, for example, processed nearly $3.2 trillion in transactions daily in 2007, a 69 percent expansion at current exchange rates and a 63 percent rise at constant exchange rates since 2004. See Bank for International Settlements, *Triennial Central Bank Survey,* 1.

8. The establishment of the World Trade Organization in 1995 led to the dismantling of these bilateral regulatory mechanisms.

9. This transition is especially stark in total merchandise trade. In 1996 the U.S.–China share of such trade was 4.4 percent of total American trade, and the U.S.–Japan share was 12.9 percent. By 2006 these ratios had reversed, to 11.8 percent and 7.2 percent, respectively, according to U.S. Department of Commerce statistics. See U.S.–Japan Business Council, *Revitalizing U.S.–Japan Economic Relations,* 8.

10. JETRO website: http://www.jetro.go.jp/.

11. Investment across the Taiwan Strait now totals well over $100 billion, with more than 70 percent of Taiwan's 2004 global foreign investment flows going to China, and 10 percent

of its entire labor force working on the mainland. Since 2003 the mainland has been a larger trading partner of Taiwan than the United States, and the gap is widening. For more details, see Calder, *Stabilizing the U.S.–Japan–China Strategic Triangle,* esp. 10–11.

12. Ministry of Defense, *Defense of Japan* (2007 ed.), 56.

13. North Korea launched a Taepodong 2 in July 2006, but it appeared to fail in midflight, without separating the first stage. See ibid., 38.

14. International Institute for Strategic Studies, *Military Balance* (2007 ed.).

15. On the redress movement of the 1980s, which secured up to $20,000 compensation for each living Japanese American displaced by the forced relocations of World War II, see Maki, Kitano, and Berthold, *Achieving the Impossible Dream.*

16. Honda, whose grandparents arrived in the United States around 1900 from Japan's Kumamoto Prefecture, chairs the Asian Pacific American Caucus in the House of Representatives. He was principal congressional sponsor of a resolution passed by voice vote in mid-2007, calling on Japan's prime minister to apologize for the treatment of "comfort women" by the Japanese in World War II. See Barone, *Almanac of American Politics* (2008 ed.), 204–06.

17. Ibid., 205. These figures are for the Fifteenth Congressional District, represented by Michael Honda.

18. See Walt, *Taming American Power.*

19. On this New York City focus, at the expense of Washington, see Calder, "A Tale of Two Cities," 1–3.

20. For details, see Edsall, *Building Red America.*

21. See Ministry of Internal Affairs and Communications Statistical Bureau website: http://www.stat.go.jp/data/nihon/zuhyou/n0200100.xls. Japan's population fell by around 20,000, from 127.79 million in 2004 to 127.769 million in 2006, 127.770 million in 2007.

22. On the details and the implications for Japanese politics and foreign policy, see Ellis Krauss and Robert Pekkanen, "Japan's Coalition of the Willing on Security Policies," *Orbis* 49, no. 3 (Summer 2005) : 429–44.

23. Three hundred of 480 Lower House districts are now single-member, while remaining Diet men are elected from large blocs of returning multiple members, which present a residual variant of the previous multimember district system.

24. Ministry of Internal Affairs and Communications website: http://www.soumu.go .jp/news/961022e.html; and the House of Representatives website: http://www.shugiin .go.jp/index.nsf/html/index_kousei.htm.

25. On the social context of this deepening disillusionment with conventional politics, see Schoppa, *Race for the Exits.*

26. The base comparison years were 2005 and 2002. See the Cabinet Office websites: http://www8.cao.go.jp/survey/h17/h17-bouei/2–1.html, http://www8.cao.go.jp/survey/ h14/h14-bouei/2–1.html.

27. Ministry of Defense, *Defense White Paper* (2006 ed.).

28. Kyodo News, "Japanese Upper House Election Results," *BBC,* 30 July 2007.

29. On the details, see Calder, "Securing Security through Prosperity."

30. See Calder, *Embattled Garrisons.* The DFAA, which served for more than four decades as

a semiautonomous affiliate of the Self-Defense Agency, was reabsorbed into the new Ministry of Defense in 2007.

31. The 2007 bribery scandal involving the former administrative vice minister of defense Moriya Takemasa, for example, substantially delayed deliberation of antiterrorism legislation, allowing for Maritime SDF refueling in the Indian Ocean after the previous antiterrorism law expired on November 1, 2007. See Kamiya Setsuko, "DPJ Rejects Fukuda's Latest Antiterror Bill Plea," *Japan Times,* 30 November 2007.

32. See U.S. Department of Defense, *Report on Allied Contributions.* The precise dollar amount continually varies, of course, since the support payments are denominated in floating Japanese yen.

33. In fiscal year 2004 the Japanese government devoted 22.1 percent of its general account expenditures to these twin purposes. See Ministry of Health, Labor and Welfare, *Kōsei Rōdō Hakusho.*

34. "SDF Troops in Iraq Cost Japan 74 Billion Yen," *Mainichi Daily News,* 16 December 2006. ¥62.4 billion was spent to support the Ground Self-Defense Forces, chiefly in Samawah, Iraq, in January 2004–July 2006 and ¥50.4 billion to fund the Marine Self-Defense Forces, mainly in the Indian Ocean, in December 2001–September 2006. Expenditures for the Air Self-Defense Forces deployment in Kuwait are not included.

35. "Defense Deal Ushers in New Era of U.S.–Japan Cooperation," *Nikkei Weekly,* 8 May 2006. Some $6 billion of this total represents Japan's prospective outlay for helping to redeploy the eight thousand Marines to Guam, the remaining $20 billion covering various aspects of the physical transformation within Japan of U.S.–Japan defense relationships.

36. On this development, see Shinoda, *Japan's Policy Process;* and Shinoda, *Koizumi Diplomacy.* Prime Ministers Koizumi and Abe, in particular, undertook major innovations in the structure of the *kantei.*

37. See Destler, Clapp, Fukui, and Satō, *Managing an Alliance,* 23–34.

38. Calder, "Turbulent Path to Social Science."

39. During the 1995–96 academic year, Japan led the way globally in sending students to American universities, with 45,531, or 10 percent of the total. By 2005–06, the number of Japanese students had fallen to 38,712, or 7 percent of the total, with Indians at 14 percent, Chinese at 12 percent, and Koreans at 10 percent. See U.S. Department of Education Institute of Education Sciences, *Digest of Education Statistics* (2007 ed.), 598.

40. Yamamoto Tadashi, "'Shimoda Kaigi' to 'Nichibei Giin Koryu Puroguramu'" [The Shimoda Conferences and the U.S.–Japan Parliamentary Exchange Program]: http://haraguti.com/bank/d006.doc.

41. Japan Center for International Exchange website: http://www.jcie.or.jp/pep/exchange/.

42. "Japan, U.S. Losing Ties that Soothe," *Nikkei Weekly,* 22 May 2006.

43. Japan Center for International Exchange website: http://www.jcie.or.jp/pep/exchange/.

44. Japan Center for International Exchange website: http://www.jcie.or.jp/pep/acypl/.

45. USJBC corporate membership reportedly fell from forty-nine members to forty-five between 2004 and 2007. Telephone interview with USJBC in May 2007.

46. Japanese statistics (Council of Local Authorities for International Relations website: http://www.clair.or.jp/cgi-bin/simai/j/02.cgi) indicated 438 U.S.–Japan sister-city rela-

tionships, compared to 256 recorded in the United States (Sister Cities International website: http://www.sister-cities.org/icrc/directory/Asia).

47. See Calder, *Embattled Garrisons,* 133–36.

48. During 2006–07 DFAA was implicated in a series of financial scandals that led to its demise as an autonomous agency and to systematic incorporation within the new Ministry of Defense.

49. For the argument that the geopolitical rationale for alliance has largely disappeared globally, see Menon, *End of Alliance.*

50. On the Anglo-Portuguese alliance, and the socioeconomic roots of its remarkable persistence, see Shaw, *Anglo-Portuguese Alliance.*

51. Reischauer, *United States and Japan,* 1.

CHAPTER 2. THE WORLD THAT DULLES BUILT

1. Santayana, *Life of Reason.*
2. Dower, *War without Mercy.*
3. Dower, *Embracing Defeat.*
4. John W. Dower, "The Eye of the Beholder: Background Notes on the U.S.–Japan Military Relationship," *Bulletin of Concerned Asian Scholars* 2, no. 1 (October 1969): 24.
5. LaFeber, *Clash,* 279.
6. Figure as of June 1953, including both Japan and Ryūkyūs. U.S. Department of Defense, *Active Duty Military Personnel* (1953 ed.). The Self-Defense Forces were not formally established as such until 1954.
7. See Johnson, *Conspiracy at Matsukawa.*
8. Yoshida, *Kaisō Jūnen* 2:180–81; ibid., 3:115–23.
9. The term "San Francisco System" is especially appropriate here because the dominant political-economic structure of Pacific affairs for the early post–World War II period was embedded in the San Francisco Peace Treaty of September 1951 and related agreements. For details, see Calder, "Securing Security through Prosperity."
10. The United States had wanted to invite Chiang Kai Shek's government on Taiwan to participate in the peace conference, but the British, who recognized Beijing rather than Taipei, had vetoed that American notion. See Swenson-Wright, *Unequal Allies?,* 82–86; and Asahi Shimbun, *Pacific Rivals,* 206.
11. For more details, see Calder, "Securing Security through Prosperity."
12. LaFeber, *Clash,* 293.
13. Asahi Shimbun, *Pacific Rivals,* 207; and Swenson-Wright, *Unequal Allies?,* 87–91.
14. See Dower, *Empire and Aftermath,* 400–414.
15. In 1950 the U.S. economy generated 27 percent of global GDP. See Organization for Economic Cooperation and Development, *Understanding Economic Growth.*
16. Fukao and Amano, *Tainichi Chokusetsu Tōshi,* 65–66.
17. LaFeber, *Clash,* 303.
18. See Allison, *Ambassador from the Prairie.*
19. U.S. Department of State, *Foreign Relations of the United States, 1952–1954* 14:1626.

20. In 2005 the foreign investment position in China was $317.9 billion, and in Japan it was $100.9 billion at book value. China's nominal GDP was around 60 percent that of Japan's. The magnitude of foreign investment in Japan may be understated because of valuation at acquisition cost, but the general point about limited inbound foreign investment seems clear. See UNCTAD, *World Investment Report* (2006 ed.). Data are from national sources.

21. U.S. troop strengths for Japan/Okinawa were as follows: 1950: 115,000/21,000; 1955: 162,000/28,000; and 1960: 47,000/37,000. See U.S. Department of Defense, *Active Duty Military Personnel* (various editions).

22. LaFeber, *Clash,* 301.

23. Valerie Reitman, "Japanese Stomp All Over Hollywood's Godzilla," *Toronto Star,* 18 July 1998.

24. LaFeber, *Clash,* 300.

25. Ishii Osamu, "Nichibei Pātonāshippu heno Michinori: 1952–1969" [A Route toward Partnership between the U.S. and Japan] in *Nichibei Kankei Tsushi,* ed. Hosoya, 222.

26. LaFeber, *Clash,* 300.

27. Significantly, Reischauer, upon becoming ambassador to Japan in 1961, later hired Fahs as his cultural minister counselor, intensifying the synergy still further and linking it formally to government policy processes.

28. Rockefeller (D-West Virginia) serves, for example, as chairman of the Intelligence Committee (2007–) in the U.S. Senate.

29. Fujiyama Aiichirō was the Japanese foreign minister of the day (Kishi cabinet), and Douglas MacArthur II was the U.S. ambassador to Japan.

30. Ohira Masayoshi was Japanese foreign minister, and Edwin O. Reischauer was, of course, U.S. ambassador to Japan. This "agreement" is said by knowledgeable observers to have been a one-way communication in which Foreign Minister Ohira indicated only the most minimal nonverbal acknowledgment.

31. See Hitoshi Yuichirō, "Hikaku Sangensoku no Konchini-teki Ronten: 'Kaku no Kasa,' Kaku Fukakusan Jōyaku, Kaku Busō-ron" [Contemporary Issues regarding the Three Non-Nuclear Principles: Nuclear Umbrella, NPT, and Nuclear Armament], *Reference* (August 2007): 48–50: http://www.ndl.go.jp/jp/data/publication/refer/200708_679/067903.pdf. Okinawa reversion thus in reality occurred on *hondo-nami* terms (i.e., equivalent to terms prevailing on the Japanese mainland), as the American government formally committed to Japan.

32. If Eisenhower had come to Japan through Moscow as originally anticipated, the Japanese Communists, who commanded major strength in the Zengakuren student movement, could not easily have opposed his subsequent trip to Tokyo. See Asahi Shimbun, *Pacific Rivals,* 217.

33. Ibid., 217–18.

34. On the details of the crisis, see Packard, *Protest in Tokyo.*

35. On the new policies evoked by the crisis, initiated under the Ikeda cabinet, see Calder, *Crisis and Compensation,* esp. 95–103.

36. Calder, *Crisis and Compensation,* 415.

37. See Edwin O. Reischauer, "The Broken Dialogue with Japan," *Foreign Affairs* (October 1960): 11–26.
38. Reischauer, *My Life,* 246–51.
39. Reischauer did, it should be noted, disagree with one important aspect of the Dulles framework—ostracizing mainland China. He argued that the United States should encourage Japan to serve as an intermediary in subtle efforts—sensitive to Cold War geopolitical realities—at rapprochement. See Reischauer, *Beyond Vietnam,* 140–80.
40. U.S. Department of State, *Foreign Relations of the United States, 1961–3* 22:707–09.
41. Ibid., 744–45.
42. Reischauer, *My Life,* 196.
43. Ibid., 173.
44. On the details, see ibid., 202, 300. The trade and economic affairs meetings continued to be held at the cabinet level for five consecutive years during Reischauer's tenure as ambassador in Tokyo, also involving Secretary of State Dean Rusk on each occasion.
45. For Reischauer's impressions of this high-level economic dialogue, see Reischauer, *My Life,* 213–14.
46. Ibid., 214.
47. U.S.–Japan Business Council website: http://www.jubc.gr.jp/eng/summary/index .html.
48. Masuda and Tsuchiyama, *Sengo Nichibei Kankei no Kiseki,* 166–67.
49. Reischauer, *My Life,* 214.
50. Ibid., 299.
51. Matsukata was home minister of Japan from 1880, finance minister from 1885, and ultimately prime minister during 1891–92 and 1896–98. He was noted for a tight fiscal policy that suppressed inflation and laid the basis for Japan's subsequent heavy industrialization. The Bank of Japan was also established while Matsukata was finance minister. On Mrs. Reischauer's family history, see Haru Reischauer, *Samurai and Silk.*
52. Reischauer, *My Life,* 171.
53. Asahi Shimbun, *Pacific Rivals,* 220.
54. Reischauer, *My Life,* 203.
55. Okinawa was not counted as a prefecture until 1972. See Asahi Shimbun, *Pacific Rivals,* 220.
56. Eight Japanese sailors were also wounded in the covert wartime demining operations in Korea, on behalf of UN forces, during the winter of 1950. See Auer, *Postwar Rearmament.*
57. On Japan's response to the Vietnam conflict, see Havens, *Fire across the Sea.*
58. LaFeber, *Clash,* 340.
59. Ibid., 341. Also see U.S. Department of State, *Foreign Relations of the United States, 1964– 68,* vol. 1.
60. Japan's imports from South Vietnam totaled only $2.8 million in 1961. Japan's reparations to South Vietnam totaled $55.6 million. See Havens, *Fire across the Sea,* 18.
61. Masuda and Tsuchiyama, *Sengo Nichibei Kankei,* 71.
62. Reischauer, *My Life,* 285.
63. Ibid, 286–87. In Senate testimony under Secretary of State George Ball and former am-

bassador Douglas MacArthur, it was reportedly implied that the reason major Japanese newspapers were so critical of America's Vietnam policy was that they were infiltrated by Communists, forcing Reischauer, in a proactive Tokyo-generated press relations step considered rare in later years, to hold a background session at the residence at which he assured editors that these reports did not reflect embassy views.

64. LaFeber, *Clash,* 348.
65. Havens, *Fire across the Sea,* 71; Reischauer, *My Life,* 285.
66. Reischauer, *My Life,* 284–95.
67. Fulbright Japan website: http://www.fulbright.jp/keikaku/chronological_history.pdf.
68. LaFeber, *Clash,* 344.
69. These ten-year renewals were automatic under the revised Mutual Security Treaty, ratified in 1960, unless one side gave notice under the treaty of intent to terminate. Yet given the tensions of the Vietnam War period and the traumatic precedents of the Security Treaty crisis of 1960, officials in America and Japan were nevertheless wary that a political explosion could occur as the renewal period approached, with Okinawa as a likely catalyst.
70. See Destler, Satō, Clapp, and Fukui, *Managing an Alliance,* 23–34.
71. Konō, *Okinawa Henkan,* 238–71.
72. Richard M. Nixon, "Asia after Vietnam," *Foreign Affairs* 46 (October 1967): 111–25.
73. Japan did have a broad range of practical reservations regarding the NPT treaty that delayed Tokyo's ratification. These included its concerns about diplomatic discrimination against nonweapons states and undue limits on its civilian nuclear programs. Japan had particular reason to be concerned in this latter area, as it envisaged extensive closed nuclear fuel-cycle programs, which burned prospectively large amounts of plutonium and thus required substantial plutonium stockpiles to be on hand. Yet Japan's uncertainties regarding American intentions to defend Japan as American forces withdrew from Vietnam and to inhibit perverse actions by Japan's neighbors both interacted with these practical concerns and also exerted an independent impact in intensifying Japan's ambivalence regarding the NPT. The current situation, it might be added, is very different from that of the 1970s.
74. Asakawa and Hanai, *Sengo Nichibei Kankei,* 132.
75. Okinawa was already, of course, under Japanese "residual sovereignty"—Dulles's delicate phrase—under the terms of the San Francisco Peace Treaty, albeit involving de facto American administration.
76. Many knowledgeable observers were predicting precisely such a response. See Isaac Shapiro, "The Risen Sun: A Gaullist Japan?," *Foreign Policy* 41 (Winter 1980–81): 62–81.
77. Asakawa and Hanai, *Sengo Nichibei Kankei,* 174.
78. Ibid., 141–43.
79. On Mansfield's role in strengthening the U.S.–Japan relationship, see Oberdorfer, *Senator Mansfield,* 457–502.
80. Terence Roehrig, "Restructuring the U.S. Military Presence in Korea: Implications for Korean Security and the U.S.–ROK Alliance" (Washington, D.C.: Korea Economic Institute, 2007); http://www.keia.org/2-Publications/Roehrig.pdf.
81. Oberdorfer, *Senator Mansfield,* 464.

82. Calder, *Embattled Garrisons,* 185–86.
83. On the program, see Calder, "Beneath the Eagle's Wings?"
84. Oberdorfer, *Senator Mansfield,* 489.
85. Ibid., 471–72.
86. Ibid., 472.
87. Ibid., 473.
88. Jimmy Carter, "Nichibei Kankei wo Koureberu ni Hikiageta Souri" [The Prime Minister Who Enhanced U.S.–Japan Relations to a Higher Level], in Kumon, Koyama, and Satō, *Ohira Masayoshi,* 361.
89. Sase, *Hakenkoku Amerika,* 138–39.
90. Oberdorfer, *Senator Mansfield,* 475. For example, Michael Armacost, then undersecretary of state for political affairs and known as a hardliner against Japan when he succeeded Mansfield as ambassador to Japan, criticized Mansfield's defending attitude for Japan as "traditional 'Cherry Blossom Protection Association' mentality, referring to an image to deride those believed to be overprotective to Japan."
91. Fukuda Takeshi, "Nichibei Bōei Kyōryoku ni okeru Mitsu no Tenki: 1978 nen Gaidorain kara 'Nichibei Dōmei no Henkaku' made no Michinori" [Three Turning Points of the Japan–U.S. Defense Cooperation: Trajectory from 1978 Guideline to 'Transformation of the U.S.–Japan Alliance'], *Reference,* July 2006, 148.
92. Pyle, *Japan Rising,* 272.
93. Ibid.
94. See Gilpin, *Political Economy.*
95. Shultz, *Turmoil and Triumph.*
96. On the FSX controversy, see Lorell, *Troubled Partnership.*
97. See Schoppa, *Bargaining with Japan.*
98. Sase, *Hakenkoku Amerika,* 146–211.
99. Hughes, *Japan's Re-Emergence,* 12; Ministry of Defense, *Defense White Paper* (2007 ed.).
100. On the details, see Ōta, *U.S.–Japan Alliance,* 115–16.
101. Ibid., 111–15.

CHAPTER 3. THE NOTION OF ALLIANCE

1. Thucydides, *Peloponnesian Wars.*
2. See Johnston, *Cultural Realism,* 109–54.
3. For details, see Sima, *Records of the Grand Historian.*
4. On this point, see Snyder, *Alliance Politics,* 1.
5. Ibid.
6. Liska, *Nations in Alliance,* 3.
7. Some of the best included Destler, Sato, Clapp, and Fukui, *Managing an Alliance;* Mochizuki (ed.), *Toward a True Alliance;* Green and Cronin (eds.), *U.S.–Japan Alliance;* and Vogel (ed.), *U.S.–Japan Relations.*
8. Holsti, Hopmann, and Sullivan, *Unity and Disintegration in International Alliances.*
9. Walt, *Origins of Alliances.* Walt's empirical data were largely limited to the Middle East, for the period from 1955 to 1979.

10. Snyder, *Alliance Politics.* Snyder's empirical base was European diplomacy for the 1879–1914 period.

11. Snyder, *Alliance Politics,* 2.

12. Mancur Olson and Richard Zeckhauser, "An Economic Theory of Alliances," *Review of Economics and Statistics* 48 (August 1966): 266–77.

13. For one preliminary comparative application to the U.S.–Japan and U.S.–South Korea alliances that accents the substantial and counterintuitive scale of HNS in both cases and stresses the explanatory role of subnational factors, see Calder, "Beneath the Eagle's Wings?"

14. Neustadt, *Alliance Politics.* Neustadt's two key cases were the Suez crisis of 1956 and the Skybolt affair of 1962.

15. J. David Singer and Melvin Small, "Alliance Aggregation and the Onset of War," in *Quantitative International Politics,* ed. Singer.

16. Gowa, *Allies, Adversaries, and International Trade.*

17. Menon, *End of Alliance.*

18. Among those subscribing to this broad, threefold definition are Morgenthau, *Politics among Nations;* Liska, *Nations in Alliance;* Fredman, Bladen, and Rosen, eds., *Alliance in International Politics;* Holsti, Hopmman, and Sullivan, *Unity and Disintegration in International Alliances;* Putnam and Bayne, *Hanging Together;* and Gowa, *Allies, Adversaries, and International Trade.*

19. See, for example, Gowa, *Allies, Adversaries, and International Trade,* 32; and Snyder, *Alliance Politics,* 4. Snyder's useful definition is that "alliances are formal associations of states for the use (or nonuse) of military force, in specified circumstances, against states outside their own membership."

20. Walt, *Origin of Alliances,* 12.

21. Snyder, *Alliance Politics,* 6.

22. Ibid.

23. Ibid., 12.

24. For an interesting theoretical consideration of the implications of asymmetry for alliance relationships, see James D. Morrow, "Alliances and Asymmetry: An Alternative to the Capability Aggregation Model of Alliances," *American Journal of Political Science* 35, no. 4 (November 1991): 904–33.

25. This appears to have been the case, as will be discussed later, with respect to the original U.S.–Japan Security Treaty of 1951, which allowed American troops based in Japan to assist in sustaining domestic order. This provision, most likely endorsed quietly by Japanese conservatives uncertain of regime stability during the turbulent post–Dodge Line, early Korean War period when the treaty was negotiated, was removed when the security treaty was renegotiated in 1959. On the details, see Packard, *Protest in Tokyo.*

26. The controversial "cork in the bottle" argument for the U.S.–Japan alliance and for forward deploying of American troops in Japan is of this character. The argument is represented by a comment in 1990 by then–U.S. Marine Corps General Henry C. Stackpole III. See Fred Hiatt, "Marine General: U.S. Troops Must Stay in Japan," *Washington Post,* 27 March 1990.

27. For an exploration of this rationale and the argument that it is especially relevant in

American relations with the broader world in the post–Cold War era, see Walt, *Taming American Power.*

28. Holsti, Hopmann, and Sullivan, *Unity and Disintegration.*

29. See Holsti, Hopmann, and Sullivan, *Unity and Disintegration,* 3–5.

30. Stephen Walt, "International Relations: One World, Many Theories," *Foreign Policy* 110 (Spring 1998): 29–35.

31. Liska, *Nations in Alliance,* 12.

32. Hans Morgenthau, "Alliances," in Friedman, Bladen, Rosen, *Alliance in International Politics,* 80.

33. Walt, *Origins of Alliances,* 12.

34. Friedman, Bladen, and Rosen, *Alliance in International Politics,* 4–5. The European Union, by this logic, would not be an alliance, while NATO, of course, would be.

35. Ibid., 65.

36. Snyder, *Alliance Politics,* 8.

37. See Nye, *Soft Power.*

38. "Constitutional" here means a prevailing political-economic regime, involving a definable set of formal or informal rules. On this notion, see Ikenberry, *After Victory.*

39. Cobden, *Political Writings of Richard Cobden,* vol. 1.

40. See Menon, *End of Alliance,* 34–36, for a summary of these points.

41. Link, *Woodrow Wilson,* chap. 2.

42. Menon, *End of Alliance,* 41.

43. For a succinct analysis of NSC-68 and an assessment of its impact on American strategy, See Leffler, *Specter of Communism,* 93–96.

44. Calder, *Embattled Garrisons,* 21–23.

45. Menon, *End of Alliance,* 48.

46. On the details, see, for example, Borden, *Pacific Alliance;* and Calder, "Securing Security through Prosperity."

47. Financial dimensions—especially the prospect of loans from the City of London—also seem to have been important. See Christina Davis, "Linkages in Economics and Security Bargaining: Evidence from the Anglo-Japanese Alliance": http://www.princeton.edu/~cldavis/files/security_economic_linkages.pdf.

48. Although the Axis Pact was greeted with passive support from those embittered by Anglo-American efforts to isolate Imperial Japan, it was also harshly criticized by many internationalists, such as the naval officers Yonai Mitsumasa and Yamamoto Isoroku, Imperial Army strategist Ishihara Kanji, Genrō Saionji Kinmochi, and Grand Chamberlain Suzuki Kantarō. See Hirama, *Dainiji Sekai Taisen;* and Kashima Heiwa Kenkyūjo, *Nihon Gaikōshi,* vol. 21.

49. For an overview of the evolving debate, see Samuels, *Securing Japan,* 13–37.

50. The views of Yoshida himself regarding rearmament evolved over time, in a direction to some extent inconsistent, ironically, with the logic of the Yoshida school. In 1946, Yoshida argued that Japan should renounce even a war of self-defense, arguing that the concept could easily be misused to rationalize invasions. Following American entry into the Korean War in 1950, however, Yoshida suggested that the "renunciation of war" specified under Article 9 of Japan's post–World War II constitution did not imply a waiver of

Japan's inherent national right of self-defense. On this evolution of Yoshida's views, see National Diet Minute Database website: http://teikokugikai-i.ndl.go.jp/; and National Diet Minute Database website: http://kokkai.ndl.go.jp/.

51. Yoshida Shigeru, "Nihon Gaikō no Ayundekita Michi" [The Path that Japanese Diplomacy has Trod], in *Sengo Nihon Gaikō Ronshū*, ed. Kitaoka, 101–09.

52. See Amaya Naohiro, "Chōnin Koku Nihon Tedai no Kurigoto" [The Complaints of Managing Merchant Nation Japan], *Bungei Shunjū* (March 1980); and Kōsaka Masataka, "Tsūshō Kokka Nihon no Unmei" [The Fate of Trading Nation Japan], *Chūō Kōrōn* (November 1975). As a believer in Japan as fundamentally a "trading nation" that should focus on national economic objectives, Amaya understood the necessity of securing global support for free trade and supported Prime Minister Nakasone Yasuhiro's military buildup of the early 1980s in that context, as a necessary quid pro quo for American support on economic matters. On this nuance in his views, see Amaya, *Sekai no Choryū*, 283–86.

53. Kōsaka Masataka, "Jiritsu no Jōken" [Conditions for Self-Reliance], in *Kōza Nihon no Shōrai III*, ed. Etō and Nagai.

54. Nagai, *Heiwa no Daishō*, 118–30.

55. Taoka, *Senryaku no Jōken*. Taoka suggested, for example, that should Japan aspire to defend its vital sea-lanes autonomously, it would need to undertake large-scale military expansion, which he saw as undesirable.

56. Funabashi, *Dōmei o Kangaeru*, 193–94.

57. Nakasone, *Nijyū Isseiki Nihon*, 154.

58. Nakasone, *Seiji to Jinsei*, 238–39.

59. Okazaki, *Shidehara Kijūrō to Sono Jidai*, 447.

60. Okazaki, *Grand Strategy for Japanese Defense*, 76–83.

61. Ozawa, *Nihon Kaizō Keikaku*, 117–19. The dimensions, which Ozawa likens to a three-story house, are as follows: (1) U.S–Japan friendship; (2) a U.S.–Japan nonaggression relationship; and (3) a military alliance. The two former elements, in short, are an essential base for military alliance.

62. Ibid., 102–08. Ozawa maintained that Venice was able to prosper for a thousand years, compared to Carthage's six hundred, because citizens in Venice bore the full security costs of controlling the Mediterranean in support of free trade, while Carthage hired mercenaries, who were easily defeated by the Romans.

63. Packard, *Protest in Tokyo*, 26; and Oguma, *Shimizu Ikutarō*.

64. Others among the thirty-five members included Rōyama Masamichi, Watsuji Tetsurō, and Yanaihara Tadao. There were a few conservative politicians also, such as the LDP's Utsunomiya Tokuma, the son of a prominent Imperial Army general.

65. For the most sophisticated version of this argument, see Maruyama, *Thought and Behavior*.

66. See Havens, *Fire across the Sea*.

67. The leader of the Socialist Party in Japan, Ishibashi Masashi, did, however, undertake a high-profile defense of unarmed neutrality in the early 1980s, arguing that the alliance was nothing but a vehicle for dragging Japan into war, and the only reason that the Self-Defense Forces were not dispatched overseas during the Korean and Vietnam wars was

the JSP's possession of enough domestic political power in Japan to compel deference to the Peace Constitution of 1947. For details, see Ishibashi, *Hibusō chūritsuron*. Interestingly, JSP Chairman Ishibashi was a former leader of Zenchūrō, the All-Japan Military Base Workers Federation, which organizes workers on U.S. military bases in Japan.

68. Saeki Keishi, "'Shin Teikoku': America ni tsuizui suru Nihon no Ayausa" ['New Empire': The Danger for Japan of Following America], *Economisuto*, 11 May 2004, 108–09.

69. Gowa, *Allies, Adversaries, and International Trade*, 36.

70. Olson, *Logic of Collective Action*.

71. On the paradox of this inordinate influence, see Robert O. Keohane, "The Big Influence of Small Allies," *Foreign Policy*, no. 2 (Spring 1971): 161–82.

72. William Burr, "The October War and U.S. Policy," National Security Archive, 7 October 2003, http://www.jewishvirtuallibrary.org/jsource/History/73wardocs.html.

73. See Ole Holsti, "Diplomatic Coalitions," in Friedman, Bladen, and Rosen, *Alliances in International Politics*, 99–101.

74. Putman and Bayne, *Hanging Together*, 15–16.

75. Liska, *Nations in Alliance*, 61–74.

76. Stephen M. Walt, "Why Alliances Endure or Collapse," *Survival* 39, no. 1 (Spring 1997): 170.

77. Putnam and Bayne, *Hanging Together*, 3.

78. Walt, "Why Alliances Endure or Collapse."

79. See Edgar Prestage, "The Anglo-Portuguese Alliance," *Transactions of the Royal Historical Society* 17, 4th ser. (1934): 69.

80. See Shaw, *Anglo-Portuguese Alliance*.

81. See especially Fisher, *Portugal Trade*.

82. Dauril Alden, "Review of *Trade and Power: Informal Colonialism in Anglo-Portuguese Relations* by Sabdri Suderi," *Journal of Economic History* 31, no. 4 (December 1971): 991.

CHAPTER 4. THE ECONOMIC BASIS OF NATIONAL SECURITY

1. Ikenberry, *After Victory.*

2. Gilpin, *Political Economy;* and Kindleberger, *World Economic Primacy.*

3. See Schaller, *American Occupation*, 6–8; and Davis and Roberts, *Occupation without Troops*, 34.

4. Schaller, *American Occupation*, 7.

5. Ibid., 8.

6. Davis and Roberts, *Occupation without Troops*, 35.

7. Ibid., 36; and Heinrichs, *American Ambassador*, 277–380.

8. On the details, see Calder, "Securing Security through Prosperity."

9. Japan, for example, obtained through the Treaty of Shimonoseki an indemnity from China of around two hundred million Kuping Taels (seventeen million pounds) of silver. This sum was used to build the Yawata steel mill in Kyūshū, which further enhanced Tokyo's economic competitiveness.

10. See Samuels, *Rich Nation, Strong Army*, 34–42. As Samuels notes, government adherence to this concept was strongest in the late Meiji and somewhat mixed during the period of

Taishō democracy, but nevertheless a persistent general theme throughout the pre-1945 period of modern Japanese history.

11. Potter, *People of Plenty.*

12. See Yergin, *Prize,* 305–27.

13. Calculations based on the figures presented in World Bank, *World Development Indicators.*

14. Maeda and Yukizawa, *Nihon Bōeki no Chōki Tōkei,* 273, 276.

15. Sudō Kazuki, "Piiku ga Semaru Nihon no Jinkō" [Japan's Population Coming Close to Its Peak], *Daiichi Seimei Report* (June 2005), at http://group.dai-ichi-life.co.jp/.

16. Much of Japan's late nineteenth-century oil came from the Caucasian oil fields of Baku, but this pattern shifted abruptly with the discovery of Sumatran fields and, with the Russian Revolution, to oil imports from Sumatra and the United States. See Yergin, *The Prize,* 58–77.

17. "Jinzō Sekiyu Keikaku no Zenbō" [Overall artificial oil plan], *Osaka Asahi Shimbun* 23 (March 1937); http://www.lib.kobe-u.ac.jp/das/jsp/ja/ContentViewM.jsp?METAID=00109621&TYPE=HTML_FILE&POS=1&TOP_METAID=00109621.

18. Asahi Shimbun Sha, ed., *Japan Almanac* (2006 ed.), 175. In 1980 the Middle East import ratio dipped to 71.4 percent owing to Japanese attempts at diversification toward Southeast Asia and China, but it rose once again as the reserves of those alternative supplies became increasingly exhausted.

19. Ministry of Economy, Trade and Industry, *Energy White Paper* (2007 ed.).

20. This calculation is based on figures from 2006; the Middle East is here considered to include Kuwait, Oman, Qatar, Saudi Arabia, and the UAE. Source: OPEC, *Annual Statistical Bulletin* (2006 ed.).

21. On this changing pattern, see Calder, *Pacific Defense,* 56–61.

22. BP, *Statistical Review of World Energy* (2008 ed.).

23. Global Security website: http://www.globalsecurity.org/military/ops/rmsi.htm.

24. U.S. Navy, Marine Corps, and Coast Guard, "A Cooperative Strategy for 21st Century Seapower" (October 2007), 11: http://www.globalsecurity.org/military/library/policy/navy/maritime-strategy_2007.htm.

25. For details on the Japanese trade of the pre–World War II period, see Ishii, *Nihon Keizai Shi 2;* Nakamura, *Senzenki Nihon Keizai Seichō no Bunseki;* Nakamura, *Meiji Taishōki no Keizai;* and Maeda and Yukizawa, *Nihon Bōeki no Chōki Tōkei.*

26. The figures depend on which GDP calculation is used. The above figures are calculated in terms of GDP (current $). In 2006, if GDP (constant 2000 $) calculations are used, United States 30 percent, Japan 13 percent, GDP (PPP, constant 2000 international/current international $), United States 20 percent, Japan 6 percent. See World Bank, *World Development Indicators.*

27. Mason, *American Multinationals and Japan,* 136.

28. Japanese trade with China in 2007 was $237 billion, while that with the United States was $214 billion. See JETRO website: http://www.jetro.go.jp/.

29. Figure for Japan, Ministry of Internal Affairs and Communications Statistical Bureau website: http://www.stat.go.jp/data/nihon/03.htm; figure for the United States, Department of Commerce Bureau of Economic Analysis website: http://www.bea.gov/national/

nipaweb/TableView.asp#Mid; figures for the rest: World Bank, *World Development Indicators.*

30. Nomura purchased the Asian and European operations of Lehman Brothers, for example, while Mitsubishi bought a 20 percent stake in Morgan Stanley. See Martin Fackler. "Wall Street Attracts Japanese Banks," *New York Times.* September 25, 2008.

31. Tokyo Stock Exchange website: http://www.tse.or.jp/market/data/sector/index.html.

32. JETRO website: http://www.jetro.go.jp/.

33. Toyota U.S.A. website: http://www.toyota.com; Honda U.S.A. website: http://www.honda.com; and Nissan U.S.A. website: http://www.nissanusa.com.

34. Department of Commerce Bureau of Economic Analysis website: http://www.bea.gov/international/xls/mousa_employment_cntry.xls.

35. On the details of Toyota's history, see Toyota, ed., *Toyota Jidōsha 30 nenshi;* Toyota, ed., *Sekai heno Ayumi.*

36. The United States, for example, promoted the concept of Japan as the "workshop of Asia," producing capital goods and construction materials essential to broader Asian development. See Borden, *Pacific Alliance,* esp. 166–219.

37. See Calder, *Crisis and Compensation,* 89–92.

38. In July and December 1989, Japanese holdings of American Treasury securities were 53.5 percent of total foreign holdings. See U.S. Department of Treasury website: http://www.ustreas.gov/tic/ticsec.shtml.

39. See Gilpin, *Political Economy.*

40. UNCTAD, *World Investment Report.*

41. World Bank, *World Development Indicators.* These flow figures are also for 2005.

42. Japan External Trade Organization website: http://www.jetro.go.jp/jpn/stats/fdi/.

43. Fukao and Amano, *Tainichi Chokusetsu Tōshi,* 159.

44. JETRO website: http://www.jetro.org/content/493.

45. Tōyō Keizai, *Gaishikei Kigyō Sōran,* 162.

46. Fukao and Amano, *Tainichi Chokusetsu Tōshi,* 65.

47. Mason, *American Multinationals and Japan,* 20–47, esp. 22.

48. Ibid., 71.

49. Ibid., 72.

50. Ibid., 96–97.

51. Ibid., 103.

52. Fukao and Amano, *Tainichi Chokusetsu Tōhi,* 65–66.

53. Mason, *American Multinationals and Japan,* 20–47, and esp. 261–62.

54. Ibid., 197.

55. JETRO website: http://www.jetro.go.jp/jpn/stats/fdi/; World Bank, *World Development Indicators.*

56. Mason, *American Multinationals and Japan,* 161.

57. Fukao and Amano, *Tainichi Chokusetsu Tōshi,* 65–66.

58. JETRO website: http://www.jetro.co.jp.

59. U.S. Department of Commerce Bureau of Economic Analysis website: http://www.bea.gov/international/bp_web/list.cfm?anon=71&registered=0.

60. On the details, see Tett, *Saving the Sun.*

61. Brian Bremner, "The Gaijin Aren't at Fault on This Deal; Ripplewood is making a bundle, and why not?," *Business Week,* 1 March 2004.
62. On general foreign investment patterns in Japan during this post–Asian financial crisis period, see Paprzycki and Fukao, *Foreign Direct Investment in Japan.*
63. Montesquieu, *Spirit of the Laws.*
64. Erik Gartzke, Quan Li, and Charles Boehmer, "Investing in the Peace: Economic Interdependence and International Conflict," *International Organization* 55, no. 2 (Spring 2001): 391–438.
65. Samuels, *Rich Nation, Strong Army,* 33–78.
66. Ministry of Internal Affairs and Communications, *Nihon Chōki Tōkei Sōran.*
67. U.S.–Japan bilateral technology trade was 0.8 percent of Japan's total trade in 2005, compared to 1.3 percent in 1995. See Ministry of Education, Culture, Sports, Science and Technology, *White Paper on Science and Technology* (various editions); and JETRO website: http://www.jetro.go.jp/. Technology trade was defined here as the magnitude of licensing fees and royalty payments for technology between two countries.
68. Japan's MOFA website: http://www.mofa.go.jp/mofaj/area/usa/keizai/pdfs/p_shipgai you.pdf.

CHAPTER 5. NETWORKS: SINEWS OF THE FUTURE

1. On the concept of policy networks, see Knoke, *Political Networks;* M. M. Atkinson and W. D. Coleman, "Policy Networks, Policy Communities, and the Problem of Governance," *Governance* 5, no. 2 (1992); and Thompson, *Between Hierarchies and Markets;* as well as Goldsmith and Eggers, *Governing by Network.*
2. See Vogel, Yuan, and Tanaka, eds., *Golden Age.*
3. See, for example, Kelts, *Japanamerica;* and Whiting, *Samurai Way of Baseball.*
4. U.S. government census figures are computed in terms of "country of origin," making no distinction between citizens and citizens. In 1970 there were 591,290 U.S. residents of Japanese origin, compared with 435,062 residents of Chinese (including Tawainese) origin. By 2000 there were 796,700 Japanese, but a much larger number of Chinese: 2,432,585. See U.S. Census Bureau, *Census of Population* (1970, 1980, 1990, 2000 eds).
5. Immigration Bureau of Japan, Ministry of Justice website: http://www.immi-moj.go.jp/index.html. The largest foreign communities in Japan are Korean (28.7 percent) and Chinese (26.9 percent).
6. The decrease was from 87,949 to 58,181. See Japan Foundation. *Survey of Overseas Organizations Involved in Japanese Language Education.* http://www.jpf.go.jp/e/japanese/survey/result/index.html
7. Ibid.
8. Japanese statistics are drawn from the Council of Local Authorities for International Relations website: http://www.clair.or.jp/cgi-bin/simai/j/02.cgi. This Japanese source, it should be noted, indicated 438 U.S.–Japan sister-city relationships, compared to 232 recorded in the United States (Sister Cities International website: http://www.sister-cities.org).
9. Sister Cities International website: http://www.sister-cities.org/.

10. International House of Japan, *Kokusai Bunka Kaikan,* 186.

11. International House of Japan, *General Activities 2006–2007,* at http://www.i-house .or.jp/en/ihj/disclo/2007/e-houkoku.pdf.

12. On the turbulence, see Calder, *Crisis and Compensation,* 71–126.

13. See Auslin, *Japan Society,* 34–37.

14. Ibid., 35.

15. Among the early recipients of support from the fledgling Grew Foundation was the young Iriye Akira, later to become a distinguished Harvard historian. See Yamamoto, Iriye, and Iokibe, eds., *Philanthropy and Reconciliation,* 50–51, 330–32.

16. Yoshida, for example, held a major support reception for International House at his official residence, attended by over two hundred distinguished visitors. See ibid., 329.

17. Ibid., 74.

18. Auslin, *Japan Society,* 99.

19. International House of Japan, *Kokusai Bunka Kaikan,* 50–52.

20. These contributions included more than $3 million to the Japan Society, including a $1.35 million property gift for its headquarters building, which is within easy walking distance of the United Nations; $1.9 million for English-language education in Japan; and $1.5 million for East Asian Studies at Princeton University, his alma mater. See Yamamoto, Iriye, and Iokibe, eds., *Philanthropy and Reconciliation,* 110–16.

21. See Auslin, *Japan Society,* 100.

22. Japan Society, *General Information* (brochure): http://www.japansociety.org/resources/ content/2/2/7/6/documents/JS%20General%20Brochure-japanese.pdf.

23. JCIE website: http://www.jcie.or.jp/japan/pe_usgk/tojhouse.htm#New.

24. Chino Kyōko, "Yabaizo Nippon: Beigiin no Ashi ga tōnoiteiru," *Sankei Shimbun,* 23 July 2007.

25. JCIE website: http://www.jcie.or.jp/japan/pe_usgk/tojhouse.htm#New.

26. On the crisis-inspired logic of engagement, see Brzezinski, *Fragile Blossom.*

27. Yamamoto, Iriye, and Iokibe, eds., *Philanthropy and Reconciliation,* 54.

28. See Prestowitz, *Trading Places.*

29. Rockefeller funding, apart from JDR III's personal activities, phased down under McGeorge Bundy after 1966. Carnegie pulled out around the same time. Ford Foundation funding, critical for building early post–World War II Japan studies in the United States, declined sharply after 1975. In total, such private American institutions spent around $60 million on Japan-related activities during the 1945–75 period. See Yamamoto, Iriye, and Iokibe, eds., *Philanthropy and Reconciliation,* 23, 108–10, 128, 144–45.

30. Although Vogel was the author of *Japan as Number One* (1979) and *Comeback* (1982), which had a strong focus broadly admiring of Japan, his later work was more critical and grew increasingly China-centric.

31. On the operation of the WTO and the changes it wrought in international trading relationships, see Narikar, *World Trade Organization.*

32. "China, U.S. Begin Trade Talks in Beijing," *BBC,* 14 December 2006; "Strategic Economic Dialogue Stumbles," *Japan Times,* 28 May 2007; "China-U.S. to Hold Strategic Economic Dialogue in Beijing 12–13 Dec," *BBC,* 29 November 2007; and "China: Finance Minister Expects Mutual Benefit from Strategic Dialogue with U.S.," *BBC,* 3

April 2008. Also see Kerry Dumbaugh, "China-U.S. Relations: Current Issues and Implications for U.S. Policy," CRS Report for Congress, 17 March 2008; and Andrew Jacobs, "Paulson's China Trip Leaves Big Issues Unresolved," *New York Times,* 6 December 2008.

33. Department of State website: http://www.state.gov/r/pa/prs/ps/2005/44616.htm. See also Kerry Dumbaugh, "China-U.S. Relations: Current Issues and Implications for U.S. Policy," CRS Report for Congress, 17 March 2008.

34. "Sino-U.S. Dialogue," *China Post,* 24 June 2007. Also see Kerry Dumbaugh, "China-U.S. Relations: Current Issues and Implications for U.S. Policy," CRS Report for Congress, 17 March 2008.

35. Japan Defense Agency, *Bōei Hakusho* (1976 ed.).

36. Ibid. (2007 ed.).

37. Ibid.

38. For details, see the NATO website: http://www.nato.int/structur/structure.htm.

39. See Iriye, *Across the Pacific,* 328–29. Iriye argues that military and economic aspects of foreign relations are much easier to define than the cultural, psychological, and emotional aspects; and yet these latter are the keys to cross-cultural understanding and ultimately to stable transpacific relations. He further contends that ideas about the past necessarily derive from formative experiences, whether personal, national, or transnational. That is the reason the future of transpacific relations depends so much on genuine intellectual communication. Iriye suggests that only when efforts are made to overcome propaganda, emotionalism, and excessive focus on narrow details of bilateral relations will it become possible to transcend the stormy past and assure a more peaceful Pacific.

40. On complex interdependence, see Nye and Keohane, *Power and Interdependence.*

41. The Japanese Special Action Committee on Okinawa (SACO), for example, filled both crisis-management functions just after the 1995 rape crisis and agenda-setting functions later as the governments in question shifted their focus toward long-term programmatic changes in their management of American bases in Okinawa.

42. Destler, Satō, Clapp, and Fukui, *Managing an Alliance.*

CHAPTER 6. AN ALLIANCE TRANSFORMED: U.S.–JAPAN RELATIONS SINCE 2001

1. Japanese Self-Defense Forces were authorized to extend "reconstruction and humanitarian assistance" (*jindōteki shien*) in Iraq and surrounding areas until December 2008, under the Iraq Special Measures Law, which was originally passed in July 2003 and extended the dispatch period of the SDF three times thereafter.

2. See CNN website: http://www.cnn.com/SPECIALS/2001/memorial/index.html; and the Prime Minister's Office website: http://www.kantei.go.jp/jp/tyoukanpress/rireki/2001/09/14-p.html.

3. Fuji Bank and Trust operated a large office on four floors at 2 World Trade Center (South Tower), accommodating 125 Japanese expatriate and 500 local American employees. Asahi Bank had an office at 1 World Trade Center (North Tower), with 94 employees. See CNN website: http://edition.cnn.com/2001/BUSINESS/asia/09/12/attack.tenants/index.html.

4. Japanese Cabinet Secretariat website: http://www.kantei.go.jp/new/23tuitou.html.

5. Itō Masami, "Afghan SDF Mission Constitutional, Ozawa Says," *Japan Times,* 11 October 2007.

6. Rejected by the opposition-dominated Upper House of the Diet, the legislation was passed twice, by two-thirds majorities, by the government-dominated Lower House and thus promulgated into law.

7. See Hughes, *Japan's Re-Emergence,* 126.

8. MSDF website: http://www.mod.go.jp/msdf/about/haken/hakenkyouryoku/sienkatu dou/index.html.

9. Hughes, *Japan's Re-Emergence,* 127.

10. On the SDF's activities in Iraq, see Satō, *Iraku Jieitai Sentōki.*

11. Ministry of Defense, *Defense White Paper* (2007 ed.).

12. Ministry of Defense website: http://www.mod.go.jp/asdf/iraq/jisseki.htm

13. On the details, see Hughes, *Japan's Re-Emergence,* 127–37.

14. The "Far East Clause" (Article 6 of the U.S.–Japan Mutual Security Treaty) limits U.S. military operations in Japan to the defense of Japan and "the maintenance of peace and security in the Far East." See Ministry of Foreign Affairs, *Diplomatic Blue Book* (1960 ed.), 127–37.

15. UN website: http://daccessdds.un.org/doc/UNDOC/GEN/No3/368/53/PDF/No3368 53.pdf?OpenElement; Ministry of Defense, *Defense White Paper* (2004 ed.).

16. "U.S. Pressure Causes Japan to Lose Rights to Develop Iranian Oil Field," *Mainichi Shimbun,* 5 October 2006.

17. International Institute for Strategic Studies, *Military Balance* (2002 and 2008 eds.).

18. Ministry of Defense, *Defense White Paper* (various editions from 1996).

19. Ibid. (2007 ed.), 54.

20. See Calder, "New Face of Northeast Asia."

21. Ministry of Economic Affairs of Taiwan, Department of Statistics website: http:// 2k3dmz2.moea.gov.tw/GNWEB/english/indicators/e_indicators.aspx?menu=2#subo5.

22. Of Taiwan's total population of twenty-three million, roughly one million are currently living in mainland China, chiefly in connection with the massive Taiwanese investment there. See Doug Young, "For Taiwan's Middle Class, A Hidden Struggle," *International Herald Tribune,* 17 January 2008.

23. Keith Bradsher, "Taiwan Elects Leader Who Seeks Closer Mainland Ties," *New York Times,* 23 March 2008.

24. International Institute for Strategic Studies, *Military Balance* (2008 ed.).

25. On the Okinotorishima controversy, see Yukie Yoshikawa, "Okinotorishima: Just the Tip of the Iceberg," *Harvard Asia Quarterly* 9, no. 4 (Fall 2005).

26. Watanabe Chisaki, "Japanese Fighter Jets Scrambled 30 Times to Turn Away Chinese Planes in Last 6 Months," *Associated Press,* 9 November 2005.

27. "Japan Detects Chinese Research Ship Near Disputed Islets," *AFP,* 4 February 2007.

28. "Foundation for Better Ties," *Japan Times,* 30 December 2007; and "Smoother Path between Rivals," *Japan Times,* 9 May 2008.

29. Chang-Gun Park, "Japan's Emerging Role in Promoting Regional Integration in East

Asia: Towards an East Asian Integration Regime (EAIR)," *Journal of International and Area Studies* 13 (June 2006): 53.

30. International Institute for Strategic Studies, *Military Balance* (2008 ed.).
31. Hughes, *Japan's Re-Emergence*, 108.
32. Ibid., 108–09.
33. Ōta, *U.S.–Japan Alliance*, 116–20.
34. "Japan Takes Cautious Stance to U.S. Missile Shield Deployment," *AFP*, 18 December 2002.
35. "Ishiba Plays Down Missile Defense Remarks," *Jiji Press*, 19 December 2002; "Japan Takes Cautious Stance to U.S. Missile Shield Deployment," *AFP*, 18 December 2002.
36. Martin Sieff, "BMD Watch: U.S., Japan Plan New BMD Base," *UPI*, 5 December 2006.
37. Martin Sieff, "BMD Watch: Japan Deploys Its Own Patriots," *UPI*, 3 April 2007.
38. The test involved a shipboard Aegis detection and tracking tool built by Lockheed Martin and a Standard Missile-3 interceptor produced by Raytheon. Japan is the leading partner of the United States in an effort by the U.S. Missile Defense Agency to build a multibillion-dollar layered system to defeat warheads that could potentially be fired by Iran and North Korea. See "Japanese Ship Downs Missile in Pacific Test," *New York Times*, 18 December 2007.
39. Hughes, *Japan's Re-Emergence*, 112.
40. See Allison, *Nuclear Terrorism*.
41. For details, see Ministry of Defense, *Defense of Japan* (2007 ed.), 283–301.
42. Around eight thousand members of the III Marine Expeditionary Force, together with about nine thousand of their dependents, are to be relocated from Okinawa to Guam by 2014, while the U.S. Carrier Air Wing, currently based at Atsugi, is to be transferred to Iwakuni by 2014. See Ministry of Defense, *Defense of Japan* (2007 ed.), 284–86.
43. Ibid., 293.
44. Jin Dae-woong, "'Japan's F-22 Buy Will Ignite Arms Race; South Korea Raises Concerns U.S. Sales Could Affect Military Balance in Northeast Asia," *Korea Herald*, 30 April 2007.
45. Hughes, *Japan's Re-Emergence*, 63.
46. "LDP Approves Bill to Set Up Japanese National Security Council," *Japan Economic Newswire*, 3 April 2007.
47. CENTCOM includes the nations of the Middle East, Central Asia, and Northeast Africa. PACOM includes East and South Asia, the Pacific, and the Indian Ocean. On the role of the regional military commanders, see Reveron, ed., *America's Viceroys*.
48. Reischauer, *United States and Japan*, 1.
49. Japan's MOFA website: http://www.mofa.go.jp/mofaj/area/usa/keizai/pdfs/p_ship-gaiyou.pdf.
50. Jim Yardley, "Berlin Talks Set the Ball Rolling; Bilateral Meeting Led North Korea Back to Negotiating Table," *International Herald Tribune*, 15 February 2007.
51. Glen Kessler, "Envoy Warns of N. Korea Deal Fallout; Ambassador to Japan Cables Bush to Outline Concerns Over Relations With Tokyo," *Washington Post*, 26 October 2007.

52. On the concept of critical juncture and its policy implications, see Calder and Ye, "Regionalism and Critical Junctures."

CHAPTER 7. THE GLOBAL CHALLENGE

1. North, *Institutions, Institutional Change, and Economic Performance;* North, *Structure and Change;* and North, *Understanding the Process of Economic Change.*
2. As late as 1960, the U.S. share of global GDP was still nearly 40 percent. See World Bank, *World Development Indicators Online.*
3. See Calder, "Securing Security through Prosperity."
4. In 1989, for example, Japan bought 45 percent of all the U.S. Treasury bonds and notes and 40 percent of other U.S. government securities issued in that year. Calculations based on the figures at U.S. Department of Treasury website: http://www.ustreas.gov/.
5. See Mann, *About Face,* 78–95.
6. Japanese aid to Indonesia, for example, rose from $161 million in 1986 to $707 million in 1987. See Japanese Ministry of Foreign Affairs website: http://www3.mofa.go.jp/mofaj/gaiko/oda/shiryo/jisseki/kuni/index.php.
7. On the deepening globalization of the 1980s, see Frieden, *Global Capitalism,* 423–76.
8. For a history of the World Economic Forum and its contribution to international agenda setting, see the World Economic Forum website: http://www.weforum.org/en/about/History%20and%20Achievements/index.htm.
9. World Bank, *World Development Indicators.*
10. Figures are for 2005. See Ministry of Economy, Trade, and Industry, *Energy White Paper* (2007 ed.).
11. Figures are for 2007. See Department of Energy Information Agency website: http://www.eia.doe.gov/.
12. BP, *Statistical Review of World Energy.*
13. GCC includes Bahrain, Kuwait, Oman, Qatar, Saudi Arabia, and UAE.
14. World Bank, *World Development Indicators;* ILO website: http://laborsta.ilo.org/.
15. Ministry of Economy, Trade, and Industry, *Energy White Paper* (2007 ed.).
16. Ministry of Foreign Affairs website: http://www.mofa.go.jp/mofaj/kaidan/s_fukuda/russia_08/gaiyo.html.
17. Calder, *Pacific Defense,* 43–61.
18. Sakamoto Shigeki, "Mareeshia: Marakka Kaikyō Ukai Genyu Paipurain Keikaku no Jitsugensei wo Kenshō suru" [Malaysia: Reviewing the Oil Pipeline Plan to Avoid the Strait of Malacca], 20 June 2007 at Japan Oil, Gas, and Metals National Corporation website: http://oilgas-info.jogmec.go.jp/report_pdf.pl?pdf=0706_01_sakamoto_malacca_r.pdf&id=1745.
19. Thomas Friedman, "The Power of Green," *New York Times Magazine,* 15 April 2007, 40–51, 67, 71–72; and Friedman, *Hot, Flat, and Crowded.*
20. Japan Coal Energy Center website: http://www.jcoal.or.jp/overview/kokusai.html.
21. UNEP website: http://www.unep.org/Documents.Multilingual/Default.asp?DocumentID=512&ArticleID=5599&l=en.

22. Stiglitz characterizes these income inequalities as "so many losers and so few winners." He points out that full global economic integration implies the equalization of unskilled wages throughout the world, putting particular pressure on unskilled wage levels in advanced nations. He further notes that although globalization does require many countries to cut taxes to enhance competitiveness, the way in which the United States has done this—awarding the bulk of tax cuts to the wealthy—compounds the perverse impact of globalization on domestic income equality. He concludes that economic globalization has outpaced the globalization of politics and mindsets, with perverse implications worldwide. See Joseph Stiglitz, "We Have Become Rich Countries of Poor People," *Financial Times,* 8 September 2006.

23. Frieden, *Global Capitalism,* 436.

24. Ibid., 454.

25. Ibid., 436. Nigeria, with 110 million people, for example, had a smaller economy than Switzerland, with 7 million people.

26. Ibid., 453.

27. See World Bank, *World Development Indicators.*

28. Indeed, Japanese defense spending, in yen terms, declined by a full 2 percent, from 4.9 trillion yen ($42.8 billion) in 2003 to 4.8 trillion yen ($41.1 billion) in 2006. See IISS, *Military Balance* (various editions).

29. On the security threat of foreign missiles to overseas U.S. bases in the absence of missile defense, see Bracken, *Fire in the East.*

30. On this dichotomy and its geostrategic implications, see Barnett, *Pentagon's New Map.*

31. Nye and Donohue, eds., *Governance in a Globalizing World;* and Vayrynen, *Globalization and Global Governance.*

32. Japanese manhood suffrage was introduced in 1925. On the nevertheless stirring, yet ultimately futile progress of Japanese democracy before World War II, see Scalapino, *Democracy and the Party Movement;* Reischauer, *Japan;* Dower, ed., *Origins of the Modern Japanese State;* and Duus, *Rise of Modern Japan.*

33. Semipalatinsk was close to one of the most important longtime Soviet nuclear test sites. Between 2000 and 2005 Japan sent numerous experts there to consult on nuclear illness issues and provided medical equipment for the hospital, valued at ¥650 million (around $6.1 million). See Japan Ministry of Foreign Affairs website: http://www.mofa.go.jp/policy/oda/data/2004/03ap_ca01.html#KAZAKHSTAN.

CHAPTER 8. ALTERNATIVE PARADIGMS

1. The decision to terminate the treaty was made at the Washington Naval Conference of 1921–22, but because of notice provisions the treaty itself formally lapsed in 1923.

2. The Anglo-American alliance is considered here to have originated in the Arcadia Anglo-American summit of December 1941–January 1942.

3. The modern U.S.–PRC relationship is considered here to have begun with Kissinger's secret trip to Beijing in July 1971.

4. The modern U.S.–German alliance relationship is considered here to have begun with West Germany's formal recovery of sovereignty and entry into NATO during 1955.

5. LaFeber, *Clash*, 76. The Triple Intervention of 1895 by Russia, Germany, and France against Japan forced Tokyo to cede China's Liaodong Peninsula back to the Chinese.

6. See Kennedy, *Rise and Fall*, 20–237; and Friedberg, *Weary Titan*.

7. Timothy D. Saxon, "Anglo-Japanese Naval Cooperation, 1914–1918," *Naval War College Review* 53 (Winter 2000): 62–92; and Kennedy, *Rise and Fall*, 262.

8. LaFeber, *Clash*, 137.

9. See Kennedy, *Rise and Fall*.

10. LaFeber, *Clash*, 139.

11. On this concept, see Calder, "Japanese Foreign Economic Policy Formation."

12. Under the bilateral Anglo-Japanese tariff agreement of 1911, Japan reduced by around one-third the duties on key British exports to Japan, such as textiles, iron, and steel. In return Britain committed to restraining tariff increases on its comparatively low prevailing levels. See Christina Davis, "Linkages in Economics and Security Bargaining: Evidence from the Anglo-Japanese Alliance" (lecture, International Studies Association, Budapest, Hungary, 2003), 30–31.

13. Ibid., 35.

14. Nagura, Onozuka, and Yokoi, *Nichiei Heiki Sangyō to Jimensu Jiken*.

15. LaFeber, *Clash*, 81.

16. Hirama, Gow, and Hatano, eds., *History of Anglo-Japanese Relations*, 46.

17. Hirama, *Nichiei Dōmei*, 162–63.

18. Hirama, Gow, and Hatano, eds., *History of Anglo-Japanese Relations*, 38–50.

19. Hirama, *Nichiei Dōmei*, 99–102.

20. Prince Komatsu was an offspring of Emperor Kōkaku of the late Edo period and thus a distant cousin of Emperor Meiji.

21. Economic relations also significantly deteriorated. Bilateral trade fell sharply after 1925, and a sharp sense of betrayal set in, especially on the Japanese side. See Christina Davis, "Linkages in Economics and Security Bargaining," 34; and Kurobane, *Nichiei Dōmei no Kenkyū*, 549.

22. Kibata, Nish, Hosoya, and Tanaka, eds., *History of Anglo-Japanese Relations*, 314–29.

23. Armitage et al., *United States and Japan*.

24. Walt, *Taming American Power*.

25. World Bank, *World Development Indicators*.

26. IISS, *Military Balance* (2007 ed.).

27. Neustadt, *Alliance Politics*.

28. Steve Marsh and John Baylis, "The Anglo-American 'Special Relationship': The Lazarus of International Relations," *Diplomacy and Statecraft* 17 (2006): 173–211.

29. PRO, FO 371 38523, "The Essentials of an American Policy," 21 March 1944; Bell, *Debatable Alliance*, 7.

30. Ibid.

31. Renwick, *Fighting with Allies*, 404–05.

32. Marshall, *Winning of the War*.

33. See, for example, U.S. Department of State, *Foreign Relations of the United States, 1952–1956* 6:704–05.

34. Marshall and Baylis, "The Anglo-American Special Relationship," 182–83.

35. Baylis, *Anglo-American Relations,* 226.

36. Kissinger, *White House Years,* 90–91.

37. Marsh and Baylis, "Anglo-American Special Relationship," 185.

38. Baylis, *Anglo-American Defense Relations,* chap. 1.

39. Ibid., 18.

40. Ibid., 41–43.

41. Baylis and Stoddart, "Britain and the Chevaline Project: The Hidden Nuclear Program, 1967–1982," *Journal of Strategic Studies* 26 (2003) 124–55.

42. Calder, *Embattled Garrisons,* 10–13.

43. Baylis, *Anglo-American Defense Relations,* 75.

44. See Neustadt, *Alliance Politics.*

45. Baylis, *Anglo-American Defense Relations,* 92.

46. On Anglo-American cooperation in establishing the highly strategic Diego Garcia bases in the Indian Ocean, see Calder, *Embattled Garrisons,* 183–87.

47. For details on Anglo-American relations, see Sasaki and Kibata, eds., *Igirisu Gaikō Shi.*

48. Renwick, *Fighting with Allies,* 394.

49. On the Suez and Skybolt shocks and related "paranoid perceptions" between Washington and London, see Neustadt, *Alliance Politics,* esp. 8–55.

50. One serious obstacle to close coordination with Japan in international finance, mentioned personally to me by a top Japanese financial official, continues to be the Diet's requirement that top officials be available for legislative questioning at any time the Diet is in session, thereby seriously constraining international travel even when the requirements of international finance demand it.

51. http://www.sfc.keio.ac.jp/china-express/01jiang/kosovo.htm.

52. Evan Thomas and John Barry, "The Conflict to Come," *Newsweek,* 23 April 2001. America indicated that it was "very sorry" the Chinese pilot died and "very sorry" that the plane entered Chinese airspace without clearance. Although China's state-run newspaper could thus claim, for domestic consumption, that the United States had apologized, Chinese leaders nevertheless took into consideration the warning by former Secretary of State Henry Kissinger that "American anger over a hostage situation could jeopardize the $116 billion of annual trade between the two countries."

53. "China and Taiwan in the WTO: At last, after 15 and 11 years of effort, respectively, China and Taiwan successfully concluded negotiations on the terms of membership of the World Trade Organization (WTO) on Sept. 17 and 18 this year," *Korea Times,* 24 September 2001.

54. World Bank, *World Development Indicators.*

55. On the historical pattern, see Shirk, *How China Opened Its Door;* and on the economic utility, see Huang, *Selling China.*

56. It appears, for example, that despite rigid U.S. exports controls and a series of Taiwanese investment restrictions, local semiconductor manufacturers are increasingly leaving Taiwan to manufacture directly in China's volatile and growing market, taking with them Taiwanese engineers and capital as well as technology that could potentially augment People's Liberation Army capabilities. On this issue, see Michael Klaus, "Red Chips: Im-

plications of the Semiconductor Industry's Relocation to China," *Asian Affairs* 29, no. 4 (Winter 2003): 237.

57. Wal-Mart, for example, imported $18 billion of merchandise from China into the United States during 2004, underpinning its low-price, high-volume strategy. Having invested $3.6 billion over twenty years in the PRC, Motorola's accumulated exports from China reached $41.7 billion, with China-based production thus accounting for more than a third of its worldwide production and nearly a quarter of global sales. See "China's Clothing Makers Hit by Order Slump from Wal-Mart," *AFP,* 30 May 2007; and "Motorola Sales in China Exceed U.S. $58.1 billion," *China Knowledge Newswire,* 18 April 2006.

58. The immediate previous governor of Washington, still influential, was Gary Locke, America's first Chinese-American governor, who chaired the planning committee for Hu's visit to the state in 2006.

59. Joseph Kahn, "In Hu's Visit to the U.S., Small Gaffes May Overshadow Small Gains," *New York Times,* 22 April 2006.

60. Peter Baker and Glenn Kessler, "Bush, Hu Produce Summit of Symbols; Protester Screams at Chinese President," *Washington Post,* 21 April 2006.

61. Calder, *China's Energy Diplomacy,* 6.

62. Keith Bradsher, "Rallying Round the China Bill, Hungrily; Rallying Round the China Bill, Hungrily," *New York Times,* 21 May 2000.

63. Ibid.

64. Elizabeth M. Gillespie, "Chinese President Extols Trade Tie Benefits at Boeing Plant," *Associated Press,* 20 April 2006.

65. Arnold Wayne, "Where the Appetite for Aircraft Is Big," *New York Times,* 28 November 2006.

66. Ann Scott Tyson, "Biggest China Boosters: Boeing, GM, Motorola," *Christian Science Monitor,* 10 June 1998.

67. On the history of the Taiwan-oriented China lobby, see Backrack, *Committee of One Million.*

68. Yizhong Sun, "The New China Lobby: China's Encounter with the U.S. Congress" (Ph.D. diss., University of Notre Dame, 2006), 147.

69. Ibid., 133.

70. Airbus's Tokyo representative since 2005 has been Glen Fukushima, formerly director of Japan affairs at the U.S. Trade Representative's Office and also formerly president of the American Chamber of Commerce in Tokyo.

71. Sun, "New China Lobby," 133.

72. While China ordered 112 new planes during 2006, Japan ordered only 2. See Boeing website: http://www.boeing.com/.

73. On the establishment of this critical cultural exchange infrastructure for the U.S.–China relationship, see Lampton, *Relationship Restored.*

74. NCUSCR website: http://www.ncuscr.org/.

75. USCPF website: http://www.uscpf.org/.

76. CSCC website: http://www.acls.org/pro-cscc.htm.

77. The China Institute was founded in 1926 by John Dewey (among others) and is the old-

est bicultural organization in the United States that focuses on China. See China Institute, *Annual Report,* 2007 edition: http://www.chinainstitute.org/pdfs/ChinaInstitute AR_2007.pdf.

78. In 2007 there were 21 Confucius Institutes distributed broadly across the United States, from Oklahoma to Illinois and New York City. Worldwide, 210 Confucius Institutes have been established in 64 countries and regions. See China Institute, *Annual Report* (2007 ed.); and "Chinese State Councillor Addresses Confucius Institute Conference in Beijing," Xinhua News Agency, 11 December 2007.

79. The Taiwan lobby, of course, didn't make the task any easier. See Backrack, *Committee of One Million;* and Garver, *Sino-American Alliance,* 248–63.

80. "Wen Makes Proposals to Promote Sino–U.S. Relations," Xinhua News Agency, 10 December 2003.

81. See Vogel, Yuan, and Tanaka, eds., *Golden Age.*

82. Mann, *About Face,* 113–14. Stansfield Turner, William Casey, and Robert Gates all visited China under this program.

83. On Kissinger's interaction with China from a comparative perspective, see Kissinger, *Diplomacy,* 703–32; and Kissinger, *White House Years.*

84. See Brzezinski, *Power and Principle.*

85. Harding and Yuan, eds., *Sino-American Relations.*

86. Ibid., 318.

87. Kerry Dumbaugh, "China–U.S. Relations: Current Issues and Implications for U.S. Policy," CRS Report for Congress, 17 March 2008.

88. See Katzenstein, *World of Regions.*

89. Hanrieder, *West German Foreign Policy;* and Katzenstein, *Policy and Politics,* 9.

90. See Calder, *Embattled Garrisons;* Sandars, *America's Overseas Garrisons,* 153–77, 199–226; also, Duke and Krieger, eds., *U.S. Military Forces,* 56–148.

91. While Germany has six international cooperative R&D programs, two foreign comparative testing programs, and two advanced concept technology demonstration programs with the United States, Japan has only one R&D program and no testing and advanced concept technology demonstration programs. See Department of Defense, *International Armaments Cooperation,* 17.

92. U.S. State Department representative interview data, November 2007.

93. Unimpeded by arms export controls, Germans have developed defense technology of high quality, which allows them to exchange engineers and scientists with the United States more than other allies, to share educational facilities and R&D costs of new defense technology, to exchange test data regarding military products and technology, and to encourage the United States to waive Buy America provisions for procurement by the U.S. military. For details, see Department of Defense, *International Armaments Cooperation Handbook* (2006 ed.).

94. JETRO website: http://www.jetro.go.jp/.

95. See UNCTAD, *World Investment Report* (2006 ed.). Cited in U.S.–Japan Business Council, *U.S.–Japan Relations,* 21.

96. German embassy in Washington, D.C., website: http://www.germany.info/phprint .php.

97. Ibid.: http://www.germany.info/relaunch/politics/german_us/facts.html.

98. Significant non-German donors in recent years have included the European Union, USAID, and the Charles Stewart Mott Foundation. See the GMF website: www.gmf us.org.

99. Helmut L. Anheier, "Der Dritte Sektor in Zahlen: Ein sozial-ökonomisches Porträt" [The Third Sector in Figures: A Social-Economic Portrait], in Anheier, Priller, Seibel, and Zimmer, eds., *Der Dritte Sector in Deutschland* [The Third Sector in Germany], 60–64.

100. Miyakawa, *Seisaku Kagaku*, 18–22.

101. As a toddler, King Harald of Norway even lived in the White House with his family; President Franklin D. Roosevelt offered them refuge following the Nazi invasion of 1940.

102. On Spaak's career, see Spaak, *Continuing Battle*.

103. Goethe Institute New York Office website: http://www.goethe.de/ins/us/ney.

104. German Marshall Fund, *Annual Report* (2006 ed.).

105. Comparison was made between German Marshall Fund, *Annual Report* (2006 ed.), and Japan Center for International Exchange, *Activity Report* (2004–05 ed.).

CHAPTER 9. PRESCRIPTIONS FOR THE FUTURE

1. Mike Mansfield, "Sharing Our Destinies," *Foreign Affairs* 68, no. 2 (Spring 1989): 3–15.

2. World Bank, *World Development Indicators*.

3. Ministry of Internal Affairs and Communications Statistical Bureau website: http://www.stat.go.jp/data/nihon/03.htm.

4. Menon, *End of Alliance*.

5. On the political-economic forces behind this stalemate, see Calder. *Embattled Garrisons*, 172.

6. For details, see Samuels, *Rich Nation, Strong Army*, 154–83.

7. Ibid., 48–52.

8. See U.S. Department of Defense, *International Armaments Cooperation Handbook* (2006 ed.); and U.S. Embassy in Germany website: http://germany.usembassy.gov/germany /odc.html. Joint production programs include NATO AWACs procurement, for which Germany is a major subcontractor. Joint R&D programs include the AV-8B Harrier II; the Future Multiband Multiwaveform Modular Tactical Radio; and the Challenging Mini-Satellite Payload (CHAMP).

9. In 2006, foreign investors accounted for 45 percent of all such transactions. Major stock exchange markets in Japan include Tokyo, Osaka, and Nagoya. See Tokyo Stock Exchange, *Factbook* (2008 ed.).

10. American and British investors together accounted for 62 percent of the total in 2006. See Bank of Japan website: http://www.boj.or.jp/theme/research/stat/bop/bop/index .htm#rdip.

11. See INVEST Japan websites: http://www.investment-japan.go.jp/statements/files/ 20030327-2.pdf and http://www.investment-japan.go.jp/jp/statements/files/20060 401-1.pdf.

12. U.S.–Japan Business Council, *Revitalizing U.S.–Japan Economic Relations,* 12. The original data reporting is from UNCTAD, *World Development Report,* with the data itself from national sources.

13. Ibid. The specific prime ministerial pledge was for a doubling of inbound foreign investment by 2010.

14. The Inter-University Center for Japanese Language Studies in Yokohama, initiated by Stanford University in 1963 and joined by fifteen other schools soon thereafter, is a significant case in point. See Inter-University Center for Japanese Language Studies website: http://www.stanford.edu/dept/IUC/about.html.

15. See Mikanagi, *Japan's Trade Policy,* on the MOSS talks of the late 1980s; and Schoppa, *Bargaining with Japan,* on the ensuing SII talks of the 1989–93 period.

16. The term CINCPAC changed to PACOM in 1992 without change of meaning. See U.S. PACOM website: http://www.pacom.mil/about/history.shtml.

17. Ministry of Defense, *Bōei Hakusho* (2007 ed.).

18. See, for example, Destler and Satō, *Coping with U.S.–Japan Economic Conflicts.*

19. Given that the Marshall Plan and the related Marshall Fund were transatlantic, a name more rooted in transpacific experience, such as GARIOA II, might be appropriate. The Government Appropriations for Relief in Occupied Areas (GARIOA) program provided $1.6 billion worth of food, medicine, oil, and fertilizer to Japan during the difficult early–World War II period (1946–51).

20. German Marshall Fund, *Annual Report* (2007 ed.).

21. The JET program has a budget of over $400 million annually and employs more than six thousand foreign nationals each year, in schools all over Japan. For a comprehensive assessment, see McConnell, *Importing Diversity.*

22. An average of 2,826 Americans, 895 British, 80 Chinese, and 64 Koreans were invited annually during 2003–07. See JET website: http://www.jetprogramme.org/j/introduction/pamphlet.html.

23. During the Nakasone era (1982–87), Gaston Sigur, senior director for Asian affairs on the NSC, and his Japanese counterpart, Kunihiro Michihiko, met periodically in San Francisco on a confidential basis to coordinate key issues in U.S.–Japan relations at the working level, for example. See Nakasone, *Seiji to Jinsei,* 43.

24. Although NHK does feature some programs with secondary audio tracks in English, these are basically just translated Japanese programs targeting Japanese audiences and thus fail to provide basic context regarding Japanese society, economy, and politics that Americans, unless they are quite knowledgeable, need in order to understand fully the visual presentations they are watching.

25. Some major Japanese newspapers, including *Yomiuri Shimbun* and *Asahi Shimbun,* publish selected articles from affiliated American papers, including the *Washington Post* and *New York Times,* in their English-language editions. Yet very few editorials are included among these reprinted selections. And owing to language barriers and lack of translation, such American stories as are reprinted in local English editions do not reach the mainstream of Japanese readers.

26. Felicitously, longtime Japanese ambassador to the United States Katō Ryōzō became commissioner of Japanese baseball in mid-2008, enhancing the prospects for expanded

sports exchanges sensitive to the larger cultural communications requirements of U.S.–Japan relations.

27. The figure is as of 2006. U.S. Census Bureau website: http://www.census.gov.

28. New York, for example, has the American headquarters of the Japan Foundation, while Washington, at the end of 2008, had no Japan Foundation representation at all—the foundation's secondary office is located in Los Angeles. The Korea Foundation, by contrast, has a major D.C. presence, as does the Korea Economic Institute. KEI's Japanese counterpart was disbanded in 2000.

29. Jean Strouse, "The Evolution of American Capitalism; Here's How It's Done, Hank: A Parable From a Crisis of a Century Ago," *Washington Post,* 28 September 2008.

30. See Buruma, *Wages of Guilt.*

31. GovTrack website: http://www.govtrack.us/congress/billtext.xpd?bill=sr110–323.

32. The conflict in Iraq has been a partial exception that demonstrates the broader point. The Bush administration strongly pressed for Japanese involvement there, and the Koizumi administration, unlike a number of America's NATO allies, such as France and Germany, acquiesced, complicating its substantial and long-standing ties with neighboring states in the region, particularly Iran. Constitutional restrictions coupled with domestic political realities within Japan, however, prevented Japan from playing a dynamic role in the conflict, and Japan withdrew its Ground SDF after five years (without casualties) in July 2006. Meanwhile, on the high seas, political pressure was making the Japanese naval presence in the Indian Ocean and Tokyo's air-supply role from Kuwait problematic and inconsistent. Formally, the United States and Japan may thus have cooperated in Iraq, but whether this constitutes an important and positive experience of solidarity for the future, by significantly reinforcing and deepening the Pacific alliance, is open to question.

Bibliography

Allison, Graham. *Nuclear Terrorism: The Ultimate Preventable Catastrophe.* New York: Times Books/Henry Holt, 2004.

Allison, John. *Ambassador from the Prairie: or, Allison Wonderland.* Boston: Houghton Mifflin, 1973.

Amaya, Naohiro. *Sekai no Choryū, Nihon no Sentaku* [The World's Challenge, and Japan's Choice]. Tokyo: PHP, 1991.

American Chamber of Commerce in Japan. *Financial Center White Paper: A Strategic Roadmap for Enhancing the International Competitiveness of Japan's Financial and Capital Markets.* Tokyo: American Chamber of Commerce in Japan, 2007.

Anheier, Helmut K., Eckhard Priller, Wolfgang Seibel, and Annette Zimmer, eds. *Der Dritte Sektor in Deutschland* [The Third Sector in Germany]. Berlin: Sigma, 1997.

Armacost, Michael H., and Daniel I. Okimoto. *The Future of America's Alliances in Northeast Asia.* Stanford: Asia-Pacific Research Center, 2004.

Armitage, Richard L., and others. *The United States and Japan: Advancing Toward a Mature Partnership.* Washington, D.C.: INSS and NDU, October 2000. At http://www.ndu.edu/inss/strforum/SR_01/SR_Japan.htm.

Asahi Shimbun, ed. *Japan Almanac.* 2005, 2006, and 2007 editions. Tokyo: Asahi Shimbun.

————. *The Pacific Rivals: A Japanese View of Japanese–American Relations.* New York and Tokyo: Weatherhill/Asahi, 1972.

Asakawa, Kōki, and Hitoshi Hanai. *Sengo Nichibei Kankei no Kiseki* [The Trajectory of Japan–U.S. Relations in the Postwar World]. Tokyo: Keisō Shobō, 1995.

Auer, James E. *The Postwar Rearmament of Japanese Maritime Forces, 1945–71.* New York: Praeger, 1973.

Auslin, Michael R. *The Japan Society: One Hundred Years.* New York: Japan Society, 2007.

————. *Negotiating with Imperialism: The Unequal Treaties and the Culture of Japanese Diplomacy.* Cambridge: Harvard University Press, 2004.

Backrack, Stanley D. *The Committee of One Million: "China Lobby" Politics, 1953–1971.* New York: Columbia University Press, 1976.

Bank for International Settlements. *The Triennial Central Bank Survey on Foreign Exchange and Derivatives Market Activity in 2007.* Basel: Bank for International Settlements, 2007. At http://www.bis.org/publ/rpfxf07t.htm.

Barnett, Thomas. *The Pentagon's New Map: War and Peace in the Twenty-First Century.* New York: G. P. Putnam's Sons, 2004.

Barone, Michael. *Almanac of American Politics.* 2008 edition. Washington, D.C.: National Journal Group, 2007.

Baylis, John. *Anglo-American Defense Relations, 1939–1984.* New York: St. Martin's Press, 1984.

————. *Anglo-American Defense Relations since 1939: The Enduring Alliance.* Manchester: Manchester University Press, 1997.

Bell, C. *The Debatable Alliance: An Essay in Anglo-American Relations.* London: Oxford University Press, 1964.

Blair, Clay. *Silent Victory: The U.S. Submarine War against Japan.* Philadelphia: Lippincott, 1975.

Borden, William. *The Pacific Alliance: United States Foreign Economic Policy and Japanese Trade Recovery, 1947–1955.* Madison: University of Wisconsin Press, 1984.

Bracken, Paul. *Fire in the East: The Rise of Asian Military Power and the Second Nuclear Age.* New York: HarperCollins, 1999.

British Petroleum. *Statistical Review of World Energy.* 2007, 2008 editions. London: BP, 2007, 2008.

Brzezinski, Zbigniew. *The Fragile Blossom: Crisis and Change in Japan.* New York: Harper and Row, 1972.

————. *Power and Principle: Memoires of the National Security Advisor, 1977–1981.* New York: Farrar, Straus and Giroux, 1983.

Buruma, Ian. *The Wages of Guilt: Memories of War in Germany and Japan.* New York: Farrar, Straus and Giroux, 1994.

Calder, Kent E. "Beneath the Eagle's Wings?" *Asian Security* 2, no. 3 (October 2006): 148–73.

————. *China's Energy Diplomacy and Its Geopolitical Implications.* Washington, D.C: Reischauer Center for East Asian Studies, 2006.

————. *Crisis and Compensation.* Princeton: Princeton University Press, 1988.

————. *Embattled Garrisons: Comparative Base Politics and American Globalism.* Princeton: Princeton University Press, 2007.

———. "Japanese Foreign Economic Policy Formation: Explaining the Reactive State." *World Politics* 40, no. 4 (July 1988): 517–41.

———. "The New Face of Northeast Asia." *Foreign Affairs* (March/April 2001): 106–23.

———. *Pacific Defense: Arms, Energy, and America's Future in Asia*. New York: William Morrow, 1996.

———. "Securing Security through Prosperity: The San Francisco System in Comparative Perspective." *Pacific Review* 17, no. 1 (March 2004): 135–57.

———. *Stabilizing the U.S.–Japan–China Strategic Triangle*. Washington, D.C.: Reischauer Center for East Asian Studies, 2005.

———. "A Tale of Two Cities: U.S.–Japan Relations in New York and Washington, D.C." *Kudan Square* (March 2008).

———. "The Turbulent Path to Social Science: Japanese Political Analysis in the 1990s." In Helen Hardacre, ed., *The Postwar Development of Japanese Studies in the United States*. Leiden: Brill, 1998.

———, and Min Ye. "Regionalism and Critical Junctures: Explaining the 'Organization Gap' in Northeast Asia." *Journal of East Asian Studies* 4, no. 2 (May–August 2004): 191–226.

Cobden, Richard. *The Political Writings of Richard Cobden*. Volume 1. London: T. Fisher Unwin, 1903.

Davis, Glenn, and John G. Roberts. *An Occupation without Troops*. Tokyo: Yenbooks, 1996.

Destler, I. M., Priscilla Clapp, Haruhiro Fukui, and Hideo Satō. *Managing an Alliance: The Politics of U.S.–Japan Relations*. Washington, D.C.: Brookings Institution Press, 1976.

Destler, I. M., and Hideo Satō, eds. *Coping with U.S.–Japan Economic Conflicts*. Lexington, Mass.: Lexington Books, 1982.

Dower, John W. *Embracing Defeat: Japan in the Wake of World War II*. New York: W. W. Norton/New Press, 1999.

———. *Empire and Aftermath: Yoshida Shigeru and the Japanese Experience, 1878–1954*. Cambridge: Harvard University Council on East Asian Studies, 1979.

———, ed. *Origins of the Modern Japanese State: The Selected Writings of E. H. Norman*. New York: Pantheon Books, 1975.

———. *War without Mercy: Race and Power in the Pacific War*. New York: Pantheon Books, 1986.

Duke, Simon, and Wolfgang Krieger, eds. *U.S. Military Forces and Installations in Europe: The Early Years, 1945–1970*. Oxford: Oxford University Press, 1993.

Duus, Peter. *The Rise of Modern Japan*. Boston: Houghton Mifflin, 1976.

Edsall, Thomas B. *Building Red America: The New Conservative Coalition and the Drive for Permanent Power*. New York: Basic Books, 2006.

Etō, Sinkichi, and Yōnosuke Nagai, eds. *Kōza Nihon no Shōrai III: Sekai no naka no Nihon: Anzen Hoshō no Kōsō* [Lessons Concerning Japan's Future III: Japan in the World: The Concept of Security]. Tokyo: Ushio Shuppan Sha, 1969.

Fisher, H. E. S. *The Portugal Trade: A Study of Anglo-Portuguese Commerce, 1700–1770*. London: Methuen, 1971.

Freedman, Julian R., Christopher Bladen, and Steven Rosen, eds. *Alliance in International Politics*. Boston: Allyn and Bacon, 1970.

Friedberg, Aaron. *The Wary Titan: Britain and the Experience of Relative Decline, 1895–1905.* Princeton: Princeton University Press, 1988.

Frieden, Jeffrey. *Global Capitalism: Its Fall and Rise in the Twentieth Century.* New York: W. W. Norton, 2006.

Friedman, Thomas L. *Hot, Flat, and Crowded: Why We Need a Green Revolution—and How It Can Renew America.* New York: Farrar, Straus and Giroux, 2008.

Fukao, Kyōji, and Toyofumi Amano. *Tainichi Chokusetsu Tōshi to Nihon Keizai* [Foreign Direct Investment in Japan and the Japanese Economy]. Tokyo: Nihon Keizai Shimbun Sha, 2004.

Funabashi, Yōichi. *Alliance Adrift.* New York: Council on Foreign Relations Press, 1999.

———. *Dōmei o Kangaeru: Kuniguni no Ikikata* [Thinking about Alliance: How Countries Survive]. Tokyo: Iwanami, 1998.

Garver, John W. *The Sino-American Alliance: Nationalist China and American Cold War Strategy in Asia.* New York: M. E. Sharpe, 1997.

German Marshall Fund. *Annual Report.* 2007 edition. At http://www.gmfus.org/doc/ GMF_AR2007.pdf.

Gilpin, Robert. *The Political Economy of International Relations.* Princeton: Princeton University Press, 1987.

Goldsmith, Stephen, and William D. Eggers. *Governing by Network: The New Shape of the Public Sector.* Washington. D.C.: Brookings Institution Press, 2004.

Gowa, Joanne. *Allies, Adversaries, and International Trade.* Princeton: Princeton University Press, 1994.

Hanrieder, Wolfram F. *West German Foreign Policy, 1949–1963: International Pressure and Domestic Response.* Stanford: Stanford University Press, 1967.

Hara, Akihisa. *Kishi Nobusuke: Kensei no Seijika* [Kishi Nobusuke: Politician of Power Politics]. Tokyo: Iwanami Shoten, 1995.

Hardacre, Helen, ed. *The Postwar Development of Japanese Studies in the United States.* Leiden: Brill, 1998.

Harding, Harry, and Ming Yuan, eds. *Sino-American Relations, 1945–1955: A Joint Reassessment of a Critical Decade.* Wilmington, Del.: SR Books, 1989.

Hastings, Max. *The Korean War.* New York: Touchstone Books, 1987.

Havens, Thomas. *Fire across the Sea: The Vietnam War and Japan, 1965–1975.* Princeton: Princeton University Press. 1987.

Heinrichs, Waldo H., Jr. *American Ambassador: Joseph C. Grew and the Development of the United States Diplomatic Tradition.* New York: Oxford University Press, 1966.

Hirama, Yōichi. *Dainiji Sekai Taisen to Nichidokui Sangoku Dōmei: Kaigun to Kominterun no Shiten kara* [World War II and the Tripartite Pact: From the Viewpoint of the Imperial Navy and the Comintern]. Tokyo: Kinsei Sha, 2007.

———, *Nichiei Dōmei: Dōmei no Sentaku to Kokka no Seisui* [The Anglo–Japanese Alliance: Choosing Allies and the Rise and Fall of a Nation]. Tokyo: PHP, 2006.

———, Ian Gow, and Sumio Hatano, eds. *History of Anglo–Japanese Relations: The Military Dimension.* Volume 3. Tokyo: Tokyo Daigaku Shuppan Kai, 2001.

Holsti, Ole, P. Terrence Hopmann, and John D. Sullivan. *Unity and Disintegration in International Alliances: Comparative Studies.* New York: Wiley, 1973.

Hosoya, Chihiro, ed. *Nichibei Kankei Tsūshi* [A Comprehensive History of Japan–U.S. Relations]. Tokyo: Tokyo Daigaku Shuppan Kai, 1995.

Huang, Yasheng. *Selling China: Foreign Direct Investment during the Reform Era.* Cambridge: Cambridge University Press, 2003.

Hughes, Christopher W. *Japan's Re-Emergence as a "Normal Military Power."* London: Adelphi Papers 368–69, 2004.

Ikenberry, John. *After Victory: Institutions, Strategic Restraint, and the Rebuilding of Order after Major Wars.* Princeton: Princeton University Press, 2001.

———, and Takashi Inoguchi, eds. *Reinventing the Alliance: U.S.–Japan Security Partnership in an Era of Change.* New York: Palgrave Macmillan, 2003.

International Energy Agency, *World Energy Outlook.* 2005 edition. Paris: Organization for Economic Co-operation and Development, 2005.

International House of Japan. *Kokusai Bunka Kaikan Go Jyū Nen no Ayumi* [The Fifty-Year Course of the International House of Japan: 1952–2002]. Tokyo: International House of Japan, 2003.

International Institute for Strategic Studies. *The Military Balance.* Annual edition. London: Routledge.

Iriye, Akira. *Across the Pacific: An Inner History of American–East Asian Relations.* New York: Harcourt, Brace, and World, 1967.

Ishibashi, Masashi. *Hibusō chūritsuron* [A Theory of Unarmed Neutrality]. Tokyo: Nihon Shakaitō Chūō Honbu Kikanshi Kyoku, 1983.

Ishii, Kanji, and others. *Nihon Keizai Shi 2: Sangyō Kakumei Ki* [History of the Japanese Economy 2: Industrial Revolution Period]. Tokyo: Tokyo Daigaku Shuppan Kai, 2000.

Japan Center for International Exchange. *Activity Report.* 2004–05 edition. At http://www.jcie.org/about.html#Annual%20Reports.

Johnson, Chalmers. *Conspiracy at Matsukawa.* Berkeley: University of California Press, 1972.

Johnston, Alastair Ian. *Cultural Realism: Strategic Culture and Grand Strategy in Chinese History.* Princeton: Princeton University Press, 1995.

Kaplan, Lawrence S. *NATO Divided, NATO United: The Evolution of an Alliance.* Westport, Conn.: Praeger, 2004.

Kashima Heiwa Kenkyūjo. *Nihon Gaikōshi.* Volume 21: *Nichidokui Dōmei, Nisso Chūritsu Jōyaku* [Diplomatic History of Japan. Volume 21: The Tripartite Pact and the Soviet–Japan Neutrality Treaty]. Tokyo: Kashima Kenkyūjo Shuppan Kai, 1971.

Katzenstein, Peter J. *Policy and Politics in West Germany: The Growth of a Semi-Sovereign State.* Philadelphia: Temple University Press, 1987.

———. *A World of Regions: Asia and Europe in the American Imperium.* Ithaca: Cornell University Press, 2005.

Kelts, Roland. *Japanamerica: How Japanese Pop Culture Has Invaded the U.S.* New York: Palgrave Macmillan, 2006.

Kennedy, Paul. *The Rise and Fall of the Great Powers: Economic Change and Military Conflict from 1500 to 2000.* New York: Random House, 1987.

Kibata, Yōichi, Ian Nish, Chihiro Hosoya, and Akihiko Tanaka, eds. *The History of Anglo–Japanese Relations.* Volume 1: *The Political-Diplomatic Dimension, 1600–1930.* Tokyo: Tokyo Daigaku Shuppan Kai, 2001.

Kindleberger, Charles. *World Economic Primacy: 1500 to 1990.* New York: Oxford University Press, 1996.

Kissinger, Henry. *Diplomacy.* New York: Simon and Schuster, 1994.

———. *The White House Years.* London: Weidenfeld and Nicholson, 1991.

Kitaoka, Shin'ichi, ed. *Sengo Nihon Gaikō Ronshū: Kōwa Ronsō kara Wangan Sensō made* [Collected Works on Postwar Japanese Diplomacy: From Peace Treaty Disputes to the Gulf War]. Tokyo: Chūō Kōrōn Sha, 1995.

Knoke, David. *Political Networks: The Structural Perspective.* Cambridge: Cambridge University Press, 1990.

Kōno, Yasuko. *Okinawa Henkan o meguru Seiji to Gaikō: Nichibei Kankei Shi no Bunmyaku* [Politics and Diplomacy concerning the Return of Okinawa: The Japan–U.S. Relations Historical Context]. Tokyo: Tokyo Daigaku Shuppan Kai, 1994.

Krasner, Stephen D. *Defending the National Interest: Raw Materials Investments and U.S. Foreign Policy.* Princeton: Princeton University Press, 1978.

Kumon, Shunpei, Kenichi Koyama, and Seizaburō Satō. *Ōhira Masayoshi Seijiteki Isan* [The Political Legacy of Ōhira Masayoshi]. Tokyo: Zaidan Hōjin Ōhira Masayoshi Kinen Zaidan, 1994.

Kurobane, Shigeru. *Nichiei Dōmei no Kenkyū* [Research on the Anglo–Japanese Alliance]. Sendai: Tōhoku Kyōiku Tosho, 1968.

LaFeber, Walter. *The Clash: U.S.–Japanese Relations throughout History.* New York: W. W. Norton, 1997.

Lampton, David. *Relationship Restored: Trends in U.S.–China Educational Exchanges, 1978–1984.* Washington, D.C.: National Academy, 1986.

Leffler, Melvyn P. *The Specter of Communism: The United States and the Origins of the Cold War.* New York: Hill and Wang, 1994.

Link, Arthur S. *Woodrow Wilson: War, Revolution, and Peace.* Wheeling, Ill.: Harlan-Davidson, 1979.

Liska, George. *Nations in Alliance: The Limits of Interdependence.* Baltimore: Johns Hopkins University Press, 1962.

Lorell, Mark. *Troubled Partnership: A History of U.S.–Japan Collaboration on the FS-X Fighter.* Santa Monica, Calif.: Rand Corporation, 1995.

Maeda, Shōzō, and Kenzō Yukizawa. *Nihon Bōeki no Chōki Tōkei: Bōeki Kōzō Kenkyū no Kiso Sagyō* [Long-term Statistics of Japanese Trade: Basic Works for Studies of the History of Trading Structure]. Kyoto: Dōhōsha, 1978.

Maki, Mitchell T., Harry H. L. Kitano, and S. Megan Berthold. *Achieving the Impossible Dream: How Japanese Americans Obtained Redress.* Urbana: University of Illinois Press, 1999.

Mann, James. *About Face: A History of America's Curious Relationship with China, from Nixon to Clinton.* New York: Alfred A. Knopf, 1999.

Marshall, George C. *The Winning of the War in Europe and the Pacific.* Biennial Report of the Chief of Staff of the U.S. Army, July 1, 1943, to June 30, 1945, to the Secretary of War.

Maruyama, Masao. *Thought and Behavior of Modern Japanese Politics.* Oxford: Oxford University Press, 1963.

Mason, Mark. *American Multinationals and Japan: The Political Economy of Japanese Capital*

Controls, 1899–1980. Cambridge: Harvard University Council on East Asian Studies, 1992.

Masuda, Hiroshi, and Jitsuo Tsuchiyama. *Sengo Nichibei Kankei no Kiseki* [The Trajectory of Japan–U.S. Relations]. Tokyo: Yūhikaku, 2001.

Matsumoto, Shigeharu. *Shōwa Shi e no Ichi Shōgen* [One Testimony about Showa History]. Tokyo: Tachibana Shuppan, 2001.

McConnell, David L. *Importing Diversity: Inside Japan's JET Program.* Berkeley: University of California Press, 2000.

Menon, Rajan. *The End of Alliance.* Oxford: Oxford University Press, 2007.

Mikanagi, Yumiko. *Japan's Trade Policy: Action or Reaction?* London: Routledge, 1996.

Ministry of Defense. *Bōei Hakusho* [Defense White Paper]. Various editions. Tokyo: Zaimushō Insatsu Kyoku.

Ministry of Economy, Trade, and Industry Agency for Natural Resources and Energy. *Enerugii Hakusho* [Energy White Paper]. 2006 edition. Tokyo: Zaimushō Insatsu Kyoku, 2006.

Ministry of Education, Culture, Sports, Science, and Technology. *White Paper on Science and Technology.* Various editions. Tokyo: Zaimushō Insatsu Kyoku.

Ministry of Health, Labor and Welfare. *Kōsei Rōdō Hakusho* [Annual Report on Health and Welfare]. 2007 edition. Tokyo: Zaimushō Insatsu Kyoku, 2007.

Ministry of Internal Affairs and Communications Statistical Bureau. *Nihon Chōki Tōkei Sōran* [Long-Term Statistics of Japan]. Volume 3. Tokyo: Nihon Tōkei Kyōkai, 2006.

Miyakawa, Tadao. *Seisaku Kagaku no Shin Tenkai* [New Developments in Policy Science]. Tokyo: Tōyō Keizai Shinpō Sha, 1997.

Montesquieu, Charles-Louis de Secondat, Baron de La Brède et de. *The Spirit of the Laws.* Translated and edited by Anne M. Cohler, Basia Carolyn Miller, and Harold Samuel Stone. Cambridge: Cambridge University Press, 1989.

Morgenthau, Hans. *Politics among Nations: The Struggle for Power and Peace.* New York: Knopf, 1960.

Nagai, Yōnosuke. *Heiwa no Daishō* [The Price of Peace]. Tokyo: Chūō Kōrōn Sha, 1967.

Nagura, Bunji, Tomoji Onozuka, and Katsuhiko Yokoi. *Nichiei Heiki Sangyō to Jiimensu Jiken: Buki Iten no Kokusai Keizai Shi* [The Japanese and British Armament Industries in the Naval Race: An Economic History of Arms Transfer and the Siemens Affair]. Tokyo: Nihon Keizai Hyōron Sha, 2003.

Nakamura, Takafusa. *Meiji Taishōki no Keizai* [The Economy during the Meiji and Taishō Periods]. Tokyo: Tokyo Daigaku Shuppan Kai, 1985.

———. *Senzenki Nihon Keizai Seichō no Bunseki* [Analysis of the Economic Growth of Japan during the Prewar Period]. Tokyo: Iwanami Shoten, 1971.

Nakasone, Yasuhiro. *Nijyū Isseiki Nihon no Kokka Senryaku* [Japan's National Strategy in the Twenty-First Century]. Tokyo: PHP, 2000.

———. *Seiji to Jinsei: Nakasone Yasuhiro Kaisōroku* [Politics and Life: Memoir of Nakasone Yasuhiro]. Tokyo: Kōdansha, 1992.

Narikar, Amrita, *The World Trade Organization: A Very Short Introduction.* Oxford: Oxford University Press, 2005.

Neustadt, Richard E. *Alliance Politics.* New York: Columbia University Press, 1970.

Nish, Ian H. *The Anglo–Japanese Alliance: The Diplomacy of Two Island Empires, 1894–1907.* Cambridge: Cambridge University Press, 1966.

Nishihara, Masashi, ed. *The Japan–U.S. Alliance: New Challenges for the 21st Century.* Tokyo: Japan Center for International Exchange, 2000.

North, Douglass C. *Institutions, Institutional Change, and Economic Performance.* Cambridge: Cambridge University Press, 1990.

———. *Structure and Change in Economic History.* New York: Norton, 1981.

———. *Understanding the Process of Economic Change.* Princeton: Princeton University Press, 2005.

Nye, Joseph. *Soft Power: The Means to Success in World Politics.* New York: Public Affairs, 2004.

Nye, Joseph, and John D. Donohue, eds. *Governance in a Globalizing World.* Washington, D.C.: Brookings Institution, 2000.

———, and Robert Keohane. *Power and Interdependence.* Glenview, Ill.: Scott, Foresman, 1989.

Oberdorfer, Don. *Senator Mansfield: The Extraordinary Life of a Great American Statesman and Diplomat.* Washington, D.C.: Smithsonian Books, 2003.

Oguma, Eiji. *Shimizu Ikutarō: Aru Sengo Chishikijin no Kiseki* [Shimizu Ikutarō: The History of an Intellectual in the Postwar Period]. Tokyo: Ochanomizu Shobō, 2003.

Okazaki, Hisahiko. *A Grand Strategy for Japanese Defense.* Lanham, Md.: University Press of America, 1986.

———. *Shidehara Kijūrō to sono Jidai* [Shidehara Kijūrō and His Era]. Tokyo: PHP, 2003.

Olson, Mancur. *The Logic of Collective Action.* Cambridge: Harvard University Press, 1966.

OPEC [Organization of Petroleum Exporting Countries]. *Annual Statistical Bulletin.* 2006 edition. At http://www.opec.org/library/.

Organization for Economic Cooperation and Development. *Understanding Economic Growth.* Paris: OECD Publications, 2004.

Ōta, Fumio. *The US–Japan Alliance in the 21st Century: A View of the History and a Rationale for Its Survival.* Folkestone, Kent: Global Oriental, 2006.

Ozawa, Ichirō. *Nihon Kaizō Keikaku* [Blueprint for a New Japan]. Tokyo: Kōdansha, 1993.

Packard, George. *Protest in Tokyo: The Security Treaty Crisis of 1960.* Princeton: Princeton University Press, 1966.

Paprzycki, Ralph, and Kyōji Fukao. *Foreign Direct Investment in Japan: Multinationals' Role in Growth and Globalization.* Cambridge: Cambridge University Press, 2008.

Pond, Elizabeth. *Friendly Fire: The Near-Death of the Trans-Atlantic Alliance.* Pittsburgh: European Union Studies Association, 2004.

Potter, David M. *People of Plenty: Economic Abundance and the American Character.* Chicago: University of Chicago Press, 1954.

Prestowitz, Clyde. *Trading Places: How We Allowed Japan to Take the Lead.* New York: Basic Books, 1988.

Putnam, Robert, and Nicholas Bayne. *Hanging Together: Cooperation and Conflict in the Seven-Power Summits.* Cambridge: Harvard University Press, 1987.

Pyle, Kenneth B. *Japan Rising: The Resurgence of Japan Power and Purpose.* New York: Public Affairs, 2007.

Reischauer, Edwin O. *Beyond Vietnam: The United States and Asia.* New York: Alfred A. Knopf, 1973.

———. *Japan: The Story of a Nation.* New York: Knopf, 1970.

———. *My Life between Japan and America.* New York: Harper and Row, 1986.

———. *The United States and Japan.* 3d ed. New York: Viking, 1965.

Reischauer, Haru. *Samurai and Silk: A Japanese and American Heritage.* Cambridge: Harvard University Press, 1986.

Renwick, Neil. *Japan's Alliance Politics and Defence Production.* London: Macmillan, 1995.

Renwick, Robin. *Fighting with Allies.* New York: Times Books, 1996.

Reveron, Derek S., ed. *America's Viceroys: The Military and U.S. Foreign Policy.* New York: Palgrave Macmillan, 2004.

Roberts, John. *Mitsui: Three Centuries of Japanese Business.* New York: Weatherhill, 1973.

Roehrig, Terence. *Restructuring the U.S. Military Presence in Korea: Implications for Korean Security and the U.S.–ROK Alliance.* Washington, D.C.: Korea Economic Institute, 2007.

Samuels, Richard J. *"Rich Nation, Strong Army": National Security and the Technological Transformation of Japan.* Ithaca: Cornell University Press, 1994.

———. *Securing Japan: Tokyo's Grand Strategy and the Future of East Asia.* Ithaca: Cornell University Press, 2007.

Sandars, Christopher T. *America's Overseas Garrisons: The Leasehold Empire.* Oxford: Oxford University Press, 2000.

Santayana, George. *The Life of Reason: or, The Phases of Human Progress.* New York, Scribner, 1959.

Sasaki, Yūta, and Yōichi Kibata, eds. *Igirisu Gaikō Shi* [A History of British Diplomacy]. Tokyo: Yūhikaku, 2005.

Sase, Takao. *Haken Koku Amerika no Tainichi Keizai Seisaku* [Economic Policy toward Japan by the American Hyperpower]. Tokyo: Chikuma Shobō, 2005.

Satō, Masahisa. *Iraku Jieitai Sentōki* [The Self-Defense Forces Battlefield Report]. Tokyo: Kōdansha, 2007.

Scalapino, Robert. *Democracy and the Party Movement in Prewar Japan.* Berkeley: University of California Press, 1953.

Schaller, Michael. *The American Occupation of Japan.* New York: Oxford University Press, 1985.

Schonberger, Howard B. *Aftermath of War: Americans and the Remaking of Japan, 1945–1952.* Kent, Ohio: Kent State University Press, 1989.

Schoppa, Leonard. *Bargaining with Japan: What American Pressure Can and Cannot Do.* New York: Columbia University Press, 1997.

———. *Race for the Exits: The Unraveling of Japan's System of Social Protection.* Ithaca: Cornell University Press, 2006.

Shaw, L. M. E. *The Anglo-Portuguese Alliance and the English Merchants in Portugal, 1654–1810.* Brookfield, Vt.: Ashgate, 1998.

Shibusawa, Naoko. *America's Geisha Ally: Re-imaging the Japanese Enemy.* Cambridge: Harvard University Press, 2006.

Shinoda, Tomohito. *Japan's Policy Process to Dispatch the SDF to Iraq.* Washington, D.C.: Reischauer Center for East Asian Studies, 2006.

————. *Koizumi Diplomacy: Japan's Kantei Approach to Foreign and Defense Affairs.* Seattle: University of Washington Press, 2007.

Shirk, Susan. *How China Opened Its Door: Political Success of PRC Foreign Trade and Investment Reform.* Washington, D.C.: Brookings Institution Press, 1994.

Shultz, George. *Turmoil and Triumph: My Years as Secretary of State.* New York: Scribners, 1993.

Sima, Qian. *Records of the Grand Historian.* Translated by Burton Watson. New York: Columbia University Press, 1961.

Singer, J. David, ed. *Quantitative International Politics: Insights and Evidence.* New York: Free Press, 1968.

Snyder, Glenn H. *Alliance Politics.* Ithaca: Cornell University Press, 1997.

Spaak, Paul-Henri. *The Continuing Battle: Memories of a European, 1936–1966.* London: Weidenfeld, 1971.

Swenson-Wright, John. *Unequal Allies? United States Security and Alliance Policy Toward Japan, 1945–1960.* Stanford: Stanford University Press, 2005.

Taoka, Shunji. *Senryaku no Jōken: Gekihen suru Kyokutō no Gunji Jōsei* [Strategic Conditions: The Changing Far Eastern Military Balance]. Tokyo: Yūhisha, 1994.

Tett, Gillian. *Saving the Sun: A Wall Street Gamble to Rescue Japan from Its Trillion-Dollar Meltdown.* New York: Harper Business, 2003.

Thompson, Grahame F. *Between Hierarchies and Markets: The Logic and Limits of Network Forms of Organization.* Oxford: Oxford University Press, 2003.

Thucydides. *The Peloponnesian Wars.* Translated by Benjamin Jowett. New York: Washington Square Press, 1963.

Tokyo Stock Exchange. *Factbook.* 2008 edition. At http://www.tse.or.jp/english/market/data/factbook/fact_book_2008.pdf.

Tōyō Keizai. *Gaishikei Kigyō Sōran* [Overview of Foreign-Affiliated Companies]. Tokyo: Toyo Keizai Shinpo Sha, 2006.

Toyota Jidōsha Hanbai Kabushiki Gaisha Shashi Hensan Iinkai, ed. *Sekai heno Ayumi: Toyota Jihan 30 Nenshi* [The Path to the World: 30-Year History of Toyota Motors Sales Company]. Tokyo: Toyota Motors, 1980.

————. *Toyota Jidōsha 30 Nenshi* [30-Year History of Toyota Motors]. Tokyo: Toyota Motors, 1967.

UNCTAD [United Nations Conference of Trade and Development]. *World Investment Report.* 2006 edition. New York: United Nations Publications, 2007.

U.S. Census Bureau. *Census of Population.* 1970–2000 editions. Washington, D.C.: U.S. Government Printing Office.

U.S. Department of Defense. *Active Duty Military Personnel by Regional Area and by Country.* Washington, D.C.: U.S. Government Printing Office, annual.

————. *International Armaments Cooperation Handbook.* 2006 edition. Washington, D.C.: U.S. Government Printing Office, 2006.

————. *Report on Allied Contributions to the Common Defense.* Washington, D.C.: U.S. Government Printing Office, annual.

U.S. Department of State. *Foreign Relations of the United States.* Various volumes. Washington, D.C.: U.S. Government Printing Office.

U.S.–Japan Business Council. *Revitalizing US–Japan Economic Relations*. April 26, 2007. At http://www.usjbc.org/.

Vayrynen, Raimo. *Globalization and Global Governance*. Lanham, Md.: Rowman and Littlefield, 1999.

Vernon, Raymond. *Storm over the Multinationals*. Cambridge: Harvard University Press, 1977.

Vogel, Ezra, Ming Yuan, and Akihiko Tanaka, eds. *The Golden Age of the U.S.–China–Japan Triangle, 1972–1989*. Cambridge: Harvard University Asia Center, 2002.

Walt, Stephen M. *The Origins of Alliances*. Ithaca: Cornell University Press, 1987.

———. *Taming American Power: The Global Response to U.S. Primacy*. New York: Norton. 2005.

Whiting, Robert. *The Samurai Way of Baseball: The Impact of Ichiro and the New Wave from Japan*. New York: Warner Books, 2004.

World Bank. *World Development Indicators Online*. At http://devdata.worldbank.org/dataonline/.

Yamamoto, Tadashi, Akira Iriye, and Makoto Iokibe, eds. *Philanthropy and Reconciliation: Rebuilding Postwar U.S.–Japan Relations*. Tokyo: Japan Center for International Exchange, 2006.

Yergin, Daniel. *The Prize: The Epic Quest for Oil, Money, and Power*. New York: Simon and Schuster, 1991.

Yoshida, Shigeru. *Kaisō Jūnen* [Looking Back over the Past Decade]. Volumes 2, 3. Tokyo: Tokyo Shirakawa Shoin, 1982.

Index

Page numbers in italic designate illustrations.

Owen, Henry, 47
Ozawa Ichirō, 81, 238, 250nn61–62

parliamentary exchange, 24–25, 26, 28, 123, 125
Partnership for Further Growth, 113, 153
Passin, Herbert, 23
Patrick, Hugh, 60
Pearl Harbor, Japanese attack on, 3, 32, 38, 122, 183
Pelosi, Nancy, 17
Perry, Commodore Matthew C., 31, 57, 79, 92, 213
Persian Gulf, 63, 95, 140, 192; global security after Cold War and, 165–68; sea-lanes and, 5, 161, 238
Philippines, 35, 160
policy networks, 52, 117, 128, 226, 228–30; alliance equities and, 73, 129–33, 179; in China, 202, 204, 205; crisis networks, 131, 132; erosion of, 127, 164, 227; German Marshall Fund and, 214; importance of, 210–13; Ivy League and, 124; Okinawa's reversion to Japan and, 23; seven-point program for development of, 228–34
Portugal, 84, 85–88, 116
Prestowitz, Clyde, 126
Putnam, Robert, 84, 85

Qian Qichen, 205
Quayle, Dan, 25

race/racism, 3, 4, 213, 231
Reagan, Ronald, administration of, 4, 12, 189; Japanese capital flows and, 101, 160; Mansfield and, 59–60; SDI program, 222; trade frictions with Japan, 61
Reischauer, Edwin O., 2, 62, 113, 130, 133; on communication and understanding, 152, 238; cultural collaboration supported, 3–4, 40; death of, 23; Democratic Party and, 64; "grunt agree-

ment" with Ohira, 41; human networks and, 65, 66; Ivy League universities and, 124; legacy of, 131; return of Okinawa to Japan and, 53; tenure as ambassador, 44–48, 245n44; on U.S.–Japan relations, 30; Vietnam War and, 50, 51
Reischauer, Haru, 47
Renwick, Sir Robin, 188, 193
Republican Party (U.S.), 19, 64
Rice, Condoleezza, 9
Rockefeller, David, 26
Rockefeller, Jay, 40
Rockefeller, John D., III, 2, 47, 65, 130, 133; cultural collaboration supported, 3–4; Japan Society and, 122, 123–25; Trilateral Commission and, 212
Rockefeller Foundation, 40, 45, 126
ROK (Republic of Korea). See Korea, South (ROK)
Roosevelt, Eleanor, 123
Roosevelt, Franklin D., 76–77, 89, 90, 188, 189
Roosevelt, Theodore, 38, 180
Rostow, Walt, 123
Rothschild, Baron Walter, 182
Rōyama Masamichi, 123
Rumsfeld, Donald, 25, 146
Rusk, Dean, 45, 245n44
Russia: czarist, 79, 92, 101, 179, 180, 181, 236; post-Soviet, 162, 165–68, 217, 218
Russo-Japanese War, 38, 101, 182–83, 185
Rwanda, 20, 64, 137
Ryūkyū Islands, 35, 142, 159, 172–73

Saeki Keishi, 82
San Francisco System, 35, 91, 160, 163–64, 172, 219, 243n9
San Francisco Treaty (1951), 1, 7, 12, 32, 63; Dulles and, 37; economics-for-security bargain, 159, 160, 161; global context of alliance and, 14; Korean War and, 122